"Udaipur … must lie, I think, within a magic circle, for it is a place of utter enchantment … it seemed as if with every step we were being drawn into another world, a world imagined in an oriental fairy tale."

Roderick Cameron

A bagpipe procession at Bikaner, with the old fort in the background.

The Rajput and the British shared a common interest: the *shikar,* or hunt. Tiger shooting became an obsession from the early 19th century.

THIS IS A BORZOI BOOK
PUBLISHED BY ALFRED A. KNOPF, INC.

Published in the United States by Alfred A. Knopf, Inc., New York,
and simultaneously in Canada by Random House of Canada Limited, Toronto.
Distributed by Random House Inc., New York.

This guide to Rajasthan is published by Alfred A. Knopf, Inc. in the English language and exclusively distributed by **Archipelago Press**, an imprint of Editions Didier Millet Pte. Ltd., Singapore, in Singapore, Malaysia, Brunei Darussalam, Thailand, Indonesia, Vietnam, Laos, and Cambodia.

Originally published in France by Nouveaux-Loisirs, a subsidiary of Gallimard, Paris, 1996. Copyright © 1996 by Editions Nouveaux-Loisirs.

RAJASTHAN – ISBN 0-679-76591-3
LC 96-77570

First published 1996
Revised and updated, March 1998, September 2001

WE ARE GRATEFUL TO THE NUMEROUS ACADEMIC AND LOCAL EXPERTS WHO HAVE CONTRIBUTED TO THE GUIDE. WE WOULD LIKE TO ACKNOWLEDGE WITH SPECIAL THANKS THE CONTRIBUTION OF ANVAR ALIKHAN AND UMAIMA MULLA-FEROZE IN THE OVERALL TASK OF PLANNING AND RESEARCHING THIS BOOK.

EDITORS: Irene Toh, Vivien Crump

DESIGNERS:
Tan Seok Lui, Norreha Sayuti

ARCHIVAL PHOTOGRAPHS/DOCUMENTALISTS:
Umaima Mulla-Feroze, John Falconer

EDITORIAL ASSISTANT:
Nadia Cornelis

WRITERS:
NATURE: Kailash Sankhala, M.K. Ranjitsinh, Kuldeep Bhan
HISTORY: Anjula Bedi, Asok Kumar Das
ARTS AND TRADITIONS : Asok Kumar Das, Anjula Bedi, Tripti Pandey, Sharada Dwivedi
ARCHITECTURE: Rahul Mehrotra
RAJASTHAN AS SEEN BY PAINTERS: Asok Kumar Das
RAJASTHAN AS SEEN BY WRITERS: Sharada Dwivedi
ITINERARIES: Anvar Alikhan
TEXTILE MOTIFS: Asok Kumar Das
THE TIGER – TOWARD CONSERVATION: Kailash Sankhala, Sherree Desai
WALL PAINTINGS OF SHEKHAVATI: Aman Nath
WEAPONRY: Anvar Alikhan
CAMEL CORPS: Anjula Bedi
SCULPTURES OF OSIYAN, RANAKPUR, AND DILWARA: Saryu Doshi
FOLK ART: Anjula Bedi
THE RAJ: Sharada Dwivedi
BIRDS OF BHARATPUR: Sherree Desai, Kailash Sankhala
PRACTICAL INFORMATION: Tripti Pandey, Anvar Alikhan, Amita Sarwal
GLOSSARY: Anvar Alikhan

ILLUSTRATORS:
NATURE: Anuar Bin Abdul Rahim, David Rankin, Lim Yew Cheong
ARCHITECTURE: Kathryn Blomfield
PRACTICAL INFORMATION: Heather Thompson

MAIN PHOTOGRAPHERS: Nitin Rai, Raghu Rai
ADDITIONAL PHOTOGRAPHERS: Benoit Juge, Roy Lewis, Jon Burbank, M.D. Sharma, Suresh Cordo, A.L. Syed, Farooq Issa, Jimmy Ollia, K.B. Jothady, Chelna Desai, Sally Holkar, Daulat Singh Shekhavat, Mahipal Singh, Kailash Sankhala, Jagdish Agawal, Nitin Jhaveri, Samar Singh Jodha, Avinash Pasricha

Thanks also to Asok Kumar Das, Kailash Sankhala, Aman Nath, Divyabhanusinh Chavda, G. H. R. Tillotson and David Stone for reviewing the various sections.

FIRST EDITED AND TYPESET BY EDITIONS DIDIER MILLET PTE LTD,
THEREAFTER BY BOOK CREATION SERVICES, LONDON
PRINTED IN ITALY BY EDITORIALE L

RAJASTHAN

KNOPF GUIDES

CONTENTS

NATURE, *15*

Natural ecosystems, *16*
Geology, *18*
Traditional agriculture, *20*
Agriculture and irrigation, *22*
Fauna, *24*
Endangered species, *26*
Birds, *28*
Flora, *30*

HISTORY, *31*

Early history, *32*
Princely States, *34*
Rajputs and the Mughals, *36*
British India and Independence, *38*
Modern times, *40*
Languages, *42*

ARTS AND TRADITIONS, *43*

Hinduism and the Bhakti movement, *44*
Hinduism in daily life, *46*
Jainism, *48*
Islam, *50*
Tribal beliefs, *52*
Folklore, *54*
Block-printed textiles, *56*
Tie-and-dye textiles and embroidery work, *58*
Costume, *60*
Jewelry and objets d'art, *62*
Miniature paintings, *64*
Wall and cloth paintings, *66*
Carpets and durries, *68*
Leather work, *69*
Stone carving, *70*
Pottery, *72*
Puppetry, *73*
Food, *74*
Sula, *76*
Music and dance, *78*
Fairs and festivals, *80*

ARCHITECTURE, *83*

Rural houses, *84*
Urban houses – Havelis, *86*
Palaces, *88*
Forts, *90*
Jaipur – A planned city, *92*
Jain temples, *94*
Styles and forms, *96*

RAJASTHAN AS SEEN BY PAINTERS, *97*

RAJASTHAN AS SEEN BY WRITERS, *105*

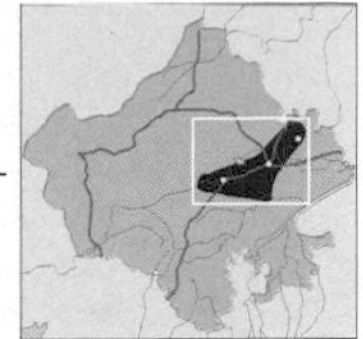
The east

THE EAST, *129*

Jaipur, *130*
Amber, *146*
Around Jaipur, *158*
Ajmer, *162*
Pushkar, *164*
Kishangarh and Makrana, *166*
Alwar, *168*
Around Alwar, *178*

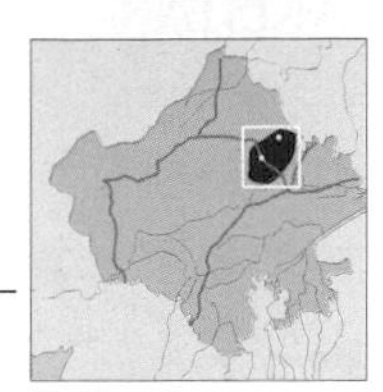
Shekhavati

SHEKHAVATI, *179*

Samode and Sikar, *180*
Nawalgarh to Baggar, *182*
Ramgarh, Mehensar and
Lachhmangarh, *190*

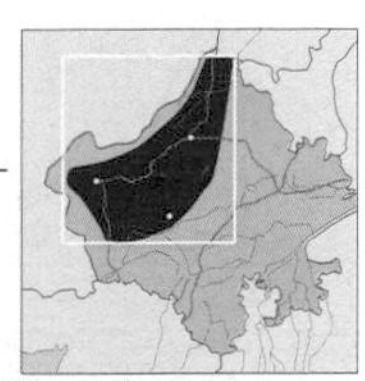
The northwest

THE NORTHWEST, *191*

Bikaner, *192*
Around Bikaner, *206*
Jaisalmer, *208*
Around Jaisalmer, *216*
Jodhpur, *220*
Around Jodhpur, *232*

The south

THE SOUTH, *239*

Udaipur, *240*
The Raj, *252*
Around Udaipur, *240*
Dharna Vihara, *262*
Mount Abu, *268*
Jain temples, *272*
Nakki Lake to Sirohi, *274*
Chittorgarh, *276*

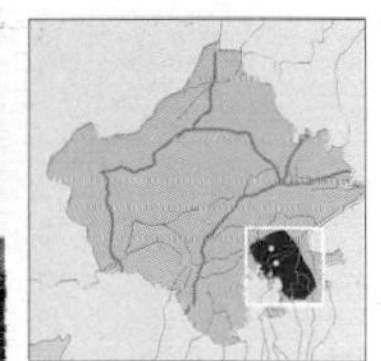
The southeast

THE SOUTHEAST, *279*

Kota, *280*
Bundi, *290*
Garh Palace, *292*

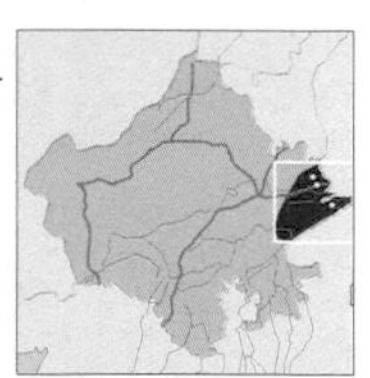
Bharatpur to Karauli

BHARATPUR TO KARAULI, *299*

Bharatpur, *300*
Ranthambhor, *304*
Birds of Bharatpur, *308*
Around Bharatpur, *310*

PRACTICAL INFORMATION, *313*

Getting there, *314*
Local transport, *316*
Getting around from A to Z, *318*
Hotels and restaurants, *326*
Places to visit, *341*
Appendices, *346*

1. Jaipur
2. Sikar
3. Sambhar Lake
4. Ajmer
5. Nagaur
6. Bikaner
7. Jodhpur
8. Jaisalmer
9. Barmer
10. Mount Abu
11. Udaipur
12. Debar Lake
13. Chittorgarh
14. Kishangarh
PAKISTAN
GUJARAT
8
6
5
7
9
10
11
13
12

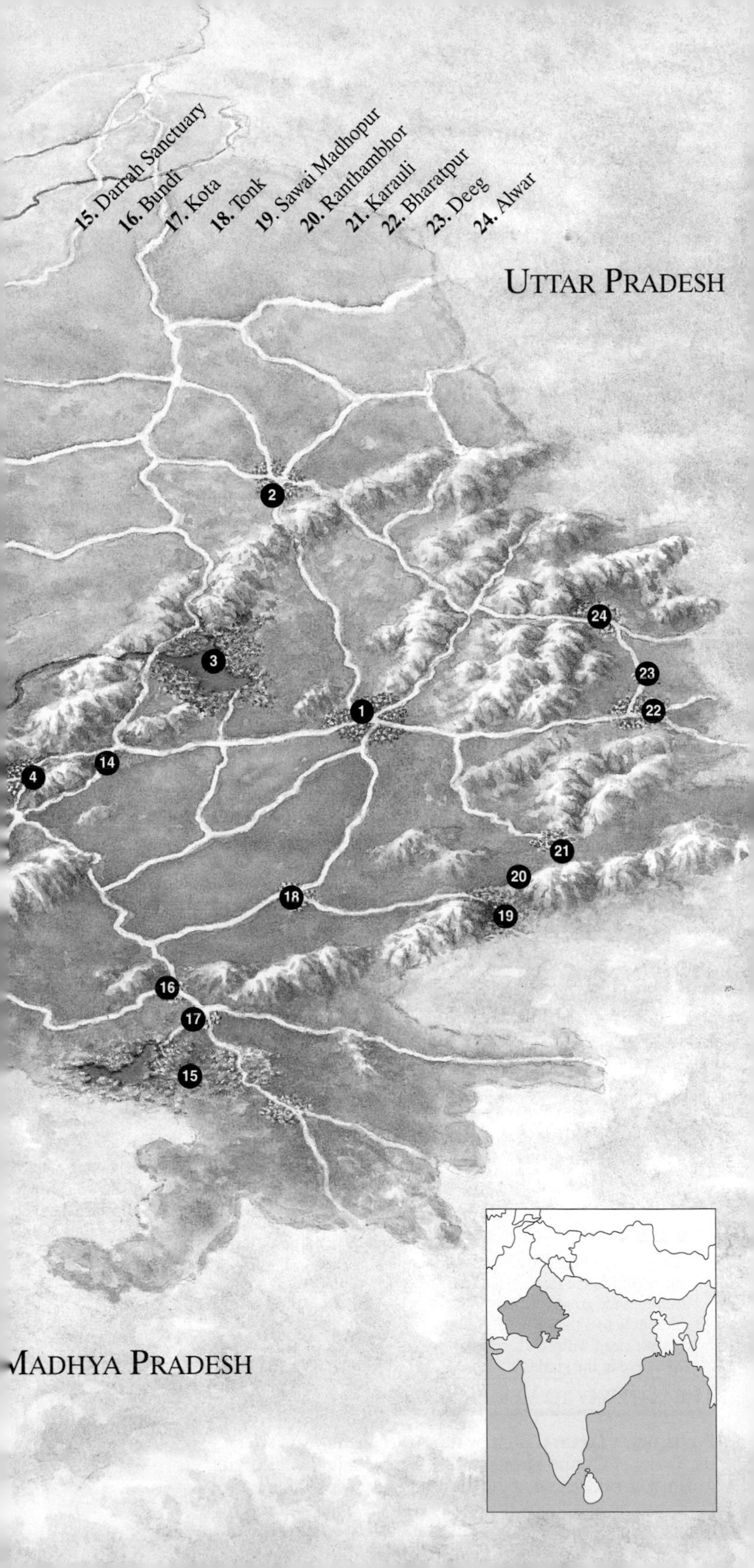
15. Darrah Sanctuary
16. Bundi
17. Kota
18. Tonk
19. Sawai Madhopur
20. Ranthambhor
21. Karauli
22. Bharatpur
23. Deeg
24. Alwar
UTTAR PRADESH
MADHYA PRADESH
1
2
3
4
14
15
16
17
18
19
20
21
22
23
24

How to Use this Guide

The symbols at the top of each page refer to the different parts of the guide.

- ■ Natural Environment
- ● Understanding Venice
- ▲ Itineraries
- ◆ Practical Information

The mini-map locates the particul itinerary within the wider area covered by the guide.

The itinerary map shows the main points of interest along the way and is intended to help you find your bearings.

Immediately outside the railway station lies Cannaregio, the first of the six sestieri of Venice. Situated at the north-west end of the city, this is the second largest sestiere after Castello ▲ 155, covering an area of 150 hectares. Nearly a third of the population of Venice is concentrated here, amounting to more than twenty thousand people. There are two theories about the origins of the name Cannaregio; according to one, it comes from *Canal regio* (the Royal Canal), meaning the broad waterway which once provided convenient access to the city from the mainland, by prolonging the lagoon canal of San Secundo (which runs parallel to the railway bridge). The other hypothesis is that the word derives from the reeds and canes which used to abound in this area. In any case, a system of straight, parallel canals, with long fondamenta abutting southwards and linked by calli, criss-cross this zone of workmen's houses interspersed with magnificent palaces. To the south, behind the palaces of the Grand Canal, a wide street known as the Strada Nuova was built at the end of the last century. Now pedestrianized, this street runs from the station to the Campo Santi Apostoli, crossing the sestiere from one side to the other and adopting a number of different names as it goes. Few people lived in this sestiere until the 11th century, and it seems to have taken form only gradually, as the process of draining and consolidating the site progressed. From the 15th century onwards, Cannaregio was a definable quarter, though it was still peripheral to Venice proper. Before the railway bridge and the station were built, manufacturing was the principal industry in the district, despite attempts to create a new area of growth with the Fondamenta Nuove. A similar project in the 16th century, the draining of the Sacca della Misericordia, was also never realized.

"The gateway to Venice, after all, is neither the station nor the Piazzale, but the Grand Canal before us, churned by propellers, turbulent as a great river."
Fernand Braudel, *Venise*

Santa Lucia Station.

136

The Gateway to Venice ★

Ponte della Liberta. Built by the Austrians 50 years after the Treaty of Campo Formio in 1797 ● *34*, to link Venice with Milan. The bridge ended the thousand-year separation from the mainland and shook the city's economy to its roots as Venice, already in the throes of the industrial revolution, saw its dependence on the mainland grow out of all recognition. **Santa Lucia Station.** The present station dates from 1955, but still bears the name of the Renaissance church demolished in 1861 to make way for it. Opposite is the green dome of the Church of San Simeone Piccolo.

Half a day

Bridges to Venice The Austrians conceived a project for a bridge between Mestre and Venice as early as 1814, but it was not until 1846 that construction of the Ponte della Liberta was finally begun. The span of this new viaduct was almost 11,500 feet, and it included 222 stone arches. On April 25, 1933, the Ponte delle Littorale was opened. Built in less than two years by the engineer Umberto Fantucci, this bridge was intended for use by motor cars.

136

★ The star symbol signifies that a particular site has been singled out by the publishers for its special beauty, atmosphere or cultural interest.

At the beginning of each itinerary, the suggested means of transport to be used and the time it will take to cover the area are indicated:

- By boat
- On foot
- By bicycle
- Duration

● ▲ ■ ◆
The symbols alongside a title or within the text itself provide cross-references to a theme or place dealt with elsewhere in the guide.

The Gateway to Venice ★

Ponte della Liberta. Built by the Austrians 50 years after the Treaty of Campo Formio in 1797 ● *34,* to link Venice with Milan. The bridge ended the thousand-year separation from the mainland and shook the city's economy to its roots as Venice, already in the throes of the industrial revolution, saw

Half a day

Bridges to Venice

Nature

16 Natural ecosystems
18 Geology
20 Traditional agriculture
22 Agriculture and irrigation
24 Fauna
26 Endangered species
28 Birds
30 Flora

Human activity, including an ever-increasing population and excessive grazing by livestock, has had a severe impact on the natural ecosystems in Rajasthan. The lack of rainfall, poor vegetation, low soil fertility, susceptibility to erosion, and a series of droughts have also left their mark on this region. Yet fascinating vestiges remain of the original topography and natural ecosystems. While the claim that Rajasthan's desert is entirely man-made is an exaggeration, the role of the human population in accentuating aridity cannot be denied.

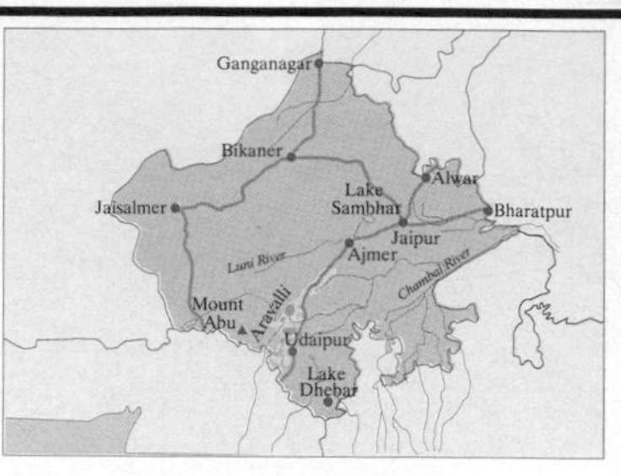

1. SANDY ARID PLAINS (MARUSTHALI)
This region, also known as 'Thar Desert', comprises sand dunes interspersed with silt-covered valleys. It extends to about 40,000 square miles.

2. SEMI-ARID PLAINS
These stretch from Shekhavati in the north to the Godawar plain, north of Mount Abu in the south, with the Aravallis to the east. Seasonal water courses, such as the Sukri-Jawai, originating in the Aravallis, flow through it. The plains, sparsely covered with trees and bushes, are studded with rocky outcrops and sand hills called *bhits*.

3. ARAVALLI RANGE
The most distinctive and ancient mountain chain of peninsular India, the Aravallis mark the site of one of the oldest geological formations in the world. Heavily eroded and with exposed outcrops of slate rock and granite, it has summits reaching 4950 feet above sea level. It bisects the State of Rajasthan.

4. EASTERN PLAINS
Sloping gradually eastward from the Aravallis, the plateau consists of undulating, once forested hills, especially in southern Mewar around the Bagad region of Udaipur, where there is more rainfall.

5. CHAMBAL VALLEY
The middle portions of the Chambal, the largest river and most reliable water source of Rajasthan, are marked by heavily eroded valleys and ravines. The region is a low plateau, cut by the Vindhya range, and covered with shallow soil, exposed rock, and coarse grasses in the upper reaches.

SECTION OF DESERT

STABILIZED SAND DUNES
Some sand dunes have been stabilized by *Calligonum polygonoides* shrubs and clumps of *Panicum turgidum*.

LONGITUDINAL SAND DUNES
The dunes, often parallel, usually run in a northeast to southwest direction, corresponding to the prevailing monsoon and winter wind directions.

WOOD FOSSILS
During the Jurassic age some 180 million years ago, the western region of Rajasthan was covered by forest. Now much of the region is desert. The forest was fossilized in geological times and buried by soil and sand in recent times. Wind and water erosion has exposed colorful wood fossils of large conifer trees. These fossils are scattered over a large area 11 miles south of Jaisalmer.

SHELL FOSSILS
Shell fossils are the remnants of the marine life which existed in the desert region of Jaisalmer some 2000 million years ago.

ARAVALLI RANGE

MOUNT ABU
The Abu massif in the southwestern corner of Rajasthan rises from the plains, a rocky outcrop separated from the Aravalli range, forming a distinctive microcosm of its own. Its highest point, Gurushikhar peak, reaches 5693 feet above sea level.

ASBESTOS
Asbestos ("rock wool") is a fibrous material used in making roof sheets and pipes.

Rajasthan is rich in mineral deposits, both metallic ones, such as copper, zinc, lead, and tungsten, and non-metallic ones, such as limestone, super lime, marble, dolomite, soapstone, sandstone, gypsum, granite, and mica, as well as carbonaceous fuel minerals such as lignite. Explorations are in progress for fossil oil since natural gas has already been found in the desert region. Precious stones such as diamonds and emeralds are also being prospected in Ajmer district. Mining of copper, zinc, and lead, and quarrying of sandstone, limestone, marble, mica, silica, and gypsum are some of the principal economic activities of the state.

DISTRIBUTION OF MINERALS

- Asbestos
- Barytes
- Beryllium
- Clay
- Copper
- Emerald
- Feldspar
- Garnet
- Gypsum
- Iron
- Kyanite
- Lead and zinc
- Lignite
- Limestone
- Manganese
- Sandstone
- Rock phosphate
- Marble
- Mica
- Salt
- Silica sand and quartz
- Steatite
- Tungsten
- Vermiculite
- Granite

4. COPPER
Copper pyrite is found in hydrothermal veins in the Delhi series of rocks in Khetri (Jhunjhunu district) and Khoh Dariba in Alwar. A large smelting plant has been established at Khetri.

SANDSTONE
Sandstone, shown in situ above, is largely found in the Vindhyan supergroup in Dholpur and Karauli and in the Marwar supergroup of rocks in Jodhpur and Nagaur districts. It is used exclusively for building construction.

7.

ROCK STRATIFICATIONS

- Recent
- Tertiary
- Deccan trap
- Triassic-cretaceous
- Permo-carboniferous
- Marwar supergroup
- Malani igneous suite
- Delhi supergroup
- Aravalli supergroup
- Bhilwara supergroup
- Vindhyan supergroup

ROCK STRATIFICATIONS
The geology of Rajasthan represents all major rock stratifications, from some of the oldest fragments of the earth's crust of the Bhilwara supergroup formed some 2500 million years ago to the sedimentary Delhi series, Vindhyan, Marwar super and Deccan trap to the recent sand-dune formations.

7. ROCK PHOSPHATE
Rock phosphate deposits have been discovered in the Aravalli supergroup of rocks and in Jaisalmer, Jaipur, and Banswara. It is a direct fertilizer, ideal for tea gardens where the climate is damp.

Left to right: Granite rock field; marble ready for cutting; mini cement plant.

1. Limestone
Limestone is found extensively in the Vindhyan supergroup deposits in Alwar, Sawai Madhopur, Chittorgarh, and Jaisalmer. It is used for cement manufacture. A high-quality limestone discovered at Jaisalmer is used in the steel industry.

2. Iron
Iron ore was known to early Iron Age civilization. It is found in Jaipur and in small deposits in Udaipur.

3. Pink quartz
Quartz varies in color according to the iron compound present in the rock. It is used for the manufacture of ceramic wares and optical instruments. Quartz is found in Alwar, Ajmer, and Sirohi.

5. Mica
Mica is a group of minerals (silicates of aluminium) which is capable of splitting in thin laminas. The commonest form, called muscovite, is used as insulating material in electric appliances and fillers in rubber tyres. Mica is found in Bhilwara, Rajsamand, and Jaipur.

6. Pink granite
Granite is predominantly a crystalized homogenous rock of quartz and feldspar with subordinate quantities of other minerals such as mica and hornblende. Granitic rock occurs in the Delhi series in Alwar and Aravalli formations in Pali, Sirohi, Ajmer, Jalore, Barmer, Bhilwara, and Banswara.

8. Garnet
Garnet, a semi-precious stone, is found in high-grade pellet-like sediments of pre-Aravalli age in Udaipur and Tonk. It is transparent and colored red, lilac, or pink.

9. Marble
Marble is a metamorphosed form of limestone rock. The marble of Makrana made the famous Taj Mahal. Marble is also quarried in Bundi, Kishangarh, Nagaur, Rajsamand, and Abu Road. Presence of iron salts creates different colors in the marble.

10. Lead ore
Lead is found in Jawar, Dariba, and the Rajpura-Agucha mines in the Aravalli series of rocks in Udaipur.

The earliest evidence of cultivation in Rajasthan comes from the excavations at Kalibangan in the northeast. A field surface dated to early 3000 BC uncovered there still retains the marks of furrows, laid out at right angles to each other, suggesting that a wooden plough had been used. Studies of archeobotanical remains of the succeeding mature Harappan civilization, dated to the middle and late third millennium BC, revealed that barley (*Hordeum*) of two varieties, wheat (*Triticum sp.*), and gram (*Cirer arietinum*) were cultivated.

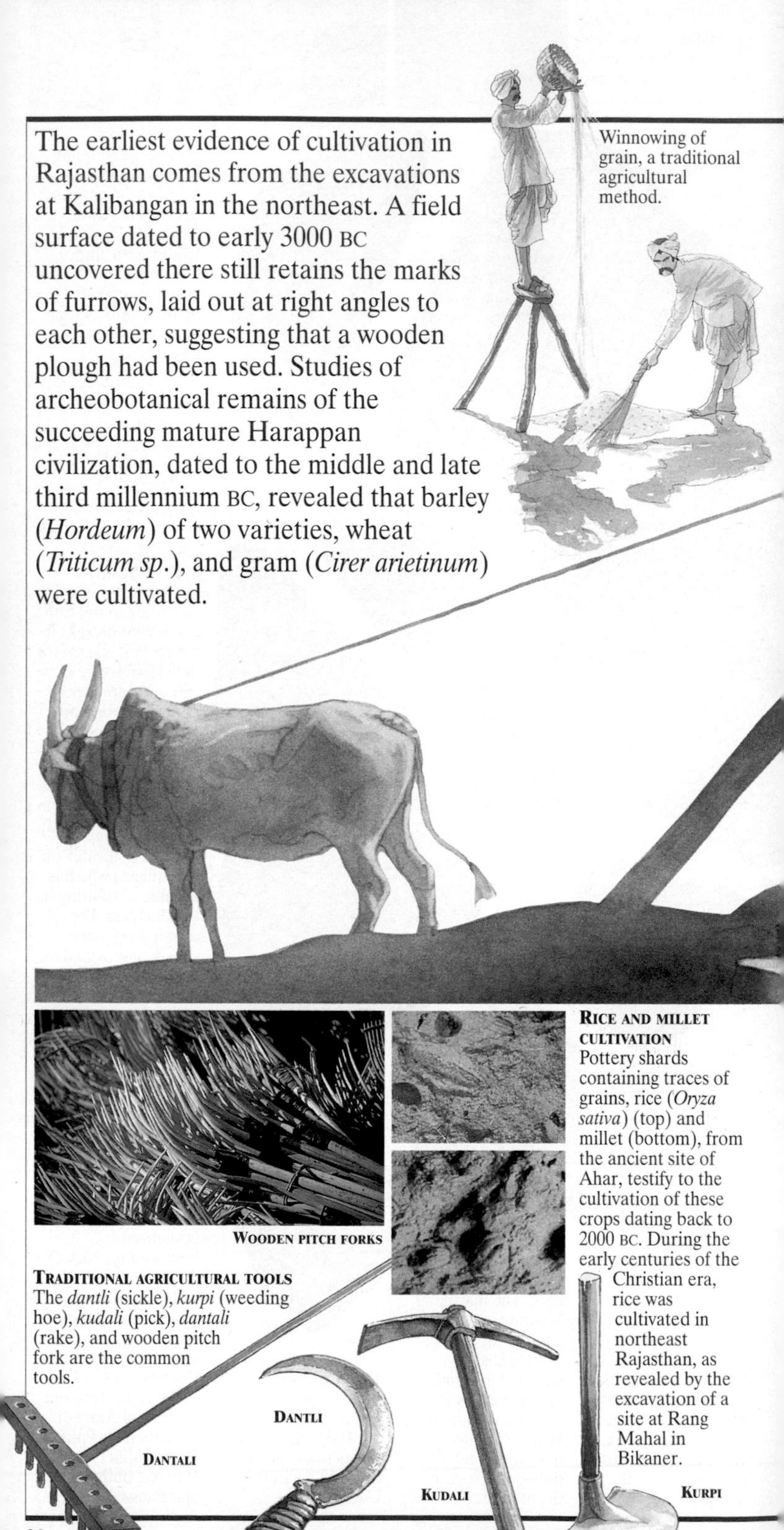

Winnowing of grain, a traditional agricultural method.

RICE AND MILLET CULTIVATION
Pottery shards containing traces of grains, rice (*Oryza sativa*) (top) and millet (bottom), from the ancient site of Ahar, testify to the cultivation of these crops dating back to 2000 BC. During the early centuries of the Christian era, rice was cultivated in northeast Rajasthan, as revealed by the excavation of a site at Rang Mahal in Bikaner.

TRADITIONAL AGRICULTURAL TOOLS
The *dantli* (sickle), *kurpi* (weeding hoe), *kudali* (pick), *dantali* (rake), and wooden pitch fork are the common tools.

Ploughing with camels (left); monsoon ploughing (right).

Irrigation using a mote (the sewn-up skin of a large domestic animal) was once a common method in the arid western region.

CROSSED FURROWS
The pattern of the crossed furrows (right), closely spaced in one direction and more widely spaced in the other, is still used for planting two crops simultaneously.

TRADITIONAL IRRIGATION METHODS
The Pratapgarh inscription of AD 946 records the various methods of irrigation prevalent at that time. The main devices include a wineskin, called a *koshavahaka*, pitchers, and the Persian wheel ■ *23*. In the 15th century, Babur also wrote about the use of a wineskin tied with a length of rope which passed over a roller, with the other end of the rope being tied to a bullock. This simple irrigation method is still practiced today.

Agriculture and irrigation

Rajasthan's economy is mainly agriculture-based. About 80 percent of the population lives in rural areas and is dependent on farming. Cereal crops such as *bajra*, *juar*, wheat, and barley cover the largest cultivated area. About 30 percent of the total cultivated area is irrigated. The Indira Gandhi (or Rajasthan) canal provides irrigation to the arid western districts of Bikaner and Jaisalmer. Ganganagar district is irrigated with water from the Ganga canal in the Punjab ▲ *194*. Irrigation projects have also developed on the Chambal and Luni rivers. The western region grows predominantly *kharif* (monsoon) crops, while the eastern belt, which has better rains and soil, grows both *kharif* and *rabi* (winter) crops. The latter is grown under rain-fed farming conditions or in irrigated areas.

Key
1. Juar
2. Makka/ Maize
3. Bajra
4. Cotton
5. Wheat
6. Gram
7. Sesame
8. Groundnut

Bajra
Bajra (*Pennisetum typhoideum*) is consumed by the rural poor, particularly the nomads. Rajasthan is the largest producer of *bajra* in India.

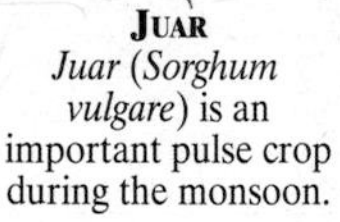

Juar
Juar (*Sorghum vulgare*) is an important pulse crop during the monsoon.

Barley
Barley (*Hordeum vulgare*) is the second largest crop in Rajasthan.

Sesame
Rajasthan provides the second highest quantum of sesame (*Sesamum indicum*) in India. One of its common uses is as an ingredient in sweetmeats.

Gram
Gram (*Cicer arietinum*) (right) is another major pulse crop grown in *rabi*.

Maize
(*Zea mays*) is a staple crop for the Bhil tribes in the Aravallis. In northern Rajasthan, maize is a delicacy eaten with butter and the green leaf of the mustard plant.

Cotton
Cotton (*Gossypium sp.*), used to make the famous Rajasthani textiles, is a major cash crop.

Wheat
Wheat (*Triticum sp.*) is cultivated on irrigated land.

Groundnut
Groundnut is a major *kharif* oilseed crop.

Sugarcane, sold in the market (right), is grown in irrigated areas, mostly in the eastern region.

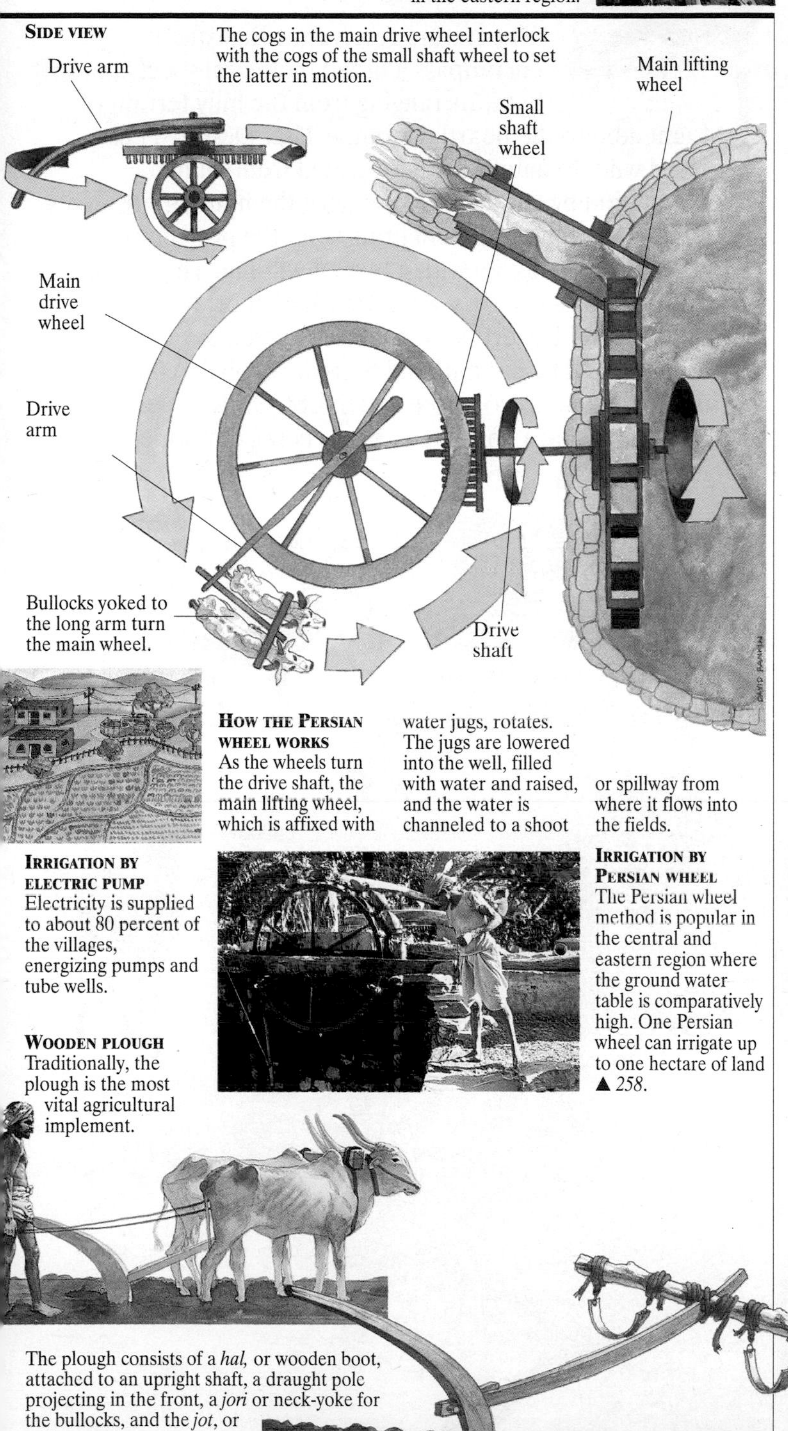

The cogs in the main drive wheel interlock with the cogs of the small shaft wheel to set the latter in motion.

Bullocks yoked to the long arm turn the main wheel.

HOW THE PERSIAN WHEEL WORKS
As the wheels turn the drive shaft, the main lifting wheel, which is affixed with water jugs, rotates. The jugs are lowered into the well, filled with water and raised, and the water is channeled to a shoot or spillway from where it flows into the fields.

IRRIGATION BY ELECTRIC PUMP
Electricity is supplied to about 80 percent of the villages, energizing pumps and tube wells.

IRRIGATION BY PERSIAN WHEEL
The Persian wheel method is popular in the central and eastern region where the ground water table is comparatively high. One Persian wheel can irrigate up to one hectare of land ▲ *258*.

WOODEN PLOUGH
Traditionally, the plough is the most vital agricultural implement.

The plough consists of a *hal,* or wooden boot, attached to an upright shaft, a draught pole projecting in the front, a *jori* or neck-yoke for the bullocks, and the *jot*, or collar strap.

COMMON LANGUR
The common langur, with its shiny, white-gray coat, jet black face, and lanky limbs with long fingers, is a leaf-eating monkey.

The nature reserves of Rajasthan encompass a broad biological spectrum, with habitats ranging from the hilly terrain of Mount Abu to the heartland of the Thar Desert. These special wildlife habitats are protected from human depredation by law. Some were once the hunting preserves of the maharajas and, benefiting from the protection afforded, now hold a wide range of wildlife. The species featured here can be seen at Ranthambhor, Keoladeo Ghana, and Desert National Park, as well as sanctuaries such as Gajner, Tal Chappar, and Sariska. Keoladeo Ghana is a World Heritage site recognized by UNESCO. Reserves such as Kumbhalgarh and Sitamata are being developed as national parks.

SAMBAR
The *sambar,* with its magnificent antlers, is the largest deer of India. When danger is sensed, it gives a high-pitched, metallic, trumpet-like call. If repeated, the call confirms the presence of a predator.

CHINKARA
The *chinkara* lives in small family herds in dry, deciduous, bracken, rocky, open country, as well as in sandy deserts.

Key
■ National park
▲ Sanctuary

Sloth bear
The sloth bear is a clumsy-looking, shaggy animal which lives in deciduous forests. It feeds on fruit and honey, but its favorite food is termites which it obtains by breaking into termite mounds using its strong claws. Sloth bears are nocturnal and do not hibernate, although they may shelter and sleep in secluded dens.

Protected areas
1. Desert
2. Wood Fossil Park
3. Kanodiawala Rann
4. Gajner
5. Tal Chappar
6. Sariska
7. Keoladeo Ghana
8. Baretha
9. Vanvihar
10. Ranthambhor
11. Chambal
12. Ramgarh
13. Darrah
14. Jawahar Sagar
15. Sitamata
16. Jaisamand
17. Mount Abu
18. Kumbhalgarh
19. Doli-Dhawa

Marsh crocodile
The Indian marsh crocodile, or mugger, is the largest aquatic predator of rivers and lakes in India. It feeds on insects, frogs, and fish, while adults prey on small mammals, birds, snakes and even deer and buffalo. The female lays forty to fifty eggs, which are buried in the sandbank to be hatched by the sun's heat.

Rock python
The rock python is a large, sluggish reptile which preys on small mammals by strangling them. It swallows its prey in one piece.

Four-horned antelope
The four-horned antelope is a solitary animal which lives in hilly regions with tall grass. It walks with graceful yet jerky movements.

Chital
In color, design and shape, the *chital* is the most handsome deer of India. It lives in forests interspersed with patchy, open meadows, in herds which swell to a few hundred.

Blackbuck
The blackbuck, with its long, pointed, spiraling horn, is an impressive creature. Males live in open, grassy wastelands in the company of ten to fifteen hornless female bucks. The bucks fight fierce territorial battles and are often seen chasing their errant females to bring them back to their harem.

Jackal
The jackal, with its conspicuous evening howling chorus, was once a common scavenger of the forests and villages. It has been heavily hunted

Nilgai
The *nilgai* is a robust antelope which lives in open country. The bull is ashy black with spiky, forward-turned horns. The female is fawn-colored. The *nilgai* moves in an ungainly fashion.

Smooth Indian otter
The smooth Indian otter, which is exclusively a fish predator, is the most common otter in India although its habitat.

For decades, over a hundred tigers were shot in the annual hunts of the maharajas of Rajasthan. Other hunts, such as the unleashing of cheetahs on blackbucks, and caracals on game birds, were also a princely pastime ▲ *176*. Even Akbar hunted antelopes with his favored cheetah in the open wastelands of Sanganer near Jaipur. But such scenes are now a thing of the past. Overhunting for trade and the loss and destruction of natural habitats constitute the main threats to wildlife. A total ban on hunting and the emergence of national parks and sanctuaries are helping to protect some of the threatened species.

LEOPARD
The leopard has a great talent for survival, feeding on deer, antelopes, and other small mammals, as well as birds. It lives in thick forests and open arid country, including rocky outcrops. Overhunting for its spotted, light golden colored coat has made it an endangered species.

STRIPED HYENA
The striped hyena feeds on carrion since its body structure is not adapted for the speed and agility needed for killing fast-running animals except when two or more corner a helpless antelope or deer.

WOLF
The wolf preys on antelopes, deer, rabbits, and livestock. It lives in pairs or small family packs in open wastelands and mountains.

DESERT FOX
The desert fox preys on gerbils, lizards, birds, and insects and, when in season, on desert fruits. It breeds in spring, commonly raising two to four pups.

Siberian crane
The Siberian crane breeds in south Siberia and arrives at the marshes of Bharatpur for feeding during the winter months ▲ *307*. It has become endangered probably as a result of hunting and the disappearance of wetlands. No birds arrived at Keoladeo Ghana in 1994.

Great Indian bustard
The Great Indian Bustard is the state bird of Rajasthan. It feeds on lizards, locusts, beetles, and small birds. These birds make a nest in which a single egg is laid. The eggs are often destroyed by cattle.

Caracal
The caracal is an agile cat of the open jungle. It feeds on small mammals and birds.

Tiger
The tiger, one of the most magnificent animals of India, has long fascinated people with its awesome power and beautifully patterned coat. Adult tigers are solitary animals. Male and female tigers remain together only for a short period when the latter is in heat. Two to three cubs are born, but on average just one survives. Cubs remain with their mother for two years, by which time they have learned to fend for themselves.

Gharial
The long, thin snout of the gharial (right) is designed for catching fish such as catfish and tilapia. The females bury their eggs in a deep nest dug in a sandy bank above the flood level; as many as sixty eggs may be laid. The female guards the nest against predators.

The metallic blue neck and open crest add grace to the peacock, India's national bird.

SARUS CRANE
In summer, they gather in their hundreds at drying lakes ▲ *307*.

The sub-tropical forests of Mount Abu, the dry, deciduous, hilly forests of the Aravallis, and the arid, open grasslands of the Thar Desert, with its dry land farming, create ideal habitats for birds and support a wide range of the birdlife of Rajasthan. But the feature which makes the State unique is its location on the bird-migration flyways: not only for water birds flying from Siberia to the tropical and sub-tropical wetlands, but also for the terrestrial houbaras, sandgrouse, larks and cranes, and their predators, the eagles, falcons, and hawks in the desert lands. Rajasthan is also on the flight path of birds flying from the south to the Himalayas.

PEACOCK
The peacock's elaborate train, with its colorful moons and crescents, allures peahens to mate during the monsoon when many mating calls can be heard.

RING DOVE
The ring dove, a common bird, is a symbol of peace and charity. It feeds on small grains and constructs a simple nest in which two eggs are laid. These are incubated alternately by both parents.

COMMON SANDGROUSE
The common sandgrouse flies for miles every morning to congregate noisily in the hundreds at waterholes to drink.

GRAY PARTRIDGE
The gray partridge is a prized bird of open scrub jungles. Its elegant walk and high-pitched challenging calls make it conspicuous. It nests on the ground and raises a covey of eight to ten chicks.

BLOSSOM-HEADED PARAKEET
It lives in small flocks feeding on shoots, flowers, and fruits.

PHEASANT-TAILED JACANA
The pheasant-tailed jacana is a wetland species. The male develops a beautiful tail as a breeding plumage. The female constructs a well-anchored floating nest and lays four eggs which are hatched by the male.

WHITE-BACK VULTURE
This scavenger lives in pairs and makes its nest on rocky peaks or on the top-most branches of large trees. It is often seen circling high in the sky in search of an animal carcase on which to feed.

CRESTED SERPENT EAGLE
The crested serpent eagle is a bird of open forests with well-distributed waterholes. Perched on a tree, the eagle keeps a watchful eye open for game birds coming to drink, as well as snakes that emerge from ponds in search of rodents and lizards.

SMALL GREEN BEE-EATER
The small green bee-eater feeds on bees and insects.

FLAMINGO
The flamingo is a mysterious bird; its nesting places are located in inaccessible, brackish marshlands. One such site is the Rann of Kachchh, where they breed. The birds live in large flocks and feed by sifting tiny plankton from the brackish waters. Their walk, flight, and landings are delightfully graceful.

STONE CURLEW
The stone curlew is a curious-looking bird, with its round, large eyes and its body perched on long legs. Living on open ground, it relies on the subtle colors of its plumage for camouflage against predators. It spends much time surveying the ground before returning to its nest.

DEMOISELLE CRANE
The demoiselle crane, or *kurja*, migrates to Rajasthan in large flocks in late September, where it breeds. The flocks scatter in search of drying lakes, and ripening gram and groundnut fields for feeding.

ANWAL
The bark of *anwal* (*Cassia auriculata*), a perennial shrub, is a source of tanning material.

The natural vegetation of Rajasthan is of two distinct types, perennial and ephemeral, the latter occurring only during the monsoon. Desert National Park in Jaisalmer provides a prime example of extant Thar flora: grassland dotted with xerophytic (arid-climate) shrubs and stunted trees. The Thar Desert was once forested, as evidenced by wood fossils near Jaisalmer ■ *17*.

KHEJRI
Khejri (*Prosopis cineraria*) is an all-purpose tree held sacred by Hindus ▲ *202*. Its pods are eaten as vegetables, while its leaves provide valuable fodder. During famines, even its bark is consumed.

BABUL
Babul (Acacia arabica), which flourishes in valleys and places where the soil is deep, is found particularly in the Chambal Valley.

AKARO
Akaro (Calotropis procera), a commonly found plant, is widely used: its fibres for making rope; its latex and root-bark for medicine; and the soft floss from its seeds for stuffing pillows.

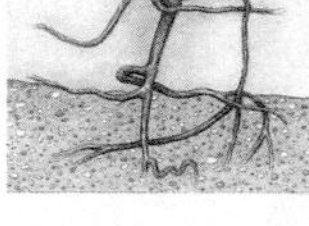

ROOT SYSTEM
Perennial xerophytic plants have deep tap roots. The roots of a 20-foot high *khejri* tree may penetrate 100 feet beneath the top sandy soil to find water.

TUMBO
Tumbo (*Citrullus colocynthis*) (above) is a perennial creeping plant. Its fruit is used in indigenous medicines and as a purgative.

BORDI
Bordi (*Zizyphus nummularia*) has delicious, red berries and leaves that are relished by camels and goats. Its dried twigs are used with the aromatic roots of the *khas* grass (*Vetiveria zizanioides*) for making screens.

DESERT GRASS
Perennial grasses such as *Eragrostis plumosa* not only help bind soil and dunes together, but are also a good source of fodder for livestock.

KER
Ker (*Capparis decidua*) is commonly found on rock, gravel and sandy plains. Its unripe fruit is eaten as pickles and vegetables. The plant flowers twice a year.

History

32 Early history
34 Princely States
36 Rajputs and the Mughals
38 British India and Independence
40 Modern times
42 Languages

Sculpture from Kalibangan (left) and Harappan seal (right).

2500 BC TO EARLY RAJPUTS

On the northwestern limits of India lies Rajasthan. The name literally means the "Land of Kings (rajas)". Since a large part of the State is covered by the arid and desolate Thar Desert, its very inhospitality had bred a race of tough and brave warriors, the Rajputs. The land fostered independent kingdoms and also attracted enterprising merchants.

2500 BC – HARAPPAN CIVILIZATION. In 1965 archeologists discovered the site of Kalibangan ▲ *207* in the Ganganagar district of Rajasthan, just 100 miles from the famous site of Harappa. Kalibangan is located on the left bank of the now dry river, Ghaggar. The excavations at Kalibangan established a link with the Harappan era, which flourished between 2500 and 1500 BC and was part of the Indus Valley Civilization, which has been traced back to 6000 BC. Harappa represented the zenith of the Bronze Age and was the apogee of the Indus Valley Civilization. Its emphasis on town planning was a mark of a well-established society.

THE ARYANS. When the Indus Valley Civilization was dying out, a new group of migrants, the Aryans, moved from Central Asia through Iran into the Indian subcontinent. They brought a new political and social organization and a new religion, the Vedic religion, based on their holy books, the *Vedas* (derived from the word *vid*, which means "to know") ● *44*. The first of these was the *Rig Veda,* believed to have been composed between 2000 and 1000 BC. The *Vedas* were written in an older form of Sanskrit, the Aryan mother tongue in India. Thus this period, from the coming of the Aryans to around 500 BC, is known as the Vedic Age.

ORIGIN OF THE RAJPUTS. According to orthodox Hindu views, the Rajputs of Rajasthan were the direct descendants of the Kshatriyas or warriors of Vedic India. They were first mentioned in the oldest Hindu stories, the *Puranas* ● *44,* about 1000 BC, as the "solar" or *suryavanshi* – those descended from Rama, the hero of the epic *Ramayana* – and the "lunar" or *chandravanshi,* who claimed descent from Krishna, the hero of the *Mahabharata*. A third clan was the *agnikula* or fire-born, said to have emerged from the ritual fire or *yajna* atop the sacred mountain, Mount Abu, in Rajasthan ▲ *269*.

HISTORICAL RECORDS. The conquests by many races have perhaps been responsible for the lack of historical records in India. For the history of

2700 BC
Date of the Indus Valley seals found at Kish.

2500–1500 BC
Indus civilization in India.

1435 BC
Aryan kings in Western Asia.

6TH CENTURY BC
Mahavira ● *49, the founder of the Jain sect.*

Harivamsha Purana manuscript (right). (Below) Colonel Tod at the Mewar court.

Chandravati stone sculptures (right and below).

Rajasthan we are dependent on the accounts of foreigners such as Alberuni, an Arab scholar, in the 11th century, or Ferishta, a Deccanese Muslim scholar, in the 16th century. Information can be also gleaned from inscriptions, old coins, sculptures and deeds commemorating the gift of land, wells, temples, and the like by the ruler to his subjects. But perhaps the best record of events and descriptions of kingdoms and battles fought between them is contained in the *khyats* or historical prose and verses written by the royal bards, the Charans and the Bhatts ● *54*, who were patronized by the rulers. The best known of these are Chand Bardai, who in the 12th century immortalized the last Hindu ruler of Delhi, Prithviraj Chauhan, and Narpati Nalha, whose earliest manuscripts date from the 14th century. With the advent of the British came Colonel James Tod, who wrote *Annals and Antiquities of Rajasthan*, which became one of the primary texts on Rajasthani history.

The first rulers. There is evidence of the Kushanas ruling western India in AD 40. The Kushanas came from Central Asia and straddled the Hindu Kush mountains in the north, establishing their capital at Peshawar on the Great North-West Road between the Indus and the Khyber Pass. Their supremacy lasted between the 1st and 3rd centuries AD. The Aryans settled down to different occupations, which later led to the creation of the caste system.

Rajput strongholds. The Rajputs were divided into thirty-six races and twenty-one kingdoms. The leaders were the Sisodias of Mewar (Udaipur), the Kachwahas of Amber (Jaipur), the Rathors of Marwar (Jodhpur) and Bikaner, the Haras of Kota and Bundi, the Bhattis of Jaisalmer and the Chauhans of Ajmer. From earliest times, the Rajput kings were called upon to play a difficult role: to defend their faith, to preserve their traditions and to protect Hindustan from the marauding attacks of the Muslim invaders. They paid a heavy price: their lands were often ravaged and their strongholds captured by the superior Muslim forces. But such was their valor and tenacity that they refused to be beaten despite the odds. The history of Rajasthan is the stuff of legends. The rajas fought for their honor, while the ranis who sent the men off to the field urged them to return victorious, or to die fighting on the battlefield. Suryamal, the royal bard of Bundi state in the 18th century, epitomized the valor of the Rajputs when he wrote, "The mother, while rocking the cradle, sings of bravery and sacrifice, preparing her son for death on the battlefield, rather than the dishonour of retreat."

327 BC
Alexander enters India.

322 BC
Accession of Chandragupta Maurya.

269 BC
Coronation of Ashoka.

AD 320
Beginning of Gupta era.

AD 500–42
Hunas rule in Malwa and Rajasthan.

Rajput noblemen.

Sun symbol of the Sisodias.

AD 629–45
Travels of Hieun Tsang.

997
Mahmud becomes Sultan of Ghazni.

1052
Red Fort at Delhi.

1163
Rise of the Chauhan Rajputs.

1192
Second Battle of Tarain. Fall of Prithviraj III Chauhan.

1206–90
The Slave Kings.

1231
Qutab Minar in Delhi.

Rao Bika transporting the heirlooms of Jodhpur.

1288
Marco Polo at Kayal.

1301
Capture of Ranthambhor by Alauddin Khilji.

1302–3
Capture of Chitor. Mongol invasion.

1325
Accession of Muhammad bin Tughlak.

1327
Transference of the capital from Delhi to Daulatabad.

1459
Foundation of Jodhpur Fort.

Battle scene at Jaisalmer Fort (right).

MEWAR. Of the Rajput states which kept alive the tradition of independence, pride of place undoubtedly belongs to Mewar and the Sisodias, who to this day are acknowledged as the first family in the Rajput hierarchy ▲ *240*. The legendary founder of this dynasty was Bappa Rawal, who established the capital city of Chittor in the 8th century AD. Because of the indomitable spirit of the rajas, the conquest of Chittor became a point of prestige for all invaders. It was attacked over the centuries by Alauddin Khilji, Sultan of Delhi, Bahadur Shah, Sultan of Malwa, and even the great Mughal, Akbar. Consequently in AD 1567, Udai Singh had to establish a new capital, Udaipur. The Sisodias produced a line of kings who became legendary heroes – Rana Kumbha, a man of letters who patronized the arts and built the Kirtistambha, or Tower of Fame, and the great fort, Kumbhalgarh ▲ *260*; Rana Sanga, who carried the scars of battle, having no less than eighty-four wounds on his body; and Maharana Pratap, who introduced guerilla warfare and refused to bow before the Mughals; he died an uncrowned king in 1597 ▲ *242*.

MARWAR. According to legend, the Rathor clan ▲ *220* is descended from a dynasty established in the kingdom of Kanauj under Jay Chaud. Conquered in 1193 by Mohammed of Ghor, the clan took refuge in Marwar, south of the Ganges. In 1459 their descendant, Rao Jodha, established the kingdom of Jodhpur, and Rao Jodha's son Bika ruled the state of Bikaner. In the 16th century, Raja Maldev annexed Bikaner state, exalting Marwar to the first place among Rajput states. When the Mughal emperor Humayun was defeated by the Afghan Sher Shah in 1540, Maldev offered him refuge in Marwar. Sher Shah took revenge and defeated Maldev. Maldev's son, Chandra Sen, succeeded him in 1562, but in 1572 Rai Singh of Bikaner attacked and occupied Marwar, severely wounding Chandra Sen. With the accession of Chandra Sen's brother, Udai Singh, Marwar's struggle against the Muslims and Mughals came to an end, and peace was established. In 1639, Jaswant Singh was the first ruler to be recognized as maharaja by the Mughal emperor, Shah Jahan.

JAISALMER. An oasis in the desert, Jaisalmer was important because it lay on the trade route from Jodhpur to Sind. The Bhattis, who founded the state in the 10th century AD, had been driven there by the pressure of the Arabs, and in 1156 Rao Jaisal founded the fort and city of Jaisalmer. For centuries it was an independent state, until Alauddin Khilji of Delhi captured the fort in 1294 and left it desolate for years. In 1570, the ruler Rawal Har Rai submitted to the Mughal emperor Akbar by giving his daughter in marriage. Consequently, from 1626 to 1702, Jaisalmer became one of the leading Rajput states.

BIKANER. In 1485, Bika, the son of Rao Jodha of Jodhpur, built the fort of Bikaner and three years later founded the

A fiscal stamp from Jodhpur State.

city. When Bika died in 1504, his influence extended to the borders of Ajmer, Delhi, and southeastern Punjab. There were frequent forays between the kingdoms of Jodhpur and Bikaner, which were suspended only with the supremacy of the Mughals. One of the most influential princes at the Mughal court was Rai Singh. Under his reign, Bikaner grew into a prosperous town, and the gigantic fort erected in 1588–92 was one of the most impressive in Rajasthan. Later Raja Anup Singh (reigned 1674–98) ▲ *199* encouraged art, science, and literature. Bikaner rose in prominence, along with Jaipur and Jodhpur.

AMBER. The erstwhile rulers of Amber (Jaipur) belonged to the Kachwaha clan, which is supposed to have migrated to Rajasthan around AD 1093. Legend has it that the founder, Duleh Rai, first had to defeat the Mina tribesmen who had lived in and ruled Amber for centuries, and that his son, Kakil Dev, established his kingdom at Amber in 1135. Amber rose to prominence in the 16th century under Raja Prithviraj, a great statesman and visionary. His son, Raja Bharmal, thought it wise to ally himself with the Mughals of Delhi, since Amber lay closer to Delhi than any of the other Rajput kingdoms. In 1727, Sawai Jai Singh II decided to establish the new city of Jaipur, which even today is considered a unique example of town planning ▲ *92*. Amber produced a number of rulers of exceptional abilities, including, among others, Bhagwan Das, Man Singh ▲ *131*, Sawai Jai Singh II (regarded as one of the most remarkable men of his age, being an astronomer, mathematician, and patron of the arts ▲ *131*), who raised the house of Amber from obscurity to prominence.

AJMER. The Chauhans of Ajmer were once a great power in northern India. Their rule extended to Delhi till AD 1192, when with the death of their ally, Prithviraj Chauhan, the last Hindu king of Delhi, they were eventually crushed by Shihabuddin Ghori in the Battle of Tarain.

BUNDI-KOTA. These two states were known as Haravati, or Province of the Haras, the most important branch of the Chauhan line. The founder was Rao Dewa, who captured the area from the Mina tribesmen. The name Kota came from Koteya, the chief of the Ujala Bhil tribe and ruler of this kingdom.

BHARATPUR. It is significant that this is the only Jat kingdom in a part of the country which has known only Rajput supremacy. Under Raja Ram the Jats were organized into a predatory power, looting caravans that passed the road from Delhi to Agra. The Jats were of peasant stock, and though they did claim descent from the moon, they were never accepted as Rajputs and could not intermarry with other Rajput clans. Historians have observed that up to the middle of the 18th century there was no Jat state, only a robber leader whose success had netted many as partners in plunder. Around 1722 Badan Singh organized these scattered units and established his supremacy ▲ *300*. His son, Surajmal, raised Jat power to the pinnacle of its glory. With the murder of Surajmal's son in 1768, Jat power declined. In 1826 the fort was captured by the British ▲ *301*, but the Jats continued to rule till 1947.

Prithviraj Chauhan (top) and Sawai Jai Singh II (bottom).

1497–98
First voyage of Vasco da Gama.

1526
First battle of Panipat. Founding of the Mughal Empire.

1556
Death of Humayun. Enthronement of Akbar.

Jat noblemen.

RAJPUTS AND THE MUGHALS

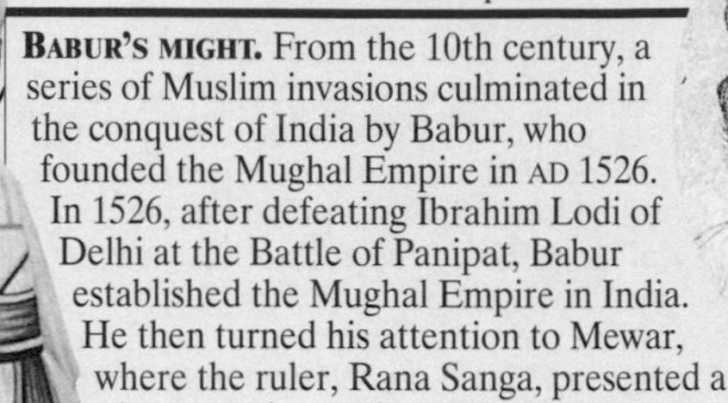

Emperor Akbar.

BABUR'S MIGHT. From the 10th century, a series of Muslim invasions culminated in the conquest of India by Babur, who founded the Mughal Empire in AD 1526. In 1526, after defeating Ibrahim Lodi of Delhi at the Battle of Panipat, Babur established the Mughal Empire in India. He then turned his attention to Mewar, where the ruler, Rana Sanga, presented a threat to his position. With better arms and military tactics, Babur won the Battle of Khanwa in 1527. The conquest of Rajasthan became one that earned prestige for subsequent Mughal rulers.

AKBAR. Babur's son, Humayun, was beset with enemies and had to take refuge at the Marwar court. But his son, Akbar, the greatest emperor of the Mughal dynasty, ascended the throne of Agra in 1556 and extended his hand of friendship to convert his inveterate foes into steadfast friends. His liberal policies and far-sightedness attracted many of the Rajput princes as vassals.

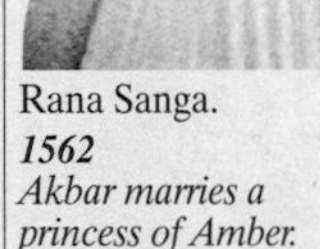

Rana Sanga.

1562
Akbar marries a princess of Amber.

1567
Fall of Chittor. Foundation of Fathepur Sikri, Agra.

1600
English East India Company founded.

1602
Dutch East India Company founded.

1615
Submission of Mewar to the Mughals.

1632–53
Building of the Taj Mahal.

MATRIMONIAL ALLIANCES. The Rajput princes realized the futility of fighting against a superior force, so they cemented their bonds through matrimonial alliances. The first alliance was that of the daughter of Bharmal of Amber with Akbar. His son, Bhagwan Das, gave his daughter Man Bai in marriage to Prince Salim, later to become Emperor Jahangir. Salim also took the Jodhpur princess, Jodha Bai, as his wife. Man Singh, Bhagwan Das' son, became one of Akbar's most trusted generals. Thus, by the time Akbar's grandson, Shah Jahan, was born, the Mughal emperor had three parts of Rajput blood.

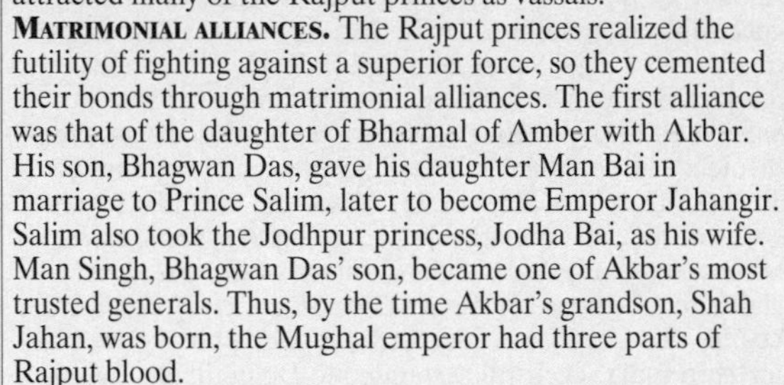

PERIOD OF PEACE. It can be said that the golden age of Rajput civilization was closely linked with the destiny of the Mughal Empire. Rajasthan's political and cultural contacts with the rest of India were considerably widened. This encouraged an assimilation of several cultures into the arts and traditions of the Rajput kingdoms, which were already renowned as centers of art and learning. *Karkhanas,* or craft workshops, were started, based on the Mughal model; Mughal miniature paintings aroused interest and Muslim artists came under royal patronage; Mughal buildings influenced Rajput architecture, and even the red sandstone color of the monuments of Agra inspired the "Pink City" of Jaipur. The musician, Behram Khan, from the Mughal court, was invited and established the tradition of *dhrupad* music in the Jaipur *gharana* style. Rajasthan still retains its position as a leader in the fields of arts and crafts, and dance and music, in India.

Shah Jahan as a prince.

THE RESISTANCE. The proud ranas of Mewar had singularly refused to bow before the Mughals. In 1572, by the time Maharana Pratap came to the throne, the princes of Amber, Bikaner, Jaisalmer, Sirohi, and Bundi had come into the Mughal orbit. But Maharana Pratap chose to take on Akbar's forces at the Battle of Haldighati in 1576 ▲ *242*. Though he was defeated, he continued guerilla warfare tactics for several years, eventually recovering a large part of his territory.

JAHANGIR. Akbar's son, Jahangir, sent a force under his son, Khurram, to subjugate the indomitable Maharana Pratap's son, Amar Singh. Amar Singh was forced to sign a treaty with the Mughals and for the first time a Mewar rana paid

Haldighati battle scene.

obeisance at the Mughal court.

SHAH JAHAN. When Prince Khurram, later to become Shah Jahan, rebelled against his father, Jahangir, he sought refuge with Amar Singh's son, Karan Singh, at the beautiful palace on Lake Pichola, Jag Mandir ▲ *251*. But when Karan Singh decided to restore Chittorgarh, Shah Jahan, as Emperor, invaded the fort and subverted Karan Singh's plans. Jaswant Singh of Jodhpur served Shah Jahan loyally for twenty years, but the civil war after Shah Jahan's dethronement forced him to join forces with the heir-apparent, Dara, who was finally defeated by another son, Aurangzeb.

AURANGZEB. In 1658, Aurangzeb deposed his father, Shah Jahan, and usurped the throne of Delhi. Initially, the Rajput vassals of the Mughals were loyal to him. But Aurangzeb's anti-Hindu policy and religious fanaticism provoked a violent reaction and once again the Rajputs renewed their conflict with the Emperor of Delhi. Aurangzeb's proposal of marriage to the Princess of Roopnagar was taken as an insult to Rajput womanhood. She appealed to Raj Singh of Mewar, who, displaying true Rajput chivalry, married her to save her honor. From then on, he assumed the leadership of the Rajputs. In 1679, when Aurangzeb escheated the property of Jaswant Singh of Jodhpur and declared Marwar a centrally established territory, Raj Singh gave refuge to Jaswant Singh's wife and restored their son, Ajit Singh, to his rightful position as heir-apparent, bringing the wrath of the Mughals upon himself. The formidable alliance he built was an example to the other Rajput states, who decided to avenge their pride after years of subjugation.

THE LAST MUGHALS. After Aurangzeb's death in 1707, the Mughal Empire showed signs of disintegration. The time was favorable for the princes of Rajasthan to regain their independence. Ajit Singh of Marwar, Sawai Jai Singh II of Amber, and Amar Singh II of Mewar made a pact in 1708 to protect their territories from the Mughals. And even though peace with the Mughals was made in 1710, in the words of the historian, Satish Chandra, "the gulf with the Rajputs was narrowed but not bridged".

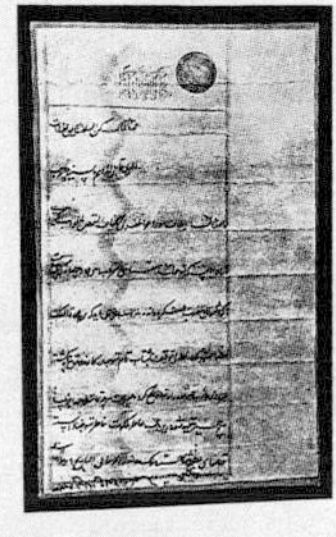

Firman, or order, dated 1605, soliciting Raja Rai Singh of Bikaner's presence at Akbar's sick bed.

1678
Marwar occupied by the Mughals.

1826
Fall of Bharatpur.

Shah Jahan's palace on the island of Jag Mandir.

RAJPUTS AND THE BRITISH

The Imperial Assemblage held at the *durbar* in New Delhi in 1877.

1829
Prohibition of sati *by Lord William Bentick, Governor-General of India.*

1853
First railway from Bombay to Thana.

1854
Lord Dalhousie introduces postal and telegraph system.

1857
The Sepoy Mutiny.

1858
British India placed under the direct government of the Crown.

1877
Queen Victoria's Proclamation as Empress of India.

1876
The Royal Titles Act.

1885
Foundation of the Indian National Congress.

THE TAKEOVER. The East India Company, which started as a trading company, eventually took over as rulers. In 1807 the Company signed a treaty of protection and paramountcy with the Rajput states. Rajputana at that time consisted of eighteen native states and the British district of Ajmer. The five important courts of Udaipur, Jaipur, Jodhpur, Bharatpur, and Kota had British Political Agents representing the Governor-General ▲ *253*, while all the other states were directly under him. In time the influence of the Company over the internal administration of the states increased considerably.
BRITISH PROTECTION. British protection restored peace in Rajasthan. Although the princes were convinced that under no government would their rights be so well-protected, they considered the British a necessary evil. The British introduced education and banned social practices such as *sati* (the burning of a widow on her husband's funeral pyre). Several reforms were made and state debts paid off. It is significant that during the Sepoy Mutiny in 1857, when armies elsewhere revolted, nearly all the Rajput princes remained loyal to the British, helping them put down the rebellion.
THE CROWN. The Rajput support of the British was rewarded when, after 1857, India came directly under the Crown, and the princely states were allowed to remain separate entities. The rule of the princes was thus perpetuated. The new policy was to punish the princes for misdeeds by deposing them, but their states could not be annexed to the Empire. One of the main points of resentment, however, was the British right to recognize a ruler's successor. All successions had to be accepted by the Paramount Power and confirmation given through a letter of authority handed over at a special *durbar*.
RAJPUT-ANGLO RELATIONS. The Rajputs believed that they had several traits in common with the British. Their traditions of chivalry and gallantry, their courtesy and large-heartedness toward their adversaries, their love of sports and horses, all combined to build a good social rapport. Despite political differences, the Political Agents enjoyed being guests of the princes, especially during the Christmas sandgrouse shooting season. Several of the rulers were sent to England to study administration and brought back Western influences to their lifestyles and government. After the first Imperial Durbar of 1877 at New Delhi, when Queen Victoria was declared

A tiger hunt in Rajasthan.

The Maharaja of Jaipur's first interview with the British Political Agent.

Maharaja Ganga Singh of Bikaner.

Empress of India, several Rajput princes, following the British royal tradition, fashioned coats-of-arms for their states.

World War One. Until 1916 the states were treated as isolated foreign units and no formal relations, either political or social, between the states, were tolerated. The permission of the Political Agent was necessary even for courtesy calls among the princely states. World War One loosened the shackles of this isolationist policy, since the princes had cooperated wholeheartedly with the British government during the war. A conference of princes was summoned by the Viceroy, Lord Hardinge, in New Delhi in 1916. The rulers of Jaipur and Jodhpur were among those who attended. In 1917, at the Imperial Conference in London to boost the war effort, the Maharaja of Bikaner, Ganga Singh, figured most prominently among the princes. He was elected the first Chancellor of the Chamber of Princes in 1921. The Indian National Congress had appealed to the princes in 1920 to permit a fully responsible government in the states. In 1927 the All India States Peoples' Conference was formed to support popular movements in the Princely States. But ordinary citizens did not respond to this attempt at politicization and the idea of power-sharing or a democratic self-government did not meet with success.

Post-World War Two. With the end of World War Two, the British days in India were numbered. The Indian Independence movement gained momentum under Mahatma Gandhi, and, with it, the idea of democracy. It was clear that the Princely States could not last long. In 1946 the rulers met with the Cabinet Mission which came to India. They were advised to organize themselves into viable units and to deal directly with the new Indian rulers. When, in April 1948, a number of states, led by Bhopal Singh, Maharana of Udaipur, merged to join the Rajasthan Union, Nathudan wrote, "Oh Eklingji [the family deity of Udaipur], why was he crippled in his legs [Maharana Bhopal Singh was paralysed from the waist down ▲ *248*]? It should have been in his hands so that he would have been unable to sign."

1914–18
World War I.

1920
Khilafat (Non-Cooperation) Movement.

1930
Civil Disobedience Movement. First Round Table Conference.

1934
Civil Disobedience Movement called off.

1939
World War II begins.

1943
Lord Mountbatten, Supreme Commander of southeast Asia.

Independence

Lord Mountbatten of Burma was appointed Viceroy to facilitate the transfer of power and the partition of the subcontinent into India and Pakistan. At first the princes were assured that they would be part of a federation and retain their states. But a month before the takeover a new State Department was formed under Sardar Vallabh bhai Patel, who urged Mountbatten to persuade the princes to sign an individual Instrument of Accession to either of the new states of India or Pakistan, according to their geographical contiguity. India became independent on August 15, 1947, and the rule of the British and the princes came to an end.

Lord Mountbatten, the last Viceroy of India.

DISBANDING OF PRINCELY STATES

ACCESSION. The first to sign the Instrument of Accession was Maharaja Sardul Singh of Bikaner. For many of the princes, a free India was the prime consideration. Others such as the Maharaja of Jodhpur (who is said to have pulled out a pistol in anger) signed because they had no choice. But by March 30, 1949, all the princes of Rajasthan had acceded.

PRIVILEGES. In return for signing over their lands, the princes were allowed certain privileges in the Indian Union. They were given privy purses annually, the percentage being worked out according to revenue collected. The Maharana of Udaipur received the highest, with 2 million rupees. The princes retained the State number plates for cars, were exempted from paying wealth tax and were allowed to import goods without paying customs duty. The Maharaja of Jaipur was named Rajpramukh, equal in status to the governor of a state. Many of the maharajas and maharanis joined politics, prominent among them being Gayatri Devi of Jaipur, who was one of the founders of the Swatantra Party.

DEMOCRACY. In 1951, India had its first general elections to the Lok Sabha, or the Central Parliament, as well as to the State Legislatures. The Congress Party, which had emerged as the symbol of the protest against the British, naturally won the elections in most states, including Rajasthan. It took about eight years for the state of Rajputana to come into its present shape, and it was only on November 1, 1956, that it acquired its new name, Rajasthan. Now India was well and truly on the road to its avowed goal of a socialist society.

WITHDRAWN PRIVILEGES. In 1970, the Prime Minister, Indira Gandhi, dealt a severe blow to the princes by withdrawing the privy purses and canceling their privileges, an act which alienated many of the princes who had joined the Indian Union with great hopes. There is no doubt that their contribution to Indian history was considerable. They had been a symbol of unity between the ruler and the ruled and were, by and large, looked upon by their subjects as their *mai-baap* (mother-father). Once the custodians of Indian tradition and culture, they were now effectively consigned to history. Several of the princes tried to adapt to the changed times and carved out careers for themselves in the armed forces or the foreign service. Sawai Man Singh of Jaipur was given an ambassadorial assignment in Spain. Karni Singh of Bikaner represented India at three Olympic Games.

1947
India gains independence on 15th August. Pandit Jawahar Lal Nehru, India's first Prime Minister. Dr. Rajendra Prasad, India's first President.

Gayatri Devi of Jaipur (above) was a candidate of the opposition Swatantra Party in 1962. She won a spectacular victory, beating the ruling Congress Party candidate by a margin of 175,000 votes.

1948
Mahatma Gandhi assassinated. Sri C. Rajagopalachari appointed Governor-General.

1949
State of Rajasthan formed.

Bhopal Singh of Udaipur (left) with Ganga Singh of Bikaner. This picture was taken in the 1920's.

Samode Palace near Jaipur, like many Rajput palaces, has been turned into a splendid hotel.

Tourism. One of the major contributions of the princes, especially after the withdrawal of their privileges, has been to the tourist industry. Many palaces and hunting lodges have been converted into luxurious hotels, and tourists from all over the world visit Rajasthan to experience for themselves the lost lifestyles of the princes of Rajputana. Some of the world's best hotels are Rambagh Palace, Jaipur, Lake Palace, Udaipur and Umaid Bhavan Palace, Jodhpur. Another great success was the Palace on Wheels, a train which ran between Delhi, Jaipur, Jodhpur and Jaisalmer, with saloons of the former rajas providing the visitor with a taste of mobile luxury. Many of the rulers took great interest in the development of the fabled handicrafts of Rajasthan. They started their own workshops for the production and export of the famous block prints, blue pottery, camel-hide items and other crafts.

1949
New Constitution of India adopted and signed.

Contemporary Rajasthan

Rajasthan supports a population of 43,880,640 in an area of 342,239 square miles. Once one of the most backward states industrially, it is fast making up for lost time. Jaipur, the capital, is one of the fastest growing cities in India. Though traditionally arts and crafts form the mainstay of the economy, natural resources such as zinc, mica, feldspar and precious stones such as emeralds and garnets are also the State's assets ■ *18*. The glorious history, myriad handicrafts, and fairs and festivals of Rajasthan ensure that its tourism industry flourishes.

Agriculture. With the building of the Rajasthan Canal, also known as the Indira Gandhi Canal, in northwest Rajasthan, the greening of the desert has been extremely successful, especially in Ganganagar and the northeastern part of Bikaner district, which boasts several lucrative farms, orchards and vineyards. Even the Kota-Jhalawar area in the southeastern region, which was mostly stony uplands, has now been successfully irrigated with water from the Chambal River and its tributaries. A state suffering a deficit in food grains in the pre-Independence years, Rajasthan has adopted a pro-agriculture economic policy and produced 110,000 tons of food grains in 1990–1. Several public-sector enterprises provide employment to thousands of people.

Industry. Cement, fertilizer, fabric and chemical plants and big public-sector companies, Hindustan Salts, Hindustan Zinc, and Hindustan Copper are just a few of the many important industrial units. Light industries, including television and precision instruments assembly, are rapidly expanding. The main industrial complexes are located at Jaipur, Kota, Udaipur and Bhilwara. Given Rajasthan's location, constant surveillance against illegal immigrants and smuggling is a high priority in the extensive, sparsely populated border area in the northeast.

1950
India celebrates first Republic Day on 26th January.

1950
Sardar Vallabhbhai Patel, India's "Iron Man", dies.

1964
Death of Pandit Nehru.

1966
Lal Bahadur Shastri, the country's second Prime Minister, dies.

1984
Indira Gandhi assassinated.

1991
Rajiv Gandhi assassinated. Narsimha Rao sworn in as Prime Minister.

HINDI AND RAJASTHANI

While Hindi is the official language of the State, there are important local dialects with regional variations. In fact the word "Rajasthani", often used to identify the local language, has emerged only after the union of the Princely States and represents the dialects spoken in those states. It is only in recent years that the issue of getting Rajasthani constitutionally recognized as the original language has been taken up by a few, but the matter remains unresolved. Since Rajasthani dialects have the same roots as Hindi, it is not difficult for locals to understand Hindi, which is widely used in the big cities of the State. Unlike some states of India, English has not really become the second language of Rajasthan, despite it being taught in the schools.

DIALECTS. The earliest reference to a dialect spoken in Rajasthan is to that of Maru Bhasha, probably dating back to the 15th century. Today the recognized dialects are Marwari, spoken in Jodhpur, Bikaner, Jaisalmer, and Barmer; Dhundhari, spoken in the entire former Jaipur state; Mewati, spoken in the Alwar-Bharatpur belt; Mewari, spoken in the Mewar, and in particular, the Udaipur-Chittorgarh region; Hadoti, spoken in the former states of Bundi, Kota, and Jhalawar; Bhili, a tribal language, the main dialect of which, Wagri, is spoken in the south (Dungarpur and Banswara); and Malwi, spoken in the southwest (Kota and Jhalawar). These dialects also vary every few miles within their particular territory. Marwari is considered the most polite and sweet-sounding dialect.

SCRIPT. The different dialects have no characteristic script and today follow the pattern of the official script of India, known as Devanagari. In earlier times, the impure version of Devanagari was used by the Mahajans or Baniyas. Because of the twisting letters, the script was also known as Muria (meaning "twisting"). It is said that the script was developed by Raja Todarmal, one of the key administrators of the emperor, Akbar.

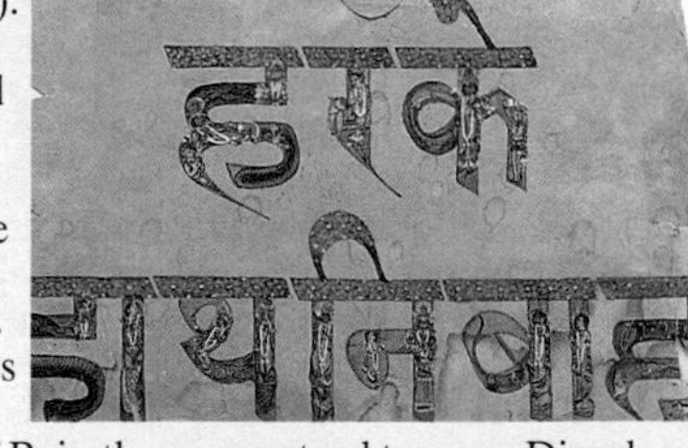

DINGAL AND PINGAL. Whenever references are made to the classical language of Rajasthan, many tend to name Dingal, as it has an extremely rich poetic heritage. Linguists have identified Dingal and another dialect, Pingal, as having two distinctively poetic styles. While the traditional bards, the Bhatts ● *54* and Charans, used Dingal to compose boastful sagas of heroic deeds, Pingal was used by the saints in their devotional writings. A salient feature of Dingal is its abundant use of adjectives. Pingal is conspicuously influenced by Brij Bhasha, the language of Krishna's land, or Brij Bhumi, which includes some parts of today's eastern Rajasthan.

LITERACY
Literacy rates are low in Rajasthan, with only about 40 percent of the State's population being literate. Female literacy is particularly low. However, in recent years, the State government has made great efforts to improve the situation, and many adult literacy programs have been implemented.

"*Talwar ko ghav bhar jat, bat ko ghav kone bhare.*" (The wound of a sword can heal but one caused by words cannot.)
Rajasthani saying

Mewari script.

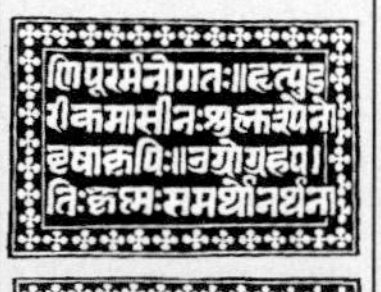

Arts and traditions

44 Hinduism and the Bhakti movement
46 Hinduism in daily life
48 Jainism
50 Islam
52 Tribal beliefs
54 Folklore
56 Block-printed textiles
58 Tie-and-dye textiles and embroidery work
60 Costume
62 Jewelry and objets d'art
64 Miniature paintings
66 Wall and cloth paintings
68 Carpets and durries
69 Leather work
70 Stone carving
72 Pottery
73 Puppetry
74 Food
76 Sula
78 Music and dance
80 Fairs and festivals

HINDUISM AND THE BHAKTI MOVEMENT

Hinduism is not a homogeneous religion but an assemblage of beliefs and practices, many of which differ markedly from one another. Classic Hinduism evolved from the Vedic religion introduced by the Aryans ● *32*. While the Vedic religion was based on sacrifice, Hinduism was concerned with mystical ideas and the concept of being, and was influenced by popular cults. The principal Vedic divinities – Agni, Mitra, Varuna and Yama, among others – were eclipsed by the *trimurti* (or trinity) of Brahma, Vishnu and Shiva, with their consorts Lakshmi and Parvati. Simultaneously, the notion of *karma* (according to which people's past deeds determine their current and future lives) was born. From the early 2nd century AD, this Brahmanic tendency was counterbalanced by the rise of a devotional religion. This was *bhakti*, or devotion to a god, most commonly one of Vishnu's avatars, Rama or Krishna.

INCARNATIONS OF VISHNU
Vishnu, the Preserver, appeared in ten principal forms known as *avataras* or incarnations in different *yugas* or ages, to save the world from the imminent danger of total destruction.

CHILD KRISHNA
Krishna is often worshiped as Bala Gopala, the Divine Child, full of childlike innocence, pranks, and playful acts despite his mighty power. Many of these stories are illustrated in the *Bhagavata Purana*, a popular and revered religious text of the Vaishnavas, the followers of Vishnu. In this detail the child Krishna is shown stealing butter from the churning pot of milkmaid Yashoda, his foster mother.

"He [Krishna] is the Father, Mother, Friend and Brother to me – there is none besides."

Meera, 16th-century saint-poetess of Rajasthan

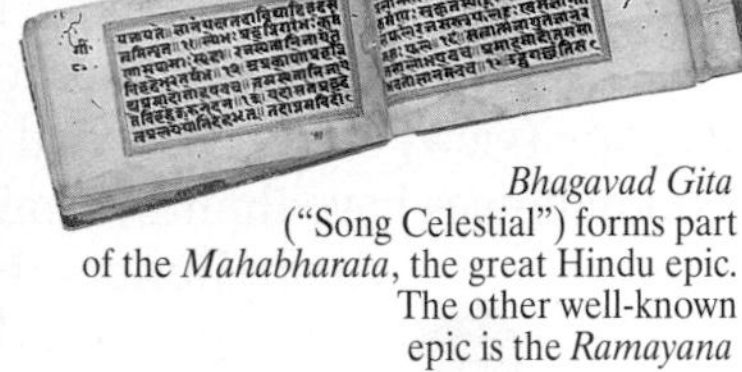

Bhagavad Gita ("Song Celestial") forms part of the *Mahabharata*, the great Hindu epic. The other well-known epic is the *Ramayana*

The Trinity
The three most important divinities of Hinduism are Brahma the Creator, Vishnu the Preserver, and Mahesvara or Shiva, the Destroyer. With the growing popularity of Shakti, the Great Goddess, Brahma has been gradually relegated to near-oblivion.

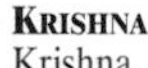

Krishna
Krishna, the eighth incarnation of Vishnu, is the most popular god in Rajasthan. Easily identified with youthful exuberance, Krishna is the eternal hero, the symbol of life and joy, and man's communion with god. Apart from the standard daily rituals, the Krishna temples observe Dola-lila, or Holi, in the spring, Janamashtami, or Krishna's birth, in early autumn, Ras-lila ● *64*, or the circular dance with the *gopis* (left), at the advent of winter, and Annakut on the day following Diwali.

Brahma
The God of Creation, Brahma, is four-headed, facing all four directions, symbolizing his presence everywhere. He is old, the prime godly spirit, and the creator of all gods and living beings. At Pushkar, in one of the only temples in India dedicated to Brahma ▲ *164*, he is worshiped as any other cult god (right).

Shakti
Goddesses were worshiped in India from the dawn of civilization. They became Shakti, the strength of her male counterpart. The consort of Shiva is Parvati. In her powerful martial form she is Durga, and in her most grim aspect she is conceived as Kali (left). She protects everybody and destroys evil.

Shiva
Shiva is a great ascetic. He wears his long matted hair in a top knot with the crescent moon, his forehead besmeared with lines of ashes round his all-seeing third eye and his neck garlanded with a black cobra.

Male and female deities
Gods are mostly worshiped with their consorts. Often the male and female traits are combined into one syncretic form known as Ardhanarisvara, half male and half female, a combination of Shiva and his consort Parvati, or Vishnu and his consort Lakshmi. Even Vishnu and Shiva combine as Hari Hara and give birth to an offspring.

Gita-Govinda is a 12th-century poetical work in Sanskrit by Jayadeva on the love of Krishna for Radha and the milkmaids.

Hindus generally visit a temple to worship a deity. On festive occasions large numbers of devotees throng a temple for a *darshan* (view) of the deity clad in suitable festive attire. Many Hindu homes have their own miniature shrine or *puja* (prayer) room. Besides the family's patron deity, small bronze or wooden images or paintings of other divinities also find a place there. One of the spouses performs all rituals, such as "waking up" the god or goddess in the morning, bathing and dressing it with appropriate clothing, and decorating it with sandal paste, vermilion, flowers, and perfumes, as well as performing the *arati* (worship) with a lighted lamp, camphor, and a yak-tail fly-whisk or *chauri*.

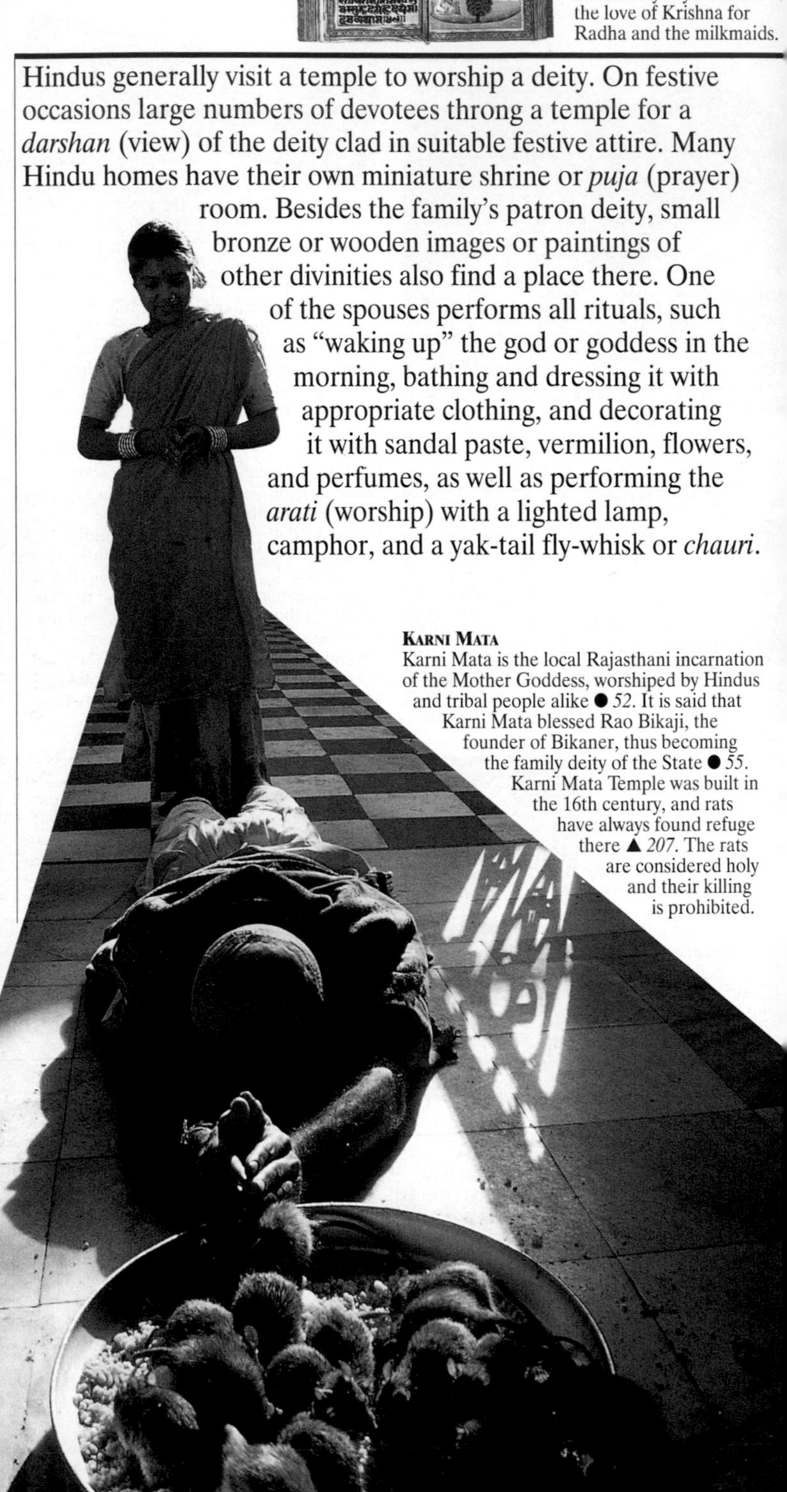

KARNI MATA
Karni Mata is the local Rajasthani incarnation of the Mother Goddess, worshiped by Hindus and tribal people alike ● *52*. It is said that Karni Mata blessed Rao Bikaji, the founder of Bikaner, thus becoming the family deity of the State ● *55*. Karni Mata Temple was built in the 16th century, and rats have always found refuge there ▲ *207*. The rats are considered holy and their killing is prohibited.

"Rituals are only the bark covering the tree of religion. Even after the bark has been shed, the tree remains."

Celebrated Vedantic philosopher, Swami Chinmayananda

PUJA
A priest offers prayers to the *Shivalinga*, or the phallic emblem of Shiva, the most popular form in which he is worshiped all over India.

DECORATED IDOLS
Hindu temples are generally dedicated to a principal cult deity whose image is installed in the sanctum chamber. Other cult deities are also present as subsidiary divinities. The image is decked in elaborate costumes and precious ornaments on special occasions. Temple idols are mostly carved from stone or metals such as copper, brass, or bronze, or even silver or gold. The use of wood and ivory is limited to miniature shrines.

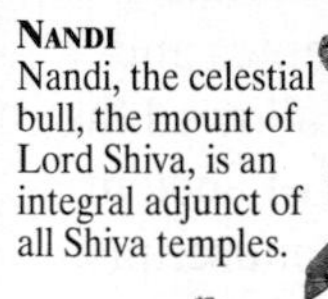

NANDI
Nandi, the celestial bull, the mount of Lord Shiva, is an integral adjunct of all Shiva temples.

ELEPHANT GOD
Ganesha is the elephant-headed son of Parvati, the wife of Shiva. He is invoked first in every ritual and as god of prosperity, he is highly revered.

BATHING IN HOLY WATERS
The lake at Pushkar is called Tirtharaj, or the King of all Holy Places. Most Hindu temples have a "holy" tank where one must purify oneself before entering the temple.

PRAYER PARAPHERNALIA
For the daily *puja* or the elaborate temple ritual, a large variety of special vessels, lamps, and bells are used. Their shapes, forms, and sizes vary according to their use as containers of holy water from the River Ganga, or the various offerings of flowers, fruits, sweets, or perfumes. Every day the deity is offered *bhog*, or food, consisting of milk, honey, dry fruit, rice, yoghurt, and ghee.

SHIVA RATRI
The most important festival for the followers of Shiva is Shiva Ratri, observed on the day preceding the new moon in the spring. Devotees observe fasting and offer special *puja* throughout the night.

The origins of Jainism are obscure. It is the religion of the Jinas, or "Overcomers" (through asceticism) and was founded by Mahavira in the 6th century BC in Bihar, eastern India. Although only about 2 percent of the population are adherents, Jainism counts among its followers influential families, wealthy people and high officials. Their wealth has funded the building of many temples and hospices, and allowed the preservation of ancient books and manuscripts. The two main Jain sects are the Digambaras, the "sky-clad ones", and the Svetambaras, the "white-clad ones". The latter scrupulously follow the original canonical texts. Their guiding principle is absolute respect for life, and therefore advocate the practice of non-violence.

MASKING THEIR MOUTHS
The mask worn by Svetambaras is to prevent them from inhaling living things accidentally. This stems from their belief that all life is sacred. *Ahimsa* ("non-violence") forms the cornerstone of Jainism.

RISHABHDEV TEMPLE
Rishabhdev Temple near Udaipur is visited by many Jain pilgrims ▲ *258*. The image of Rishabhdev is of black marble. Hindus also visit the shrine.

ASCETICISM
Jainism is a highly ascetic religion. Jains, who are strict vegetarians, do penance through fasting. During the holy week of Pajoshan, Jains abstain from leafy vegetables, roots, and unboiled water. They ask for forgiveness on the last day of penance from any living creature they have wronged.

TIRTHANKARAS
Jains revere the twenty-four *tirthankaras* ("ford-makers"), saints who have attained immortality. Mahavira, who reformed Jainism, was the last *tirthankara*. His predecessor, Parshvanatha, lived 150 years earlier.

DIGAMBARAS
Digambaras believe that man has to renounce all earthly possessions, including clothes, to achieve salvation. Thus their temples are more stark than the temples of the Svetambaras and their idols (above) unadorned.

FIVE ESSENTIAL ITEMS
Pious Svetambaras carry all their earthly belongings with them: the *dhoti* (sarong), for a change of clothes which doubles as bedding, the *odhni* (mantle), as a covering and to sit on, the *rajo haran* (broom), to gently dust resting places without harming living creatures, the *patra* (vessel), to accept food given in alms (they do not accept money), and the eight-fold *muhpatti* (a mask) to cover the mouth.

JAIN STATUE
The images of the Svetambaras have prominent enameled eyes, sometimes studded with precious gems, and an auspicious *tilak* or vertical mark on the forehead.

PROCESSION
Smaller images from temples are brought home for special prayers with great ceremony and after ritual cleaning of the home. They may not be carried in any modern conveyance, only on foot or in bullock carts. After the prayers, they are returned to the temple. Jain processions are also held to felicitate those who have fasted for Pajoshan, or holy month (August to September). This rigorous fast is undertaken by adults and even children for as long as a month.

MONK
A Jain monk totally renounces all worldly possessions and attains ultimate discipline of mind and body by practicing twenty-two forms of endurance and penance.

JAIN BELIEFS
Jains believe that the practice of austerity will prevent a fresh inflow of *karma* (action) and destroy the undesirable existing *karmas*. The soul then realizes its inherent supreme knowledge, attains unlimited happiness and salvation (*kevalgyan*), and becomes the perfect being (Siddha).

Muslims paying obeisance at the *dargah* at Ajmer.

From the 11th century, Northern India was repeatedly ransacked by Muslim invaders from the north and northwest. It was at this time that various Sufic orders, the most widely known being that of the Chistiyyas, were founded. The influence of orthodox Islam, tempered by popular Islamic beliefs and by Sufism, increased in the 6th century during the reign of Akbar, who formed alliances with the principal Rajput kingdoms. Today, about 8 percent of the population of Rajasthan is Muslim. Muslims believe in one God, Allah, and follow the teachings of the prophet Muhammad and their holy book, the Qur'an. Most Indians belong to the Sunni sect, although some are Shias.

FLORAL OFFERINGS Muslim shrines use only fragrant flowers such as roses and jasmine, unlike the Hindus who offer all kinds of flowers, especially marigolds.

COVERING THE GRAVE It is customary to offer flowers at the grave of Muslim *pirs* (saints). In return for granted wishes, devotees even offer *chaddars*, or sheets of glittering satins, to cover the grave.

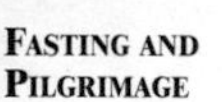

FASTING AND PILGRIMAGE The month of Ramadan is the month when Muslims observe a fast from dawn till evening. Many Muslims go to Mecca for the Haj pilgrimage on this occasion and return home with the title "Haji", which they add to their name, a coveted distinction.

Arabic inscription at Arhai din ka Jhonpra ▲ *163*.

DARGAH KHWAJA SAHIB
Ajmer is the principal center of the order of the Chistiyyas among the mystic Sufis, which has a large following throughout the Indian subcontinent. The most venerated saint Khwaja Mu'in-ud-din Chisti ▲ *162* settled and died here. The *urs*, the death anniversary of the Khwaja, is observed annually by Muslims, and even by Hindus, in the month of Rajab. Thousands of devotees from all over India and neighboring Bangladesh, Pakistan, and Maldives attend.

MUHARRAM
For the Shia Muslims, Muharram is the month of mourning for their assassinated leader Husayn, grandson of the prophet Muhammad. The festival is also celebrated by Sunnis and Hindus. The culmination of Muharram is a mourners' procession through the towns. Picturesque replicas of mausoleums (*tazia*), as tall as two-storied buildings, are carried during the procession.

SUNNI MUSLIMS
The majority of Muslims in Rajasthan are Sunnis, the sect to which the people of Arabia, North Africa, South and Southeast Asia, and Turkey belong. The basic tenets of Sunnism are: donating a certain portion of their income as *zakat* (charity), abstaining from liquor, eating only *halal* food, refraining from charging loan interest, and fasting during the month of Ramadan. The Islamic insistence on social homogeneity contrasts with the Indian tradition of rigid stratification according to caste. The tenet of equality, however, is limited to men, and women are not allowed to pray in mosques.

Rajasthan is the home of many tribal communities, such as the Bhil, Girasia or Garasia, Mina or Meena, and Gujar. As most nomadic and pastoralist castes (for example the Kalbelia, Banjara, Rebari, and Gujar), they have assimilated well with contemporary Hindu society. Some of these tribal communities still retain their traditional ways of life, social structure and religious beliefs. Belief in evil spirits, magical and supernatural phenomena, local gods and goddesses, heroes and demi-gods, and tree and snake spirits, together with the practice of ancestor worship, are by no means exclusive to these tribal people, however. Most of these traditional beliefs and practices are shared by Hindus of various castes, from the Brahmins to the untouchables.

SNAKE CULT
The snake cult has a wide popular following. In Tantric Shivaism the serpent represents dormant energy and the source of all spiritual conquests. In popular belief the snake god Gatodji or Gogaji ▲ *203* is believed to have the power to protect man and his cattle. Most villages have a temple dedicated to the snake god.

TRIBAL PRACTICES
The Bhils believe in witchcraft and resorted to many esoteric practices to get rid of the evil spirits. They – both men and women – tattooed their bodies (right). Now such practices are becoming rare.

SNAKE GOD IN PROCESSION
The Kalbelias, a nomadic snake-charmer tribe, carry the snake god in procession on the day of Nag-Panchami. People offer milk to snakes and alms to snake charmers on this day.

HINDU INFLUENCES
The Garasia, a tribe living in areas near Udaipur and Dungarpur, have adopted Brahmin deities and revere the cow. They were originally believers in ghosts, spirits, and black magic.

ANCESTOR WORSHIP
Most tribes believe in honoring their ancestors. The icon of a male ancestor (*chira*) is wrapped in white cloth, and that of a female (*mathori*) in red. Large numbers of tribes from southeast Rajasthan and the adjacent regions of Gujarat and Madhya Pradesh assemble at Baneshwar in Dungarpur district to immerse the remains of their dead ancestors at the confluence of rivers Mahi and Som in February. The fair held there, known as Kumbh Mela, is the largest congregation of tribes in Rajasthan.

Sadhu
A mendicant who has renounced earthly possessions, the Sadhu has an accepted role in orthodox hinduism.

Jats
The Jats, an important agricultural community in northern and western Rajasthan, generally worship their own village deities (above) rather than the orthodox Hindu pantheon. Their temples include a number dedicated to deified heroes of the community.

Lingam and yoni
The temple of the cattle-breeding Rebaris sometimes consists of small stones representing the *lingam*, the phallic symbol, and the *yoni*, the female symbol, placed under a tree, on which a few green petals are strewn occasionally. Water is too scarce to be poured over the shrine.

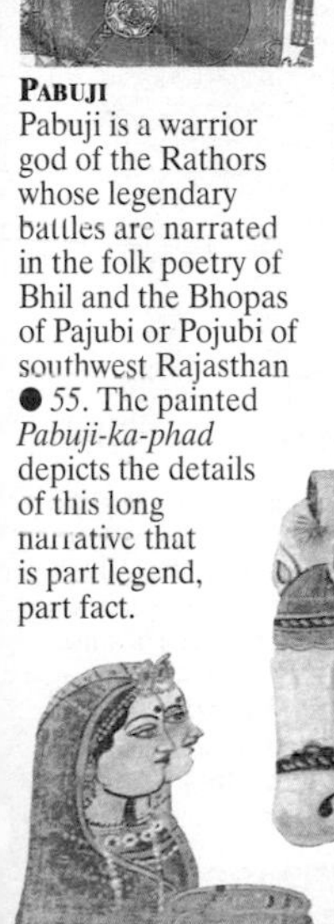

Pabuji
Pabuji is a warrior god of the Rathors whose legendary battles are narrated in the folk poetry of Bhil and the Bhopas of Pajubi or Pojubi of southwest Rajasthan ● *55*. The painted *Pabuji-ka-phad* depicts the details of this long narrative that is part legend, part fact.

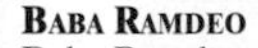

Baba Ramdeo
Baba Ramdeo (below), worshiped by Hindus and Muslims alike, helps the poor and those of lowest caste. The untouchable Meghwars revere him as a god. Ramdeo-ka-Karni, a fair held every year near Pokharan, between Jodhpur and Jaisalmer ▲ *219*, attracts a large number of devotees, both tribal and non-tribal.

Rajasthani folklore, which developed over the centuries, was closely linked with the nomadic existence of a large part of the population. Moving from court to court and village to village, the professional story-tellers, the Bhopas, Bhatts, Charans, and Bandis, developed their distinctive styles. Rajasthani folklore contains examples of some of the oldest handwritten tales. The common man was exposed to the oral, written, and pictorial versions of folk legends. In a land where heroism, valor, honor, and chivalry were given pride of place, it was but natural that many legends were created around heroic rajas, as well as ranis, whose beauty inspired superlative descriptions.

ITINERANT STORYTELLERS
The Bhopa of Pobuji, from the Navak caste, are the balladeers and storytellers of Rajasthan. A Bhopa, accompanied by his wife, the Bhopi, travels from village to village, narrating the stories of legendary heroes, usually tales of valor, through song and mime. They use the *ravanhatta*, a twelve-stringed instrument with a long neck.

"One tale from another differs in course,
Yet art is one and single its source."

Rajasthani ritual verse

Love reunion
The story of Prince Dhola of Malwa in central India and Princess Maru of Marwar in Rajasthan (left) is a saga of love, written in *dohas,* or couplets. Betrothed when they were very young and then separated, Dhola was forced to marry a princess of his own clan. The lovelorn Maru regarded Dhola as her husband and sent several messages to him to come and bring her away. These were intercepted by his second wife. Desperate, Maru asked a Dhadi (a wandering minstrel) to tell her sad story in song. Dhola heard the plaintive singing, and recognizing it as a call from Maru, he mounted his camel and, after overcoming several obstacles and defeating his rivals, was reunited with his betrothed.

Karni Mata
Karni Mata was the daughter of a 15th-century Charan (bard). Married at twenty-seven, she refused to have children and became a *sanyasin* (ascetic), devoting her life to the service of the poor. She is the Kuldevi (family deity) of the rulers of Bikaner who built the Karni Mata Temple ● *46* ▲ *206*.

Romantic warrior
Prithviraj Chauhan (right) ● *35,* son of the powerful Someshwar, the ruler of Ajmer, excelled in riding, war strategy, and the use of weapons. Fiercely independent, he refused to acknowledge the supremacy of Raja Jaichand of Kanauj. He is said to have received a message that Jaichand's daughter, Sanyogita, had chosen him as a husband, even though he was her father's enemy, and carried her off from her father's court, as she sat surrounded by suitors from among whom she had to choose a husband. Prithviraj rode through the gates into the court and vanished with Sanyogita on his horse before Jaichand's very eyes.

Honorable Pabuji
The sacrifice of Pabuji ● *53*, recounted in song by the Bhopa of Pobuyi, is one of the favorite subjects of Phad painters (left) ● *67*. Legend has it that Pabuji, the son of a nymph and a 14th-century Rajput ruler, promised a Charan woman who had lent him a horse that, in return, he would come to her aid if she ever needed his help. She later called upon Pabuji to save her cattle from a thieving neighboring clan, disrupting his nuptial ceremony in the process. True to his word, Pabuji left the ceremony to ride forth to her defence and sacrificed his life in the ensuing battle. Elevated to divine status, Pabuji became the principal deity of the Nayak and Rabari.

Handblock printer from Barmer (left); prints from Sanganer and Bagru (right).

Rajasthan is an important producer of textiles in India, especially the printed and tie-and-dye varieties. Textile printing is practiced in many areas of the State, with each having its special color scheme, design, and technique. The most important centers are Sanganer, Bagru, Jodhpur, Akola (in Chittorgarh district), Nagaur, Jaisalmer, and Barmer. In the last century, many printers of the Chhipa community, the traditional dyers and printers, came from Alwar, Sikar, Jhunjhunu, and other places to work in these cities. Handblock printing is perhaps the most popular kind of textile decoration as it allows the printer to produce a wide range of fabrics in bright colors and attractive designs to be made into saris, *odhnis*, bedcovers, and tablecloths.

AJRAKH PRINTS
Ajrakh prints are based on a special design in dark shades of blue and red geometrical patterns. These prints are used mostly for making turbans, coverlets, and *odhnis*, besides various other useful items. The designs of Jaisalmer and Barmer are similar to those seen in the *ajrakh* textiles of Sind in Pakistan.

PRINTING BLOCKS
The printing blocks used by the Chhipas are procured from the Khatis (carpenters) of Jaipur or brought from Delhi, Mathura, Farrukhabad, and Pethapur, where traditional woodcarvers create intricate traditional designs from blocks of *gurjun* or teak wood, as they have done for many generations.

BLOCK PRINTING
The process of printing is undertaken by the printer in his small workshop sitting before a low, wooden table.

DYEING
Reams of dyed cloth are hung on racks to dry. Black dyes are prepared by fermenting iron oxide with molasses and gum; red by extracting alizarin from madder roots and mixing with the locally available *dhawai* flower in lukewarm water in a large copper pot; blue from indigo extracted from the leaves of the *nil* plant (*Indigofera tinctoria*); yellow from pomegranate rind and raw turmeric. The millmade bleached cloth is prepared for handblock printing by washing and desizing for many hours.

SANGANER
With the foundation of Jaipur, the handblock printing industry in Sanganer flourished, enjoying phenomenal growth as a commercial center. Its origin as a textile producing center, however, remains shrouded in mystery. In the last few decades, the handblock printers who had been working in Sanganer for centuries received a renewed impetus. Now, sadly enough, most of the printers have resorted to screen painting instead of the time-consuming and costly block printing by hand.

DRYING BLOCK-PRINTED TEXTILES
The printed pieces of cloth are dried in the sun, and after the dyes are fixed, the cloth is given one or more washes and finally sized and dried before it is ready for the market.

Tie-and-dye Textiles and Embroidery Work

Tie-and-dye textiles, called *bandhej* or *bandhani,* are an important Rajasthani craft. From the 18th century, embroiderers from Delhi and Gujarat arrived in large numbers to work in the *toshakhanas* (royal wardrobe section) of the palaces at Amber-Jaipur, Jodhpur, Bikaner, and Udaipur. An array of court costumes and furnishings with elaborate and gorgeous golden embroidery works was produced for the Rajput courts. The main production centers today are Jaipur, Jodhpur, Udaipur, Alwar, Ajmer, Kota, Jaisalmer, Barmer, Sikar, and Jhunjhunu.

Mirror work
In the areas adjoining Gujarat and Kutch, traces of the *mochi* technique, which uses small pieces of mirrors in cross-stitched designs, can be seen.

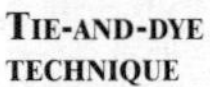

Turban cloth
Multi-colored turbans are often worn at festivals and weddings. Presents of bright, multi-colored turbans for respected elders are a must at a traditional Rajasthani wedding.

Tie-and-dye technique
The outline of the design is drawn or painted onto the cloth using a fugitive, or non-permanent, dye. The cloth is then tied with strings, usually by women who perform this task with remarkable ease. They pinch the cloth with their long fingernails and tie strings around the spots of the design. When the cloth is dipped in dye, the tied areas remain unaffected. The process is repeated according to the intricacy of the design and the number of dyes used. The light and more fugitive dyes are used first, followed by red, chocolate brown, and black, or any other combination of colors.

Royal costume
The costumes of royal ladies and their attendants show a profusion of *zari* and *gota* embroidery. In this replica of a court lady of Jaipur, an original 19th-century court costume made of tie-dyed cloth is shown. The borders and main field are in contrasting colors. The field is designed with dots and petals of stylized flowers.

Embroidery
The Jat women of Sikar and Jhunjhunu embroider various geometric motifs as well as animal designs on long, flowing *ghagras* and on *orhnis*. Other handicrafts such as wall hangings, table cloths, purses, and coverings of palanquins are also richly embroidered.

Laharia
A special process of tie-and-dye creates the stylized wave pattern, or *laharia*, symbolizing water or the monsoon rain. Turbans and *orhnis* with *laharia* patterns are generally used on festive occasions, especially Teej.

Embroidered detail.

Gota work
Gota work is a special kind of embroidery using the appliqué technique. Small pieces of *zari* ribbon are applied onto the fabric with the edges sewn down to create elaborate patterns. Lengths of wide, golden ribbons are similarly stitched on the edges of the fabric to create an effect of gold *zari* work. The *gota* method is commonly used for women's formal costumes. Khandela, in Shekhavati, is best known for its manufacture.

Embroidery and appliqué work
Examples of embroidery work produced in Rajasthan (clockwise from bottom left): an animal-embroidered cloth from Jaisalmer, a quilt from Jaipur, and appliqué work with animal motifs.

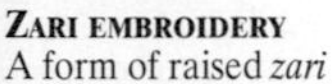

Zari embroidery
A form of raised *zari* metallic thread embroidery known as *karchobi* is created by sewing flat stitches on cotton paddings. *Zari* embroidery (above) in bridal and formal costumes is still common. The wedding costume of a Rajasthani prince would invariably be of thick, brocaded silk with elaborate *zari* embroidery. The technique is also commonly used for velvet coverings, tent hangings, curtains, and the coverings of animal carts and temple chariots.

Tie-and-dye fabrics
Rajasthani *bandhej* pieces are generally of fine *malmal* (delicate cotton cloth) for saris and *orhnis*, and medium or coarse cloth for the traditional *ghagra* (skirt), *kurti* (shirt), and *choli* (bodice). The designs are not as elaborate or delicately drawn as those in Gujarat.

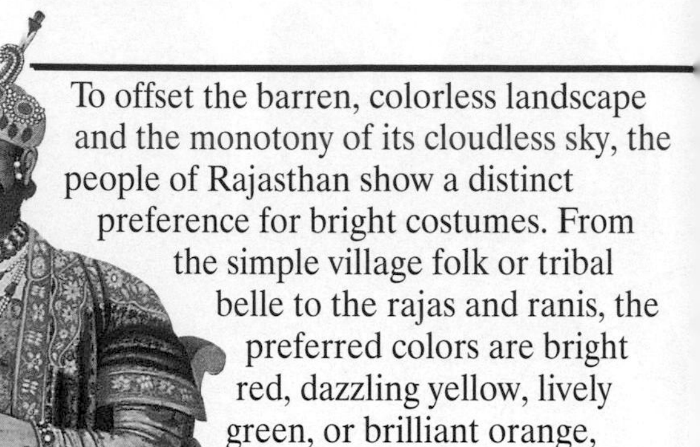

To offset the barren, colorless landscape and the monotony of its cloudless sky, the people of Rajasthan show a distinct preference for bright costumes. From the simple village folk or tribal belle to the rajas and ranis, the preferred colors are bright red, dazzling yellow, lively green, or brilliant orange, highlighted by a lavish use of sparkling gold and silver *zari* or *gota*. The dyers of Rajasthan and neighboring Gujarat (many of whom migrated here) were masters of their craft from the dawn of history. Their unsurpassed skill is still evident in the costumes worn by the Rajasthani people, both rich and poor.

RAJPUT COSTUME

The Rajput kings, owing to their close proximity to the Mughal throne, adopted the Mughal court style in their formal dress. Richly brocaded materials from Benaras and Gujarat, embossed velvets, patterned silks, embroidered and woven Kashmiri shawls, and delicate cottons from Chanderi and Dhaka were procured at great cost. This formal dress made for Maharao Banai Singh of Alwar (1815–57) shows a strange admixture of Mughal and traditional styles.

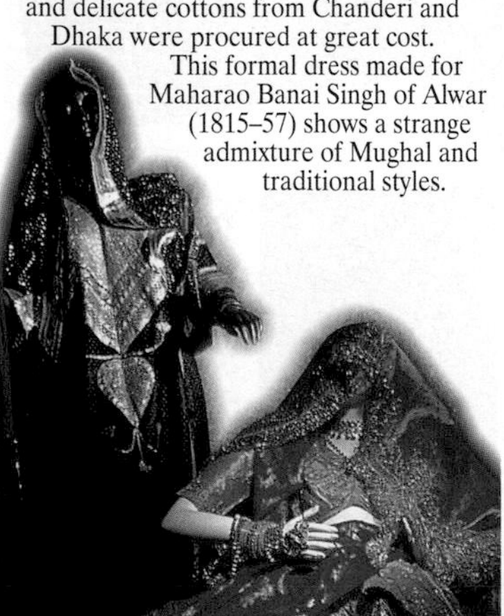

ORHNI

Many Hindu and some Muslim women wear an *orhni*, a piece of fine cloth, 10 feet long and 5 feet wide. One corner is tucked in the skirt while the other end is taken over the head and right shoulder. Colors and motifs are particular to caste, type of costume, and occasion.

ROYAL WARDROBE

The state records of Jaipur mention special departments in charge of royal costumes. While the *rangkhana* and the *chhapakhana* are departments that took care of dyeing and printing the fabrics respectively, the *siwankhana* ensured its immaculate tailoring. Two special sections, the *toshakhana* and the *kapaddwara*, took care of the daily wear and formal costumes of the king.

WOMEN'S ATTIRE
The standard design is a three-piece dress which includes the *ghagra* (skirt), the *kanchli* (a small bodice) or the *kurti* (a long, loose blouse), and the *orhni.*

MEN'S ATTIRE
The turban, variously called *pagri, pencha, sela,* or *safa,* depending on style, an *angrakhi* or *achakan* as the upper garment, and *dhoti* or pyjamas as the lower garment make up the male outfit.

TRADITIONAL TEXTILES
Rajasthani daily wear such as saris, *odhnis*, and turbans are often made from textiles using either block-printed (above) or tie-and-dye techniques ● *56, 58.*

TURBAN STYLES
Varying styles of turban denote region and caste ▲ *295*. These variations are known by different names such as *pagri, pecha*, *sela*, *ori* and *safa*. A *pagri* is usually 82 feet long and 8 inches wide. A *safa* is shorter and broader. The common man wears turbans of one color, while the elite wear designs and colors according to the occasion.

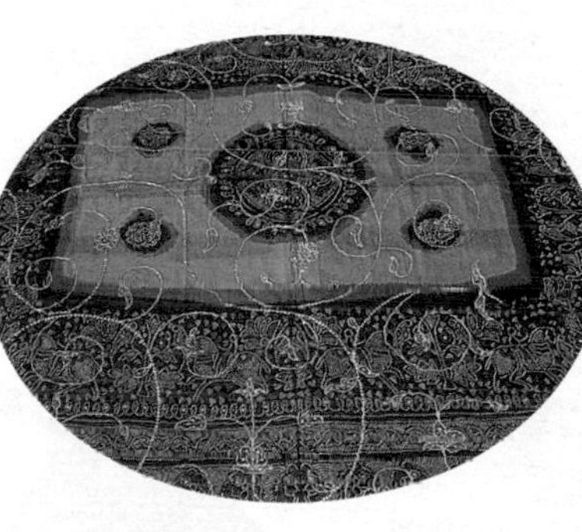

PILA
An *orhni* with a yellow background and a central lotus motif in red, called a *pila*, is a traditional gift of parents to their daughter on the birth of a son.

TYING THE TURBAN
Achieving different styles with just a length of material requires great skill. Specialists in this art, called *pagribands*, were employed by the royal courts, but Rajasthanis generally take pride in practicing and perfecting the art of turban-tying themselves.

Enameled liqueur sipper.

Rajasthan became famous for its jewelry industry from very early times, being an important source of precious and semi-precious stones ■ *18*. Sophisticated jewelry, set with precious stones using the *kundankari* technique, or decorated with bright enamel work, known as *minakari*, were made for the Rajput court and affluent people. Skillful artisans from Lahore, Delhi, Gujarat, and Bengal, attracted by the liberal patronage of the rajas, came to work in Jaipur, Bikaner, Udaipur, and Jodhpur.

THRONE
Silver was used extensively in the court to make cradles, carriages, *howdahs*, utensils, door panels, and thrones. The lion motif, as seen in this silver chair from Fateh Prakash Palace in Udaipur, could only be used for the throne or other formal furniture of the ruler.

ENAMELING
A lithograph of 1884 showing a typical workshop of a *minakar*. While three young assistants shape the ornament and engrave the design on it, the old master craftsman carefully fires it in the earthen *bhatti* (kiln) fired with charcoal. The process is not much different today.

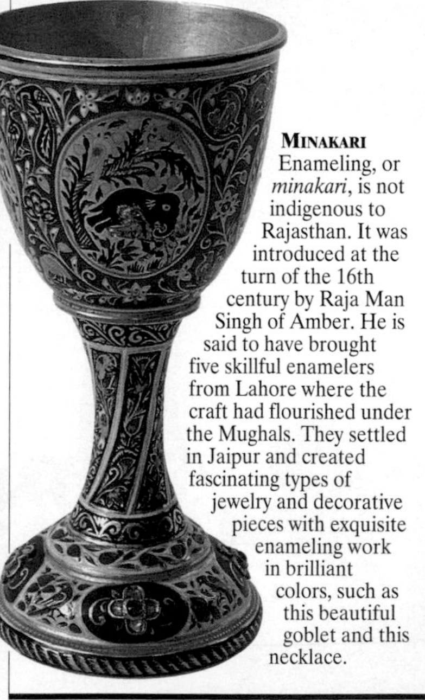

MINAKARI
Enameling, or *minakari*, is not indigenous to Rajasthan. It was introduced at the turn of the 16th century by Raja Man Singh of Amber. He is said to have brought five skillful enamelers from Lahore where the craft had flourished under the Mughals. They settled in Jaipur and created fascinating types of jewelry and decorative pieces with exquisite enameling work in brilliant colors, such as this beautiful goblet and this necklace.

VILLAGE GOLDSMITH
In every small town or village, the resident *sunar* (goldsmith) produces traditionally designed ornaments to meet the needs of the the tribes living in the surrounding areas and those of the ordinary village folk. He also works as the repair expert, money lender, and pawnbroker.

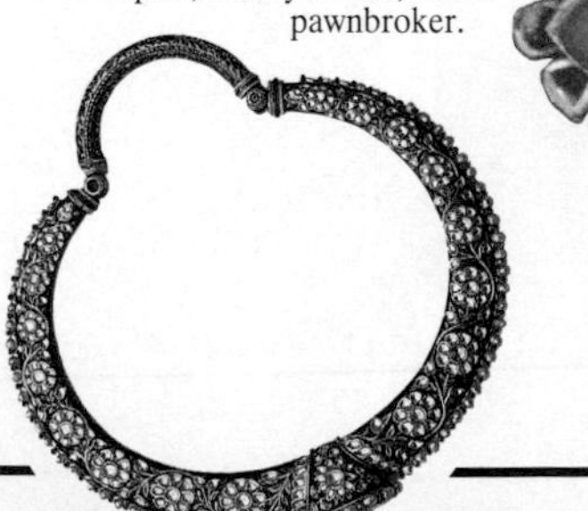

Enameled chess pieces.

KUNDANKARI TECHNIQUE
The Jaipur lapidary displays superior skill in carving from hard stones such as jade, rock crystal, agate, garnet, emerald, topaz, amethyst, and spinel. The *jadiyas* (stone-setters) create fabulous pieces of jewelry using the age-old *kundankari* technique. In this typically Indian technique, the gemstones are set within solid walls of gold.

TRADITIONAL JEWELRY
Silver ornaments help identify the cast, social or marital status of a person. They are also thought to have healing powers. The pressure from the weight of an earring, for instance, is believed to have a beneficial effect on certain organs.

TURBAN JEWELS
1. Following the Mughal emperors, the Rajput rulers wore costly turban ornaments, or *jigha*, made of dazzling, enameled gold and set with rare rose-cut diamonds, rubies, emeralds, sapphires, and pearls. Turban jewels like this one are still made by the jewelers of Jaipur.
2. The *sarpati*, made of enameled gold, is tied around the turban on formal occasions. The reverse of this piece is beautifully enameled in white, red, and green.

1.

2.

BODY JEWELRY
Women wear jewelry on many parts of their body. Personal ornaments include specific types worn on the feet, head, forehead, ear, nose, neck, arm, wrist, fingers, toes, and waist. Nose rings are attached to the earrings by fine gold chains. Widows have to renounce any such adornment, however.

Rajasthani painting combines the exuberance of bright primary colors with the vigor of strong, bold lines. Early paintings illustrated religious and rhetorical texts such as the *Bhagavata Purana, Gita Govinda, Ramayana,* and *Ragamala*. From the mid-17th century, court portraiture and genre scenes gained in importance. The style of Rajasthani painting differs from state to state and from *thikana* to *thikana* (minor fiefdom). A variety of social, religious, and ethno-cultural differences gave rise to many distinct schools, the four major ones being Mewar, Marwar, Hara (Bundi-Kota), and Dhundhar (Amber-Jaipur). Several minor ones include Kishangarh, Alwar, and Ajmer.

AMBER–JAIPUR
Despite a close association with the Mughals, the early painting style of Amber reveals little of their influence. The foundation of Jaipur by Jai Singh II in 1727 resulted in a new wave of paintings comprising religious and popular subjects, such as this splendid painting of Ras-lila (the circular dance of Krishna and *Gopi*, the cowherd women).

KISHANGARH
This small state produced perhaps the most distinctive religious paintings in Rajasthan. Nihal Chand, a highly innovative painter, transfigured his patron Maharaja Sawant Singh as Lord Krishna, his lady Bani Thani as Radha, and the lakes and gardens of Kishangarh as Vrindaban. Stylized linear distortions of the Mughal style were his hallmark, such as the curving elongation of the eyes and the sharp angular nose.

MEWAR
By the end of the 16th century Mewari painting had developed its distinctive style as revealed by a fabulous group of *Ragamala* paintings. Between 1649 and 1653 a seven-volume *Ramayana,* profusely illustrated, was prepared for Maharaja Jagat Singh. From the 18th century the Mewari artists started to portray the patron maharajas in court scenes of a vast scale with innumerable courtiers.

This is a beautiful example of Mewar painting showing Maharana Fateh Singh of Udaipur crossing a swollen river in the rain during a hunting trip.

The west

The most important centers in Marwar were Bikaner and Jodhpur, ruled by two collateral branches of the same family. The rulers employed Mughal-trained artists whose works display a distinct style – cool palette, delicate drawings, and restrained expression. This is particularly evident in Bikaner. Many paintings illustrating the seasons and manifold moods of lovelorn heroines as described in Hindi literature were produced, as were portraits of royal splendor. In Jodhpur paintings developed a robustly conservative Rajput style, full of verve and passion.

Hara

The rulers of Bundi were also close to the Mughal *durbar* and imbibed much court culture. The palette of the Bundi painters is often quite muted with patches of strong color for contrast (above). Court scenes, portraits, illustrations of religious and classical poetry, and the *Ragamala* were produced in large numbers in the 18th and 19th centuries. Much fauna, and flora such as banana trees and flower beds were often introduced as if to recreate the green verdure of this eastern Rajasthani state.

Kota

The neighboring offshoot court of Kota, recognized as a separate kingdom from the early 17th century, continued the Bundi idiom. Later Kota works exhibit exceptional vitality and versatility. Hunting and wildlife scenes abound.

The small states of Uniara and Kaurali and the *thikanas* of Sarola, Indargarh, Antarda, and Karwar also reveal the strong impact of the distinct Hara style of Bundi and Kota.

GATHERING OF GODS
This interesting detail painted on a wall of a palace in Jhalawar depicts "Ram Durbar", an imaginary assembly of gods and goddesses – the five-headed Brahma, Shiva, Vishnu, elephant-headed Ganesha, Rama and Sita seated on a golden throne. The monkey god, Hanuman, is shown in the foreground seated with folded hands.

Kota mural.

Walls embellished with colorful paintings are a common sight in Rajasthan. The tradition of wall painting goes back to early times when the interiors of caves and temples were painted with religious scenes. Many towns contain numerous palaces, forts, temples, *chhatris,* and *havelis* with the walls covered in paintings. Some of the finest wall paintings are to be seen in the ancient towns of Bundi and Kota and the small fiefs of Shekhavati. In the temples, painted or printed cloths called *pichhvais,* which are hung behind a deity, serve as objects of devotion. As esthetic objects, they also provided a new genre in Rajasthani art.

KOTA SCHOOL
This mid-18th century picture is a superb example of the Kota school ● *65*. Two female dancers accompanied by musicians perform before the enthroned Brijnathji, the presiding deity of Kota State.

MOTIFS
Pichhvais may be embroidered or woven with motifs derived from a vast repertoire of Vaishnava rituals. This design depicts the cowherd girls frolicking with Lord Krishna.

BUNDI STYLE
The paintings in the Chitrashala (painted pavilion) in Garh Palace are exquisite examples of the Bundi style ▲ *293*. Popular subjects include the Krishnalila (above) and *Ragamala* scenes.

SHEKHAVATI STYLE
Shekhavati has its own distinctive style ▲ *184–9*. Scenes of Krishnalila and *Ragamala*, erotic paintings, modern inventions, and genealogical portraits are common subjects. In this detail the painter has reproduced a familiar and popular subject, Lakshmi, the goddess of wealth, flanked and revered by four white elephants.

PICHHVAIS ▲ *257*
Pichhvais are large canvases painted with sacred scenes and placed in Vallabha temples dedicated to Krishna ▲ *257*. The canvas, of woven cotton, is covered with a mixture of gum arabic and rice flour. The colors, made from pigments obtained from plants or animals, are then applied with a brush.

PHAD
This is a kind of hand-woven cotton cloth, known as the *khadi*, used on certain occasions by the folk minstrels of the Bhopa caste to assist their performances. Illustrated with episodes of folk legends, the *phad* (above) ▲ *54* is still being produced by a few surviving families of *phad* painters from the Chhipa Joshi communities at Bhilwara.

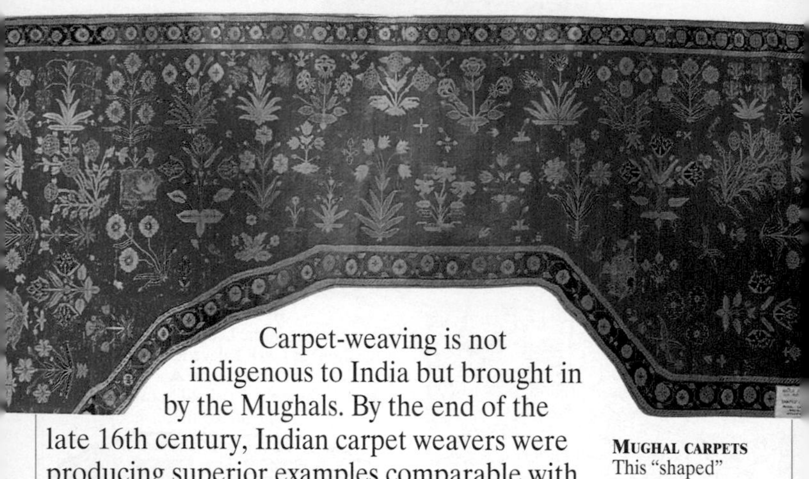

Carpet-weaving is not indigenous to India but brought in by the Mughals. By the end of the late 16th century, Indian carpet weavers were producing superior examples comparable with the finest products of Persia. The rulers of Amber-Jaipur took a great interest in carpets and built up a large collection of 16th- and 17th-century Persian and Mughal carpets. The carpet industry in Jaipur started only in the mid-19th century when carpet-making was introduced as a jail craft. Ajmer and Bikaner were also selected as carpet-weaving centers.

MUGHAL CARPETS
This "shaped" Mughal carpet is from the Shah Jahani looms of Lahore. Mirza Raja Jai Singh bought a large number of such individually shaped carpets for spreading in his garden at Amber. The design shows rows of flowering plants of delicate hues similar to the design used in the palaces of the Red Fort and the Taj Mahal. Some representative Mughal carpets are on display at the Central Museum and the Maharaja Sawai Man Singh II Museum, Jaipur.

RAJASTHANI CARPETS
Modern Rajasthani carpets follow north Persian designs. Often dictated by the buyers' tastes, such designs frequently incorporate hunting scenes or romantic themes from Persian poetry.

DURRIES
A *durrie* is a cool, light rug. Rajasthani *durries* are smooth and closely woven. Pastel shades and a sparse use of geometrical and vegetal motifs are popular.

DURRIE-MAKING
Durries are woven all over the country where skilled labor is available cheaply ▲ *232*. Durrie-making, which dates back to very ancient days in India, had been popular in eastern and northern Rajasthan, meeting a steady demand from the court and the general public.

WEAVING CARPETS
Carpet-weaving entails the combined efforts of the designer, dyer, weaver, and the knotter, whose skillful and deft fingers apply the delicate knots of different shades to bring out the design. The knots are then trimmed with a pair of carpet scissors, and the carpet is ready after a wash.

Leather saddles.

In every village of Rajasthan there are families of Chamars (who skin the hides of animals), Regars (tanners) and Mochis (cobblers). The quality of craftsmanship of these poor, neglected artisans – who are regarded as being on a level with untouchables – in this trade is amazingly high. The hides are processed by an indigenous method, and the processed leather is used to make shoes, sandals, bags, saddles, pouches, and other items.

SURAHI
Camel hide has many uses for the people of western Rajasthan. The tanned, soft inner hide is processed and polished till it is translucent and then molded to the desired shape to create various designs with gesso work. Tastefully painted flasks, jugs, *surahis* (long, narrow-necked water pots), like this example (right), and the lampshades of Bikaner, are made from camel hide.

KNUCKLE PAD
Knuckle pads, with padded inner lining for protecting the knuckles, are delicately turned out works of art. This example shows geometrical and floral patterns embroidered with delicate silk yarn.

SHIELD
A shield was not only essential armor; a specially made animal-hide shield, polished and decorated with painting and embellished with gold and silver bosses, or a shield of special steel with golden damascened decoration, was a symbol of high status for a Mughal and Rajput king or noble. Kota, Karauli, and Bikaner produced some of the finest animal-hide shields. Processing the toughest buffalo, rhinoceros and crocodile hides, and shaping them into shields was a difficult, time-consuming process. This shield (right) from the Maharaja Sawai Man Singh II Museum, Jaipur, with its lacquered painting, is a masterpiece.

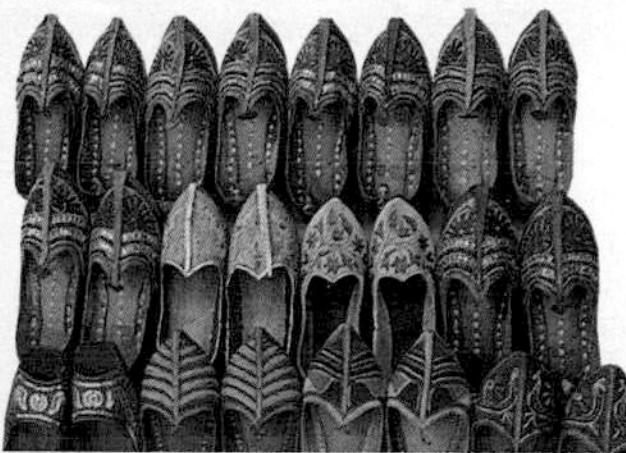

JOOTIS
In Jodhpur, Jaisalmer, and Barmer, soft processed goat or sheepskin is decorated with colorful needle work. From these hides, *jootis* (leather sandals) (above), pouches, purses, belts, and saddle accessories are fashioned.

MUSICAL INSTRUMENTS
The Dagbar people specialize in making traditional musical instruments in leather. Examples include percussion instruments such as the *dholak* or the *tabla*, and stringed instruments as the *kamaycha* ● 79, and the *sarangi* (left).

A panel of dancing figures decorate Jagdish Mandir in Udaipur (below left). Fine *jali* work from Jaisalmer (below right).

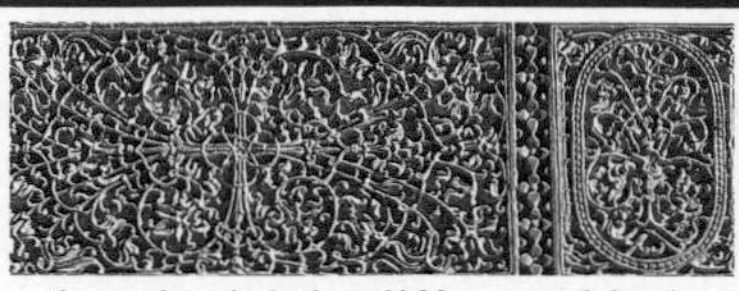

The geologically old land of Rajasthan is rich in different kinds of hard rocks, yielding granites, marbles, quartzites, slates, and other metamorphic rocks ■ *18*. With the ready availability of high-quality stone (the use of brick was almost unknown), it was easy for the Rajasthani builder to construct strong and beautiful forts, palaces, and temples. The full extent of the Rajasthani stone-cutters' skill can be seen in the richness and beauty of the large number of sculptures found in the temples built in ancient and medieval times in Bharatpur, Abaneri, Baroli, Ramgarh, Nagda, Ajmer, Chittor, Mandore, Osiyan, Jaisalmer, Bikaner, and Udaipur.

STONES FOR BUILDINGS
While Makrana produces white marble, Rupbas (near Agra) and Karauli produce red sandstone used by the Mughals to build their forts and palaces at Agra, Delhi, and Fatehpur Sikri; Kota in east Rajasthan produces gray stone for floor making; Barmer produces yellow marble for delicate carvings; and Ajmer produces granites.

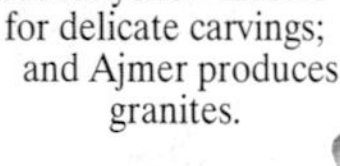

STONE CARVING
The *silavat* (stone carver) carefully selects the stone, draws the design in charcoal and chips away the unwanted stone to create superbly reliefed *jali* works used to adorn temples, palaces, and forts.

FEMALE DANCER
This intricately carved sculpture is from Karni Mata Temple in Deshnoke, Bikaner ▲ *207*. Though it does not have the free-standing or high-relief sculptural decorations found in the earlier temples of Abaneri, Baroli, Ramgarh, or Mandore, its delicate embellishments are no less striking. Stylized birds, flying, craning necks, or perching, form the border of this niche, with a female dancer hidden behind large leaves carved with immense care.

Dedicated to gods
A row of figures (above) embellishes the Surya temple, Jhalarapatan, in southern Rajasthan. The stone carvers of this region, like their counterparts in north Gujarat and western Madhya Pradesh, produced some of the finest temples dedicated to Devi, Shiva, Vishnu, and the Sun God, adorning the buildings with many delicately carved figures of human and celestial beings.

The genius of jali
The genius of the Rajasthani *silavat* is seen in architectural pieces such as pillars, lintels, *jalis* (latticed grilles), and friezes. Some of the finest examples of *jali* work reign at Jaisalmer in unique mansions such as Patwon-ki-haveli, Nathmalji-ki-haveli, and Salim Singh-ki-haveli, where the stone carver has effectively transformed the hard surface of the yellow sandstone into soft, transparent traceries.

The Mughal style
During the 16th and 17th centuries the Rajput lords built marble cenotaphs in the Mughal style, as well as superb *Diwan-i-Khas* in their palaces. At the beginning of the 20th century, during the reign of Shah Jahan (1628–1658), the Mughal style was still in evidence. Such palaces and monuments as the Mubarak Mahal and the imposing gateway of City Palace, in Jaipur, flanked by two monolithic white elephants (right), provide typical examples from this period.

Elephants in high relief
This pair of elephants forms part of a sculptured panel from a Jain temple, Sat Bis Deorhi, in Chittorgarh. Hindu and Jain temples, Victory towers, and the palace coexist within the sprawling fort of Chittorgarh. Various panels within the temple display figures of men, women, and animals in high relief. The majestic figures of elephants abound everywhere.

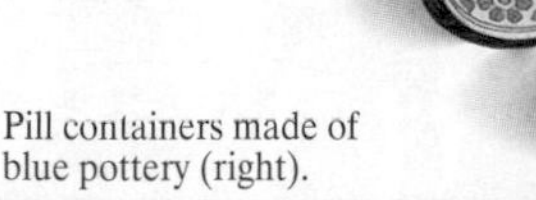

Pill containers made of blue pottery (right).

Clay – which could be obtained easily, shaped with little effort, and given some permanency after firing – is used extensively for making pots, dolls, and other objects in Rajasthan. Alwar, Pokharan, and Nohar near Bikaner are famous for pottery-making. Many beautiful terracotta plaques and figures come from the ancient sites of north and northwest Rajasthan. Some of them, discovered along the dried up Ghaggar basin at Rang Mahal near Bikaner, have excellent artistic merit and have been preserved in the Bikaner Museum.

BLUE POTTERY
Jaipur became a flourishing center of blue pottery from the middle of the 19th century. Vases, flower pots, plates, bowls, ewers, water pots, and other objects are produced in many workshops. Though traditional geometrical and floral motifs are used extensively, decorative water pots with hand-painted details of Rajasthani heroes and heroines are also common.

PREPARING BLUE POTTERY
The materials used are Multani clay or fuller's earth, quartz, raw glaze, and sodium sulfate. Once the piece is made, partly in molds and partly on the wheel, the artist draws the design with a soft brush on the surface using a copper sulfate pigment for turquoise blue and a cobalt oxide pigment for deep blue. The piece is then fired carefully in the kiln.

PAINTED EARTHENWARE
Images of folk divinities are sold in village fairs during festive times such as Teej, Gangaur, and Diwali. These icons are brush-painted.

THE POTTER (KUMHAR)
The potter uses clay to make *surahis* (water jugs) and *matkas* (water pitchers). Each area in Rajasthan creates its own special shape and design, as much depends on the quality of the clay and the expertise of the potter, or *kumhar*.

MOLELA TERRACOTTAS
Like the large clay horses of Bankura in West Bengal or the different kinds of *gramadevata* figures found in Tamil Nadu, Karnataka, Maharashtra, and Andhra Pradesh, the clay plaques of Molela, a small town not far from Udaipur, are votive objects made in very high relief.

"...their faces, with large accentuated eyes and bold features, conform to the genre of the folk paintings of the region."

Uma Amand, *Mansions of the Sun*, 1972

Puppetry is an ancient, popular form of folk entertainment. The string puppets in Rajasthan are called *kathputlis*, or marionettes. The riveting histrionics of the puppeteers (*kathputlivale nat*), like the full-throated songs of the Mirasis, Langas, and Manganiyars ● *79*, belong to old times, and epitomize a traditional, leisurely pace of life. No village fair, no religious festival, and no social gathering would be complete without them.

CONTROLLING THE PUPPET
The puppet is manipulated by strings which are looped into the puppeteer's hands and fingers. The puppets lie inert on the stage until they come to life when the strings are pulled. The puppeteers are usually from one family, such as a father-and-son team.

NARRATING FOLK LEGENDS
Heroic stories of folk divinities and Rajput heroes are popular with the Rajasthani puppeteer. This illustrated text (above) is of the love story of Dhola-Maru ● 55, a popularly narrated tale.

PUPPET THEATER
The traditional puppeteers are from the wandering community of the Bhatts. They move from village to village with their box of *kathputlis*, accessories, and *dholaks* during the festive seasons, returning to their villages to cultivate their small patch of land during the short rainy season.

MAKING A PUPPET
The typical Rajasthani *kathputli* has a brightly painted face and a rough torso. Appropriate brightly colored male or female costumes are fashioned by the puppeteers themselves from patches of old cloth.

The daily fare in Rajasthan typically comprises *chappati* (unleavened bread made of wheat, barley, millet, or maize), *dal* (a soup of legumes) flavored with red chili peppers, yogurt, or milk, and sometimes a vegetable such as *okra*, jackfruit, eggplant, mustard green, or fenugreek leaf. The martial Rajputs are traditionally a meat-eating people, but many abstain for religious or economic reasons. In the deserts of Bikaner or Jodhpur spices and water are considered a luxury and are used sparingly; people use scraggly roots, the seeds of grasses, and *ker-sangri* (a vegetable extracted from trees or a thorny bush).

MUGHAL-INSPIRED DISHES
The Mughals influenced the eating habits of the Rajput courts. From the simple grilled meats served on leaves, the royal kitchen introduced elaborate curries, *kebabs,* and *pulaos* (rice prepared with clarified butter, spices, meat or vegetables) served on silver platters.

LASSI
Natural yogurt is churned to remove the butter content for the making of *lassi*, or buttermilk, a cooling summer beverage. The painting (left) shows Krishna's mother preparing a pot of *lassi*.

CHAPPATI-MAKING
The *chappati* is a flat, unleavened bread which serves almost as a spoon, for it is used as a scoop to transfer food to the mouth. It complements both the texture and flavor of the food, balancing strong flavors and pleasing the palate with its smoothness. The *chappati* forms an integral part of the meal, like the millet cake or *bajre ki roti*, typical of Rajasthan.

"Eat flesh and you will grow stout, eat butter and you will grow strong; eat greens and you will grow pot-bellied and have no strength at all".

Old proverb of the Rajputs

FRYING PURIS
In this painting (left), a woman in the upper floor kitchen is frying *puris*. *Puris* are delicious, fried wheaten bubbles which have varied uses: as snacks, scoops for food, and as a complement to hot spices. Family members typically sit on the floor and are served piping hot food by the lady of the house.

KHAR KHARGOSH
Khar khargosh (hare or rabbit meat cooked in a pit) is a Rajput specialty during summer, when the hare is lean. The hare is skinned and stuffed with spices, wrapped in dough, and finally in layers of mud-soaked cloth. The ambrosial result is meat perfectly blended with the spices and dough.

THE INDIAN KITCHEN
The simple Indian kitchen has a brick-and-mud fireplace. Food is usually cooked over a wood or charcoal fire, in clay, brass, or copper utensils.

HOME-COOKED DESERT COOKING
Very little produce grows in the desert. Daily food mainly comprises *daal-bati* (cooked lentils and roasted balls of dough), accompanied by a variety of dried or pickled berries cooked in different ways.

● SULA

The painting below portrays a picnic, with *sula* being prepared in the foreground. Right, cooking *sula*, tender morsels of skewered meat.

In Rajput cuisine, *sulas* refer to tender morsels of meat, the most prized being wild boar cutlets (*pasla*), marinated in a mixture of dry yogurt, browned onions, garlic, ginger, coriander, red chili, and *kachri*, a small pod which tenderizes meat and lends a particular sharp-sour flavor to many dishes. The marinated meat is smoked, spitted on skewers, and grilled over hot coals. Now that *shikar* (hunt) is a sport of the past, *sulas* are made of chicken, pheasant, mutton, or fish.

1. Pound *garam masala* ingredients and strain.

2. Pound *tandoori chaat masala* ingredients and strain.

3. To prepare mint sauce: grind cumin seeds and mango or pomegranate seeds. Add garlic paste, green chilis, and salt. Finally add mint and coriander leaves. Strain. Taste for saltiness and sourness. If needed, add lemon juice and lime cordial.

4. Fillet lamb leg and cut into thin one-inch strips (same as for *shashlik*). Sprinkle salt and marinate with half of malt vinegar. Put aside for two hours.

5. Mix ginger and garlic paste, red chili paste, salt, *garam masala*, mustard oil, pineapple juice, and the rest of malt vinegar with the curd (curd has to be hung in muslin cloth for two hours to obtain the solid coagulated substance, allowing the liquid to drain). Marinate mutton pieces in mixture and keep in the refrigerator for at least eight hours.

INGREDIENTS FOR TANDOORI CHAAT MASALA
$2\frac{1}{4}$ oz cumin seeds
$2\frac{1}{4}$ oz black pepper corns
2 oz black salt
$31\frac{1}{2}$ oz dry mint leaves
a pinch of ajowain
a pinch of asafoetida
one drop of tartaric acid
$\frac{1}{2}$ oz mango, pounded
2 oz salt
$\frac{3}{4}$ oz ginger, ground
$\frac{3}{4}$ oz yellow chili, ground

INGREDIENTS FOR GARAM MASALA
2 lb cumin seeds
$3\frac{1}{2}$ oz cloves
$3\frac{1}{2}$ oz green cardamom
2 lb black cardamom
$3\frac{1}{2}$ oz cinnamon
$3\frac{1}{2}$ oz fennel seeds
150 g dry ginger
$3\frac{1}{2}$ oz bay leaf
$5\frac{1}{4}$ oz black pepper corns
10 pieces nutmeg
$3\frac{1}{2}$ oz mace

INGREDIENTS FOR PUDINA (MINT) CHUTNEY
$1\frac{3}{4}$ oz cumin seeds
2 lb raw mango or or 7 oz pomegranate seeds
$3\frac{1}{2}$ oz garlic paste
$5\frac{1}{4}$ oz green chili
salt to taste
2 lb mint leaves
$6\frac{1}{2}$ lb green coriander

Ingredients for Sula
2 lb lamb leg (mutton, boneless)
salt to taste
1 oz malt vinegar
$^3/_4$ oz ginger and garlic paste
$17^1/_2$ oz curd
$^3/_4$ oz red chili paste
$1^3/_4$ oz mustard oil
$1^3/_4$ oz pineapple (raw) juice
$1^3/_4$ oz butter
2 lemons
$^1/_2$ oz *garam masala*

6. Skewer mutton pieces. Allow eight to ten pieces per skewer.

7. Place skewered mutton in a moderately hot charcoal clay oven. After seven to eight minutes, turn over the skewer so as to ensure uniform cooking on both sides. Cook for another seven to eight minutes. Baste with butter using a brush. Place in oven for another two to three minutes' cooking.

8. Sprinkle with *tandoori chaat masala* and lemon juice. Serve with lemon wedges, onion rings, tomato quarters or slices, mint sauce, and Indian bread.

Music and dance are deeply ingrained in Rajasthani life. The stillness of the desert evening and the upsurge of life in the short-lived rainy season or spring are filled with soulful, full-throated music and rhythmic dance. Instruments such as *sarangi*, *kamaycha*, *satara*, *nad,* and *morchang* create a wide range of lilting and melodious sound in accompaniment to the music of the Bhopas ● *54*, Kalbeliyas, Langas, and the Manganiyars as well as the lively and spontaneous dances, *ghoomar*, *gair,* and *chari*.

MORCHANG
The *morchang* (above) resembles a jew's-harp. The plaintive, melancholic twang of the *morchang* adds a desolate dimension to the songs of the Manganiyars.

OF BAMBOO, BRASS AND BELLS
The vast array of Rajasthani folk instruments is made ingeniously from a variety of materials. Shells of dried gourds of all shapes and sizes are used for stringed and wind instruments, thick gorse stems or bamboo segments for flutes, and baked clay pots for drums.

Conch shells are blown to produce full, resonant sounds; sticks create a rasping rhythm; and *ghungroos* (brass bells) jingle on waists and ankles.

KANJAR DANCE
It is only recently that the Kanjar women have come out of their villages to perform on the stage. Their dance, referred to as *chakri*, has the dancers moving in fast swirling movements.

SNAKE DANCE
The dance of the Kalbeliyas, the snake charmers' community, is a recent discovery ▲ *216.* The dancers accentuate supple and snake-like movements.

FIRE DANCE
In the fire dance, devotees of the Jasnathi sect dance on a platform of smoldering embers. Their movements grow more frenzied as the music reaches a crescendo. The dance is performed in Bikaner and Churu.

KAMAYCHA
The *kamaycha* has a big, circular resonator which produces a deep, booming sound. It is used exclusively by the Manganiyars, a caste of traveling singers, in the Jaisalmer-Barmer region.

DHOLI
The name of these minstrels comes from the Dhole drum (above), which is their main instrument. Both singers and musicians play an important role in marriage ceremonies.

CHARI DANCE
Pots topped with lighted lamps are balanced on the head, and gentle steps and graceful hand movements come together in the *chari* dance of the Kishangarh area.

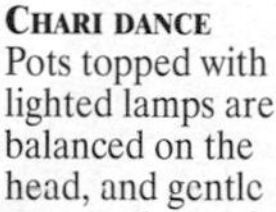

SATARA
This double flute, with its melodious and haunting sound, is evocative of the desert environs. It is played by both the Langas and Manganiyars.

FESTIVE DANCE
Rajasthani folk dances are performed during festivals and other ceremonial occasions. Each community and region has its own variations and the dances are accompanied by a particular type of music.

GAIR
The *gair* dance is performed during Holi, and the dancers are exclusively men. A series of half-swirls make up a simpler version. Based on the dancers' proficiency, the dance can build up to a series of intricate patterns. The striking of sticks gives the dance a vigorous character.

Camel polo (left) and folk dances (right) are featured during the Desert Festival.

There is a local saying that "Rajasthanis celebrate nine festivals in a week". In this State, seasons are heralded with a festive fervor; and cattle marts turn into delightful fairs. While some traditional *melas* (fairs and religious festivals) have a mythological origin, others commemorate a local hero or god. Most of the traditional festivals fall in "the bright half of the month" (or when the moon is seen). To provide visitors with the opportunity to enjoy the romance of the full moon in the desert, new festivals such as the Desert Festival at Jaisalmer have been organized.

GANGAUR
Gangaur is based on the myth concerning the reunion of the goddess Gawa (another name for Shiva's consort, Parvati), and Lord Shiva after a long penance. Women revere the two deities to seek conjugal bliss. In Jaipur, following an age-old tradition, processions of stately elephants, camels, bullock carts, and caparisoned horses, all decorated in festive dress, emerge from the Tripolia Gate of the City Palace, accompanied by music.

ELEPHANT FESTIVAL
On the day of Holi, the entire elephant population of Jaipur assembles in the Chaugan stadium in a festive mood. The *mahouts* (elephant keepers) decorate their elephants with beautiful, colorful designs and dazzling attires.

"Among many remarkable festivals of Rajasthan kept in peculiar brilliance in Oodipur is that in honor of Gaur."

Lieutenant Colonel James Tod, 1820

URS GHARIB NAVAZ
Devotees celebrate the death anniversary of the venerated Sufi saint, Khwaja Mu'in-ud-din Chisti, in the Muslim month of Rajab. Rich offerings of profusely embroidered tomb covers, fragrant flowers, and the lilting melody of Qawwali, devotional songs composed in honor of the saint, create a mystical atmosphere ● *51* ▲ *162*.

BOAT PROCESSION
In Udaipur, a boat procession on the serene waters of Pichola Lake is a magical sight during Gangaur. The glittering lights of the boats and their manifold reflections in the water create an unforgettable scenario.

TEEJ, THE MONSOON FESTIVAL
Teej (July–August) celebrates the onset of the monsoon. There is a spectacular procession in reverence to the goddess Parvati, known as Teej Mata. As in Gangaur, the procession emerges from the Tripolia Gate in Jaipur on both days of the Teej festival.

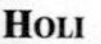

DESERT FESTIVAL
For three days in February, traditional performers gather in Jaisalmer to celebrate with folk music and dances. The sandstone city provides a golden backdrop to the popular festival, which was started in 1979.

HOLI
This festival welcomes the advent of spring with songs and dances, and with the colored powders participants spray over each other on the night of the full moon of Phagun (in February or March).

Traveling to Pushkar fair (left); Ravana effigy being prepared to be burnt on Dashhera festival, Kota (right).

From ancient times the fairs provided the best opportunity to buy and sell livestock and other essential items not available in nearby places. More than a dozen animal fairs, including large ones such as the Pushkar or Nagaur fairs, are held in the State. These are not only important trade events but also events of social and cultural interaction.

NAGAUR FAIR
Thousands of animals are gathered at the cattle fair of Nagaur, a small town in the Thar Desert ▲ *238*. The cattle fair is reputed to be one of the best in the subcontinent. Nagaur itself is famous for a special breed of bull. There are two fairs annually, in February and August, named after local heroes.

PUSHKAR FAIR
Thousands of devotees take a dip in the sacred lake of Pushkar during the Full Moon of Karvik (October–November) ● *47*. Camels, horses, and bullocks are bought and sold in the hundreds. The bazaar sells camel decorations, saddlery, apparel for cattle, and handicrafts. Cattle races, plays, a fun fair, and a circus, with performers such as tightrope walkers, are other highlights.

SHEETLA FAIR
Devotees make offerings at the shrine of the Mother Goddess at the Sheetla fairs of Chaksu near Jaipur (below), and Kanana near Barmer. The Mother Goddess is believed to manifest her anger in diseases such as smallpox.

Architecture

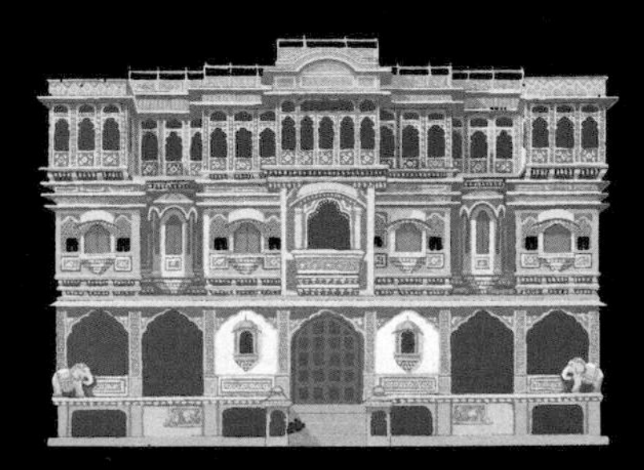

84 Rural houses
86 Urban houses – Havelis
88 Palaces
90 Forts
92 Jaipur A planned city
94 Jain temples
96 Styles and forms

The architectural style of the rural house in Rajasthan is clearly a product of climatic conditions of intense, dry heat, desert storms, and a lack of building materials. The forms that emerge, mud or rubble masonry buildings, are firmly rooted in the landscape. Perhaps because of their remoteness from urban areas, they are expressive of the intuitive knowledge of materials held by local people and are ideally suited to the climate.

HOUSE
Every house in a typical Rajasthani village resembles a tiny fortress. Each is organized around an open courtyard, typically 400 to 600 square feet in area. This configuration is a response to sandstorms in the area, which blow drifts up against external walls, often to roof height.

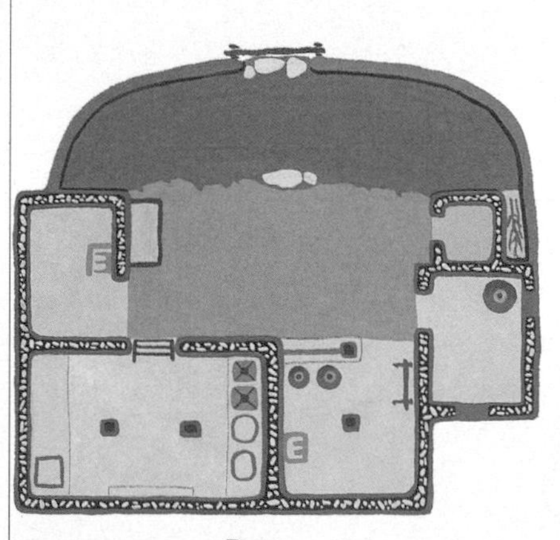

PLAN
The house is divided into a series of rooms, living, store, kitchen and so on, all oriented to face the internal, open-to-sky courtyard.

FAÇADE
The rural house usually has blank exterior walls, as most rooms are positioned facing the internal courtyard.

ROOF
The sloping roof is made with dried hay and supported by unplaned wooden rafters.

STORAGE UNITS
Rooms usually contain a variety of storage elements (below) which, besides their utilitarian function, serve as ornamental objects. Often these units comprise wooden chests, clay granaries of various sizes, clay storage units, and clay shelves with intricate decorative designs and inlaid colored glass and mirrors.

DECORATIVE MOTIFS
The homogeneity of building materials is broken by the motifs that decorate the openings of the houses. Doors and windows are outlined by colored bands, giving the houses a certain individuality.

The *haveli* is a prototype of the Rajasthani urban house – a superb response to the dense urban structure that characterizes towns throughout the State. Settlements usually comprise houses huddled together, collectively creating a micro-environment and shielding their inhabitants from the hot, dry climate. The *havelis* form a unit and have their entrances off the shady, narrow, winding streets which are lined with offices and temples. Within a city there is a consistency of building material, which ensures some unity despite variations in details. In Jaisalmer, for example, yellow sandstone unifies dwellings right across the fortified town ▲ *214*.

STREET GATEWAY
Galis (alleys) are often punctuated by *darwazas* (gateways) which act as security devices, shutting off entire streets and defining enclaves.

These gateways are wonderful architectural elements in themselves. The gateway usually has a small room above it, presumably for the guardsman, and a large ornamental door – a monumental feature within the street.

BALCONY
A common feature adorning *havelis*, with *chajjas* (sunshades) protecting against the desert glare.

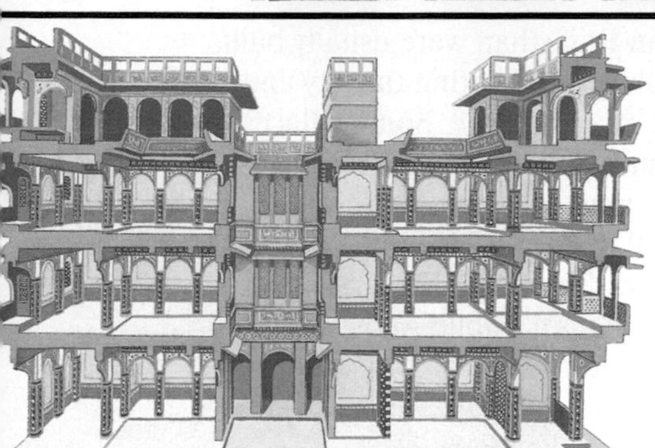

Viewing window
Jarokhas (balcony windows) are diverse in form, but often include elaborately carved *jalis*, brackets and *chajjas,* the latter sometimes curved like a *bangla* roof.

Side section
Although *havelis* can vary widely in plan, configuration, and scale, each is usually built around a courtyard, or several courtyards, at different levels. The *haveli* "breathes" through the courtyard, which provides adequate light and ventilation to the adjacent rooms, and it is topped by a roof terrace.

Haveli façade
The façades of *havelis* vary in richness, texture, and detail from city to city and neighborhood to neighborhood. Usually, the buildings in the poorer quarters are simply white-washed, with some color to accentuate openings, cornice bands, brackets, and other decorative features. In affluent precincts, elaborately carved elements ornament the façade in the form of faceted *jarokhas*, while arches and recessed areas add to the variation in profile of the varied *haveli* façades.

Street façade
The street façade of the *havelis* comprises elements such as balconies, *jalis* (screen windows), *jarokhas* (view windows), gargoyles, and decorated thresholds. The territory of each house is slightly extended toward the street by a raised platform or *otla*. In some areas, the richly carved wooden doors of individual *havelis* add yet another texture to the streetscape.

Palaces in Rajasthan were usually built as citadels located within the city and fortified by a high wall. Some palaces, such as those in Bundi and Udaipur, were built over several generations, and were therefore incremental, yet well integrated to create a whole. Public areas within the palaces consisted of the Diwan-i-Am (Hall of Public Audience), where the raja heard petitions from his subjects, the Diwan-i-Khas (Hall of Private Audience) for the council of ministers, the Sileh Khana for the display of armory, and the Daulat Khana, or treasury.

HAWA MAHAL, JAIPUR
Jaipur's Hawa Mahal, or Palace of the Winds ▲ *139*, makes use of elements such as *jalis* (intricately carved stone lattice screens). The *jali* has in a sense come to characterize Rajasthani architecture and with time has evolved an astounding variety of patterns.

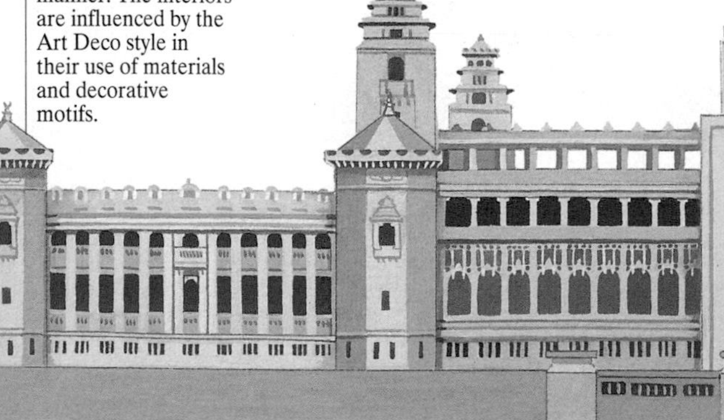

UMAID BHAWAN PALACE, JODHPUR
In colonial times, the need for fortified palaces disappeared, and many of the traditional-style retreats were abandoned in favor of stately mansions based on the Western model, such as the Umaid Bhawan Palace in Jodhpur. The Umaid Bhawan Palace ▲ *230* was built between 1929 and 1944. Its extended façade is clad in sandstone and is conceived in the grand, classical manner. The interiors are influenced by the Art Deco style in their use of materials and decorative motifs.

"One of the most curious features of the palace of Oudeypoor is, undoubtedly, its extensive hanging garden."

Louis Rousselet, *India and its Native Princes*, 1878

City Palace, Udaipur
The City Palace in Udaipur ▲ *246* was built over some three hundred years, and consists of individual palaces connected by a labyrinth of corridors. This sprawling quality is what makes Rajput palaces different from those of the Mughals, who employed an architecture of perfect, preconceived symmetry. But later in the 18th century, the Rajput style changed under Mughal influence to become more formal in its planning and building concept, as exemplified by the City Palace in Jaipur.

Cupola
Cupola-domed *chhatris* characterize the skyline of palaces and major public buildings in Rajasthan. *Chhatris* or pavilions were most often located at the highest corner points of the buildings.

Door
Doors are usually made of wood, with decorative studs in metal.

Parapet
Stone filigree allows the breeze to penetrate the interior.

Bracket
Ornate carved stone brackets support balconies and *chajjas*.

Panel
Made in stone relief, panels usually echo the patterns of openings, such as arches, in the rest of the building.

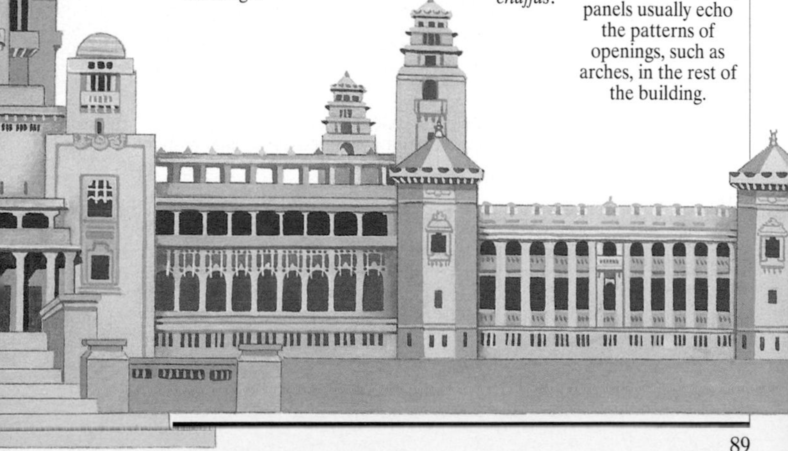

The fortresses of Rajasthan are strategically located on hilltops, rising abruptly out of the desert landscape. The defensive walls of the fort are often contiguous with the raja's palace (and sometimes other houses) contained within it, forming a single structure. The desert location of some of the forts influenced their architecture, which developed into interesting variations of the Rajput style. The fort symbolized power, and its function was to provide accommodation, a retreat for the Rajput warriors. The forts of Bikaner, Jodhpur, and Jaisalmer are some of the most dramatic and invincible in Rajasthan, having sheltered their inhabitants from numerous attacks.

JAISALMER FORT'S PLAN
Within the fort walls are the raja's palace, consisting of several buildings, *havelis*, a temple, and a bazaar. Like all forts, it is designed to be a self-sufficient entity, a city in the desert.

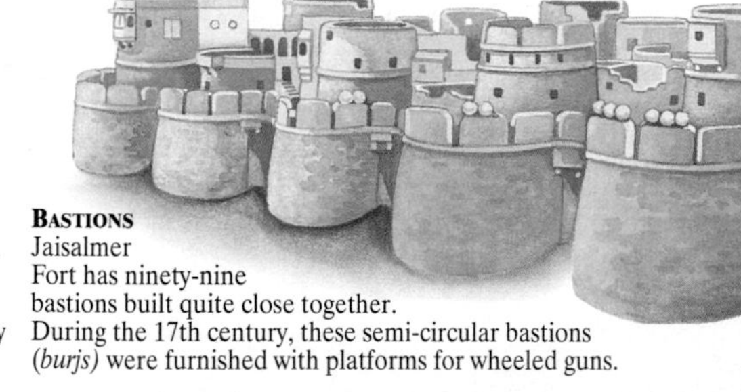

BASTIONS
Jaisalmer Fort has ninety-nine bastions built quite close together. During the 17th century, these semi-circular bastions (*burjs*) were furnished with platforms for wheeled guns.

WALL OF JAISALMER FORT
The snake-like fort wall ▲ *212*, which is several miles long, is made of local stone and built without any mortar. The shifting sands of the desert cover the base of the bastions, creating the illusion of a fort rising out of the desert.

Mehrangarh Fort
The fort wall is 6 miles long and sits 400 feet above the plain. It has 101 bastions and seven gateways ▲ *224*. The main gate, like most fort gates, is heavy and spiked. Five to seven gates are often strung together, each a short turn to the next, and some with paths leading to dead ends to trick invaders.

Gateways
These gateways (*darwazas*), studded with iron spikes to prevent elephants charging against them, provide a series of protective locks along the main access route to Mehrangarh Fort.

Sati marks
Found in both the Mehrangarh and Bikaner forts are these hand prints of women who committed *sati* (the practice of widows immolating themselves on the funeral pyre of their warrior husbands), a poignant reminder of a Rajput tradition.

Galleries
The western range of the Mehrangarh Fort-Palace is capped with tiered galleries. The soft sandstone of the region was ideal for fashioning the intricate lacework of the *jali* screens. The sandstone was easy to carve, and over time, hardened. Sandstone was also used to build the dramatic fort walls.

Jaipur was one of the first examples in the world of city planning. In the 1720's architect Vidyadhar planned for Raja Sawai Jai Singh II a city of rectangular shape aligned on a grid pattern. The east–west axis of the new city was preordained by the existence of a ridge running from the Galta Hills in the east to Chandpole in the west. Following standard practice, Vidyadhar took the *haveli* or dwelling house as the smallest unit. Imposing multi-courtyarded *havelis* with impressive façades were built along the main bazaars and more modest ones along the smaller lanes.

CHANDRA MAHAL
The seven-storied Chandra Mahal, or Moon Palace, is the residential palace of the ruling family. Some of its floors, especially the upper ones, adhere to characteristically Rajput styles of decoration, while the lower floors also incorporate some Mughal and even European embellishments.

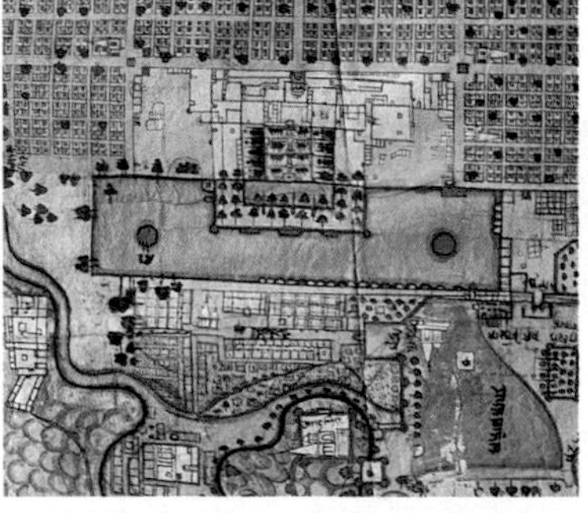

PLAN
Among the most far-sighted features of Vidyadhar's planning are the wide and straight axial roads dividing the nine *chokris* (city sectors), and the imposing gateways at the intersections of these roads. The two northern *chokris* were allotted mostly to high-caste officials, while the southern *chokris* were reserved for commercial activities and residences. Two *chokris* were added later, bringing their number to a magical nine.

SITE OF CITY PALACE
The palace complex ▲ *136* and all royal buildings, Jai Niwas garden, and the temple of Govinda Devji were constructed near the square-shaped Lake Talkatora, on the north of the east–west axis. Two city sectors lie on either side and four sectors of unequal size lie to its south.

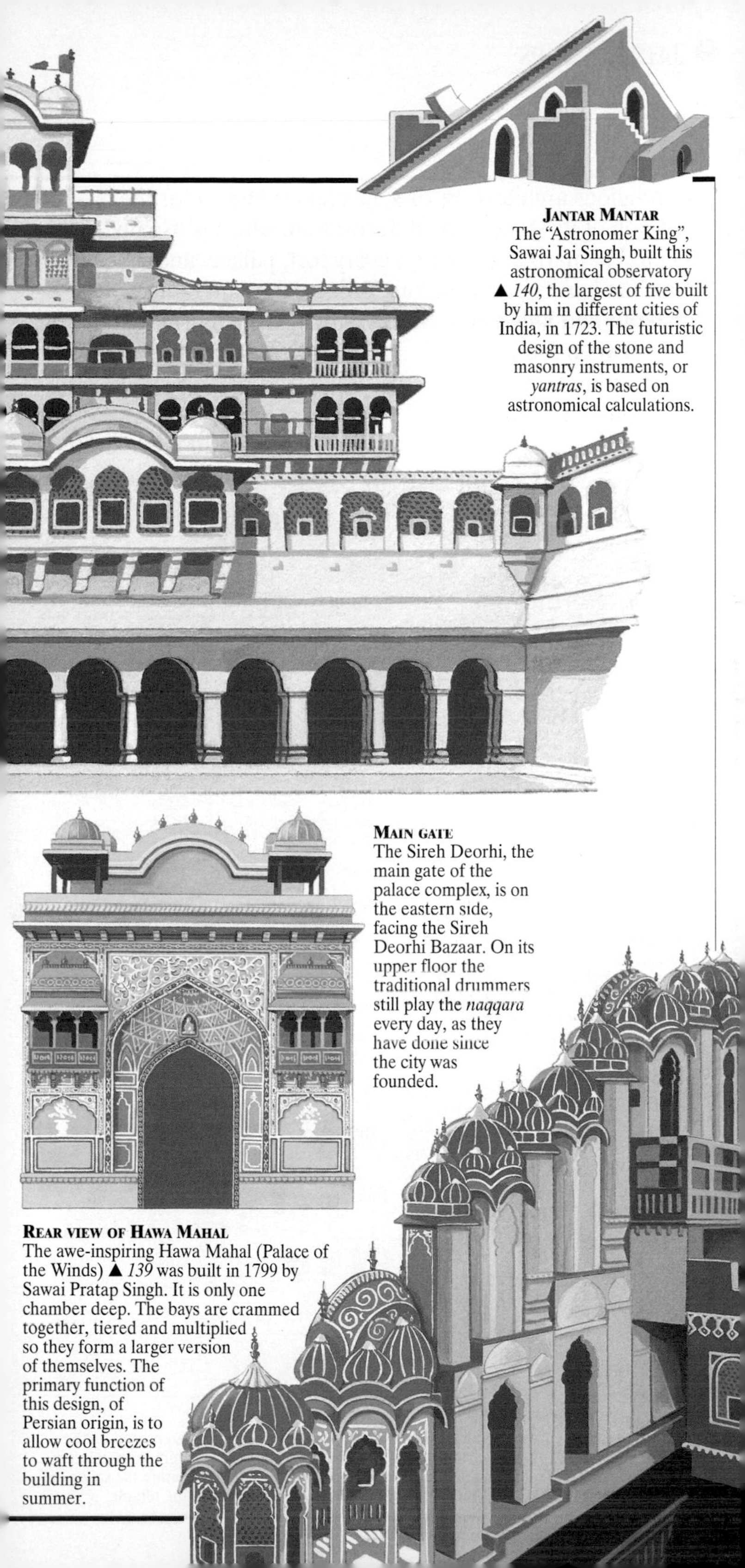

JANTAR MANTAR
The "Astronomer King", Sawai Jai Singh, built this astronomical observatory ▲ *140*, the largest of five built by him in different cities of India, in 1723. The futuristic design of the stone and masonry instruments, or *yantras*, is based on astronomical calculations.

MAIN GATE
The Sireh Deorhi, the main gate of the palace complex, is on the eastern side, facing the Sireh Deorhi Bazaar. On its upper floor the traditional drummers still play the *naqqara* every day, as they have done since the city was founded.

REAR VIEW OF HAWA MAHAL
The awe-inspiring Hawa Mahal (Palace of the Winds) ▲ *139* was built in 1799 by Sawai Pratap Singh. It is only one chamber deep. The bays are crammed together, tiered and multiplied so they form a larger version of themselves. The primary function of this design, of Persian origin, is to allow cool breezes to waft through the building in summer.

The religious architecture of Rajasthan is known for the profusion of its stone-carved decoration, which is usually executed in marble. Although every fort, palace, and city in Rajasthan has its own religious shrines, the Jain temples of Ranakpur and Dilwara at Mount Abu are the most outstanding. Built between the 11th and 13th centuries, the Dilwara temples are set within rectangular courts lined with rows of small shrines and a double colonnade ▲ *270–3*. The chief glory of the 15th-century Ranakpur Temple, set in the beautiful Aravalli hills, is its profusion of marble carvings ▲ *262–5*.

CEILING
The ceilings of the Dilwara temples are examples of the unsurpassed delicacy and complexity of marble carvings.

PLAN OF THE TEMPLE OF ADINATHA AT RANAKPUR ▲ *262*
The *cella*, at the center of the temple, contains four identical images of the deity. It is surrounded by four vestibules. This cruciform plan, that of most Jain temples, is based on the concept of the *samavasarana*, an audience-hall where the *tirthankaras* ● *49* gave their discourses.

RANAKPUR TEMPLE
The outer walls carry depictions of Jain saviors. A striking feature of the interior is the extraordinary quality of the light, with the sun's rays streaming in through the clerestories created by the multiple-level domes supported on the numerous columns within the space of the temple.

Sculptured panel from Ranakpur Temple.

DILWARA TEMPLES
The exuberant decoration of the interiors is in stark contrast to the unadorned outer walls. The wall niches of the sanctuaries house images of Jain saviors. The cool, white marble and the airy style of architecture symbolize an aloofness that defines the Jain aspirations of detachment and introspection.

PILLAR
The columns of the Dilwara temples are intricately decorated with figures of celebrating soldiers, dancers, and musicians.

PARSHVANATHA VOTIVE PLAQUE
This stone disk in the temple at Adinatha ▲ *264–5* represents Parshvanatha, the 23rd *tirthankara* of the Jains.

DOORWAY
The doorways to the Dilwara temples are covered with finely carved friezes.

Jaswant Thada, Jodhpur.

ARCHITECTURAL PORTFOLIO
Architect Sir Swinton Jacob ▲ *134*, who lived in Jaipur, produced a celebrated portfolio of Indian architectural details (below) which virtually became the blueprint for British colonial designs all over India.

Albert Hall Museum, Jaipur.

Lallgarh Palace, Bikaner.

Gopal Bhawan Palace, Deeg.

Mehrangarh Fort, Jodhpur.

Bara Bagh cenotaph, Jaisalmer.

Balsamand Lake Palace, Jodhpur.

City Palace, Jaipur.

Chandravati Temple, Kota.

Amarsagar, Jaisalmer.

Umaid Bhawan Palace, Jodhpur.

Salim Singh ki Haveli, Jaisalmer.

Rajasthan as seen by painters

98 Mughal paintings
100 Rajput paintings
102 William Simpson
104 Mortimer Menpes

"The fort is very lofty and strong, so that the lasso of the imagination cannot reach its battlements, nor the catapult."

Abu'l Fazl

The Mughal emperors often included painters in their entourage so as to have firsthand records of their campaigns and other activities. Some works are preserved in manuscripts and albums. One such is the *Akbarnama*, dating from the late 16th century, a chronicle of Akbar's life, written by his principal counselor, Abu'l Fazl. This is the first and most important artistic record of Rajasthan. Among the paintings of battles and sieges the most splendid is *Akbar directing the attack against Ranthambor Fort* (1), painted by Khem Karan, a master in Akbar's extensive studio. The painting comes from part of the *Akbarnama*, now at the Victoria and Albert Museum, London. At least fifty-seven painters were employed, with most of the miniatures being a joint work; the master drawing the composition, the junior artists applying pigments, and the portraitist often adding the important people. *Akbar visiting the shrine of Khwaja Mu'in-ud-din Chisti at Ajmer* (2), is also from the *Akbarnama*. The shrine is that of the patron saint of the Mughals. In *Akbar making a pilgrimage to Ajmer* (3), he is shown going on foot to give thanks for the birth of his son, Salim ▲ *162*.

1	2
	3

"These pictures also represent the continuing achievement of an ancient artistic tradition."

Andrew Topsfield

Some of the rulers of the different states of Rajasthan took a similar interest to that of the Mughal emperors in recording their activities. From the early 18th century the court painters of Udaipur prepared many large paintings showing the ruling maharaja holding court, visiting temples, and hunting and traveling in the countryside. Though their primary concern was to paint the ruler, they managed to portray monuments and landscape details with great vividness. The palaces of Udaipur, especially the two beautiful ones built on the islands in Pichola Lake ▲ *250*, received careful attention. *Maharana Ari Singh with his ladies at Jag Mandir*, c. 1767, by an unknown artist, shows the maharaja promenading with female attendants among the courtyards and gardens (1). Hunting trips in the hill country south of Udaipur were common, as shown in *Maharana Jawan Singh hunting tigers*, c. 1830, by an unknown artist (2). *Maharana Bhopal Singh inspecting the royal animals at Dassehra*, c. 1939, is attributed to Pannalal G. Sharma (1880–1950) and Chhaganal G. Sharma (1900–84) (3). It is one of the last pictorial records of the Dassehra festival at Udaipur.

1	
2	3

William Simpson (1823–99) was a Scottish painter and lithographer who first visited India between 1859 and 1862 to record the aftermath of the Indian Mutiny. His second visit was as a correspondent on *The Illustrated London News* with the party of the Prince of Wales in 1875. He was not much interested in formal court scenes and ceremonies. As a sensitive observer, he preferred the picturesque and subjects of human appeal. He was fascinated by the beauty of the deserted fort-palace of Amber, especially at the first light of dawn. The painting, *The Palace of Amber* (1863), shows the palace and its reflection in Maota Lake (1). He was attracted by the simple life of the villagers in their colorful dress and painted the striking *The Village Well* (1863) (2). To the water-starved Rajasthani the well has great significance. It is a common meeting point, with women coming to gossip and exchange information. *Dust storm coming on near Jeypore, Rajportana*, (1863), shows the startling beauty of a swirling dust storm or *andhi* enveloping the afternoon sky near Jaipur (3). Here at the edge of the vast Thar Desert dust storms are common at the height of summer.

1	
2	3

Oil paintings of Rajasthani scenes are comparatively rare as most of the visiting painters were amateurs or minor artists. Mortimer Menpes (1860–1938), was a professional artist who came to India from Britain to cover the grand Indian *durbar* of Lord Curzon in 1902–3 at Delhi for various London journals, such as *The Illustrated London News*, *The Pall Mall Gazette,* and *Punch*. He prepared a large number of paintings of the *durbar*. Following this work he traveled extensively in northern India and Rajasthan. Though he was more enthusiastic about the cities and monuments, many of his small-format oils show the love he developed for the rural scenes and landscapes of Rajasthan. Jaipur attracted him most and he prepared as many as eleven views of it, covering a wide range of subjects. In this street scene, *Jaipur*, c. 1900, Menpes shows a group of women clad in colorful, traditional clothing, covering their faces, emerging from a narrow lane. The pinkish *havelis* with small green windows belong unmistakably to Jaipur.

Rajasthan as seen by writers

106 Images and color

110 Palaces – A slice of history

112 Jaipur sketches

114 Grand old Rajputs

116 Game and wildlife

118 Landscape and legacy

RAJPUT TRAITS

The magnum opus of Lieutenant-Colonel James Tod (1782–1835) is considered to be the most authoritative account in English of the history and culture of the Rajputs and their traditions of valor, romance, and sacrifice. Tod joined the service of the East India Company as an army cadet. In 1818 he was appointed Political Agent to the western states.

“The Rajpoot worships his horse, his sword and the sun, and attends more to the Martial Song of the Bard than to the Litany of the Brahmin.
A pledge once given by the Rajpoot, whether ratified by the ‘eating opium together’, ‘an exchange of turbans’, or the more simple act of ‘giving the right hand’, is maintained inviolable under all circumstances.
The Rajpoot is fond of his dog and his gun. The former aids him in pulling down the boar or hare, and with the stalking-horse he will toil for hours after the deer.... The practice of the bow is likewise a main source of pastime, and in the manner there adopted it requires both dexterity and strength. In these martial exercises, the youthful Rajpoot is early initiated, and that the sight of blood may be familiar, he is instructed, before he has strength to wield a sword, to practise with his boy’s scimitar on the heads of lambs and kids. In this manner the spirit of chivalry is continually fed, for everything around him speaks of arms and strife. His very amusements are warlike; and the dance and the song, the burthen of which is the record of his successful gallantry, so far from enervating, serve as fresh incitements to his courage.”

JAMES TOD, *ANNALS AND ANTIQUITIES OF RAJASTHAN*, LONDON, 1829–32

A PROFUSION OF TURBANS

Aldous Huxley (1894–1963) has published poetry, critical essays, short stories and works of an ethical and philosophical nature. His writings portray a witty satire on the moral anarchy of the times he lived in. “Jesting Pilate” was the diary he maintained while traveling through India, Burma, and America.

“The long days of travelling through Rajputana seemed to me, as I sat entranced at the window, at once short and eternal. The journeys occupied only as much time as it took to fall into my trance, to eat lunch and relapse, to change trains and, once more settled, to relapse again. The remaining hours did not exist, and yet were longer than thousands of years. Much passed before my eyes and was seen; but I cannot pretend that I remember a great deal of what I saw. And when I do remember, it is not so much in terms of individual objects as of processes. Innumerable separate images, seen during hours of contemplation, have blended and run together in my mind, to form a single unit of memory, just as the different phases of the growth of plants or the development of caterpillars into butterflies are selected and brought together by the photographer so as to be seen as a single brief process in a five-minute cinema film. Shutting my eyes I can revisualise, for example, the progressive changes in colour, across the breadth of Rajputana, of the horns of the oxen; how they started by being painted both green, how the green gradually melted out of one and became red, how, later, they were both red, then both parti-coloured, then finally striped like barber’s poles in concentric circles of red, white and green. More vividly still I remember a process connected with turbans, a gradual development, the individual phases of which must have been separately observed here and there through hundreds of miles of country. I remember that they started, near Jodhpur, by being small and mostly white, that

they grew larger and larger and redder and redder, until, at a certain point where they came to a climax, touched an apogee of grandeur, they were like enormous balloons of dark crimson muslin with a little brown face peeping almost irrelevantly out of the middle of each. After that they began to recede again from the top of their curve. In my memory I see a process of gradual waning, culminating at Ajmere in a return to the merely normal. The train drew up in the midst of the most ordinary Indian headwear. I had seen the rise, I had been the entranced spectator of the decline and fall of the Rajput turban.”

ALDOUS HUXLEY, *JESTING PILATE: THE DIARY OF A JOURNEY*, PUB. CHATTO & WINDUS, LONDON, 1927

UDAIPUR STREET SCENE

A member of the French aristocracy, Baron Jean Pellenc traveled extensively through Royal India in the years before the outbreak of World War Two. As a friend of many distinguished Indian maharajas, the Baron was afforded an intimate view of princely states, palaces, and royal family life.

“Queer streets indeed they are, driving straight uphill, then shooting off at a sharp angle; beginning spacious as a market-place and dwindling into narrow alleys; coiling around the houses and rambling into footpaths, sand-tracks or merely dead-ends; plunging lakewards or soaring to the palace; fretted with flights of steps or escalating temple-crowned heights; drenched in sunlight and bright dust, and loud with chaffering voices – the marvellous streets of Udaipur where now as ever for a thousand years the daily pageant of Rajputana is enacted.
No turbulence was here, only composed disorder, reminiscent rather of a fairy ballet than a market-fair. With the serenity of immemorial routine a motley cortege streamed through the bazaar: cloven-bearded Rajput clansmen in rich brocades coming down from the palace, holding themselves haughtily erect, their swords enveloped in silken scarves; merchants in coloured turbans, their shirts dangling over their long white drawers; naked starveling “untouchables”, members of the sweeper caste; Mohometan women, their faces veiled, in gaudy pantaloons looped in above their tinkling anklets; conventional Hindu matrons swathed in orange saris, or bold young Rajput beauties moving with a supple, dancing movement of the hips, dressed in the pleated Rajput skirt, their bellies bare to the navel, their firm breasts pointing under bodices of crimson silk.”

BARON JEAN PELLENC (TRANS. STUART GILBERT), *DIAMONDS AND DUST: INDIA THROUGH FRENCH EYES*, PUB. JOHN MURRAY LTD., LONDON, 1936

THE ENCHANTED LAND

Satyajit Ray (1922–92), film director from Bengal, gained worldwide recognition as one of the most important film-makers of the 20th century. Among his outstanding films are the "Apu Trilogy", *a poetic presentation of the life of a Bengali peasant, "Teen Kanya", "Devi", and "Mahanagar".*

"When we were very young, a Bengali book we were much taken with was called *Rajkahini*, or *Princely Tales*. The tales were about real kings and real princes; but so filled were they with the stuff of romance and chivalry that they didn't seem real. We read of a land of desert and forest and mountain fastnesses; of marble palaces rising out of lakes like gem-studded lotuses; of brave Hindu warriors on faithful, fearless steeds charging into battle against invaders; and of their womenfolk who threw themselves into the flames rather than be snatched away as prizes by alien conquerors.

I doubt if I'd have ever got to know Rajasthan well if I hadn't decided to become a film-maker. As a student of painting in Santiniketan, I had already discovered the exquisite world of Rajput miniatures, and realized that it wasn't just the martial arts that the Rajputs excelled in. And, of course, even as a child I knew some of the beautiful devotional songs of Mira, the Queen of Chittor who shed her finery to become a lifelong devotee of Krishna. Indeed, the lure of the enchanted land had grown over the years, and as soon as I found an opportunity, I decided to go filming in Rajasthan.

...The contrasts are enough to take one's breath away. In a country where for miles one sees nothing but sand and rock and brambles and camels, I have seen a seven mile stretch of marshland where thousands of birds from across the continents come and make their seasonal homes on treetops and tiny islets, filling the air with their calls and spattering the landscape with colour. I have seen fortresses perched on hill tops, fortresses rising out of barren plains, fortresses in forests, fortresses in the middle of cities, and fortresses nestling in the lap of mountains. I have seen palaces and *havelis* of marble and stone, airy ones and massive ones, all with exquisite carvings on them; and I have seen the ruins of a village of stone dwellings which go back a thousand years. In the museums I have seen swords and shields and lances the warrior kings fought with, some studded with jewels, all impeccably crafted; and I have seen paintings on the walls of present-day dwellings where the colour and the brushwork strike one dumb by their sweep and gaiety. And, of course, the women – and this goes for the whole of Rajasthan – women stepping straight out of the miniatures, decked out in brilliant reds and greens and yellows, disporting themselves with a grace that would rouse a queen's envy, and striking a joyous note in the drabbest of surroundings."

SATYAJIT RAY, FOREWORD TO RAGHUBIR SINGH'S
RAJASTHAN: INDIA'S ENCHANTED LAND,
PUB. PERENNIAL PRESS, BOMBAY, 1981

THE MIRROR ROOMS AT AMBER

Aldous Huxley (1894–1963) has published poetry, critical essays, short stories and works of an ethical and philosophical nature. His writings portray a witty satire on the moral anarchy of the times he lived in. "Jesting Pilate" was the diary he maintained while traveling through India, Burma, and America in the 1920's.

"There is a mirror room in the fort at Agra; there are others in almost all the palaces of Rajputana. But the prettiest of them all are the mirror rooms in the palace of Amber. Indeed, I never remember to have seen mirrors anywhere put to better decorative use than here, in this deserted Rajput palace of the seventeenth century. There are no large sheets of glass at Amber; there is no room for large sheets. A bold and elegant design in raised plaster work covers the walls and ceiling; the mirrors are small and shaped to fit into interstices of the plaster pattern. Like all old mirrors they are grey and rather dim. Looking into them you see 'in a glass darkly'. They do not portray the world with that glaring realism which characterizes the reverberations of modern mirrors. But their greatest charm is that they are slightly convex, so that every piece gives back its own small particular image of the world and each, when the shutters are opened, or a candle is lit, has a glint in its grey surface like the curved high-lighted in an eye.

They are wonderfully rich, these mirror rooms at Amber. Their elaborateness surpasses that even of the famous mirror room at Bagheria, near Palermo. But whereas the Sicilian room is nothing more than the old-fashioned glass-and-gilding merry-go-round made stationary, the Indian rooms are a marvel of cool and elegant refinement. True, this form of decoration does not lend itself to the adornment of large areas of wall or ceiling; it is too intricate for that. But fortunately the rooms in Indian palaces are seldom large. In a country where it rains with a punctual regularity and only at one season of the year, large rooms of assembly are unnecessary. Crowds are accommodated and ceremonials of state performed more conveniently out of doors than in. The Hall of Audience in an Indian palace is a small pillared pavilion placed at one end of an open courtyard. The king sat in the pavilion, his courtiers and petitioners thronged the open space. Every room in the palace was a private room, a place of intimacy. One must not come to India expecting to find grandiose specimens of interior architecture. There are no long colonnaded vistas, no galleries receding interminably according to all the laws of perspective, no colossal staircases, no vaults so high that at night the lamp-light can hardly reach them. Here in India, there are only small rooms adorned with the elaborate decoration that is meant to be looked at from close to and in detail. Such are the mirror rooms at Amber."

ALDOUS HUXLEY, *JESTING PILATE: THE DIARY OF A JOURNEY*,
PUB. CHATTO & WINDUS, LONDON, 1927

THE PALACE OF BUNDI

Born in Bombay, Rudyard Kipling (1865–1936) is renowned as a novelist, short-story writer, and poet. He is best remembered for his tales and poems portraying British imperialism in India and his stories for children. Kipling toured Rajasthan in search of "copy" for "The Civil & Military Gazette", for which he worked in Lahore as an assistant editor.

"It has been written 'the coup d'oeil of the castellated Palace of Boondi, from whichever side you approach it, is perhaps the most striking in India. Whoever has seen the Palace of Boondi can easily picture to himself the hanging gardens of Semiramis.' This is true – and more too. To give on paper any adequate idea of the Boondi-ki-Mahal is impossible. Jeypore Palace may be called the Versailles of India; Udaipur's House of State is dwarfed by the hills round it and the spread of the Pichola lake; Jodhpur's House of Strife, grey towers on red rock, is the work of giants; but the Palace of Boondi, even in broad day-light, is such a Palace as men build for themselves in uneasy dreams – the work of goblins more than the work of men. It is built into and out of hill side, in gigantic terrace on terrace, and dominates the whole of the city. Like all the other Palaces of Rajputana, it is the work of many hands, and the present Raja has thrown out a bastion of no small size on one of the lower levels, which has been four or five years in the building. Only by scaling this annex, and, from the other side of the valley, seeing how insignificant is its great bulk in the entire scheme, is it possible to get some idea of the stupendous size of the Palace. No one knows where the hill begins and where the Palace ends. Men say that there are subterranean chambers leading into the heart of the hills, and passages communicating with the extreme limits of Taragarh, the giant fortress that crowns the hill and flanks the whole of the valley on the Palace side. They say that there is as much room under as above ground, and none know the whole extent of the Palace. Looking at it from below, the Englishman could readily believe that nothing was impossible for those who had built it. The dominant impression was of height – height that heaved itself out of the hillside and weighed upon the eye-lids of the beholder. The steep slope of the land had helped the builders in securing this effect. From the main road of the city a steep stone-paved ascent led to the first gate – name not communicated by the zealous following. Two gaudily painted fishes faced each other over the arch, and there was little except glaring colour ornamentation visible. This gate gave into what they called the chowk of the Palace, and one had need to look twice ere realizing that this open space, crammed with human life, was a spur of the hill on which the Palace stood, paved and built over. There had been little attempt at leveling the ground. The foot-worn stones followed the contours of the ground, and ran up to the walls of the palace smooth as glass."

RUDYARD KIPLING, *LETTERS OF MARQUE*, PUB. H.M. CALDWELL CO., LONDON, 1899

THE LAKE PALACE AT UDAIPUR

Roderick Cameron, who traveled in India in the 1950's, has a remarkable eye for detail, as is evident from his description of the former summer palace of the rulers of Mewar, the Bari Mahal or Lake Palace at Udaipur, which he visited in the years before its conversion into a hotel.

“I hesitate to describe the Bari Mahal, frightened that I shall be accused of exaggerating. Even now, when trying to recapture it, I wonder if I have not imagined the whole thing. Not that it is a particularly remarkable building, lots of it, in fact, being in rather questionable taste. Rather it is the poetry with which the whole thing has been conceived. Had Giraudoux's Ondine become a lady of fashion round about the eighteen-nineties, this is the kind of place one would have expected her to live in. Oscar Wilde might have stayed here, or Whistler. But even this does not give one quite the right idea, for they would have been figures met in one's dreams, where places and people are never quite real.

The drawing room is called 'The Light of the Moon'. The rooms are small and most of them have bay-windows that jut out over the lake, set on a skirting made of transparent alabaster. In 'The Light of the Moon' the doors are of mahogany but inlaid with panels of mirror, and all the table-tops are of glass. Fingers of sun crept in through the shutters, liquid sun that rippled over the crystal drops of the chandeliers.

We were shown His Highness's private sitting-room, reached by a lift connected with the landing-stage below. It is a pretty room, plastered in shining, ivory-colored *chunam* into which had been worked a pattern of green and amber roses made from flat pieces of glass. It is a happy, gay house and full of light. The Maharana's bedroom is minute, hardly more than an alcove, and frescoed all over with a landscape showing mountain scenery and rushing waterfalls cascading down between tightly packed mango trees in which perch peacocks which leopards stalk, while tigers prowl around below. It is naively rendered, precise and detailed in the manner of Mogul painting, and has something about it of a miniature Douanier Rousseau.

We were fortunate in being shown the women's quarters, for visitors, I believe, are not often taken into this part of Bari Mahal. The rooms are more or less the same, except that they have shutters instead of doors. There appear to be a great many Bohemian chandeliers and all the windows are coloured.

There is a small section of the palace that is earlier than the rest and in it, in a rather dilapidated state, is the most enchanting courtyard planted with orange trees and jasmine. The walls are inlaid with seventeenth-century Persian glass mosaics made into panels of flowers, worked in a loose pattern with brown, green, blue, and silver mirrors. The surface of the walls has been made uneven purposely, so that no piece of mirror is quite flat, and in this way there is a play of light and the whole cloister shines.”

RODERICK CAMERON, *TIME OF THE MANGO FLOWERS*,
PUB. HEINEMANN, LONDON, 1958

JAIPUR POMP

Sir Stanley Reed, editor of "The Times of India", lived in India for several years and was a popular and prominent citizen of Bombay. He accompanied the Prince and Princess of Wales during their tour of India in 1905–6 and recorded his colorful impressions in "The Royal Tour in India".

❝From the station a broad straight road stretches for two or three furlongs before it turns sharply to the right towards the Residency, and this was lined with the retainers of the Maharaja and his feudatories in their most picturesque and characteristic garb. Here were the Maharaja's runners, lithe, active, bare-legged Nagas in green jerkins edged with gold, white turbans with feather aigrettes, and striped as to the lower extremities like a Muharram tiger. Their musician bore a noble war-horn on which he blew a weird conch-like blast. There were apparitions by the score, gorgeously dressed in scarlet and bearing silver staves; orange-robed messengers, spearmen by the hundred, and match-lock men in olive green, the guardians of the Maharaja's sleep. Now came camels with huge kettledrums, horses with kettledrums, and dancing horses gaily caparisoned in tinsel and green. A score of elephants themselves made a brave sight, with their gilded howdahs, trailing cloths of green and red and gold, and painted foreheads. And these served but as a further introduction to palanquins manned by red-coated bearers, bullock palanquins in red and in green, with the horns of the splendid Gujarati oxen brightly enameled. Then came a bullock battery with the tiniest of guns and camelmen with great swivel blunderbusses mounted on the pommels of their saddles and Sirdars on boisterous stallions.
Through this fascinating throng drove His Highness the Maharaja, in a carriage...to receive his royal guests, and he alighted at the station to the braying of war-horns and the strains of a most original anthem.❞

STANLEY REED, *THE ROYAL TOUR IN INDIA*,
PUB. BENNETT, COLEMAN & CO., BOMBAY, 1906

THE BAZAAR

Ralph Oppenhejm's experiences as an inmate in a German concentration camp resulted in his first novel, "The Door of Death". The Danish author traveled extensively in India in the mid-1950's. "A Barbarian in India" was judged the best reviewed book of the year in Denmark.

❝The bazaar, the town's great news-bureau, is the liveliest and gaudiest in all India, largely as a result of the Jaipur costume, which is a firework-display of colours. The men's turbans, overdoing all the rest of the peninsula in their volume – they take nine yards of material – are findant-pink and pistachio-green, cloud-white and sea-blue. The women's skirts, a blaze of yellow and puce, are set with little mirrors, coruscating in rivalry with such an abundance of silver ornaments that arms and legs, fingers and toes are stiff with them. Only women of the people move about the streets, but they move like queens, accompanied by the gay tinkling of their ankle-bells. They are among the handsomest in the country, the same golden-brown shade as the frescoed women in the thousand-year-old caves of Ajanta, with the same bewitching half-moon eyes. Though one is not often allowed to see their faces, which are usually screened by the big headcloths that make many Rajputana beauties look like walking ship's funnels.

Jodhpur has not the glamour of Jaipur. But perhaps it has more character, and more shades of character. Dazzling beauties are apt to come easily by everything, to excite immediate rapture – which often gives place to a certain effect of emptiness, one day when we have looked our fill; whereas the more modestly equipped, who have to struggle for much the others take as a right, a matter of course, often develop far more personality, and have always fresh surprises to offer. While Jaipur is the only city in India, except New Delhi, to have been built on a plan, Jodhpur – and this is not its least attraction – has grown out of the varying taste and caprices of the generations. And if it yields to Jaipur in purity of features and beauty of form, as a set-off it has a spontaneous, natural charm, as it were a feminine inconsequence; it seems to have 'lived' – the feeling which makes it so stimulating to meet certain women past their first youth.”

RALPH OPPENHEJM, *A BARBARIAN IN INDIA*,
PUB. PHOENIX HOUSE, LONDON, 1957

JAIPUR LIFE

R.N. Currey spent three years in India and was prize-winner of Lord Wavell's All India Poetry Competition. Many of his poems have been broadcast and published in various periodicals.

JAIPUR (III)

The men had colour in their lives and movement.
Around the carpeted square durbar floor
That held the jewelled and enamelled hour
Flowered the rows on rows of intent turbans,
Ochre, and mauve, and scarlet; a disturbance
Of rumour like a breeze swept through the court;
And, in a gateway, swaying like their thought,
The howdah of an unknown elephant.

Outside was poverty. These roseate lives
Sucked blood from hungry men, but made a start
Between their gem-hilt wars upon the art
And building that are our inheritance:
Grant them aesthetic standards, positives
Yet to be made mankind's experience.

JAIPUR (IV)

Here in Jaipur the old and new worlds meet;
The forts, the temples, and the palaces
Look out on legislative offices
And schools and hospitals. This wide grave street
Worn by three centuries of slippered feet
And tripping pads of camels branches out
In roads that go impartially to meet
Old pleasure-gardens and new factories.

Here is a future growing from past beauty
Owning past inspiration – and a duty
To all men of all trades to build a city
Known for flourish of its industries;
Its roads made smooth for ordinary men
And knowledge climbing stairs to soar again.

R.N. CURREY, *INDIAN LANDSCAPE: A BOOK OF DESCRIPTIVE POEMS*,
PUB. ROUTLEDGE, LONDON, 1947

SIR PRATAP SINGH OF JODHPUR (1845–1922)

Maud Diver traveled through the Princely States in the years before World War Two. A prolific writer, her works include "The Englishwoman in India" as well as a series of novels about British life.

❝In almost every Indian State there is some special feature – building, personality, legend – that seizes one's interest and imagination. In Udaipur, it is the Palace and the tragic ruin of Chitor. In Jaipur, it is the deserted city of Amber. In Jodhpur, it is that work of demi-gods, the Fort; fit birthplace of the incomparable Sir Pratap Singh, whose name aptly signifies 'Lion of Glory'. Dead nearly twenty years, his influence still lives. Still they can say of him, 'He has no equal – he must have lived many times. Perhaps he will never need to live on earth again.' His record is unique among the Princes of India; and before his death he added lustre to a brilliant beginning. Far-famed and widely loved, intimate friend of three British sovereigns, he has been aptly named 'the first gentleman in the British Empire', using the demoded word in its higher meaning. A Rajput of bluest blood, he reckoned himself beyond all rules and codes except those dictated by his own sense of fitness, which was of the most exacting; a trait finely shown in the familiar story of an English subaltern who died at Jodhpur, and whose coffin could not be moved because one of the officers detailed to carry it was down with fever. No Hindu of caste could touch a coffin without defilement. An outcast scavenger seemed the only solution; but the officers reckoned without Sir Pratap. The young man had been his friend; and he promptly offered himself as pall-bearer with the characteristic remark, 'A soldier knows no caste with a brother soldier.' Perhaps only a Hindu could appreciate the spiritual significance of that simple courteous action. Rightly he belonged to the warrior desert tribe of Rajputs, the Rathores. 'Famous in battle,' and Sun-descended like the Seesodias of Udaipur, they trace back their pedigree for over fourteen hundred years. According to legend, the first Rathore sprang from the spine of Indra, god of storms and thunder-bolts; a legend in keeping with their history, that is mainly a red page written in their own blood. Always in the thick of danger or trouble, they welcomed any sacrifice that might save their land from the fanatic fury of Islam; and their unshaken courage has been embodied in the proverb, 'A wall may give way: a Rajput stands fast'.❞

MAUD DIVER, *ROYAL INDIA: A DESCRIPTIVE AND HISTORICAL STUDY OF INDIA'S FIFTEEN PRINCIPAL STATES AND THEIR RULERS,* PUB. D. APPLETON-CENTURY CO., LONDON, 1942

MAHARANA FATEH SINGH OF MEWAR (1853–1934)

Charles Allen, author of "Plain Tales from the Raj", and Sharada Dwivedi recorded the recollections of many of the former maharajas and nawabs and their family members and those of employees and officials.

❝A contemporary of Sir Pratap Singh who was as much concerned with Rajput honour – although displaying this in a very different way – was the ruler of Udaipur, Maharana Fateh Singh of Mewar. As Sir Pratap was the personification of the Rajput warrior, so Fateh Singh was the essence of Rajput kingship, a worthy occupant of the premier gadi in the land: 'The old man knew his power, he knew his position not only as the ruler of Udaipur but as the head of the Rajputs and virtually as the head of the Hindus. He could not accept his position

"TO CALL FATEH SINGH AN EXTRAORDINARY MAN IS ALMOST TO BELITTLE LANGUAGE. ONLY SUPERLATIVES APPROACH ADEQUACY IN DESCRIBING HIS QUALITIES, YET ONLY SIMPLICITY CAN PROPERLY CONVEY HIS VIRTUE."

BRIAN MASTERS, *MAHARANA – THE STORY OF THE RULERS OF UDAIPUR*

as head of the Indian fighting class and yet subservient to a foreign power, so at every opportunity he went against the British.'... Maharana Fateh Singh also had a low opinion of the honours and dignities handed out by the British for which so many Princes vied. During the First World War he was one of the few rulers who failed wholeheartedly to support the British war effort: 'He refused point-blank. He said, "When there is a fight in India, Europeans don't come here to die, so why should we send our Indians to die when Europeans fight?" But at the end of the war the British sent him the highest decoration for war services and when they brought this G.C.I.E. in a velvet case he looked at it and said to his interpreter, "It is the sort of thing that pattawalas (attendants) in offices wear. Put it on the horse. It looks better on a horse than a king." The interpreter on his own told the British officials that this was not an auspicious day, so His Highness would put it on some other time. Later when somebody asked him why he had got such a high honour for doing nothing, he said, "Because I rendered the British the highest service. While the British were away fighting the war in Europe, I didn't take over in Delhi. Isn't that a big enough service? " ' ”

MAHARAJA GANGA SINGH OF BIKANER (1880–1943)

“'What a towering man!' remarks M.M. Sapat, who came from Jaisalmer in 1924 to work in the Bikaner Secretariat. 'If you were to see him in just a vest and pyjamas among thousands of people you'd say, "Yes, there's a personality". What a man he was – with a voice like a tiger's.' But it was not character alone that distinguished him. 'My grandfather was the patriarch,' declares the present Maharaja of Bikaner. 'The people treated him like a father figure. Consequently he treated them like children. He always said to them, "I see no difference between my son and my grandchildren and you. You are all my children and your welfare is my first responsibility." He believed that, because he was a proud Rajput and the Rajput tradition means to protect. He could be a tyrant if he wanted to but at that time it was the only way to get work done. Anybody who stood in the way of progress he had to sweep to the side.'... Progress for Ganga Singh meant transforming Bikaner from a desert state into the granary of Rajasthan, a challenge that he first faced as a youngster in 1898: 'We had this terrible famine called the Chapna Kaal when my grandfather as a youth of eighteen went on camel-back from village to village and saw how hundreds were dying because of famine. He came to the conclusion that the only answer to this was canals – and railways so that you could bring in food quickly. So when he got his powers the first thing he worked on was the canals and the railway. Bikaner had no riparian rights but because he had that magnetism and personality he was able to influence the King and the Viceroy to gain access to the river Sutlej. That's how the Ganga Canal, which irrigated a thousand square miles, came about.' The Ganga Canal system was finally opened in 1927. 'The whole of that part of the country turned green,' remembers M.M. Sapat. 'As far as the eye could see there were green fields where the desert had been. And what a matter of pride it was, not only for him, but for all of us who went there and saw it.'”

CHARLES ALLEN AND SHARADA DWIVEDI,
LIVES OF THE INDIAN PRINCES, PUB. CENTURY, LONDON, 1984

PIG-STICKING AT BIKANER

One of the most brilliant diplomats of his time, Lord Hardinge of Penshurst was a close friend and trusted advisor of King Edward VII. He was Viceroy of India from 1910 to 1916. His memoir, "My Indian Years", was published in 1948.

"It was a glorious winter's day with a bright sun, and as we stood on rising ground, watching a battalion of Bikaner Imperial Service Infantry beating a thick jungle, one felt, with the anticipation of exceptional sport, that life was really worth living. Presently an enormous herd of pig, estimated at over four hundred, emerged from the jungle, and immediately a dozen or more young Rajput horsemen belonging to the Maharaja's Staff galloped off and dashed into the herd, scattering them in every direction, and having spotted the old boar with the torn ear, gradually separated it from the rest of the herd. We followed slowly, and when it was clear that the old boar had become entirely detached from its associates, the Maharaja called out to me, 'There is your pig!' I started at once to gallop after the pig, but when I had approached it to within about a hundred and fifty yards the pig suddenly stopped, turned round and charged me at full gallop. I reined in my horse, and holding low the point of my spear, I pierced its tongue. The pig gave an angry shriek and dashed off in another direction. I followed at once in hot pursuit and on nearing the pig after a short distance, I dashed past, and my spear passed right through its body. I was disgusted to find that although, in spite of the heavy weight of the pig, I was able to retain hold of my spear, it broke in two, leaving half in the body of the pig. The impetus of my horse carried me on two or three hundred yards and I could see the pig on the ground with half my spear projecting on each side of its body. Happily my orderly galloped up to me and gave me the spare spear that he was carrying. Then, to my great surprise, I saw the pig suddenly get up and again charge me at full gallop. As I was unprepared I avoided the charge by quickly moving to one side, fearing that it might wound my horse, as often happens. The pig having missed me and my horse, turned and again charged, but this time I was prepared to receive the charge which was directed with such violence and speed that my spear entered the pig's chest and transfixed its body to such a depth that the pig, in its final struggle, was actually able to reach my boot and bite it. It was a fine pig of thirty inches, and most gallant. I felt profound sympathy for my brave victim. There is no doubt that the Indian wild boar is one of the bravest and most gallant of animals. It is absolutely fearless and will not hesitate to attack a tiger, and the latter is always afraid of a pig, while a panther stands no chance against a wild boar."

LORD HARDINGE OF PENSHURST, K.G., *ON HILL AND PLAIN*, PUB. JOHN MURRAY, LONDON, 1933

THE SPLENDOR OF PEAFOWL

E. P. Gee has spent half a lifetime studying and photographing animals and birds in India. His book portrays a unique panorama of the wildlife resources of India – her sanctuaries, the animals that inhabit them, and the people who have helped to preserve them.

“Peafowl are everywhere in this area, and cock birds do not let you forget their existence, with their loud screams of may-awe in the evenings and early mornings. These birds are protected in most parts of west, central and north India by legislation and, more significantly, by popular and religious sentiment. For the peacock is the vehicle of Saraswati (goddess of learning), Kartikeya (god of war) and Subrahmanya (god of yogic powers).

Consequently these spectacular, and to Westerners, exotic birds have become quite common in these parts, often proudly wandering and even nesting in villages totally unafraid of man.

It is recorded in history that Alexander the Great took back with him from India to Greece two hundred peafowl, and from Greece the birds spread to other countries of western Asia, north Africa, Europe and eventually to America. The Mogul emperors were greatly attracted by the beauty of this bird, and Shah Jehan's famous Peacock Throne was designed 'its pillars of emerald being surmounted by the two figures of two peacocks, ablaze with precious stones'.

Incidentally, the splendid ocellated 'train' of the peacock is not really its tail, but its upper tail-coverts enormously lengthened. For display these are erected and fanned out before admiring hens. Its crest feathers have fan-shaped tips, while those of the Burmese subspecies have pointed tips.

Peafowl, as well as langurs, are well-known as being among the first wild creatures to notice the approach of a tiger or leopard in the jungle and to sound their call of alarm, warning their fellow creatures that a predator is on the prowl.

Peacocks shed all their tail feathers each year and grow new ones. The old shed feathers are picked up and made into fans and widely sold in bazaars and elsewhere.

'The gorgeous peacock is the glory of God', said a Sanskrit verse, and in a country of pageantry and colour it is only fitting that the peacock has been officially proclaimed as the national bird of India.”

E. P. GEE, *THE WILDLIFE OF INDIA*, PUB. COLLINS, LONDON, 1964

PADMINI OF CHITTORGARH

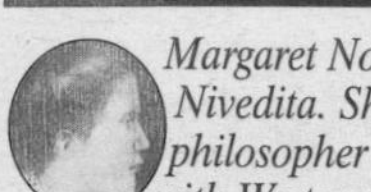

Margaret Noble came to India from Ireland and assumed the name of Sister Nivedita. She became an ardent disciple of Swami Vivekanand, the Hindu philosopher who attempted to combine the concepts of Indian spirituality with Western materialism.

“It was almost midnight, as the moon grew near the full, when we looked for the first time on the fortress of Chitore. The lights in the village at its foot had been extinguished, and the hill with its great length stood dark and isolated against the sky. Silently we sat on a low stone a mile off and drank in the scene.

Architecturally the splendour of the city justifies her pride. The rock on which she stands slopes inwards from all sides, with the result that there are innumerable tanks and a water supply practically unlimited. Within the walls are the remains of what has been virtually two cities, one to the north-east, the ancient capital of the time before Bappa Raoul, and one more modern which grew up between his accession in AD 728 and the evacuation under Akbar in 1568.

Long and narrow, like some lean grey lion crouching for the spring, lies the walled Chitore on its craggy hill. And the newly arrived traveller watching it may see it tonight, as the returning escort may have seen it when Padmini's marriage procession halted for the last time on the homeward way, more than seven centuries ago. Little can the “lotus fair” Padmini have slept that night, the last of the long journey from her father's distant stronghold. Rather must she have gazed on through hour after hour of waking dreamfulness, counting the tale of the turrets and bastions of the fortress that tomorrow she would enter as bride and queen. Within her was the confidence of the Indian wife, who thinks of herself as beginning what is only a new chapter in an old story, as recovering a thread that was held but a while ago, and dropped at death. Not for the first time were they to take up tomorrow the tale of life together – it was an ancient comradeship of the soul. Did no vision of the future cast its shadows across the path before her to make Padmini shrink and pause, in the glory of this her great homecoming? Had the bard whispered no word above her cradle of the tragedy of greatness that lay before her? Did she know that as long as winds should wail over Chitore they would sing her name, that with her would every stone and every building be associated in the world's memory till the end of time? To her, what would be was the following of the path of Rajput honour. Was it not always said that, in the hour of birth, the eyes of a boy were set upon a knife and those of a girl upon a lamp – for the man must leave life by way of the sword and woman by that of fire?”

SISTER NIVEDITA, *STUDIES FROM AN EASTERN HOME*, PUB. LONGMANS, GREEN AND CO., LONDON, 1913

"... SHE WAS THE FAIREST OF ALL FLESH ON EARTH. HER FAME WAS SUNG THROUGH THE LAND BY THE POETS, AND SHE BECAME, IN SOME SORT, THE HELEN OF CHITTOR."

RUDYARD KIPLING ON RANI PADMINI

LAKE PUSHKAR

The Frenchman Louis Rousselet traveled extensively throughout India, and in particular, in the kingdoms of Rajputana in the middle of the 19th century. Profusely illustrated with fine drawings, his book acquaints the reader with the heroic traditions as well as the daily lives of the Rajputs.

"One of the most sacred lakes in India is that of Poshkur, which is only rivalled by the lake of Mansourwar, in Tibet. It is situated in a narrow valley surrounded by immense mounds of shifting sand; and a few isolated peaks stand out on its borders with great effect. Its form is nearly a perfect oval, and at its southern extremity it empties itself by a narrow canal into an immense marsh. The origin of this lake is attributed to Lord Bramah. The story goes that the god, wishing to celebrate the sacrifice of Yug, stopped for that purpose in the valley, having first placed genii at the entrance of all the passes to keep off the evil spirits. Just as he was going to perform the ceremony, he perceived that his wife Sarasvati had not accompanied him; and, as the presence of a woman is necessary, he employed one of the Apsaras. Sarasvati was so grieved at this infidelity that she hid herself in the mountains to weep, and was transformed into a fountain. Several centuries after, one of the Purihara kings of Mundore lost his way while hunting, and, feeling thirsty, came to drink at the fountain of Sarasvati. He felt himself instantaneously healed of a disease previously incurable, and recognised the miraculous property of the spring. Shortly afterwards he returned, and had a basin dug out to receive the waters, which now form the lake of Poshkur.

This lake soon became a favourite resort of pilgrims, and during the Middle Ages the princely families of India vied with one another in covering its banks with temples and cenotaphs. Gradually quite a town of religious buildings sprang up, peopled by Brahmins. The wealthy pilgrims from all parts of India brought untold riches to Poshkur, and the princes spared no expense to enrich the holy inhabitants of the sacred town."

LOUIS ROUSSELET, *INDIA AND ITS NATIVE PRINCES*, PUB. BICKERS, LONDON, 1878

THE THAR DESERT – A DAILY PRESENCE

Born in Bombay in 1938, Dominic Frank Moraes was educated at Jesus College, Oxford. He is a prolific writer and has published several books of poems, essays, biographies, and travel books. He was awarded the Hawthornden Prize in 1958.

“Time is very fixed. The courses of the sun are fixed. Night may be cold, as the heat evaporates from the sand, but from the second the blood-red rim of the sun appears on the horizon, and a pinkish light spreads swiftly over the sand, one is conscious once more of the heat filling and occupying the air. Within an hour everything is a single sterile blaze, intensifying until at noon, the sun at meridian, a bitter whitish glare blinds one. Dark spectacles are of little help against this, but squinting through them you may see the occasional penurious hamlet with its beehive haystacks; camels sitting with their legs folded under them, resting, or camels loping down the road, sometimes attached to carts of firewood and fodder; lean thrifty men with fierce moustaches and colourful turbans, women with their long skirts, longsleeved tunics and veils, the vivid clothes as stains of brilliance on the sand.

In the desert one meets people who have spent their whole lives here, and have lost the habit of speech. Memorable for their silence, they can find food, and even liquid from a species of cactus, or simply by knowing where to dig. But unlike Saint Exupery, most people find the desert unfriendly, and prefer not only not to live in it, but not to cross its borders into anarchy. For the desert is anarchic, in that it upsets the accepted convention of civilised man, that nature is friendly and a provider. For the people of Rajasthan, the desert is a daily presence for they live near it or around it or in it and it determines the patterns of their lives. The turbans of the men are not only ornamental but necessary, since they have to protect their heads from the hot wind and the sand it carries. The women wear the amount of clothing they do because it is sensible: it protects the body from the sun and wind, and it acts as insulation against heat.

There is a reason for everything one does in the desert. Nothing is or can be done except out of necessity. Desert economy is different. A cupful of water has an importance all its own. A plant means something quite different from what it does far from the dunes. Cattle and their fodder are to be protected by every means possible. Rain is a marvel sent directly from the deity. Most prayers are to do with rain. Most desert people who come to a place like Udaipur, seem awed, and amazed, childlike as they quench their eyes with the very sight of an element they hardly know. Many people have seen the immense luxury of the palaces, and this remains the image they hold of Rajasthan. Others find in the gaunt, grim, hill forts symbols of history – a history of passionate love, warfare, guns and swords and suicide charges, women rising in smoke from fiery pyres. But none of these is the truth. The truth is the desert, which made hard men cut their way to kingdoms, and turn from soldiers to sybarites in a generation.”

DOMINIC MORAES, PHOTOGRAPHS BY GOPI GAJWANI, *RAJASTHAN* *PUB.* HIMALAYA BOOKS, DELHI, 198

Itineraries

129 The east
179 Shekhavati
191 The northwest
239 The south
279 The southeast
299 Bharatpur to Karauli

▲ Jaisalmer city.

▲ Ajmer city.

Jodhpur Fort and city. ▼

City Palace, Udaipur. ▲

Amber Fort, Jaipur. ▲

▲ Ramdeora Fair near Pokharan.

▲ Pushkar Fair.

▼ Thar Deser

▲ Udaipur.

▼ Barmer.

▲ Tilwara horse fair, near Luni River.

▲ Pushkar Fair.

Sariska Wildlife Sanctuary. ▼

▲ "Ships of the desert".

▼ Nagaur Fair.

▼ The desert at Samm.

The east

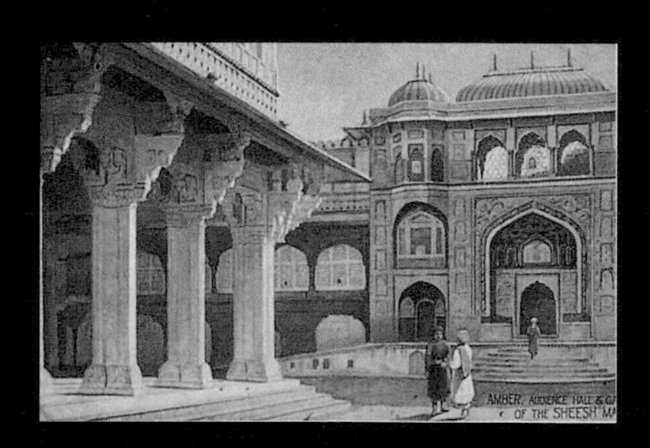

130 Jaipur
146 Amber Fort
154 Jaigarh and Nahargarh forts
156 Sisodia Rani ka Bagh to Jal Mahal
158 Around Jaipur
160 Textile motifs
162 Ajmer
164 Pushkar
166 Kishangarh to Makrana
168 Alwar
174 Around Alwar
176 The tiger: toward conservation

1. JAIPUR 2. AMBER 3. JAIGARH FORT 4. SISODYA PALACE 5. GALTA 6. SANGANER 7. BAGRU 8. TONK 9. KISHANGARH 10. MAKRANA

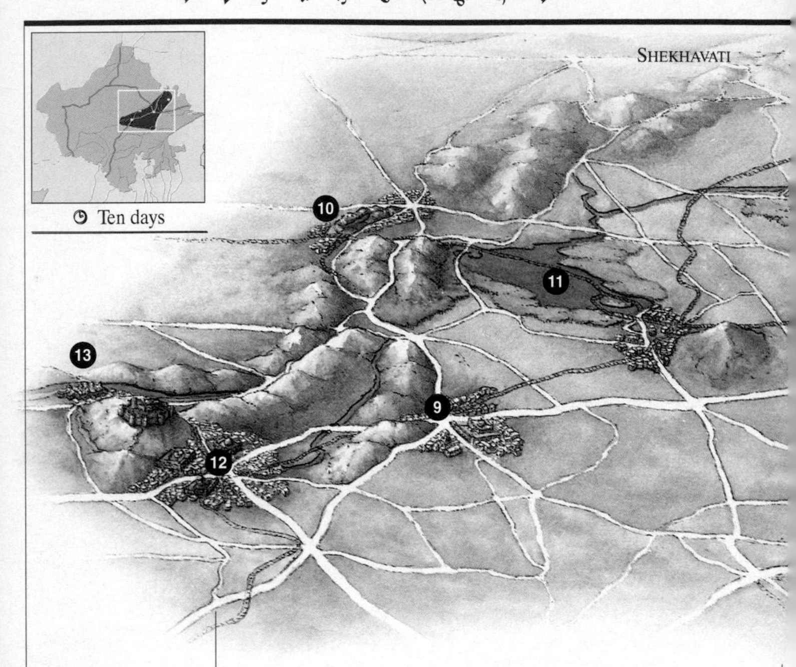

RAJPUTANA
The old name for Rajasthan was "Raputana" or "the land of the Raputs". Two years after India's independence in 1947, the Princely States of this region were merged, and the new political state that resulted was named "Rajasthan" or "the land of the rajas" ● *39.*

The city of Jaipur is the logical starting point for anyone traveling in Rajasthan because of its central location and good air, road, and rail connections. To the West lies the desert region of Marwar (Bikaner, Jaisalmer, and Jodhpur), to the north and south run the craggy Aravalli hills. From Jaipur it is an easy drive to Alwar and the Sariska Tiger Reserve ▲ *174* in the northeast, or to Ajmer, Pushkar, and Kishangarh in the Southwest. Also within reach is the Shekhavati region in the northwest ▲ *180* and Ranthambhor National Park in the east ▲ *305.*

HISTORY

The kingdom of Jaipur was originally known as Amber, which was also the name of its ancient capital, situated 7 miles away. Its history can be traced back to the 12th century, when Amber was the stronghold of the fierce Mina tribesmen. According to legend, the Minas once gave shelter to a young Rajput prince called Duleh Rai. But the prince later betrayed them by getting them drunk one night, slaying them, and taking over Amber. In the 16th century, Amber suddenly came to the fore when in 1562 Bharmal, threatened by Akbar ▲ *36,* his powerful neighbor from Jodhpur, gave him his daughter in marriage. This forged an alliance between Jaipur's Rajahs and the Mughals.

Street scene, Jaipur, c. 1902.

11. SAMBHAR LAKE
12. AJMER
13. PUSHKAR
14. BAIRAT
15. SILISERH
16. ALWAR
17. SARISKA
18. RAJGARH
19. VIJAY MANDIR
20. NIMRANA

RAJA MAN SINGH I. Akbar appointed Raja Man Singh I of Amber (reigned 1590-1614) as the Commander-in-Chief of the Mughal armies. Raja Man Singh I won a series of splendid victories for the Mughals all over India and helped them establish a vast empire, stretching from Kabul in the north to the Deccan plateau in the south. Apart from being an outstanding warrior, Raja Man Singh I was a great builder and a patron of the arts. It was he who built much of the impressive fort-palace complex at Amber. He was succeeded by Mirza Raja Jai Singh (reigned 1621-67), another great warrior and esthete cast in a similar mold.

RAJA SAWAI JAI SINGH II. The most brilliant of Amber's rulers was Raja Sawai Jai Singh II (reigned 1699-1743) ● *35.* The story goes that when, as a young boy, he was presented before Emperor Aurangzeb, the latter suddenly grabbed both his wrists and said, "Of what use is your sword now?" Jai Singh II calmly replied, "Your Majesty, when a bridegroom takes a bride's hand, he is duty-bound to protect her. Now that I have you to protect me, why do I need my sword?" Impressed by the repartee, Aurangzeb gave him the title "Sawai", which means "The One-and-a-Quarter", indicating that he was a notch above other men in spirit and bravery. Sawai Jai Singh II was a man of many parts: he was a statesman and an excellent strategist, and it was he who, in 1707, reunited the Rajputs against the Mughals after Aurangzeb's death. With the turmoil of the last days of the Mughal Empire, Jaipur became a haven for the merchants, bankers, and jewelers of northern India and flourished, becoming, as a British visitor later wrote, "a sort of Lombard Street of Rajpootana".

THE GREAT CONQUEROR
Raja Man Singh I was a brilliant general who led Emperor Akbar's Mughal armies in campaigns from Afghanistan in the east and the Deccan in the south, contributing greatly to the rapid growth of the Mughal Empire. He amassed enormous wealth from his conquests which made Jaipur the powerful kingdom it was. According to legend, when Akbar once asked him what had happened to all the treasures of Deccan, Raja Man Singh I pointed to his battle wounds and said, "They're inside here."

Coin used during the reign of Maharaja Sawai Man Singh II.

COAT-OF-ARMS
Jaipur's coat-of-arms (right) incorporates the ancient five-colored flag of Amber. The central shield is flanked by a lion (a symbol of Rajput valor) and a horse. It is topped by a sun (representing descent from the sun god), or an image of Lord Krishna or Shiva, or a helmet.

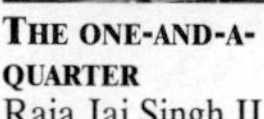

THE ONE-AND-A-QUARTER
Raja Jai Singh II was given the title of "Sawai", meaning "The One-and-a-Quarter", by Emperor Aurangzeb for his intelligence. Ever since, the rulers of Jaipur have flown two flags, one full and one quarter-sized, to symbolize this title.

THE BUILDING OF JAIPUR. In the 1720's Raja Sawai Jai Singh II, realizing that his kingdom had outgrown its old capital at Amber, began to dream of a new city which would be more powerful and more beautiful than any other – a great, flourishing center of commerce, the arts, and religion. He started work on building Jaipur ● 92 in 1727. The city, based on the ancient Hindu treatise on architecture and sculpture, the *Shilpa Shastra* ● 71, was astonishingly well-planned. The town planner was a talented young scholar and engineer, Vidyadhar Bhattacharya (below), whose family had been invited to settle in Jaipur from the distant state of Bengal by Raja Man Singh I. Jaipur was built on a grid system. Its main streets, 119 feet wide, were intersected at right angles by secondary streets, 60 feet wide, which were further criss-crossed by lanes and bylanes, 30 feet and 15 feet wide respectively. The streets were lined with fine buildings of uniform design and shaded by trees. In the middle of the main road run an aqueduct, and there were wells for drinking water at regular intervals, many of which are still used today. The city was divided into nine rectangular sectors (representing the nine divisions of the universe). Different streets were allotted for different professions such as potters, weavers, dyers, jewelers, and bankers. Louis Rousselet, the 19th-century French traveler, wrote, "The town is built in a style of unusual magnificence... I doubt whether at the time it was built there were many cities in Europe which could compare with it." The 19th-century English bishop, Heber, wrote that it was comparable to the Kremlin in Moscow. Raja Sawai Jai Singh II named the new city after himself (fortuitously Jaipur also means "City of Victory").

Jaipur, c. 1900.

"...the good people of America builded their towns after this pattern, but knowing nothing of Jey Singh, they took all the credit themselves."

Rudyard Kipling, *Letters of Marque*, 1899

Jaipur and the British. During the early 19th century, plagued by the depredations of the Marathas from the south, the kingdom was thrown into confusion. In 1818 it signed a treaty of "defensive alliance, perpetual friendship, protection and subordinate cooperation" with the British. In the years that followed, the British handled Jaipur, and all the other Rajput kingdoms, with great shrewdness, drawing them into their fold. They elevated the major rulers from rajas to maharajas ("great rajas"), dished out gun salutes, and even had Robert Taylor, a heraldic novice in the Bengal Civil Service, design ornate, if slightly bogus, coats-of-arms for them, which Rudyard Kipling found "curious" and "interesting".

Maharaja Sawai Man Singh II, portrait (left) and in his carriage (right).

Maharaja Sawai Man Singh II. The 1930's saw the beginning of a golden age in Jaipur, following the reign of Maharaja Sawai Man Singh II (reigned 1922-49), a glamorous young polo player and jet-setter. When he took his celebrated polo team to England in 1933 ▲ *144*, a newspaper breathlessly reported, "This Prince, who might have stepped straight from the pages of the Arabian Nights, is a slim, broad-shouldered Adonis. Champion polo-player of India, he can ride his horse like a Cossack, and has brought a team of princes, all of whom are related to him." Perhaps appropriately, he married in true fairy-tale. His third maharani was Gayatri Devi ● *40,* an exquisite princess of Cooch Behar, who was once listed, along with Vivien Leigh, as one of the ten most beautiful women in the world. The 1930's in Jaipur was an era of polo matches, tiger hunts, and fabulous royal parties. When a prince was born, for instance, he was promptly named "Bubbles", after the vast quantities of champagne that were downed in his honor. And when a princess was married, the wedding was so lavish that it was listed in the *Guinness Book of Records* as the most expensive wedding in the world. In 1949, after India's independence, all princely states of this region were merged ● *39.* Jaipur was made the capital of the newly formed state of Rajasthan.

Firman
Raja Sawai Jai Singh II's *firman,* or order for the building of his dream city of Jaipur, was issued in 1726. In its planning 18th-century Jaipur recalled the legendary city of Ayodhya, described in the epic *Ramayana* as such: "A great and glorious city, divided into large fine streets, embellished with a royal avenue that cuts through it admirably ....The city has arched gates, well-placed markets and is occupied by all sorts of craftmen. Bards and heralds abound."

1. CITY PALACE
2. HAWA MAHAL
3. JANTAR MANTAR
4. AMBER FORT
5. JAIGARH FORT
6. JAL MAHAL
7. NAHARGARH FORT
8. GAITOR
9. ALBERT HALL MUSEUM
10. RAMBAGH PALACE
11. MOTI DUNGRI PALACE

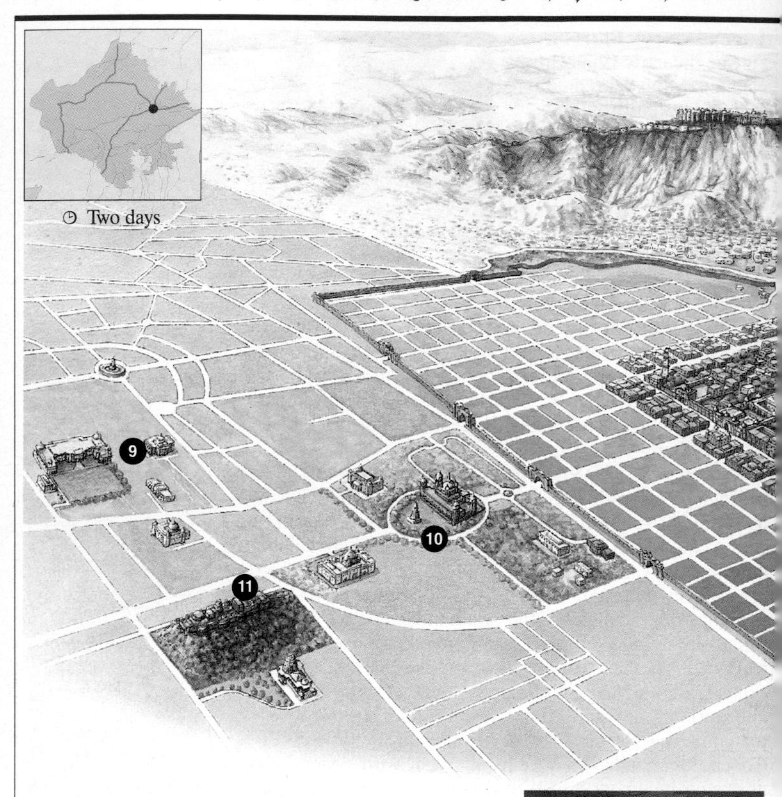

JAIPUR TODAY

Jaipur is the capital of Rajasthan, as was foreseen long ago by Raja Sawai Jai Singh II. It has a population of over 1½ million. Jaipur is called the "Pink City", for by law, all the buildings in the old city must be painted a deep saffron-pink. The practice follows a tradition that dates back to the visit of the Prince of Wales in 1876, when the entire city was freshly painted in his honor. (It might very well have been called the "blue" or "white" city, for these were some of the other colors that were apparently experimented with before pink was chosen.) Apart from being an important administrative, commercial, and educational center,

SIR SWINTON JACOB
Several of Jaipur's buildings were designed by the architect Sir Swinton Jacob, who had produced a famous portfolio of Indian architectural details in the 19th century ● *96*.

A miniature painting (above right) shows one of Jaipur's gates last century. The photograph (right) shows one of the gates of Jaipur today.

> "Highly oriented curiosity...
> all in the soft, rich tint of strawberry ice cream."
>
> Mark Twain, *Around the Equator*, 1879

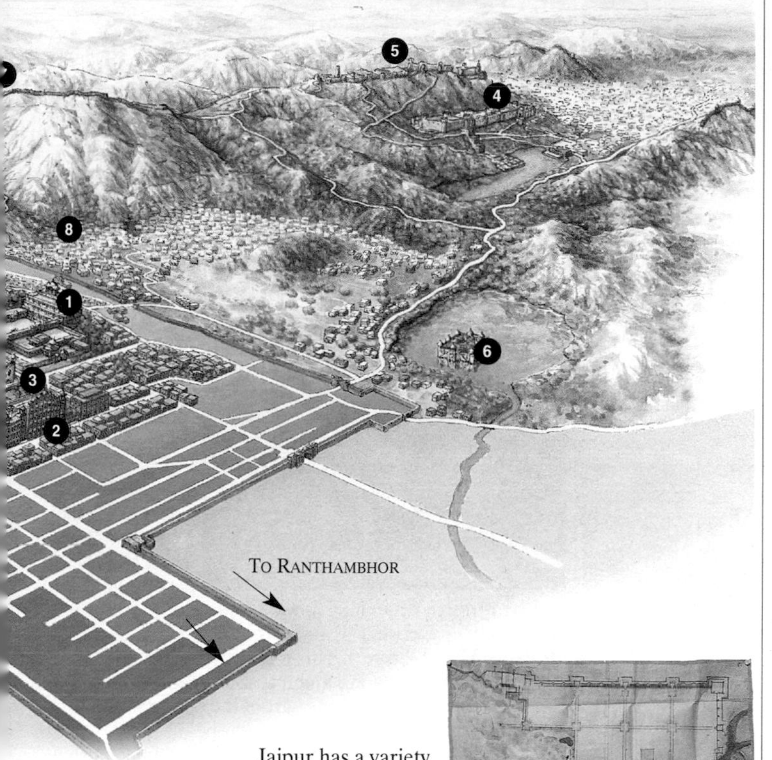

Old map of Jaipur.

Jaipur has a variety of manufacturing industries. It is especially known for its arts and crafts: jewelry, enamel work, hand-printed fabrics, and stone sculptures. Above everything, Jaipur is an extraordinary colorful place. On its streets you see women in their brilliant red and orange *orhnis* (head coverings) and sweeping skirts, and men in their equally vivid turbans and upturned mustaches. Both turbans and mustaches have an entire non-verbal vocabulary of their own: for instance, twirling one's mustache while looking at a woman constitutes making a pass at her. And, as for a turban, it can tell you the wearer's hometown, caste, profession, and various other personal details besides ▲ *295*. If Jaipur is a city of turbans and mustaches, it is also a city of polo, which has curious variants: while usually played on horseback, it is also played on elephants and, times being what they are, on bicycles! The important sights to see in Jaipur are the City Palace, the Jantar Mantar Observatory, and Amber Fort. But do not miss the city's other fine public buildings such as the Albert Hall Museum. While on the subject of architecture, remember to take a look at the grandiose Raj Mandir cinema, whose style could only be described as "Cecil B. De Mille-Rajput Rococo"!

Stone sculpture on a wall in the city of Jaipur.

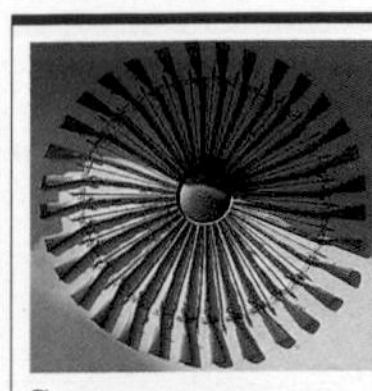

SUN EMBLEM
This sun icon, composed of antique firearms and a Rajput shield, symbolizes the belief that the rulers of Jaipur trace their descent, through Lord Rama, hero of the great epic *Ramayana* back to the sun god himself.

Tripolia Gate.

CITY PALACE ★

The sprawling City Palace was an integral part of Raja Sawai Jai Singh II's new city of Jaipur ▲ *132.* Of the nine blocks in the city plan, two were apportioned for the palace. It is almost a city within a city. The City Palace is a superb marriage of the Rajput and Mughal styles of architecture. The basic layout is in the Mughal style, with open, airy buildings designed for different functions, each one set in a geometrical garden of its own. But there is also a great deal, especially in the details of the palace, that results from centuries of Rajput (and Jain) architectural tradition. As you walk deeper into the palace complex, you come to buildings of an increasingly private function.

MUBARAK MAHAL. You enter through Atish Pol, or "Stable Gate" (the palace's great triple-arched Tripolia Gate is now reserved for the Maharaja's family, which still lives in a part of the palace). Passing through Chandni Chowk ("Square of Moonlight") and Gainda ki Deorhi ("Rhinoceros Gate"), you come to Mubarak Mahal (above). This was a royal guest house built in 1900 by Maharaja Madho Singh II. Designed by Sir Swinton Jacob ▲ 134, it now contains part of the palace museum. Here, in the *toshakhana* ("royal wardrobe" section), you can see some of the sumptuous brocade, silk, and fine muslim costumes of the royal family dating back to the 18th century.

The City Palace.

"Jeypore Palace may be called the Versailles of India."

Rudyard Kipling, *Letters of Marque*, 1899

THE MAHARAJA'S SILK ROBE
An enormous silk robe worn by Raja Sawai Madho Singh I (reigned 1750-68) is on display in the museum at the City Palace. The Raja is said to have stood at over 6½ feet tall and weighed over 500 pounds.

TAKING THE WATERS
When Maharaja Madho Singh II (reigned 1880–1927) (above) was going to England for King Edward VII's coronation in 1902, he had two enormous, solid silver urns made to carry sufficient sacred Ganges water for him to bathe with every day for four months! Measuring 5 feet high, they are listed in the *Guinness Book of Records* as the largest silver objects in the world. In addition, the devout Maharaja had the S.S. *Olympia*, a brand new ship that he had chartered, specially washed and purified, and had a temple to Lord Krishna made on board for the voyage across the "black waters".

SILEH KHANA. Nearby are the old women's quarters (*zenana*), now converted into an armoury with one of India's finest collections of antique weapons, including Raja Man Singh I's massive cutlass (weighing 11 pounds) ▲ *200* and an interesting turban-shaped helmet that belonged to Mirza Raja Jai Singh I. Some of the weapons are real curiosities such as the dagger (*katar*) that has two miniature pistols built into its handle, hence leaving absolutely nothing to chance ▲ *201*! There is also a bloodthirsty sword-like weapon – a predecessor of the dumdum bullet concept perhaps – that would spread open on being plunged into the unfortunate victim's body.

SINGH POL. Opposite Mubarak Mahal is Singh Pol ("Lion Gate"). This impressive gateway, with its ornate brackets, carved balconies, and brass-studded doors, is a fine example of the typically Hindu architectural elements that fill the City Palace. On either side of it are enormous white marble elephants (above) ● *71*. They were moved here from the *zenana* (private maharanis quarters) to mark the birth of Maharaja Bhawani Singh in 1931, the first direct male heir to the Jaipur throne in two generations.

Chandra Mahal.

A portrait of Jesus Christ as an infant in the City Palace Museum.

Hall in Chandra Mahal.

DIWAN-I-KHAS. Beyond Singh Pol lies Diwan-Khas ("Hall of Private Audience"), a large, breezy, typically Mughal, pillared hall. Set within an impressive, deep pink courtyard, it has elegant rows of marble pillars and arches supporting its beautiful pavilion roof. Today, as a sign of the times, it is surmounted, incongruously, with a satellite dish antenna.

DIWAN-I-AM. To the right is Diwan-i-Am ("Hall of Public Audience"). Its ceiling, painted in the 1870's, is decorated with floral motifs in gilt, green, and red. Along one side are latticed galleries provided so that the maharanis of the household could watch the proceedings below without being seen themselves. Today Diwan-i-Am houses a major part of the City Palace Museum, known especially for its rare manuscripts, miniature paintings and splendid carpets. The manuscripts include a beautiful, illustrated scroll of the *Bhagavad Gita* and a copy of the ancient *Shiva Purana,* rendered in almost microscopic calligraphy. The illustrated *Geet Govinda* is also worth seeing. Among the miniature paintings, of which there are some wonderful examples here, two are particularly interesting. One is a painting of the Madonna and Child, in which Joseph is depicted in a European Renaissance style, but the Madonna, curiously, is wearing a typically Mughal headdress and earrings! Another outstanding painting is *Lovers at Night,* executed almost entirely in black and white, and brilliantly capturing the glimmer of moonlight on marble. The carpets dating back to the 17th century, came from Herat and Lahore. They are exquisitely woven, and measure up to 28 feet by 10 feet. The collection includes a carpet that is said to have been the throne carpet of the Mughal emperor, Jahangir.

Peacock gateway leading to Pritam Niwas Chowk.

Pritam Niwas Chowk. Nearby is Pritam Niwas Chowk ("Square of the Beloved"). It is an enchanting enclosed courtyard with four 18th-century gateways, elaborately decorated in brilliant colors. This courtyard was originally used for royal dance performances. The balcony above one of the gates was used by performing singers.
Chandra Mahal. Beyond Pritam Niwas Chowk lies the seven-storied Chandra Mahal ("Palace of the Moon"), with its Wedgewood-blue Chhabi Niwas hall, its beautiful, floral painted Sukh Niwas hall, and its even more beautiful Rang Mahal, an ornate Hall of Mirrors, based on the one at the Red Fort in Delhi. However, the Chandra Mahal complex is where the present Maharaja lives and is closed to the public.
Govind Devji Temple. Walking back toward Sireh Deorhi Gate, you come to the large Jaleb Chowk. Here you will find Govind Devji Temple, the temple of Lord Krishna, in whose name the Kachhawaha kings used to rule Jaipur. The idol was brought back from Mathura, the birthplace of Lord Krishna, by Raja Sawai Jai Singh II and installed here in the 1730's.

Hawa Mahal

Nearby is the ornate Hawa Mahal ("Palace of the Winds") ▲ *88, 93.* It is a delightfully idiosyncratic five-tier composition of arches and balconies with 953 casements set in a wide curve. However, it is little more than a façade, as most of the building is just one chamber deep. It was built in 1799 for the ladies of the royal household to enjoy the breeze and to look out to the outside world, without flouting the confines of *purdah.* The design of Hawa Mahal is said to have been inspired by Jain temple architecture, with its tradition of taking a single structural motif and repeating it, tier after tier, for the bold vertical thrust that it creates. The 9th-century Hindu temple, Teli ka Mandir, in Gwalior Fort is said to have been the model on which it was based.

Rare photographs
Maharaja Ram Singh (reigned 1835-80) was a passionate photographer in the 1860's who set up his own studio and darkroom within the City Palace. His photographs were praised by critics of his time. As a result, the City Palace Museum has a great collection of old photographic equipment, including Ram Singh's camera (above) and photographs. These include rare photographs of ladies of the royal family. (Normally, no aristocratic Indian lady of the time would allow herself to be photographed.)

Hawa Mahal.

▲ JAIPUR JANTAR MANTAR ★

Jaiprakash Yantra.

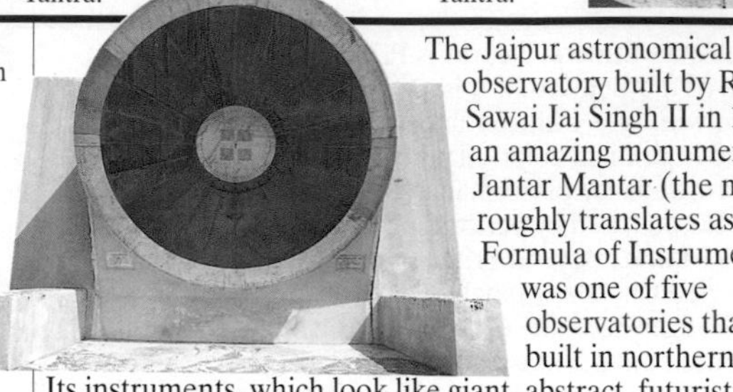

Narivalaya Yantra.

SPREADING FAME Raja Sawai Jai Singh II's observatory prompted the Portuguese Viceroy in Goa to send an emissary to Jaipur in 1729 to study it. Later, as its fame spread, French and German scholars, astronomers and priests also came here. Through his Portuguese friend, Padre Manuel de Figueredo, Raja Sawai Jai Singh II procured the latest astronomical texts and instruments from Europe. Using his huge masonry instruments, he was able to detect errors in the well-known astronomical tables of Père de la Hire, who, like other European astronomers, used only standard-sized brass instruments.

The Jaipur astronomical observatory built by Raja Sawai Jai Singh II in 1827 is an amazing monument. Jantar Mantar (the name roughly translates as "The Formula of Instruments") was one of five observatories that he built in northern India. Its instruments, which look like giant, abstract, futuristic sculptures, are actually highly sophisticated devices that could, among other things, mark time accurate to one second. The first observatory was built in Delhi. The second and more sophisticated one is at Jaipur. In addition, three smaller ones, in Varanasi, Ujjain, and Mathura, were built to supplement the observations made in Jaipur. (The Mathura one has since been destroyed.)

IN PURSUIT OF ASTRONOMY. Raja Sawai Jai Singh II eagerly devoured every known work on the subject written by Indian, Arab, and Greek astronomers and even went to the extent of having Ptolemy's *Almagest* and Newton's *Principia* specially translated into Sanskrit for him. He greatly admired the work done by the Turkish royal astronomer, Ulugh Beg, who had built an observatory in Samarkand in the 15th century, which had produced the most accurate astronomical readings to date. In the introduction to his own comprehensive treatise, he wrote that since nobody had done any significant work in the field since Ulugh Beg, he would undertake the daunting task himself. He sent out his emissaries to collect all the most advanced astronomical instruments that were being used by 18th-century European and Islamic astronomers. During the course of his studies he discovered inaccuracies in the existing astronomical tables of the time. In the tables of the French astronomers, Père de la Hire, for example, he was able to detect a discrepancy of half a degree in the placement of the moon and planets. He was outspoken in his criticism and once wrote. "Ptolemy is a bat... the demonstrations of Euclid are an imperfect sketch of the forms of his contrivances." He concluded that the inaccuracies in the existing tables were all a result of mechanical limitations of the instruments used at the time - they were too small in size to be accurate, and their moving parts made them unreliable. His solution, therefore, was to build gigantic instruments from stone, masonry, and

Jantar Mantar.

Samrat Yantra.

marble instead of the conventional brass ones.

Samrat Yantra. His great Samrat Yantra, for example, is basically a sundial, except that it is a massive 89 feet high and 148 feet wide. As a result, when the sun moves across the sky it casts a shadow on the finely calibrated quadrants on either side, which moves at a precise and measurable 0.08 inch every second. It was designed to measure local time as well as such things as zenith distances, meridian pass times and the declination of the stars with remarkable precision. Interestingly, the Samrat Yantra at each of his five observatories varies slightly in shape in order to ensure that the hypotenuse of its great triangle is aligned perfectly with the axis of the earth and the flanking quadrants are perfectly parallel to the Equator.

Other instruments. In all, Raja Sawai Jai Singh II invented fifteen different instruments, all of them based on his principle of accuracy through gigantic size. They ranged from Ram Yantra (below), which determines the azimuths and altitudes of various heavenly bodies, to Misra Yantra, which, among other things, tells the time at four different foreign observatories. The instruments are in such a good condition that, surprisingly, they are still used today. Samrat Yantra, for instance, is consulted every year on the full moon night of *Guru Purnima*, along with the ancient Sanskrit texts, to predict the onset of the monsoon. One of the instruments on display at Jantar Mantar and the City Palace Museum is a telescope, indicating just how aware the Raja was of the latest technology of his time. For all his brilliance, however, Raja Sawai Jai Singh II was touchingly ignorant of one little point: he thought, till the end, that the sun revolved around the earth.

Smaller Samrat Yantra (left).

Manuscript on astronomy
Raja Sawai Jai Singh II's eclectic collection of astronomical instruments and manuscripts from all over the then known world are displayed at Jantar Mantar and the City Palace Museum.

King of all instruments
The astrolabe, a kind of celestial map engraved on a 7-foot wide metal disc, was one of the most sophisticated astronomical instruments of its time in the Western world. Raja Sawai Jai Singh II managed to get himself one, which he named Raj Yantra ("The King of All Instruments"). He wrote two volumes on the principles and utility of the device, which became one of his proudest possessions.

▲ Jaipur Bazaars

Wandering through the bazaars of old Jaipur is an experience in itself, whether you buy anything (and there's lots to choose from) or not. They are colorful, noisy, and happily chaotic, and you can buy anything here, from Jaipur's famous *minakari* jewelry to bars of soap, marketed under the unique promise that they are made from holy Ganges water, to give you a holy Ganges water bath every time. The most interesting bazaars lie within the Pink City quarter. The best way to tackle them is perhaps by first taking a slow "recce" by cycle-rickshaw and then coming back to the parts you find most interesting.

Sireh Deorhi Bazaar. A convenient place to start is Sireh Deorhi Bazaar, just outside Hawa Mahal. At street level is a jumble of colorful stalls, and above are the pink cupolas and ornate latticed windows of Raja Sawai Jai Singh II's old city. Here the shops selling brightly colored textiles begin. By the way, don't miss the little shop here that sells ready-made turbans, or the quiant, old Ramprakash cinema.

Johri Bazaar. Johri Bazaar ("The Market of the Jewelers") is the place to buy Jaipur's famous *minakari* or *kundan* jewelry ● *62* or silver jewelry, which is traditionally sold by weight. If it is serious, expensive jewelry you are looking for, however, try Gem Palace or one of the other shops on Mirza Ismail Road. On your right, from where the tap-tapping sounds emanate, is a little shop of silver beaters who beat the delicate silver foil that is used to top traditional Indian candies. Nearby is Lakshmi Mishtan Bhandar, a restaurant known for its delicious *dahi wadas* and *kachoris.* Inside, in the narrow maze of bylanes near Gopalji

Minakari jewelry
Jaipur's *minakari* jewelry is gold jewelry that is lavishly enameled with glowing reds, greens, and turquoise blues ● *62.* Often, this technique is combined with *kundan* work and the

jewelry is further studded with gems. It is a painstaking craft (a single pendant can take months to make). Each piece passes through at least four master craftsmen. First, a goldsmith to craft the item (*kundan*), then a *minakar* to enamel it, then a jeweler to set the gems, and, finally, another jeweler to add on the dangling pearls. It is said that Raja Man Singh I originally brought five master *minakar* jewelers here from Lahore in the 16th century. Some of today's well-known *minakaris* are directly descended from them.

Locally made handicrafts (left) and ready-made turbans (right) can be found in Jaipur's bazaars.

ka Rasta, are more tiny jewelry workshops and candy shops.

Bapu, Nehru, and Indira bazaars. Past Haldiyon ka Rasta, you turn at Sanganer Gate into the textile shops of Bapu Bazaar, Nehru Bazaar and Indira Bazaar. This is the place to buy Jaipur's well-known hand-block prints and vivid tie-and-dye fabrics ● *56*. It is also the place for mirrored embroidery work and the embroidered goat-skin slippers called *mojris*, with their upturned toes. If you look up you can see the crenelated battlements of the medieval city wall running all the way along your left.

Kishanpol Bazaar. Turning up at Kishanpol Bazaar, you come to the shops selling decorative brassware and *ittar,* the heavily scented traditional Indian perfume. There are different seasonal fragrances that are supposed to cool you in summer and warm you in winter. Wander into Rangwalon ki Gali and you can see the textile dyers at work, tying and dyeing their flamboyantly colored fabrics. There is also an interesting old *haveli* here of the Commander-in-Chief of Jai Singh II: Natani ki Haveli (above), with its seven courtyards, now converted into a girls' school.

Chandpol Bazaar. Past Khazanewalon ka Rasta, with its marble artefacts, you come to Chandpol Bazaar and its colorful little stalls selling everything from spices to delightfully kitschy lithographs of popular gods and goddessess. Stop by the little *haveli* here with its curious British-Rajput architecture. At the top of the tall classical columns, where you would expect to see Greek gods, are Indian deities instead! Inside, on your right, is Maniharon ki Gali, with its brightly colored displays of wedding bangles, where they specially twist lacquer bangles for you while you wait.

Tripolia Bazaar. Down Tripolia Bazaar are shops selling Jaipur's famous blue pottery and simple earthen water pots. There are two interesting, old *havelis* here - the *haveli* of Vidyadhar Bhattacharya, the architect of Jaipur, (now converted into a museum), and the *haveli* of Nawab Faiz Ali Khan. Beyond Chaura Rasta, you come to Bari Chaupar, a good place to buy chunky rustic silver jewelry and traditional *mojri* slippers. Jaipur is also, by the way, an excellent place to buy carpets.

Famous textile prints

For more upmarket hand-block printed garments than the ones in the bazaars, try Anokhi at Tilak Marg. Featured in the pages of *Vogue* and *Elle* over the years, and with regular famous clients ranging from actress Felicity Kendall to author Doris Lessing, Anokhi has its own exclusive prints and designs. Most of what it makes is exported.

(Above) Models at an Anokhi fashion show.

Manak Chowk, Jaipur (center).

Candy treat

Jaipur is known for its delicious traditional candies. A favorite is *ghevar,* a crunchy orange honeycomb-like disk made from fine-ground flour soaked in syrup. Probably the best-known candy shop in town is within the restaurant Lakshmi Mishtan Bhandar, said to have operated from the same premises since the 18th century.

A thoroughfare (left) with the gate, Chand Pol, at the far end.

Rambagh Palace.

RAMBAGH PALACE

Rambagh Palace was the palace of Maharaja Sawai Man Singh II ▲ *133* in the closing decades of princely rule in India. A sprawling building with cupolas designed by Sir Swinton Jacob ▲ *134,* its gardens were once featured in Peter Coat's *The Most Beautiful Gardens of the World.* It has the unique distinction of being the only residence in the world with a polo field attached. Built originally as a garden house for a wet nurse of the prince, Ram Singh II, it later became a hunting lodge. (A princely guest once actually discovered a panther inside the palace and promptly speared it.) But by the 1930's, Rambagh had become the maharaja's official palace, with interiors furnished by Hammonds of London, including a magnificent red-and-gold Chinese room, Lalique crystal, Lalique chandeliers, Lalique fountains, and illuminated Lalique dining tables. It played host to a galaxy of international celebrities, from the famed Argentinian playboy (and polo player) Porfiro Rubirosa to Lord Mountbatten ● *39* and unexpectedly, the former U.S.S.R. premier, Nikita Khrushchev. Now it has been converted, like many Rajput palaces, into a splendid hotel. It is filled with the heirlooms of the last maharaja, including , in the Polo Bar, the mementoes of Jaipur's legendary 1930's polo team. Everywhere, you'll find details that speak volumes of the lifestyle of its former occupants.

Albert Hall Museum.

ALBERT HALL MUSEUM

Set in Jaipur's spacious Ram Niwas Gardens, this stately building also designed by Sir Swinton Jacob, was modeled on London's Victoria and Albert Museum. It houses a collection of exhibits of Rajasthani folk arts. Take a look at the wonderful 30-foot long *phad* painting, for instance, depicting the ballad of the folk hero, Pabuji.

WINNING POLO
The Maharaja of Jaipur's polo team which visited England in 1933 was supposed to have been one of the finest the world has seen. It trounced the English teams so badly that this was how *The Tatler* depicted them.

Drawing of Rambagh Palace.

Various other exhibits include rare stone carvings dating back to the 2nd century and some fine miniatures. You will also discover, slightly unexpectedly, an Egyptian mummy. But the prize possession is a magnificent late 16th-century Persian garden carpet, considered one of the finest carpets ever woven.

Rajmahal Palace

This charming 18th-century palace was built as a summer resort for the ladies of the royal household. Later it became the home of the British Resident in Jaipur, and ultimately the palace of the last ruling maharaja. Set in 52 acres of grounds, this was where the royal family lived till 1976.

Havelis

Jaipur probably had more nobles and wealthy landlords than any other Indian Princely State, except Hyderabad. And the *havelis* were the townhouses where they lived when they were in Jaipur ● *86*. Between them, these *havelis* give you a peep into the lifestyle of the old feudal chieftains, with their chandeliers, hunting trophies, antique weaponry - and hybrid Rajput-British decor.

Narain Niwas. Narain Niwas, one of the best examples, was the 19th-century *haveli* of the chieftains of Kanota. One of its occupants was Amar Singh of Kanota, a cavalry officer who fought with the Jodhpur Lancers in the Boxer Revolution in China in 1901 ▲ *220*. His diaries, which consist of eighty-nine volumes covering the period 1898-1942, give a brilliant portrait of life in old Rajputana. Other interesting old *havelis* are Samode Haveli and Bissau Lodge. There are other well-known *havelis* in Tripoli Bazaar and Kishanpol Bazaar, but they are not in as good a condition.

Moti Doongri Palace

Moti Doongri Palace stands out eccentrically among the old Rajput palaces. Originally a small fort called Shankar Garh ("Shiva's Fortress"), it was renovated by Maharaja Sawai Man Singh II – and idiosyncratically restyled to look like a Scottish castle! It was one of Maharaja Sawai Man Singh II's favorite palaces and was the location for glittering parties that he hosted for his intimate circle of friends. It had a rather grisly history, though, and is said to have been briefly used in the 1930's as a prison for a princeling who had cut off a boy's testicles in a fit of anger.

Indian cinema
The Raj Mandir (above) is one of the country's finest movie theaters. Going there is a good way of gaining in insight into the Indian movie-making industry, which is the most prolific in the world. The building's impressive décor, with pinks and blues offset by sparkling chandeliers, carpeting, mirrors, and moldings, is in the same spirit as the popular locally made movies, known as *masala* (a blend of spices), that are shown there. They have a saccharine and guileless romanticism, and feature spectacular staged fights and gaudy sets. Episodes of dancing and singing systematically punctuate the storyline. Going to the movies is a favorite form of entertainment for Indians, and the show is not confined to the screen. The audience, made up of people from every social class, enthusiastically participates in the action, applauding the heros, booing the "bad guys", and joining in the songs. Surprisingly, having guessed the outcome, no one stays until the end.

Ghats leading to Maota Lake.

GANESH POL
This superb gateway (right) is covered with delicate frescos and mosaics and set with finely carved lattice screens (left). From behind the privacy of these screens the royal ladies could watch the ceremonial functions held in the "Diwan-i-Am" courtyard below.

Amber Fort.

AMBER FORT ★

Amber lies about 7 miles northeast of Jaipur. The name is derived from the goddess, Amba Mata, the Mother Earth, whom the Mina tribe used to worship at this site before the Kachhawaha Rajputs took it over and made it their capital. Amber remained the capital of the Kachhawahas till 1727, but even after that it was never completely abandoned. When the Mughal emperor Aurangzeb once asked Raja Sawai Jai Singh II what his capital looked like, it is said the latter cut open a pomegranate – to demonstrate how it lay in a protected valley. All around Amber, the hills are ringed with battlements and watchtowers, and within the valley lie the remains of the ancient capital. Much of it is now in ruins, including the 13th-century palace (only Bala Bai ki Sal is somewhat intact). There remains an ornate 17th-century water tank nearby, Panna Mian ka Kund, built by a eunuch, and Jagat Shiromani Temple, a fine marriage of north and south Indian architectural styles, with a superbly carved *torana* archway over its entrance. In addition, there is the 18th-century Chamwarvalon ki Haveli ("Mansion of the Fly Whisk Attendants"), which has now been painstakingly restored to its original condition. It is a private home, but worth seeing from the outside at least.

SHEESH MAHAL
Virtually every major Rajput palace boasts a Sheesh Mahal ("Hall of Mirrors"), but the most lavish of all is the one at Amber ● *109*. Its walls and ceiling are entirely covered with an intricately patterned inlay of mirrors and colored glass. When a candle is lit in the darkness, the effect of an infinite starscape is created.

Jagat Shiromani Temple.

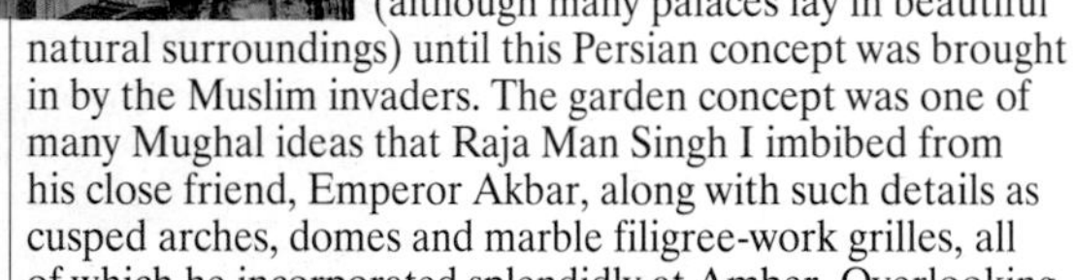

GARDENS OF DILARAM BAGH AND MOHAN BARI. By the waters of Maota Lake lie the beautifully laid out old gardens of Dilaram Bagh and Mohan Bari. A formal garden was an idea largely unknown in traditional Indian palace architecture (although many palaces lay in beautiful natural surroundings) until this Persian concept was brought in by the Muslim invaders. The garden concept was one of many Mughal ideas that Raja Man Singh I imbibed from his close friend, Emperor Akbar, along with such details as cusped arches, domes and marble filigree-work grilles, all of which he incorporated splendidly at Amber. Overlooking

Jaleb Chowk.

"...A living palace where the sightseer knows and feels that... he is being followed by scores of unseen eyes."

Rudyard Kipling, *Letters of Marque*, 1899

Maota Lake is the old Raj Mahal Palace, built from 1600 onward.

JALEB CHOWK. A steep cobbled path from Dilaram Bagh takes you up to Suraj Pol and Jaleb Chowk. Often mistakenly referred to as "Jalebi Chowk", or "The Candy Square", it actually means "The Square where Horses and Elephants are Tethered." Here lies Singh Pol ("Lion Gate"), an impressively fortified double gate, incorporating a blind turn and guard rooms on three sides. This was once richly painted with frescos, the fading remains of which you can still see.

SHILA DEVI TEMPLE. Nearby is the beautiful temple to Kali, its pillars carved in the form of banana trees in delicate green marble. The image of the goddess was brought back from Bengal by Raja Man Singh I in 1580. The temple's priests had traditionally been Bengalis but now they are from Bihar.

DIWAN-I-AM. Opposite the Kali Temple lies the marvelous Diwan-i-Am ("Hall of Public Audience"), built by Mirza Raja Jai Singh I. On the southern side of Diwan-i-Am lies the splendid Ganesh Pol ("Elephant Gate"), described as one of the finest gateways in the world. It leads you into a lovely little Mughal garden, around which the royal apartment complex was designed.

JAI MANDIR AND JAS MANDIR. Jai Mandir, used as a hall of private audience, is created in white marble. Its floral ceiling is inlaid with intricate mirror-work. The walls are decorated with fine murals of leafy scrolls and flowers. The magnificent Sheesh Mahal ("Hall of Mirrors") has walls and ceilings entirely covered with intricate inlay-work of mirror and colored glass. The stained-glass windows here, by the way, were a later 18th-century addition, imported from Europe. Just above Jai Mandir is Jas Mandir, the "Room of Glory", its walls ablaze with spangled mirrors, backed and bordered with gold leaf. Its façade is a filigreed marble screen, with a stunning view over Maota Lake and the rugged hills below, specially designed to catch the summer breezes and draw them in to cool the hall.

SUKH MANDIR. Opposite this complex, across the gardened courtyard, is Sukh Mandir ("Temple of Contentment"), an aptly named pleasure chamber, cooled by a marble water cascade. Do not miss the doors here, which are made of fragrant sandalwood, inlaid with ivory.

ZENANA. Beyond this lies the Zenana ("Palace of the Ranis"). Here, clustered around a large central courtyard, were what used to be the self-contained suites of twelve ranis, with chambers for concubines on the upper floor. There is a device for grinding millet in the floor of the favorite rani's suite: it apparently served as an exercising device to help keep her figure trim! In the courtyard is a fine *baradari* (pavilion) supported by stately carved pillars.

Mohan Bari.

PLASTERED OVER
Diwan-i-Am has a double row of red sandstone pillars with elephant capitals, and gray Mughal-style columns holding up its vaulted roof. The hall's magnificence is supposed to have provoked the jealousy of the Mughal emperor Shah Jahan, causing the Raja to prudently cover up the marble columns with plaster just before an imperial inspection. The plaster was finally removed only about fifty years ago, but if you look closely at the columns, you can still see traces of it. Nearby is a remarkable row of traditional *arayish* (lime stucco plaster) columns, so smoothly finished that you might mistake them for marble.

Jaigarh Fort.

JAIGARH FORT

High in the hills above Amber is the magnificent Jaigarh Fort. It was built in the 18th century to reinforce the defenses of the Kachhawaha capital. Its mighty ramparts stretch, seemingly for miles, across the hillsides, with embrasures cunningly designed to give the defenders a choice of three different angles for shooting down at their attackers. Also on the ramparts is an enormous watchtower, Diva Burj. Once it was seven stories high, but legend says that the lightning, jealous of the height of its flaming lamp, struck down the top two stories. The most interesting thing about Jaigarh Fort, however, is the legend of its buried treasure. Raja Jai Singh II is said to have buried inside here the booty from his various campaigns, worth, according to one account, 1 080 million rupees (US$ 35 million) in the 1720's. The treasure was guarded by fierce Mina tribesmen. Over the centuries, each successive maharaja was led blindfold to the treasure by the Minas, once in his lifetime, and allowed to choose just one piece from it. In the 1970's the government of India launched one of the world's most ambitious treasure hunts ever to unearth his legendary treasure. It was, according to one theory, hidden inside the fort's huge water-tanks, but nothing was ever found. Some say the treasure is still in there, somewhere...

JAIGARH PALACE. Inside the fort is a palace with a complex of royal apartments, build by various maharajas over a period of two centuries. In Lakshmi Vilas, there are some beautifully painted blue frescos, the remains of a lovely old Mughal garden and an interesting little theater where the maharajas used to watch dance, puppet shows, and music recitals – the ranis watched from an adjacent room, hidden behind a filigree screen (*jali*). From here there is also an interesting view of a special fortified passage snaking down to a nearby lake which provided access to water in times of siege.

WORLD'S LARGEST WHEELED CANNON
The giant Jaiban cannon is the largest wheeled cannon in the world. Cast in 1720 in Jaigarh Fort's foundry, it is 9 feet high, over 20 feet long and weighs 50 tons. It took four elephants to swivel it around on its axis. Its sound was said to have been so terrifying loud that it caused the water in the nearby wells to dry up.

Wall painting in Nahargarh Palace.

ecorative *rayish* lasterwork in he palace of ahargarh Fort.

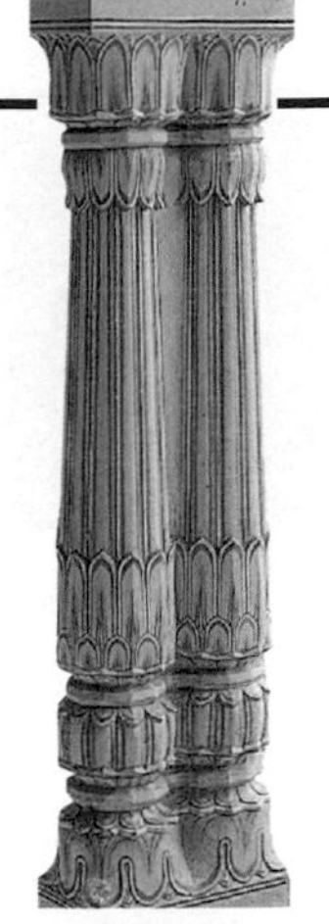

CANNON FOUNDRY. The remains of Jaigarh's famous 16th-century cannon foundry, one of the few surviving medieval cannon foundries anywhere in the world, are here at Jaigarh Fort. You can see some of its products, including the mighty Jaivana cannon. Despite its awesome firepower, it is delicately decorated with scrollwork, birds, foliage and a roaring elephant at its mouth. There is also a point called Damdama ("continuous firing"), where a battery of ten great cannons was positioned to stop any approaching enemy with a furious fusillade. The curious thing is that this formidable battery was facing the approach from Delhi, leading one to believe that Raja Jai Singh II was secretly preparing for a showdown with his Mughal allies.

NAHARGARH FORT

If Jaigarh was one of the hill forts guarding the approach to Amber, the other was Nahargarh, the "tiger Fort". Originally this site was thickly forested and inhabited by deadly accurate Mina archers. It also happened to be the site of the cenotaph of a Rathor prince, Nahar Singh. However, in 1734, Raja Sawai Jai Singh II decided that this was the precise spot on which he wanted to build a new fort. According to legend, Nahar Singh, a Bhomiya or ancestral spirit with supernatural powers, would not allow the fort to be built: whatever walls were erected by day fell down by night. Finally, tantric rites were performed to appease the disturbed spirit, and the fort, once completed, was named after the prince. The fort's thick crenelated ramparts and arches make it a superb example of Rajput military architecture. Over by the edge of the precipice is Hazari Burj, an artillery emplacement ideally positioned for the Kachhawaha guns to decimate any would-be attackers on the killing fields far below.

MADHAVENDRA BHAWAN. By the 19th century, Nahargarh Fort was converted to more peaceful purposes, and a palace was built here, with delicately cusped arches and ornately frescoed walls (above). As you enter, you can see the suites of the maharaja and his nine queens. All of them are notable for the beautiful florally painted *arayish* on their walls, which is still amazingly well-preserved. The palace complex is laid out with courtyards and terraces, and a Hawa Ghar ("breeze chamber"), from where the ranis could get a view of the city.

"MARBLE" FINISH
At Nahargarh (as at other old Rajput palaces), you can see a unique plasterwork technique called *arayish,* which had a finish as smooth as marble. *Arayish* is made from highly refined limestones, mixed with various exotic substances, including egg, *jaggery* (hardened palm syrup), gum and marble powder. Preparing it was an extremely painstaking process. The final stage was hand-polishing with a piece of agate. The finish was so smooth it was sometimes almost indistinguishable from marble.

Nahargarh Fort (left). Fresco in palace (above).

HOLY CLEANSING
Galta is a pilgrimage center for Hindus, and the waters of its seven tanks are considered to be as holy as those of the River Ganges. A dip in the tanks is said to cleanse believers of their worldly sins.

SISODIA RANI KA BAGH

Located 6 miles east of Jaipur is Sisodia Rani ka Bagh, a little palace laid out in formal terraced gardens with fountains (right). It bears the name of the clan of a princess from Udaipur who was married to Raja Sawai Jai Singh II. It was merely a political marriage between the two antagonistic states, one of the terms of which was that the son born of this union would succeed to the Jaipur throne. But tired of the constant intriguing against her at Jaipur's City Palace and fearful for the life of her son, the unhappy princess came away here to live under its domed and canopied roof. The upper storey of the palace has some charming murals of hunting scenes, polo matches, mythical beasts and episodes from the life of Lord Krishna and Radha.

View of Galta (above). Cenotaphs of Gaitor.

GALTA

Just beyond Sisodia Rani ka Bagh, in a picturesque gorge, are the temples of Galta (left). This is the spot where the great sage Galav is supposed to have lived and performed his penance. On the ridge there is an 18th-century temple of Surya, the sun god, built by one of Raja Sawai Jai Singh II's courtiers. The view of the city from here is splendid. It is said that the temple's sacred tanks never run dry because of a spring that flows out of a rock carved with the shape of a cow's face.

Gaitor

The graceful white marble cenotaphs of the Kachhawaha rulers lie in a valley beneath Nahargarh Fort, 4 miles north of Jaipur. The most impressive of them is that of Raja Sawai Jai Singh II, the great mathematician and astronomer-king ● *35, 131.* Here, on his death, as Colonel Tod records, "his wives and several concubines ascended on his funeral pyre, on which science expired with him." The cenotaph or *chhatri* (the word literally means "umbrella") has a marble dome and surrounding cupolas, all supported by twenty pillars, lavishly carved with mythological figures. Raja Madho Singh II's *chhatri,* with its beautiful frieze of carved peacock, is also worth seeing. By the time you come to the *chhatri* of the last ruling maharaja, who died in the early 1970's, however, you will see how the standards of craftsmanship have sadly waned in recent times. What is particularly touching at Gaitor are the miniature *chhatris* in the complex: these are the shrines of the two sons born to Madho Singh II by his concubines. The tombs of the Jaipur princesses lie not far away, beside Lake Man Sagar.

A taste of Rajasthan
Choki Dhani, en route to Sanganer, is a novel "food village" (one can't call it a mere restaurant) serving authentic Rajasthan food on dishes made of plaited leaves in a charming rustic setting, complete with puppeteers, ballad singers, bangle-makers and potters. Its sprawling campus is lit entirely by flickering hurricane lamps. The food is served on leafplatters while you are seated on the floor in the traditional manner.

Jal Mahal

In the middle of the lake of Man Sagar, en route to Amber, lies Jal Mahal ("Water Palace") with its graceful cupolas and *bangaldar* eaves reflecting prettily in the waters. Built at the end of the 18th century by Madho Singh I (reigned 1750–68) ▲ *137,* this palace seems to have been copied from the famous Jag Mandir in Udaipur ▲ *251,* where the raja spent his childhood. In the 19th century, it was turned into a hunting lodge.

Jal Mahal.

Origin of Cenotaphs
The idea of eracting beautiful marble *chhatris* or cenotaphs (like the ones at Gaitor) probably originated from the impressive tombs that the Raiput kings saw their Muslim counterparts leave behind. Since they themselves were cremated (and had the remains after cremation dispersed in the Ganges or in another holy River), they developed the concept of memorials like these to mark the spot where they were cremated. Every Raiput kingdom had a hauntingly beautiful complex of cenotaphs for its rulers.

HANDMADE PAPER
If you've ever used handmade paper from India, chances are it was made in Sanganer. The craftsmen are the descendants of those who, for generations, made paper for the Rajput princes, and the technique hasn't changed: the raw material is ordinary scrap paper, which is ripped up, stamped into pulp by foot, and washed. Then it is bleached, dyed, and very dexterously lifted out, layer by layer... each layer, of course, being a fresh sheet. The sheets are then dried, either by hanging them from clothes-lines, or by sticking them up on the walls of the town's houses. (The latter gives a more interesting texture.) Finally, they are smoothed out with heavy stones and speckled, if necessary with gold.

SANGANER

The old walled town of Sanganer, 10 miles south of Jaipur, is known for its traditional textile printing. It was named after a Kachhawaha prince, Sangaji. You enter the town through the ornate tripolia (triple arched) gateways in the ruined walls. Here you can see fabric being printed with hand-blocks, as has been done for centuries ● *56.* The printers here were under the patronage of Jaipur's royal family and therefore developed a highly sophisticated sense of style. The printed calicoes of Sanganer are said to have been so popular in Britain in the 18th century that they began to affect the sales of woolen flax, and were therefore actually banned by statute in 1721. They are still exported to various fashion centres all over the world and are known for their delicate motifs of flowers, foliage, peacocks, and other animals. It is fascinating to wander through the sandy, winding alleyways of Sanganer and watch the hand-block printers at work. The entire town is one large, bustling, colorful workshop that often spills out into its narrow lanes. The printing, done with intricate, hand-carved wooden blocks, is an enormously laborious process: each yard of printed fabric may call for up to thirty separate blocks and up to 350 separate impressions. Sanganer is also a well-known center for blue pottery and handmade paper. There are some old temples here as well (above), the most beautiful being a 15th-century Jain temple with stone carvings so intricate that they are reminiscent of the great Dilwara temples at Mount Abu ● *94,* ▲ *270.*

BAGRU

Beyond Sanganer, 20 miles southwest of Jaipur, is another old textile-printing town, Bagru. The hand-block printing technique here is similar to that of Sanganer ● *56,* but what makes Bagru unique is that it is one of the last bastions of printers still predominantly using traditional vegetable dyes. For example, blues are often derived from indigo, greens from indigo mixed with pomegranate rinds, reds from the madder root and yellows from the turmeric root. For black, an iron horse-shoe is placed with molasses or vinegar in a clay pot and made to stand in the sun for several days. The printers of Bagru are said to have been brought here in the late 17th century by the local raja from various different

Hand-block printer at Bagru.

Decorative details in the palace complex at Tonk.

parts of northern and northeastern Rajasthan. Over the centuries they became known for the earthy, rustic printed fabrics they created for the villages of this region. In recent years, however, their unique use of vegetable dyes and their dramatic designs have put this sleepy little town on the international fashion map. As always, in Rajasthan, there is a legend behind this craft of printing. It is said that Surasen, the son of Arjuna, the hero of the epic *Mahabharata,* had to renounce his warrior caste for a small misdeed. In order to give him an alternative trade (and caste), a goddess appeared in his dreams and revealed the heavenly secret of making dyes from the vegetables and minerals of the earth. The craftsmen of Bagru thus considered theirs to be a divinely ordained craft. There is also a small deserted 17th-century fort here in Bagru, one of the girdle of garrison forts that provided Jaipur's first line of defence.

A magnificent armored coat belonging to the nawab of Tonk.

WORD OF HONOR

Once, a sword was as essential a part of an Indian nobleman's costume as his turban. According to legend, Amir Khan, the first nawab of Tonk, once appeared at the British Resident's *durbar* without his sword. When eyebrows were raised at this impropriety, he apparently said, with a mixture of sarcasm and menace, "You British have taken away my sword. But if you say so, I'd be happy to strap it back on again."

TONK

The small town of Tonk, 58 miles southeast of Jaipur, was the capital of what was once the only Muslim state of Rajasthan. The first nawab of Tonk, Amir Khan, was a fierce Pathan warlord who had once served the powerful Maratha ruler of Indore, in central India. When he became a threat to British interests, they attempted to subdue him by creating this new state for him in 1817, prudently ensuring that it was divided into three separate pieces, rather than one contiguous chunk. The town of Tonk is rather unattractive, but one thing that makes a visit here worthwhile in itself is the Sunehri Kothi ("Mansion of Gold") (below). It is a magnificent hall within the old palace complex, whose walls and ceilings are one sumptuous expanse of enamel mirror-work, gilt and painted glass illuminated through stained-glass windows. The entire effect is that of an exquisite piece of enamel jewelry blown up to the size of a hall. The work is similar to that in Samode Palace ● *41* and the Sheesh Mahal in the Maharaja's private suites of Jaipur's City Palace. It is possible that they were, all three, executed by the same craftsmen in the 19th century. Nearby are a couple of other old palaces with quaint, if rather kitsch, frescos. Tonk is also known for its library, which houses a superb collection of Arabic and Persian manuscripts, some of them lavishly ornamented with gold, rubies, emeralds, and pearls.

Rajasthani textiles, whether tie-dyed, woven, block-printed, appliquéd, embroidered, or hand-painted, use certain motifs not generally seen elsewhere. The motifs are mostly derived from the flora and fauna found in the region. Some flowers, like the marigold, jasmine, rose, *champa*, or *raibel*, have sacred associations, and some animals such as the elephant, lion and monkey are considered more important than others. Caparisoned elephants and camels, peacocks, or a girl holding a flower or in a dance pose, add more Rajasthani character than other motifs. However, motifs based on geometrical forms, trellises (*jalis*), symbolic patterns used in age-old paintings, or decorations in daily rituals by the village women (for example the *mandana* motifs used to decorate mud houses during Diwali in certain parts of Rajasthan), and flowers and flowering plants are also common.

FLORAL MOTIFS
The Rajasthani block printers cater to the needs of an ever-expanding market and use numerous floral motifs, specially for the field design. In these fifty-year-old specimens (top), where the printers still used vegetable colors and printed with hand-blocks, four popular floral motifs are shown, clockwise from top left, *kela* (banana), *nimsher* (*neem* flower), *bade phool* (large flower), and *nargis.*

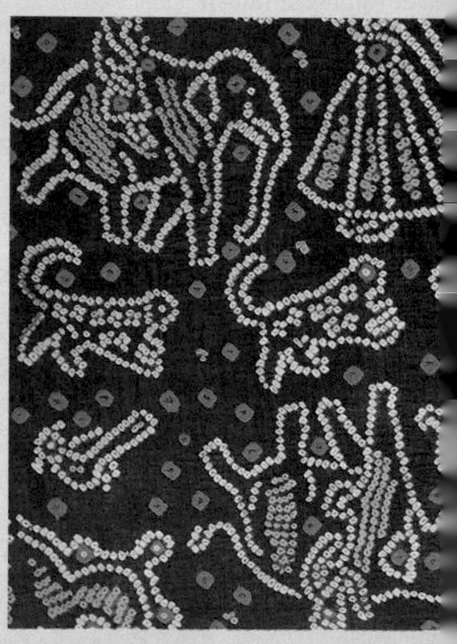

ELEPHANT, LION, BIRD, AND DANCING GIRL
Elephants are very much an integral part of the Rajasthani festive scene. Be it a royal procession or a religious festival, or the wedding of a prince or a nobleman, rows of well-decorated elephants would steal the show. The skillful dyers of Rajasthan have combined elephants, lions, birds, and a dancing girl in this 19th-century piece of tie-and-dye work. Such intricate designs are not common now, though not impossible to find.

CHAMPA (FRANGIPANI)
Besides large flower heads of lotus, marigold, hibiscus, chrysanthemum, and various bulbiferous flowers such as *nargis*, lily tuberose, and local flowers such as rose, *champa (Michelia champeca)*, and *raibel* are also popular. This motif is from a woven silk material used for the royal wardrobe.

Dots and flowers. The tie-dyed veil, or *chunari,* used by the traditional Rajasthani women, has designs of dots and petals of two or three colors arranged like rows of bright flower heads. This exquisite piece was used for a Diwali outfit, as revealed by its deep blue ground color. The design is known *kamal phool* or lotus flower.

Hajara (Chrysanthemum) This 18th-century work (right) shows the *hajara* motif at its finest and best with the outlines overprinted with gold leaf.

Woman with flower Women appear in Rajasthani textiles in various forms, standing, holding a flower, or a parrot, or a garland, dancing or worshipping in a shrine. Some of the motifs are derived from Mughal figured silks and brocades. This is an early piece from the border of a *kanat* (tent wall) segment or a curtain.

Arabesqued façade of Arhai Din ka Jhonpra (right).

Pilgrims at the *dargah* (below).

The small town of Ajmer, 78 miles west of Jaipur, played a surprisingly important role in India's history. Set at the point where the rocky Aravalli hills end and the Thar Desert begins, this was originally the stronghold of the powerful Chauhan dynasty of Rajputs ● *35*, who built India's first ever hill fort here in the 7th century, Taragarh ("Star Fort"), whose ruins you can still see today. Ajmer was ruled by the great Raja Prithviraj Chauhan ● *35, 55*, the last Hindu king of Delhi, until his defeat in 1192. After having changed hands several times, in 1556 Ajmer finally came under the Mughal Emperor, Akbar, who used it as the headquarters for his vitally important operations in Rajasthan. It was here, a generation later, that the first British Ambassador, Sir Thomas Roe, had an historic meeting with Emperor Jahangir in 1615. And it was here, half a century later, that the critical battle between the Mughal crown prince, Dara Shukoh, and the usurper, later Emperor, Aurangzeb, took place. (If the former had in fact won, along with his Rajput allies, as seemed very likely at one point, historians say India's entire history would have turned out very differently indeed.) In the 19th century, Ajmer became a little British enclave, from where the British Chief Commissioner for Rajputana kept an eagle eye on all the Rajput kingdoms. Today Ajmer is, frankly, not the most charming of towns, unlike its heyday in the 17th century when it was Emperor Shah Jahan's pleasure resort. You can still see the white marble pleasure pavilions the Emperor built by the Ana Sagar Lake. There are also various buildings of historical interest to visit here.

EMPTYING THE CAULDRON

There are two enormous *degs* or cauldrons at Ajmer's *dargah*, one of them nearly 10 feet in diameter. During the saint's annual festival, food is cooked in them. During the ritual of "looting the *degs*", attendants empty the entire cauldron at lightning speed, leaping into the steaming hot interiors to scrape out the dregs. The whole process takes just three to four minutes! The food is then distributed to the devotees.

Fortress and town of Ajmer (right).

ETON OF THE EAST

Mayo College in Ajmer is a fabled institution, once described as "the Eton of the East". Modeled on a British public school, it was set up in the 19th century to prepare young Rajput princes for their royal duties. Today it is a well-known public school, run on rather more egalitarian lines. Its white marble main building was designed by Sir Swinton Jacob ▲ *134*.

DARGAH SHARIF

Dargah Sharif is the shrine of the 12th-century Muslim saint, Khwaja Mu'in-ud-din Chisti (1142–1236), perhaps the most important Muslim shrine in the entire Indian subcontinent ● *51*. The saint was greatly venerated by the Mughal emperors, and Emperor Akbar is said to have made two pilgrimages here on foot all the way from Agra: once when an heir was finally born to him, to fulfill a vow that he had made ● *99*, and again when he won against Chittor. The shrine is believed by people of different faiths to have the power to make their prayers come true. During the saint's *urs* (death anniversary celebrations), celebrated between the first and sixth of Rajab, the seventh month of the lunar calendar, tens of thousands of pilgrims come here from all

"Ajmer is the Frankfurt of Rajasthan and its numerous Rothschilds have rivalled each other in enriching it with superb monuments."

Louis Rousselet, *India and its Native Princes*, 1878

over the sub-continent. Female pilgrims often sweep the shrine's courtyard with their long hair – as the Mughal princess, Jehanara, is said to have once done when a prayer she made here was fulfilled.

Arhai Din ka Jhonpra

This was originally a Sanskrit college, which was destroyed and converted into a mosque by Sultan Qutbuddin Aibak of Delhi in 1198. According to Cunningham, an eminent 19th-century archeologist, "For gorgeous prodigality of ornament, richness of tracery, delicate sharpness of finish... this may be one of the noblest buildings the world has produced." Its ornately carved sandstone façade is a masterpiece, and it is interesting to see how the original Hindu columns were re-erected in triple layers during its reconstruction in 1198. The name Arhai Din ka Jhonpra literally means "The Hut of the Two-and-a-Half Days", referring to the two-and-a-half days in which it was hurriedly demolished and built, or perhaps to the two-and-a-half days that *fakirs* (mendicants) would gather here during an *urs* in the 18th century.

Scent of roses
It is not commonly known that the famous perfume, "Ittar of Roses", was invented here in Ajmer, during the reign of Emperor Jahangir. Today the roses of this area are exported to perfumiers all over the world.

Arhai Din ka Jhonpra (above).

Akbar's Palace

This sandstone palace lies in the heart of the old walled city. It has a beautiful gateway, through which you can see the window where the Mughal emperors used to sit and listen to public petitions. Today it houses the Rajputana Museum, which has an interesting collection of 6th and 7th-century sculptures, including a fine black marble image of Kali and a 13th-century Jain *tirthankara* carving.

Nasiyan

Nasiyan Temple (right) is an ornate 19th-century Jain temple. It has a splendid double-storied hall, with a rich display of gilded figures from Jain mythology. Visiting it is a fascinating experience. You can see how Jain temple architecture has evolved over the centuries from the medieval temples of Dilwara and Ranakpur ● *94* ▲ *262, 270.*

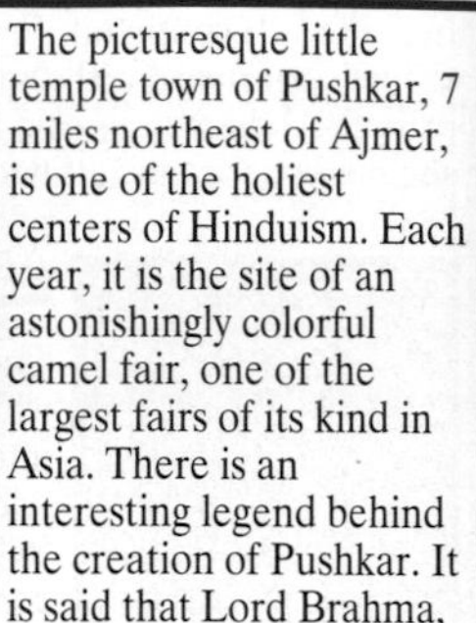

Holy lake and town of Pushkar.

The picturesque little temple town of Pushkar, 7 miles northeast of Ajmer, is one of the holiest centers of Hinduism. Each year, it is the site of an astonishingly colorful camel fair, one of the largest fairs of its kind in Asia. There is an interesting legend behind the creation of Pushkar. It is said that Lord Brahma, the Creator of the Universe, once did battle with the demon, Vajra Nabh, and slew him with a lotus blossom. The petals of the lotus floated down to earth and landed at three places in and around Pushkar, where three beautiful lakes immediately gushed forth. Brahma thereupon performed a *yagna*, an elaborate sacred rite, which was attended by all of the gods and goddesses. A temple was developed around this site, which is one of the five essential pilgrimage centers that a Hindu must visit in his lifetime, along with Badrinath, Puri, Rameshwaram and Dwarka. The town of Pushkar has been written about over the centuries by writers as diverse as the immortal Sanskrit poet Kalidasa (in his great classic *Abhigyan Shakuntalam*), the 6th-century Chinese traveler, Fa-hsein, and the 11th-century Arab traveler, Alberuni ● *33*. Later in the 17th century, Emperor Jahangir wrote in his memoirs, "While in Ajmer I visited nine times the mausoleum of the revered Khwaja, and fifteen times went to look at Pushkar Lake." Pushkar is said to have nearly five hundred temples, large and small, dedicated to various deities, and fifty-two palaces (as several rajas and maharajas from all over India maintained palaces here for their pilgrimages).

A WIFE'S WRATH
Brahma Temple is, surprisingly, virtually the only temple dedicated to Brahma, the Creator of the Universe ● *45*. According to one legend, when Brahma was performing a great *yagna* (sacred ritual) ceremony at Pushkar, his wife Savitri was absent. Since the presence of a wife was essential for the ritual, Brahma hastily married a local maiden, Gayatri. Savitri flew into a rage about this and cursed Brahma, saying that henceforth he would not be worshiped anywhere except at Pushkar.

BRAHMA TEMPLE

Brahma Temple (left) is probably the most important of all the temples at Pushkar – and one of the very few Brahma temples in existence in India. This is curious as Brahma (the Creator) is one of the Hindu Trinity; along with Vishnu (the Preserver), and Shiva (the Destroyer), and there are numerous temples dedicated to the latter two all over India. There are several interesting legends and intellectual theories to explain this fact. Inside the temple's sanctum is a fine, four-armed life-sized statue of Brahma. Another interesting feature are the coins studded in the floor of the temple, placed by devotees from all over India to commemorate the births and deaths of their loved ones.

Temples of Pushkar.

VARAH TEMPLE

Originally built in the 12th century, Varah Temple was, like many others, destroyed by the bigoted Emperor Aurangzeb (who, it is said, was particularly upset by the huge idol here of Varah, the god with the body of a man and the head of a boar). Reconstructed by Raja Sawai Jai Singh II of Jaipur in 1727, the temple has an interesting and richly ornamented image house.

CAMEL EXTRAVAGANZA
During the exuberant camel fair every year, ● *82* numerous contests, such as camel races and the traditional "loading of the camels" contest, are held. The aim of the latter is to see how many riders can pile onto a single camel. Camel polo, is of course, *de rigueur*.

MAHADEVA TEMPLE

A beautiful temple built in the 19th century, it was described by a British traveler of the time as "by far the most remarkable, for the elegance of its structure and the nature of its ornaments, of all the temples Pushkar boasts of." It owes its name to its white marble sculpture of Mahadeva (one of Shiva's names), which has five faces and the characteristic ascetic hairstyle.

RAMAVAIKUNTH TEMPLE

One of Pushkar's largest and most intricate temples is Ramavaikunth Temple (left), built in the 1920's. It has a beautifully sculpted stone *gopuram*, or pagoda, sculpted with the images of no less than 361 different deities. The ornate outer *gopuram* over the entrance is said to have been built by a team of masons specially brought here from south India.

BAZAAR

Pushkar's fascinating old bazaar is a maze of narrow lanes interspersed with little temples, *ashrams* and picturesque old homes with archways and ornate balconies. Every few yards there are broad, formal stepped *ghats* that lead off the side, down to the pretty Pushkar Lake ● *47*.

SHOPPERS' DELIGHT
Pushkar's bazaars are one of the best places in Rajasthan to buy vivid embroidery and painted textiles. It is also a great place to shop for old silver jewelry.

▲ KISHANGARH AND MAKRANA

Darban (royal retainer) outside Kishangarh Fort.

INDIAN MONA LISA
In the 18th century a Kishangarh court artist immortalized the love of Raja Sawant Singh for the beautiful court singer, Bani Thani, and the two are depicted as Radha and Krishna. Bani Thani, with her enormous, languorous eyes, curved eyebrows and tiny waist, appears frequently in Kishangarh miniature paintings, and the people here are particularly fond of referring to her as "the Mona Lisa of Rajasthan"!

Miniature of the Maharaja of Kishangarh (above).

KISHANGARH

Kishangarh, 18 miles north of Ajmer, was the capital of one of the smaller Rajput kingdoms, but one whose unique cultural heritage belied its small size. Founded in 1597 by a Rathor prince from Jodhpur, the kingdom of Kishangarh remained on friendly terms with the Mughal emperors, and the peaceful conditions that resulted from this relationship made for a great flowering of culture and the arts here – and the emergence of one of India's most celebrated schools of miniature painting. One of the great patrons of the arts was Raja Sawant Singh (reigned 1699–1764), a remarkable combination of warrior, poet and mystic.

KISHANGARH SCHOOL. The Kishangarh school of miniature paintings ● *64* is known for its elegant and graceful depictions of the divine lovers, Radha and Krishna. These splendid paintings are imbued with a rare tenderness and lyricism. They are rich with layer upon layer of meaning, the love of Radha and Krishna being a metaphor for the soul in its quest for the Divine.

PHOOLGARH FORT. The fort is reflected in the waters of a pretty little lake. Entering through its lofty, arched gateway, flanked on both sides by elephant murals, you come upon its courtyards, now in splendid decay, surrounded by delicate pavilions and latticed windows. The royal family of Kishangarh have recently restored Rupangarh Palace, an earlier seat of power and refinement for over a century. This is now a hotel with rooms the size of tennis courts.

MARBLE SUPPLIER
Makrana has become synonymous with the beautiful marble yielded up by its quarries ■ *18*. It was this marble that was used for monuments all over India – from the Taj Mahal in Agra to the Victoria Memorial in Calcutta.

MAKRANA

Makrana, which lies 36 miles from Kishangarh, is famous for its beautiful white marble, which has been mined here for centuries. As Colonel Tod noted in the 1820's, "to the marble quarries of Makrana...all the splendid edifices of the imperial cities owe their grandeur. The materials used in the palaces of Delhi and Agra, their mosques and tombs have been conveyed from (here)." The marble quarries of Makrana, where quarrying methods have changed little in the last thousand years, are interesting to visit. There are also numerous little marble workshops here, where traditional craftsmen carve delicately shaped marble artefacts, many of which are later sent to Agra for its famed marble inlay work. The vast salt lake of Sambhar is close by, creating a very eerie white landscape.

आपका
हार्दिक स्वागत है

The temple tank at the Banai Vilas Palace.

COAT-OF-ARMS
The Alwar coat-of-arms shows a shield bearing a traditional Rajput *katar*, or dagger. It is flanked by a tiger and a bull, the symbols of Rajput bravery and piety respectively (the maharajas of Alwar took their role as descendants of the Hindu god, Lord Rama, very seriously). The coat-of-arms is topped by the curiously shaped Alwar crown.

"[Maharaja Jai Singh] is the centre of innumerable stories... of hideous cruelty, and sometimes darker inferences that remind one of tales of black magic and evil possession. You may think of him as Poet and Hero – until you catch the gleam of that wild animal smile or hear the goat wail once too often."
Yvonne Fitzroy, *Courts and Camps of India*, 1926

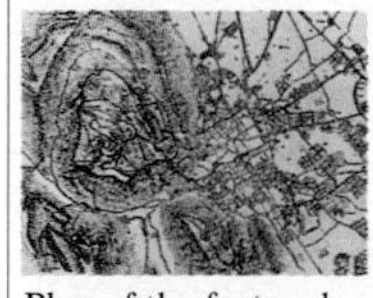

Plan of the fort and city.

HISTORY

Alwar, paradoxically, was both the oldest and newest of all the Rajput kingdoms. On the one hand, it traced its traditions back to the kingdom of Viratnagar that flourished here around 1500 BC. On the other, it was officially created – carved out of the Maratha territories – by the British as late as the 1770's. The rulers of Alwar were distantly related to the Kachhawaha dynasty of Jaipur and, until the mid-18th century, were merely the chieftains of two villages in Jaipur state. But, by skillfully aligning themselves with the right party at the right time – the Jats of Bharatpur, the Kachhawahas, the Mughals and, finally, the East India Company – they rapidly jockeyed themselves into a position of political consequence.

THE MAHARAJAS OF ALWAR. As a result of their relatively junior status, perhaps, the maharajas of Alwar conducted themselves with great ostentation: their palaces were the most ornate, their pageantry the most spectacular, and their tiger *shikars* the most elaborately organized. They even affected the title of Sawai, "The One-and-a-Quarter", following their grander cousins from Jaipur. It was this innate desire on their part to outshine their fellow princes that made Alwar the picturesque place it is today, with its splendid palaces. But since Alwar was a poorer state than many others, the maharajas also made themselves fairly unpopular with their subjects in the process. Alwar and its surrounding areas are one of the most interesting and undiscovered parts of Rajasthan. And one of the things that contributes toward making it so are the tales of Maharaja Jai Singh (reigned 1892–1937), its brilliant but weird ruler in the early part of this century.

Street scene, Alwar.

"The conical-shaped mountains of Ulwur, crowned with battlements..., leaving only a narrow strip of land crowded with fairy-like palaces and temples."

Louis Rousselet, India and its Native Princes, 1878

ALWAR TODAY

The town of Alwar lies at the point where the Aravalli hills of Rajasthan flare up one final time before subsiding into the plains of northern India. A significant part of the town was built between these craggy hills by Raja Banai Singh (reigned 1815–57), an esthete and builder of renown. In medieval times, Alwar was a town of great strategic importance because of its commanding position on the southern approach to Delhi. Today, however, it is a modest little trading center for the gram, barley and wheat grown in this region. It has a few industries, including textiles and glass-bangle making, but what is quite amazing here is the craft of double-sided dyeing, practiced by a handful of Alwar artisans: they are able to dye one side of a sari in one color and the other side in a totally different color.

OLD MONUMENTS. The layout of the town clearly reflects its turbulent history. One side of the town was protected by the steep, rocky hills, topped by the fort, Bala Qila; the other three sides were guarded by strongly fortified walls and, in addition, a deep moat, the latter being a rare feature in Rajasthan. Alwar has some fine old monuments, chief among them being the sumptuous Banai Vilas palace complex and the rugged Bala Qila Fort, with its eagle's eye view of the surrounding plains. But in addition to these, there are various other sights, including the splendid cenotaph of Raja Bakhtawar Singh; the imposing, domed, 17th-century mausoleum of Fateh Jung; the graceful, old, pink sandstone railway station; and various palaces built by the maharajas of Alwar.

PRINCE "CHARMING"
Maharaja Jai Singh of Alwar was one of the most fascinating princes of his time. He was brilliant, urbane, erudite, always gorgeously dressed, and was gifted with a magnetic personality. However, there was a dark side to him, and he was described by someone who knew him well as "sinister beyond belief". He was known to be an eccentric and a sadist, and was rumored to practice black magic. He was finally deposed by the British when, unhappy with one of his polo ponies after a match, he doused it with petrol and set fire to it.

Seal of Alwar State.

SHAKESPEARE WALLAH
One of the more unusual moments in the history of the City Palace occurred when it was used for the shooting of Merchant and Ivory's *Shakespeare Wallah*. The "Anthony and Cleopatra" scene was shot in a courtyard of Zenana Mahal, with the actors appearing out of its cupolaed pavilions and trellised balconies.

CAR FANATIC
Maharaja Jai Singh was apparently very fond of blue Bugattis, which he bought in threes. When he tired of the cars, it is said that, in his own eccentric fashion, he had them buried in the hillsides around Alwar, where, presumably, their remains still lie.

CITY PALACE ★

The City Palace ("Vinay Vilas", as it is officially called) (left) was built in 1793 by Raja Bakhtawar Singh at the foot of a rugged, towering hill and was added to over the centuries by his successors. The palace is a marriage of Rajput and Mughal styles – an almost baroque profusion of arches, balconies, pavilions and porticos, with this preference for *bangaldar* roofs that are characteristic of Mughal and Rajput architecture. Once, this palace was part of the maharajas' ornate lifestyle and housed, among other things, a drinking cup cut out of a single emerald in its treasury and a mammoth, double-storied, four-elephant carriage in its stables. Today, however, the palace has been converted into the district's collectorate, and its halls and chambers have been turned into government offices.

CENTRAL COURTYARD. The central courtyard of the palace (below) is impressive, with its graceful marble pavilions set on lotus-flower bases, its inner walls lined with canopied balconies and its dramatic marble checkerboard floor. Once dancing girls performed here by moonlight, but today it is often the venue for rowdy teenagers' cricket matches.

DURBAR HALL. Beyond the marble pavilions lies the splendid, old *durbar* hall, its walls and ceilings richly covered with gilded arabesques still remarkably fresh. In an antechamber beyond is an exquisite frieze of miniature paintings, sealed under glass and set in gilt, running along the wall. Permission to see this section, however, has to be obtained from the maharaja, who now lives in Delhi.

RANI MOOSI CHHATRI. Behind the palace lies the old temple tank and the cenotaph of Raja Bakhtawar Singh and Rani Moosi, who performed *sati*. It is a superb example of early 19th-century Rajput architecture, with its graceful brown Karauli

A view of the City Palace.

Miniature paintings from the Alwar school (below).

sandstone structure and its nine white marble canopies. Its style is completely different from those of other cenotaphs in the rest of Rajasthan. Beneath the dome you can see interesting frescos of scenes from the epics *Ramayana* and *Mahabharata*.

THE MUSEUM. The palace museum has a wonderful collection of exhibits, reflecting the eclectic tastes – and the personal wealth – of the maharajas of Alwar. There are some excellent manuscripts here, including an illustrated *Mahabharata*, on a 200-foot-long scroll, made from a single length of paper, with writing so tiny it must be read with a magnifying glass. Other prize pieces here are illustrated manuscripts of *Gulistan*, *Shah Nama*, and on Emperor Babur's life. There are also some fine *Ragamala* paintings and miniatures from the Alwar, Bundi, and Mughal schools. (Don't miss the miniature of the incarnations of Vishnu.) In the armory section you will find several historic swords, including those belonging to Sultan Mohammad Ghori, as well as the Mughal emperors Akbar and Aurangzeb. You will also find a fascinating collection of armor (including a suit of crocodile leather armor) and the usual strange Rajput weapons, such as a *nagphas*, a carpet-beater shaped weapon ingeniously designed for strangling the enemy. There are various other heirlooms from the maharajas' collection, from perfumed sandalwood fly-whisks to a solid silver dining table (with *trompe-l'œil* waves shimmering across it for good measure). One thing that is *not* here, however, is Maharaja Jai Singh's favorite car: a gold Lanchester, shaped in the form of the King of England's coronation carriage, but without the horses!

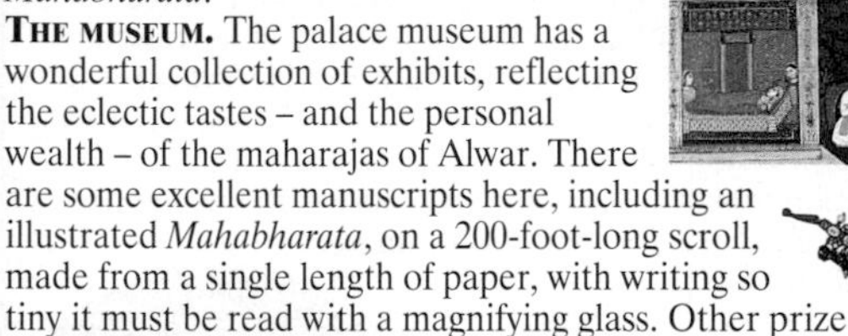

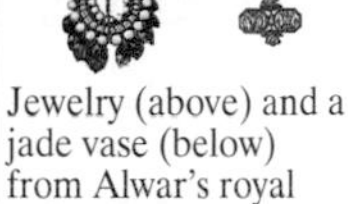

Jewelry (above) and a jade vase (below) from Alwar's royal collection.

This miniature painting shows the presentation of *Gulistan* to Maharaja Vinay Singh of Alwar. *Gulistan* is the most valued manuscript in the Alwar Museum.

Remains of Moti Doongri Palace.

Bala Qila ramparts.

Interior of Nikumbh Mahal Palace (center).

MILITARY BACKING
Bala Qila and Rajgarh Fort were held by the great founder of Alwar, Raja Pratap Singh (above). Originally a nobleman of the Jaipur court, he achieved great fame after an astrologer, seeing the rings in his eyes, predicted, "Take your armies wherever you will, victory will always be yours."

MOTI DOONGRI

Visiting Moti Doongri ("Pearl Hill") is a bizarre experience. All that now exists is a massive fortified wall, with a flat, empty space at the crest of the hill. The elegant hundred-roomed palace that stood here was dynamited out of existence by Maharaja Jai Singh. The reason remains a mystery. Was he looking for buried treasure here, as some people say? Was it in grief at the suicide of his favorite wife? Was it to destroy the tomb of a *fakir* nearby? Or was it merely his eccentricity? Nobody knows. The fact is that the demolition took two years and cost more than the building of the palace itself. Jai Singh possibly wanted to build another palace here.

BALA QILA ★

Towering on a craggy hill that dominates the town is Bala Qila ("Young Fort"). Built on the foundations of an ancient mud fort constructed in AD 928 by the Nikumbh Rajputs, it has had a turbulent history and was successively occupied by the warring Mughals, Pathans and Jats before finally being captured by Raja Pratap Singh in 1775. Bala Qila is accessible only by jeep (with special permission from the Superintendent of Police, for there is a police wireless station located in its citadel today). As you drive up the steep slope you can see the amazing fortifications that run all the way along the hill, often at crazy, seemingly impossible, angles. Passing through a series of massive gates, you finally enter Nikumbh Mahal Palace at the top. Built in the early 19th century, it has graceful *bangaldar* eaves, carved marble columns and delicate latticed balconies opening onto a central courtyard (where the police wireless station is now incongruously sited). Inside the *baradari* (pavilion), there are some beautiful gilded frescos on the walls and ceilings (above). And outside, beneath the canopies surrounding the courtyard, are traces of other delicately painted panels. From here there is a stunning view of the surrounding countryside, and you can also see the miles of ramparts that enclose the fort: a feat of military engineering, sometimes running vertically up the hill, and provided with literally thousands of steps

Frescos in Bala Qila.

built for the sentries who patrolled its top. You can also see, on a nearby ridge, the palace of the Mughal prince Salim, later Emperor Jahangir, who was exiled here for three years for trying to assassinate Abu'l Fazal, one of the celebrated "Nine Gems" of his father Akbar's court.

Painting of Akbar and Abu'l Fazal in court.

PAPER-THIN POTS
Alwar is known for its delicate *kagazi*, or literally "paper-thin", pots. Crafted from roots, these unique pots have beautiful patterns carved into their delicate double walls.

VIJAY MANDIR

Vijay Mandir, a sprawling, cupolaed palace with 105 rooms and a beautifully laid out garden, lies 6 miles outside Alwar. Reflected picturesquely in the waters of Vijay Sagar Lake, it is said to have been designed along the lines of a ship. Like all the ventures of its builder, the sinister and dazzling Maharaja Jai Singh, it has a curious history. The Maharaja had earlier commissioned another lovely Italianate palace, Yeshwant Niwas. When it was completed, he promptly decided he didn't like it. He never lived in it and immediately began work on Vijay Mandir instead. You need permission from the present Maharaja of Alwar to see this palace, but it is worth viewing from the outside anyway.

RAJGARH

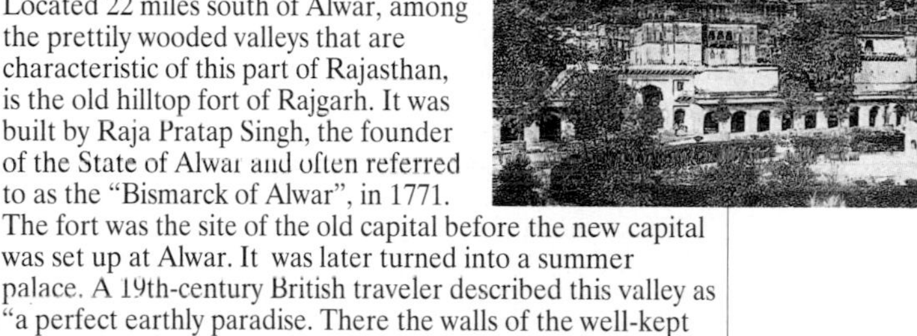

Located 22 miles south of Alwar, among the prettily wooded valleys that are characteristic of this part of Rajasthan, is the old hilltop fort of Rajgarh. It was built by Raja Pratap Singh, the founder of the State of Alwar and often referred to as the "Bismarck of Alwar", in 1771. The fort was the site of the old capital before the new capital was set up at Alwar. It was later turned into a summer palace. A 19th-century British traveler described this valley as "a perfect earthly paradise. There the walls of the well-kept fort of Rajgarh are picturesquely perched on a hill which rises out of a green and fertile tree embowered valley." Today the fort is somewhat dilapidated, but still worth visiting, with its curious fading frescos, its old Sheesh Mahal and its tales of secret passages. (Peep into the old toilets with their quaint disposal system!) At the bottom of the hill is a town with narrow alleyways and old *havelis* set amid the citrus groves. The entire surrounding region is dotted with the ruins of old hill forts, standing like silent sentinels.

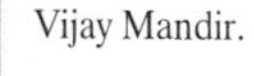

Vijay Mandir.

Siliserh Palace.

SILISERH

En route to Sariska, 8 miles southwest of Alwar, is the water palace of Siliserh and a pretty lake ringed by low, wooded hills. There is a romantic legend about this palace. Once, a young raja of Alwar was out riding when he heard a beautiful village maiden singing. He immediately fell in love with her. She seemed to reciprocate his feelings, but her brothers suddenly arrived on the scene and, infuriated at what they saw to be an insult to their sister's honor, were about to kill the raja. The raja then revealed his identity and promised to marry the girl. He built this palace for her so that she could look out at her old village across the lake's waters. The palace is now a rather shabby hotel, but it's worth stopping here briefly, sitting on the lovely terrace, and watching the cormorants diving for fish in the waters of the lake.

SARISKA ★

HUNTING STRATEGY
The eccentric Maharaja Jai Singh's tiger hunts in the Sariska forest were perhaps the most elaborate in India. He would combine these hunts with the military exercises of the Alwar army, using whole battalions of his infantry to drive the tigers toward the *shikaris*. He had superb hunting elephants, whom he spent years training, and he also took pride in his prowess in the highly dangerous sport of hunting wild boar on foot with a knife.

SARISKA TIGER RESERVE. This game sanctuary, 20 miles southwest of Alwar, was once the personal hunting ground of the maharajas of Alwar. It became a sanctuary in 1955 and was taken up under Project Tiger in 1979. It covers an area of 320 square miles (with a core area of 192 square miles). The forested hills of Sariska are among the best places to view tigers in India. There is a tiger population of approximately thirty here. Unlike other sanctuaries, the tigers here can sometimes be sighted by day. These daytime sightings are on the increase, with the tigers gradually becoming more confident with human beings around. The best time of the year to see the tigers is during the summer months, when they come out to the water-holes to drink and when there is less jungle foliage to provide them with cover. Other animals here are panthers (which tend not to overlap in the same areas with tigers), jungle cats, and caracals. In addition, there are the *nilgai, chital, sambar*, wild boar, and porcupine. The reserve is also rich in birds, including gray partridge, quail, sandgrouse, and white-breasted kingfisher. The best way to see the animals is to drive through the reserve either in the early morning or in the late

Kankwari Fort.

evening. While there are paved roads within the reserve, you can only explore the reserve in one of the large shared jeeps run by the Tourist Office, which follow fixed routes into the interiors of the forest. In the core areas, especially, you can see from the lovely forests what much of the Indian countryside must have looked like, right up to the first half of this century. Also, it is a unique experience to visit the remote little villages in the outer areas of the reserve to see how the way of life, totally untouched by outside influences, remains virtually the same as it has been for centuries. The villagers still live, for instance, with the daily threat of their cattle being carried away by leopards!

Sariska Palace. Set inside the Sariska Tiger Reserve, this was actually Maharaja Jai Singh's hunting lodge, where he would bring the guests whom he particularly wanted to impress. It has beautiful, sprawling lawns and contains some of the original antique furniture, but mercifully the Maharaja's tiger-skin patterned wall paper has been taken down. There are also some very interesting old photographs of the royal *shikar* parties of the 1920's here. (Incidentally, one of the Maharaja's eccentricities was that, being an ultra-orthodox Hindu, he always wore silk gloves to avoid touching either cow-hide or "untouchable" foreigners. It is interesting to note from these photographs that these gloves were not taken off, even when he was out hunting!)

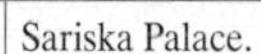

Sariska Palace.

Kankwari Fort. Within Sariska Tiger Reserve, 12 miles from the gate, lies Kankwari Fort. It is a superb example of a *vanadurg,* or jungle-fort, as described in the ancient Indian texts. Even today it is so inaccessible, deep in the tiger-infested forests (and approachable only by jeep), that one can only wonder at how it was built, back in the 17th century, and how it was supplied. It was here, apparently, that the heir to the Mughal throne, Prince Dara Shukoh, was held captive by his usurper brother, Aurangzeb, after the fateful Battle of Deorai, near Ajmer, in 1659. The fort is still impressive, though the interiors are overgrown with weeds. In the citadel is a fine old painted *baradari*, now in ruins.

Neelkanth

Beyond the Kankwari Fort, 20 miles from the Sariska Reserve's gate, and approachable only by jeep, lies the ruined ancient temple town of Neelkanth. Once there were over eighty beautifully carved temples here, which, some say, date back as early as the 6th to 9th centuries. However, the town was abandoned, and the temples are now covered by forest. It was only in the 1950's that the town was rediscovered (local villagers were using the old sculpted pillars and statues to build their huts) and excavations began. Today perhaps just a quarter of the temples have been excavated. Neelkantheshwar Temple is still in use, but what is really interesting is the superb pink sandstone monolith of the Jain *tirthankara*, Parshvanath, in Naugaza Temple. There are several other little ruined temples dotting the landscape.

Access to water
Kankwari Fort has an unusual feature: a fortified double wall projects out of its ramparts and runs down to the lake at the bottom of the hill to provide the garrison with access to the water supply even in times of siege. The double wall is narrow and runs zig-zag, so that it was easy to defend.

Sacred antelope
The *nilgai*, the largest of all Asian antelopes, is a singularly fortunate animal. It has somehow acquired the name "*gai*", which means "cow", and by virtue of its name, is sacred to Hindus. In addition, it has the prefix "*nil*", which means "blue", and is therefore associated by some with the blue-complexioned deity, Lord Krishna. This makes it doubly sacred: it cannot be killed, despite the damage it often causes to crops.

The private and privileged nature of the royal hunts of the past resulted paradoxically in the careful nurturing of forests to ensure the supply of regular sport, and many of today's national parks, such as Ranthambhor, were exclusive royal shooting preserves ■ *24*. Devastation for the tiger in India came post-Independence, when it was caught in the cross-fire between the *shikar* (hunt), trade in ingredients for traditional medicine, and widespread habitat destruction.

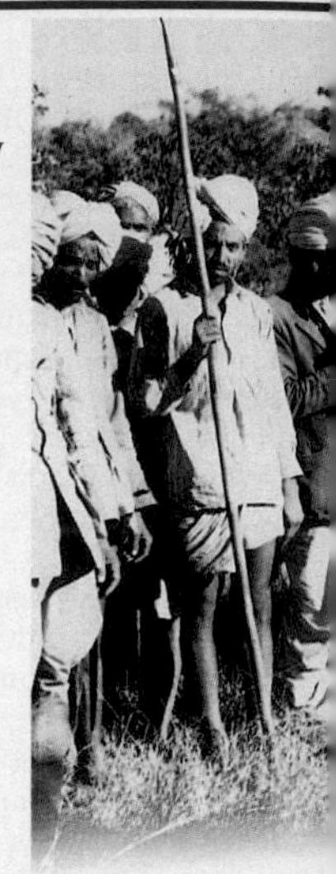

SHIKAR GUESTS
The British were the royal *shikar* guests of the maharajas, alongside fellow princes. Hunting was an exclusive privilege conferred by the maharajas.

TIGER TRADE
The destruction of the tiger's habitat, its prey species, and the species itself for skins, trophies, and bones threatens the tiger population. Whereas tiger skins were much in demand earlier, the trade has been overtaken by the demand for bones and other parts, including fat and whiskers, in oriental medicine, for ailments such as arthritis and as potency charms.

PROJECT TIGER
Project Tiger was launched in 1973 to save the species. Ranthambhor and Sariska, the past hunting reserves of the maharajas of Jaipur and Alwar respectively, are among the twenty tiger reserves in India listed under Project Tiger ▲ *304*.

ENDANGERED SPECIES
A widely accepted estimation of the tiger population in India at the turn of the century is 40,000. By 1972 this figure had dropped to an all-time low of 2000. The tiger count in India today is officially in the region of 4000, with experts placing it far below official estimates.

Gate of Sariska Tiger Reserve.

Shikars
Rajasthan was once the home of the tigers. The maharajas preserved the species and its habitats as royal reserves for *shikar* parties. The more elaborate hunting methods involved many men, mounts, and *machans* (platforms), as well as beaters and baits.

Hunting strategy
A standard hunting practice was to surround a forest with hundreds of beaters and a line of elephants in order to bring the tiger to a point where the hunter waited for a sure shot.

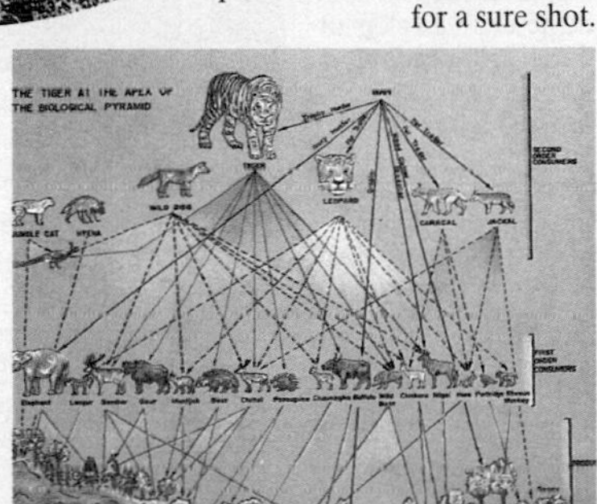

Fight for survival
The tiger is not a doomed species in the evolutionary process. It is highly adaptive to climate, terrain, and even food. In procuring its prey, the tiger adheres to the law that the intake of energy should exceed the output of labor.

Hunting portraits
The Maharaja of Kota hunting from a boat in the Chambal Valley (right). Royal hunts were a popular subject for court artists ● *65*.

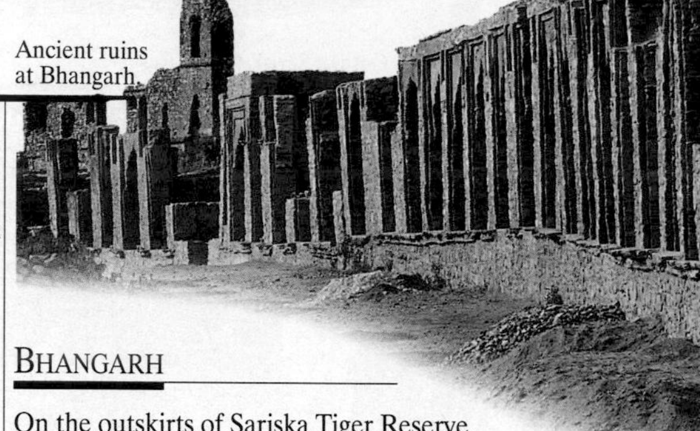
Ancient ruins at Bhangarh.

NEEMRANA – A LABOUR OF LOVE
The story of Neemrana Palace, situated 40 miles northwest of Alwar and Rajasthan's closest palace to New Delhi, is a fascinating one. Built in 1464, it was abandoned by its rajas in 1947 and slowly fell into ruins. A few years ago, it was rediscovered by Aman Nath and Francis Wacziarg, from Delhi, both of them enthusiasts for old buildings, and they have since restored it, using local village craftsmen. Neemrana Palace has been turned into an elegant hotel. It has become a favorite retreat of Indian high society and the international jet set, who come for the calm and beauty of the location.

BHANGARH

On the outskirts of Sariska Tiger Reserve, 33 miles from its gate, lies the splendid, old, ruined town of Bhangarh – its crumbling pavilions, walls and temples silent in the wilderness, against the backdrop of the forested hills. Built in the early 17th century by Raja Madho Singh, the brother of Amber's celebrated Raja Man Singh I, this was once a city of ten thousand homes. The medieval bazaar, recently restored, is fascinating and evocative of the town's ancient prosperity. Beyond it, at the foot of the hills, lie the ruins of the old palace and Someshwar Temple, with its fine carvings and its tank (where the villagers still come to bathe). Nearby is the temple of Gopinath (left), with its carved pillars and corbeled dome. Not far away is another ruined monument, now indelicately labeled "Randiyon ka Mahal" ("Palace of the Prostitute"). Overlooking all of this is a cupola on the hill, from where, if you are adventurous, you can get a great view of the superb landscape. According to legend, the town was cursed by an evil magician and had to be abandoned. The curse is still believed to operate and the local villagers tread warily.

BAIRAT

The village of Bairat, 40 miles southwest of Alwar, has a remarkably rich history, boasting monuments and legends from at least three different epochs. Here, on a low hill, are the ruins of a 3rd-century BC Buddhist *chaitya*, or chapel, the oldest freestanding structure anywhere in India. You can see the foundations of the circular building and the niches for the twenty-six octagonal wooden pillars that once supported it. Among the huge rock overhead are the remains of a monastery. Not far away is a rock edict of Emperor Ashoka, also from the 3rd century, indicating that this was an important town in that era. However, the history of Bairat goes back even further, to the time of the epic *Mahabharata,* and this is said to have been the site of the great city of Viratnagar, where the Pandava heroes, with their wife, Draupadi, spent the thirteenth year of their exile. Nothing remains of the ancient city, although archeological finds do indicate the area's great antiquity. Nearby is a little-known, neglected, but charming 16th-century *chhatri* where Emperor Akbar is said to have hunted and stayed overnight en route on his pilgrimage to Ajmer. (It is worth seeing for the elegant murals that adorn its chambers.)

EARLIEST KNOWN MURALS
The frescos at Bairat's Mughal hunting lodge are especially interesting: dating back to the early 17th century, they are probably the very earliest of their kind in Rajasthan and, directly or indirectly, a model for all the other later frescos in the region.

Shekhavati

180 Samode and Sikar
182 Nawalgarh to Baggar
184 Wall paintings
190 Ramgarh, Mehensar and Lachhmangarh

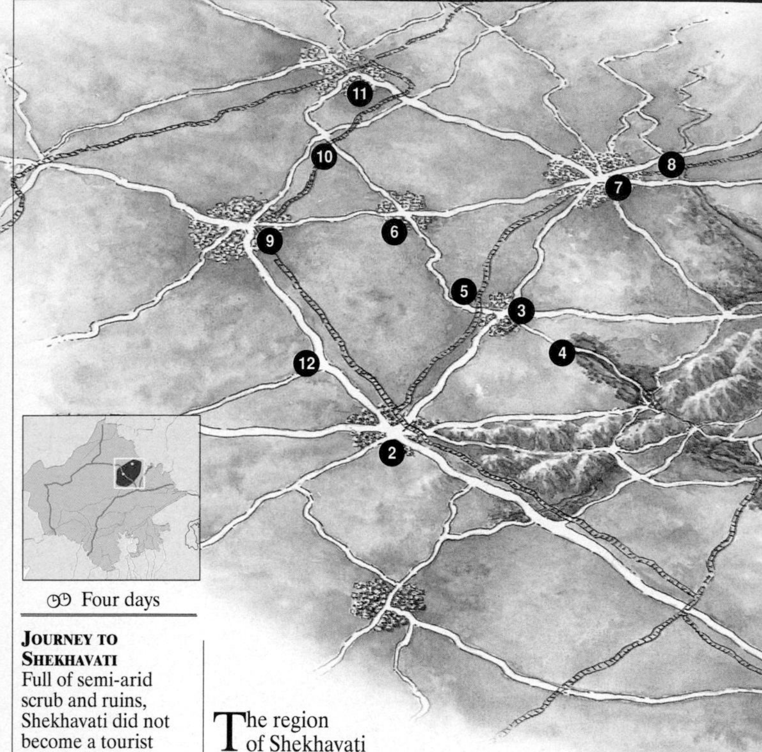

Four days

JOURNEY TO SHEKHAVATI
Full of semi-arid scrub and ruins, Shekhavati did not become a tourist destination until its attractions were publicized in *Rajasthan – The Painted Walls of Shekhavati*. The authors, Francis Wacziarg and Aman Nath, traveled extensively throughout the region before publishing their book in 1982. It sparked off new interest in the cultural heritage of the local people and the wealthy Marwari community, who still own the painted *havelis*.

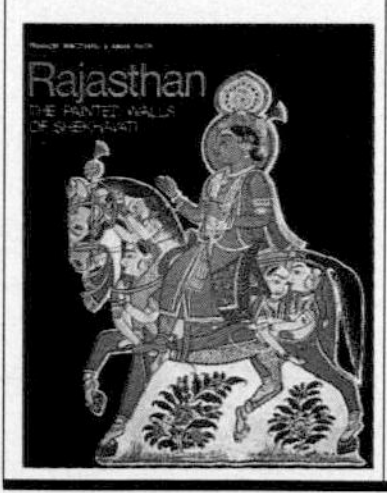

The region of Shekhavati ("Province of Shekha") was originally a part of the Amber-Jaipur kingdom. Its founder was Rao Shekha (reigned 1433–88) who made it independent till 1738 when it reverted back to Jaipur. His descendants ruled their small kingdoms as vassals of the maharajas of Jaipur till after India's independence in 1947 ● *39*.

HAVELIS OF THE MARWARIS

These mansions were built mainly between 1860 and 1900 by the *bania* (merchants) of Shekhavati who had ventured out to Calcutta and other emerging commercial centers of India, and had become famous under the name of Marwari. With their business success came a spirit of architectural one-upmanship, and each sought to outdo the other with the lavishness of his *haveli*. Gradually, the Marwaris and their families began to leave their *havelis* behind. Today the little towns of Shekhavati are strange ghost towns, packed with their splendid *havelis*, all of them empty, but for a lonely caretaker or two. The busy owners return for perhaps only a couple of days in the year for some family ceremony and then go back to Calcutta, Bombay, or wherever it is they are now settled.

SAMODE ★

En route to the region of Shekhavati, 24 miles from Jaipur, lies Samode, with its fairy-tale palace ● *41*. Samode Palace

"At present the tradition is rapidly degenerating....Houses are decorated with copies of pseudo-Gothic scrollwork...."

Herman Goetz, end of the 19th century

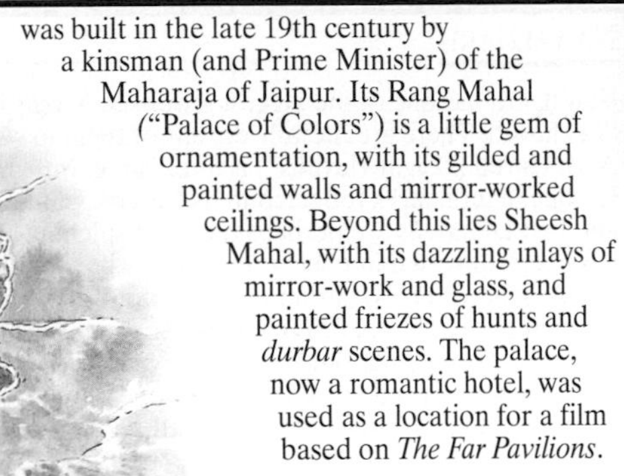

was built in the late 19th century by a kinsman (and Prime Minister) of the Maharaja of Jaipur. Its Rang Mahal ("Palace of Colors") is a little gem of ornamentation, with its gilded and painted walls and mirror-worked ceilings. Beyond this lies Sheesh Mahal, with its dazzling inlays of mirror-work and glass, and painted friezes of hunts and *durbar* scenes. The palace, now a romantic hotel, was used as a location for a film based on *The Far Pavilions*.

SIKAR

A former caravan stop, Sikar has become, together with Jhunjhunu, a main city in one of the two Shakhavati districts. Its unusual Biyani Haveli, with its blue painted frescos (below), adds a different palette to the Shekhavati frescos. It represented a new level of one-upmanship because blue was a color that was traditionally difficult to achieve on wet lime plaster – and was only made possible by the expensive, new synthetic dyes imported from Germany in the 1870's. The Hindu temples of Gopinath, Raghunath and Madan Mohan, too, have some interesting frescos. Sikar Fort, now in decay, is also worth a visit.

AGE-OLD MERCHANTS
The Marwari business community, which hails from Shekhavati, is an amazing sociological phenomenon. According to an American sociologist "it is estimated that more than half the assets in the modern sector of the Indian economy are controlled by the trading castes originating in the northern half of Rajasthan." And of these, a majority originate in just a dozen little towns of Shekhavati (including four out of India's eight largest business houses). They trace their ancestry back to the merchants who did business at this ancient meeting point of the camel caravans from the Middle East, China and India. As the old trading routes dwindled away in the late 18th century, the Marwari merchants moved to the new emerging commercial centers of British India, where their trading genius, honed over generations, made them enormously successful.

Poddar Haveli (above); cenotaph of Shardul Singh (below).

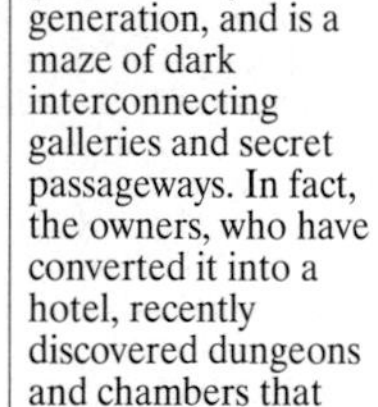

MYSTERIOUS FORT
The mysterious little desert fort at Mandawa was originally built in the 1750's. It was (in the manner of all Rajput forts) added to, generation by generation, and is a maze of dark interconnecting galleries and secret passageways. In fact, the owners, who have converted it into a hotel, recently discovered dungeons and chambers that they never knew existed.

Mandawa Castle.

NAWALGARH

Nawalgarh has one of the biggest groups of *havelis* in Shekhavati. There are literally dozens of them to wander into. Aath Haveli ("Eight Havelis") is interesting, with amusing European influences reflected in its frescos. Chhawchhariya and Poddar *havelis* are perhaps the most splendid. The latter has been converted into what must surely be the world's most picturesque school. Uttarian Haveli is notorious for its resident ghost. Here, even the telephone exchange has frescos that are worth seeing. But the *pièce de résistance* is Bala Qila Fort, whose frescoed kiosk is perhaps one of the finest examples of the art in all of Shekhavati.

PARASRAMPURA

It is worth driving out to Parasrampura from Nawalgarh, just to see the cenotaph of Sardul Singh, the eighth descendant of Rao Shekha, the founder of Shekhavati. On the ceiling of its cupola are some of the oldest frescos in the region, dating back to the mid-18th century, depicting scenes from the epics *Ramayana* and *Mahabharata*.

DUNLOD

Dunlod, off the road from Nawalgarh to Mandawa, is noted for its two impressive Goenka *havelis* and its painted Goenka *chhatri,* or cenotaphs. There is also a quaint fort here, almost Scottish in its design. Inside is an interesting Mughal-style *diwan khana,* or hall, with copies of Louis XIV furniture and old family portraits of the local *thakur*'s (chieftain's) family. The fort has now been converted into a hotel.

MANDAWA

One of the very earliest frescos in all of Shekhavati, dating back to the 1760's, is within Mandawa Castle. The castle is now a hotel of great charm and character. It was guarded in the past by a cannon and a wickedly spiked gate that served as a defense against elephant attacks. Here, in the old desert tradition, time is still kept by the striking of a gong every hour (right). Chokhani, Saraf and Goenka *havelis* in Mandawa are also worth seeing. By the way, do not miss the way the artist of Goenka Haveli has skillfully integrated the mansion's windows into the design. There are also some frescos influenced by the British East India Company style of art at the Madanlal and Newatia *havelis*. In the former, an Englishman rides a bicycle, but the artist, obviously never having seen one of these contraptions, has got its details delightfully wrong. In the latter, you can see the Wright Brothers in a strange-looking flying machine

Murals from a *haveli* in Mandawa.

with only one wing, and one of the poor brothers left suspended in mid-air.

Jhunjhunu

Jhunjhunu is known for its Chhe Haveli ("Six Havelis") complex. Tibdiwala and Modi *havelis* are particularly interesting, while Khatri Haveli is unusually elegant in its artistic approach. Rani Sati Temple is also worth seeing for its riotously colorful frescos and kitschy cement sculptures.

Fatehpur

Fatehpur has one of the largest groups of *havelis* in this region. Devra, Singhania (bottom picture), and Goenka *havelis* are especially worth visiting. Devra Haveli has a superbly painted ceiling, with a series of medallioned portraits: everybody from a Mughal emperor to an English gentleman with a dog! Goenka Haveli has an intricately painted chamber. Don't miss the curious painting here of Lord Krishna riding an elephant which is actually composed of eight maidens. Two other quirky *havelis* were built later, perhaps in the 1920's, by the Jalan and the Bhartia families. The latter has some amusingly kitsch mirror-work and Japanese tiles.

Baggar

Known for a large white gate built to honor the Maharaja of Jaipur's visit in 1928, Baggar is the only painted town of Shekhavati where you can stay in a traditional Marwari home. Piramal Haveli (above) serves excellent vegetarian cuisine and is a charming eight-roomed hotel, built in the colonial Rajasthani style. When driving from Delhi, Baggar is the gateway to Shekhavati.

Portraits of the maharajas of Jaipur, Sawai Ram Singh II (reigned 1835–80) and Sawai Madho Singh II (reigned 1880–1927) ● *137*, on the walls at Dunlod Fort. Except between 1471 and 1738, the Shekhavati chieftains served under Jaipur.

SWANKY DUDES
Two Englishmen in hats and shoes pose with their walking sticks on a mid-19th century *haveli* façade.

Stylistically the frescos of Shekhavati, which date between 1750 and 1930, follow a folk-Mughal or sub-imperial beginning, through a provincial Jaipur school development into the Company School eclecticism with British influences. The style decays into a kitsch, calendar art form made popular with the arrival of the printing press in India. The technique of painting began with the more tedious fresco *buono* painted on wet plaster, ending with the simpler fresco *secco* where paint is applied on dry lime-faced walls.

RAMA AND HANUMAN
An early fresco in natural pigments shows Rama and his brother helped by the monkey god Hanuman and his army, en route to Sri Lanka to battle the demon-king Ravana.

HINDU MYTHOLOGY
Mythological scenes of the popular god Krishna show him with his beloved Radha (above), on a swing with the cowherd girls who were eternally and metaphorically charmed by his flute (opposite, top), and with royal devotees (right, above).

Since the migrant merchants of Shekhavati amassed fortunes which were largely disproportionate with the times, besides building their elaborate *havelis* and cenotaphs, each erected at least five things to be well remembered by posterity: a temple, a well or reservoir, a school, a shelter for abandoned cows, and a garden, which was indeed a luxury in the desert. Yet they remained socially modest, seldom commissioning a portrait of themselves. The Rajputs who were the warrior rulers of this region, however, followed the example of the imperial rulers of Delhi. They commissioned grand portraits of themselves with royal attributes such as horses and arms, as well as peacetime versions with flowers.

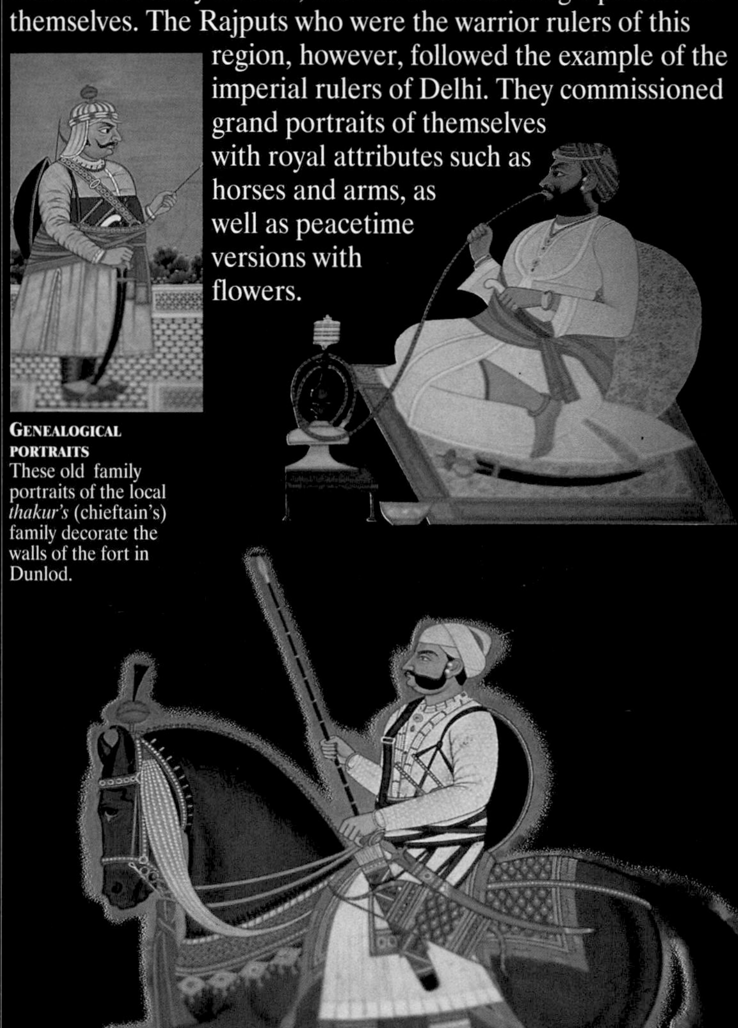

GENEALOGICAL PORTRAITS
These old family portraits of the local *thakur's* (chieftain's) family decorate the walls of the fort in Dunlod.

Royal visit
George V and Queen Mary (above), who sailed to India in 1911 for the Delhi *durbar* – among the most ostentatious celebrations of this century – are popularly represented in lithographs and frescos.

In the late 19th century it became fashionable to introduce European elements into the frescos. Thus Hindu deities were replaced by angels, and elephants were replaced by automobiles and airplanes. Gentlemen on bicycles and ladies with low necklines began to make an appearance. The inspiration for these was all second-hand, from European lithographs and photographs, which is why so many of the details, particularly of mechanical objects, are amusingly incorrect.

Ladies in a carriage
European ladies driven in a carriage car which does not appear to have an engine.

WEDDING
The bridesmaid seems to fall off her chair in this fresco which is obviously copied from a wedding photograph.

MERCENARIES
Foreign mercenaries with European headgear often helped decide the fate of battles in the early 19th century. An Irishman George Thomas was one such mercenary famous in Shekhavati.

FLYING KRISHNA
Lord Krishna, the divine charioteer in the epic battle of the *Mahabharata*, depicted in a flying car ▲ *45*.

FAMED FRESCOS
The pigments used in Shekhavati were natural ores: saffron for the oranges, a kind of terracotta for the reds, antimony for the black and indigo for the blues. The brilliant yellows were derived from the urine of cows that had been fed solely on a diet of mango leaves! The frescos in Soné Chandi ki Haveli are lavishly embellished with gilt.

RAMGARH

Two *havelis,* belonging to the Poddar and Ruia families respectively, are worth seeing. There are more delightful paintings here of new-fangled mechanical devices that the artists had obviously never actually seen, like a car whose wheels are shaped like flowers. Also, do take a look at the local *chhatris* or cenotaphs, particularly the frescos around their entrance. The scenes from the *Ramayana* in Poddar Haveli are worth noticing. There is also an interesting old mud fort here, supposed to have once been a stronghold of local dacoits.

MAHENSAR

Mahensar is one of the less visited towns of Shekhavati, perhaps, but definitely one of the most rewarding. Soné Chandi ki Haveli ("Mansion of Gold and Silver") (left), which belonged to the Poddar family of jewelers, has the finest frescos in Shekhavati, bar none. The artists are said to have been the descendants of those who painted the spectacular Anup Mahal in Bikaner, and the similarity is evident. Don't miss the frieze of the battle scene, as delicate as a miniature painting.

LACHHMANGARH

The sprawling Char Chowki Haveli ("Haveli of the Four Courtyards"), belonging to the Ganeriwala family, is arguably the grandest in Shekhavati. Rathi Haveli is also interesting. Take a look, for instance, at the fresco of the *memsahib* playing a gramophone (left). The walk from Murlimanohar Temple to Chokhani Haveli is interesting. Don't miss the quaint painting in one of the *havelis* of a European incongruously holding up an umbrella at a ceremonial function and labeled, perhaps unnecessarily, "Foreigner". There is also an interesting fort in Lachhmangarh, perched on a hill, with a good view of the town and an unusual aerial view of the great Char Chowki Haveli.

ANTIQUES
Ramgarh is one of the best places in Shekhavati to buy antiques and replicas, especially ornate Rajasthani woodwork, although the prices aren't necessarily cheap.

Lachhmangarh Fort.

The northwest

192 Bikaner
200 Weaponry
204 Bikaner Camel Corps
206 Around Bikaner
208 Jaisalmer
216 Around Jaisalmer
220 Jodhpur
232 Around Jodhpur
234 Mahavira Temple
236 Folk art

1. Bikaner
2. Deshnoke
3. Gajner
4. Kolayat
5. Nagaur
6. Khimsar
7. Jodhpur
8. Mandore
9. Osiyan
10. Pokharan
11. Jaisalmer
12. Samm
13. Khurri
14. Lodurva
15. Akal Fossils P[ark]
16. Barmer

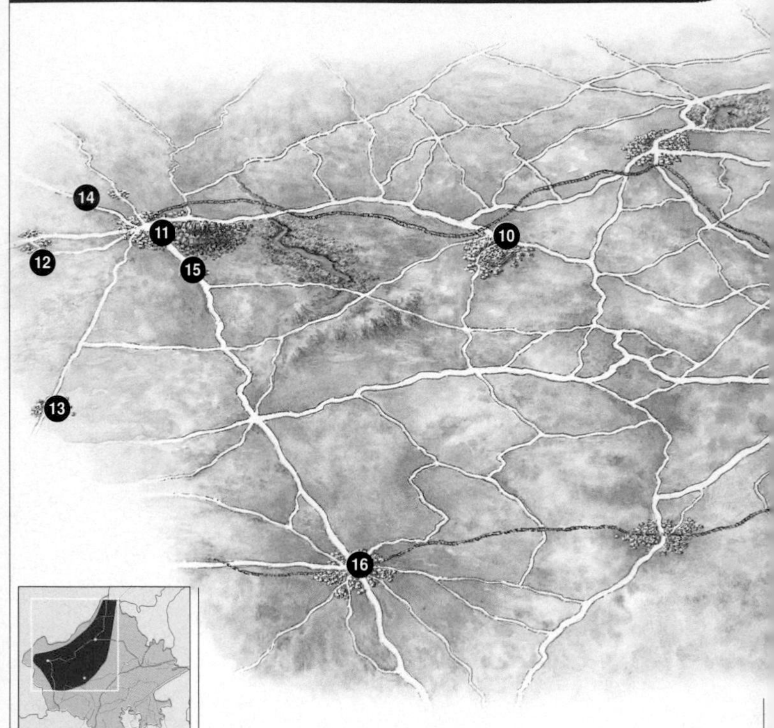

◷ Twelve days

WRITING ABOUT THE DESERT
Colonel Tod wrote in 1829 that if the North African desert could be likened to a leopard's hide, spotted with oases, the Marusthali Desert was more like "that of the tiger, of which the long dark stripes would indicate the expansive belts of sand, elevated upon a plain only slightly less sandy."

Marwar, or Marusthali, literally means the "Land of the Dead." It broadly comprises the harsh desert region of western Rajasthan, stretching from Bikaner in the north, down to the hills of Mewar in the south. It is an especially interesting part of Rajasthan; its relative remoteness tends to attract the genuine traveler keen to explore areas a little off the beaten track. There are three main destinations around Marwar – Bikaner, Jaisalmer and Jodhpur. From Bikaner you can drive out to Gajner, Deshnoke, or the archeological ruins of Kalibangan. From Jaisalmer, you can go on a camel safari, visit the Desert National Park or make side trips to Samm, Khurri, and Barmer. From Jodhpur you can take an excursion to the temples of Osiyan or to Khimsar and Nagaur.

HISTORY

Bikaner was founded in the 15th century by Rao Bika, the son of the Rathor Raja of Marwar (or Jodhpur) ● *34*. Taking offence at a stray comment that his father made, he left with a small band of horsemen to set up his own kingdom in the deserts of the north. Spurred on by the blessing of a great female mystic, Karni Mata, whom he had met along the way and who had predicted that his fame and glory would some day exceed that of his father, Rao Bika fought the local desert clans for thirty years, and ultimately carved

The desert in Bikaner.

"Out of the silken darkness of a desert dawn emerged the dream of Bikaner."

Traditional ballad

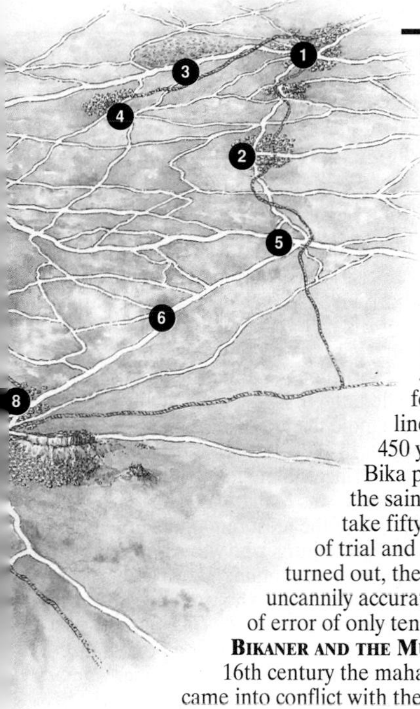

1
3
4
2
5
6
8

out a kingdom approximately the size of England. Not all the prophecies made about him were entirely optimistic, though. Another saint whom Rao Bika met, Jambhoji, foretold that his line would rule for 450 years. When Rao Bika protested at this, the saint said, "All right, take fifty years more, but of trial and tribulation." As it turned out, the prediction was uncannily accurate, with a margin of error of only ten years.

BIKANER AND THE MUGHALS. In the 16th century the maharajas of Bikaner came into conflict with the Mughal emperors in Delhi, who were in the process of setting up their new empire in Hindustan. Being located closer to Delhi, Bikaner spent much more time fighting the Mughals than other desert kingdoms, such as Jaisalmer or Jodhpur. With the harsh desert terrain on their side, the Bikaner armies soundly defeated the Mughals in their early encounters. By the late 16th century, however, they had been won over by the diplomacy of Emperor Akbar. As a result, several of Bikaner's rulers commanded the Mughal armies, fighting with distinction from Gujarat in the west to the Deccan in the south. One great ruler, Raja Prithviraj Singh, a poet and warrior, in fact, became one of the celebrated "Nine Gems" of Akbar's court. Bikaner, meanwhile, had become a flourishing town and an important trading post along the centuries-old caravan trails that connected India with the Middle East and China. As the town prospered, it became known for the handiwork of its gold and silversmiths, weavers, perfumiers and leather craftsmen, and grew into an important center for the arts and music. Bikaner's school of miniature paintings, which were a delicate fusion of the Rajput and Mughal styles ● *65*, acquired great fame.

BIKANER AND THE BRITISH. However, with the eclipse of the Mughals in the 18th century, Bikaner, along with the rest of Rajasthan, fell into a slow decline, although its desert barriers at least spared it the depredations that the Marathas were wreaking on its other Rajput neighbors. This situation continued until the treaty with the British in 1818, in which "perpetual friendship, alliance and a unity of interests" were pledged.

COAT-OF-ARMS
Bikaner's coat-of-arms depicts two tigers, which symbolize the bravery of the Rajputs, and a shield containing three sacred kites, associated with Karni Mata, the dynasty's patron goddess ● *55* ▲ *206*. The motto, which translates as "Hail, King of the Wastelands!", recalls an episode when the Raja of Bikaner agreed to spearhead a Rajput revolt against the Mughal Emperor Aurangzeb, provided the other rajas first accepted him as the overlord of the desert.

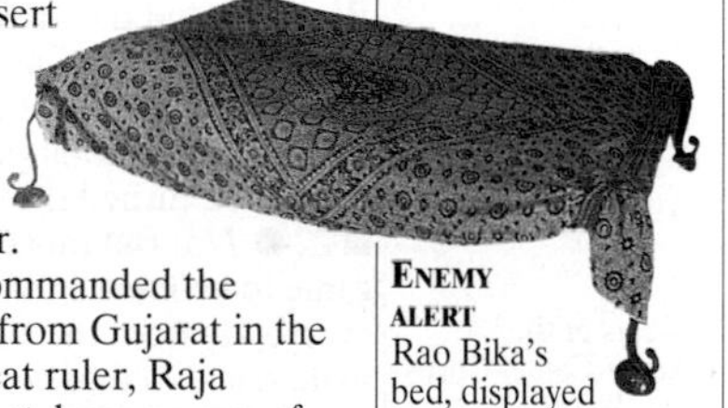

ENEMY ALERT
Rao Bika's bed, displayed in Phul Mahal within Junagarh Fort, has a strangely austere shape. The reason is that Rao Bika never forgot how his grandfather had been tied to his bed with his own turban and murdered. Hence his own bed was short, light and designed so that his feet projected well beyond its edge while he slept. The idea was that even if his enemies should ever tie him to the bed, he could still stand up and fight with it on his back!

VISIONARY RULER Maharaja Ganga Singh was a man of extraordinary vision and character. At the end of World War One he was one of the signatories to the Treaty of Versailles. He presciently objected to the terms, noting that any treaty that "imposed such a burden upon the vanquished foe could not be the harbinger of a lasting peace".

TURN OF FORTUNE. By the mid-19th century the years of internal strife and the financial and military pressures being put on Bikaner by its new allies, the British, had put the kingdom into debt. It became a shabby and backward province. But, curiously, it was Bikaner's famous camels that triggered off a process of economic and political recovery. The British were involved in fighting the Afghan War at the time and it was realized that the only "vehicles" that could deliver their supplies in that terrain were camels. The Maharaja of Bikaner cannily cashed in on this opportunity by supplying the British army with a steady stream of Bikaner's camels, long known for their hardiness and load-carrying capacity. This resulted in a turnaround in Bikaner's fortunes. A modern administrative system was soon installed, the first hospitals established, and a police force set up to handle the lawlessness and banditry that were becoming rampant. In 1886, this remote desert kingdom became the first Indian Princely State to introduce electricity.

MAHARAJA GANGA SINGH. It was Maharaja Ganga Singh (reigned 1898–1944), one of the most remarkable rulers India produced in the early 20th century, who was responsible for putting Bikaner in a position of prominence on the map of India ● *39*. Maharaja Ganga Singh, who was educated at the celebrated Mayo College in Ajmer ▲ *162* (like most of the other later Rajput maharajas), gave Bikaner a prominence far beyond its size. First, he created the famous Bikaner Camel Corps, or Ganga Risala, a flamboyant fighting force that he personally led, on behalf of the British, first to China to help put down the Boxer Rebellion in 1900, then to Somaliland to quell the Somali Uprising in 1903, and finally to Egypt during World War I ▲ *204*. (At the Suez Canal in 1915 the Ganga Risala routed the Turks in a daredevil camel cavalry charge.) Maharaja Ganga Singh also built up Bikaner's economy, promoting, among other things, the Ganga Canal, an ambitious irrigation project that was years ahead of its time, and which turned the deserts of Bikaner into rich farmland ■ *22* ● *115*. But most of all, perhaps, Maharaja Ganga Singh came to be known for his spectacular grouse shoots, to which everybody from the Viceroy downward, including fellow maharajas, vied to be invited. Maharaja Ganga Singh very

Officers of the Bikaner Camel Corps circa 1902.

"It appeared like an immense walled town with bastions, nor could we give credit to our guides when they talked of the siya kot ('castle in the sky')..."

Colonel Tod, *Annals and Antiquities of Rajasthan*, 1829

shrewdly treated these hunts as a diplomatic tool, using the opportunity to charm selected guests and win their support. His guests at the great shoots included the Prince of Wales, later King George V, and French President, George Clemenceau. Maharaja Ganga Singh later became something of an international political figure, going on to lead the Indian delegation to the League of Nations. In 1949 the kingdom became part of the new state of Rajasthan in independent India ▲ *39*.

BIKANER TODAY

Bikaner is still, at heart, a medieval, walled desert town. The thick crenelated walls encircling it are still there, studded with five huge gates that were once locked at night. Like Jaipur, it is also a "Pink City", in fact, perhaps even more so, as its impressive fort, palaces, mansions and public buildings are all carved from the rich pink-purple sandstone that is characteristic of this region. It has always been a surprisingly wealthy town because of its trade. An old saying talked of its "five famous treasures": its camels, wealthy merchants, rich candies, gold jewelry, and beautiful women. Bikaner was also, until the turn of the century, India's "Wild West" – plagued by bandit chieftains and robber barons. All that changed with the rule of Maharaja Ganga Singh, who created a modern administration and developed the kingdom's agricultural system and mineral industries. But the lingering flavor of the old, wild desert town is still there. Wander around the bazaars of Bikaner (near the walled town's old Kot Gate). Shops sell everything from camel-hair blankets to flamboyantly colored tie-and-dye fabrics ● *58*. As you wander, you're constantly jostled by supremely arrogant-looking Bikaneri camels and camel carts. The latter have now gone high-tech: they now have truck tires instead of the old creaking wooden wheels. Bikaner is known particularly for its excellent *durries* and carpets, its ornately decorated lacquer-work and its delicate, translucent hand-painted lampshades to quaint *mojri* slippers (made of goat or buffalo skin, and not camel skin as the vendors would have you believe), which, with wear, mold around the shape of your foot like a second skin (above). Bikaner is now an important military base. The surrounding region is no longer a desert wasteland, but thanks to the Ganga Canal and, later, Indira Gandhi Canal, one of the world's largest projects of its kind, it is now fertile farmland.

WATER POTS
With the scarcity of water in this desert area, water containers naturally assume a major importance. Bikaner is known for its graceful clay *kunjas*, traditionally shaped with narrow necks to prevent loss of water through evaporation.

A LEGACY OF THE PAST
The ancient sandalwood throne of the kings of Kannauj (the old dynasty from which Rao Bika was descended), is considered to be the oldest piece of furniture in India today, probably dating back to the fifth century AD. Along with a state umbrella, a diamond studded shield, war drums and an image of the family goddess, it was one of the dynasty's heirlooms, brought by Rao Bika from Jodhpur in 1486 ● *34*.

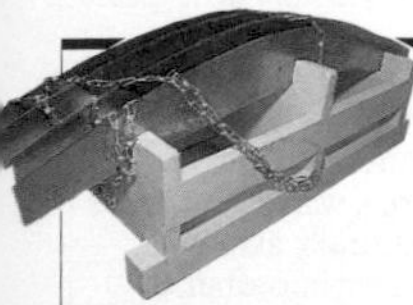

Miraculous feats
In Junagarh Fort, you can see curious platforms made of swords on which the professional magicians of Bikaner would dance. Lady Reading, the Viceroy's wife, wrote in 1922 of "a wizard who walked with bare feet on swords I could not touch, so sharp were their points...it was hopelessly uncanny, but wonderful and gorgeous."

Junagarh Fort

Junagarh Fort is one of the most interesting forts in Rajasthan. Its sumptuously decorated interiors are much better preserved than in almost any other in the region. Wandering through the halls of its palace complex, you can easily imagine what life must have been like in those medieval times. Built in 1588 by Raja Rai Singh (reigned 1571–1611), it is unusual in the sense that it was one of the few major forts of Rajasthan that was not built on a hilltop. Instead, it was built on the desert plains, perhaps using the very inconspicuousness of its location as a defense. Its rugged sandstone bastions and graceful pavilions and balconies are silhouetted against the sky. As you enter through the main gateway, Suraj Pol, you can see the twin statues of the fort's guardians, Jaimal and Patta, the warrior-heroes of Chittorgarh's defense. Beyond this lies a complex of splendid palaces, each one built by a different ruler over the centuries. The last portions were added on as recently as 1943.

Suraj Pol.

Karan Mahal. This lies in the second of the palace complex's courtyards. It is remarkable for its walls, which look like marble *pietra dura* inlaid with semi-precious stones but which actually turn out, on closer inspection, to be a superb example of gilded *arayish* ▲ 155 plaster-work.

Durga Niwas. Beyond Karan Mahal is Durga Niwas, a beautiful enclosure with superbly painted walls and a white marble pool. The pool was built to cool this part of the palace in summer. During the spring festival of Holi it would be filled with colored water, with which the maharajas and their ranis would riotously splash each other in the customary manner.

Lal Niwas. Nearby is Lal Niwas, the oldest part of the palace complex, dating back to 1595. It is notable for the richly painted stylized floral motifs in red and gold that cover its walls. Another notable feature is the revolutionary absence of columns to support the ceiling, which accounts for the narrowness of the hall. As you go upstairs, you come to Gaj Mandir and, right at the summit, the breezy Chhattar Niwas. Built in the 1880's,

Lal Niwas (top) and its red-and-gold frescos (bottom).

Chandra Mahal.

it has walls idiosyncrati-cally decorated with Dutch porcelain plates bearing old prints of "Oriental Field Sports".

Anup Mahal. One of the truly exceptional parts of Junagarh's palace complex is Anup Mahal. Built in 1669, it has a magnificent coronation room with ornately lacquered walls in red and gold and panels of dazzling colored glass inlay set over a throne. The marble columns are covered with delicate paint work, and the entire effect is simply breathtaking. Do not miss the small side chamber with its aquamarine blue walls, richly inlaid with gold leaf.

Chandra Mahal and Phul Mahal. Almost as impressive are Chandra Mahal ("Moon Palace") and the nearby Phul Mahal ("Flower Palace") built in the mid-18th century, with their superbly painted walls and elaborate mirror inlay work (below). A member of the Viceroy's party which visited Junagarh Fort in the 1920's wrote of the Maharaja's jewelry collection once housed here, "those of the Maharajah of Benares are splinters in comparison. Such pearls and emeralds, the latter in strings of about six chains and then knobs of uncut emeralds and diamonds…I tried everything on and blazed like a chandelier." Another, rather different, observation was that of the famous film director, James Ivory (who shot part of his film, *The Guru*, here at Junagarh), who noted, "So much has happened in these palaces. Nearly every story has violent death as a theme; there are terrible tales of revenge, poisonings, patricides, mass widow burnings. Finally, it is all – well, just weird and unnerving."

Anup Mahal.

Water fantasy

In a desert kingdom like Bikaner, where rain is a rare phenomenon, this fresco of rain clouds in Badal Mahal represents a fantasy.

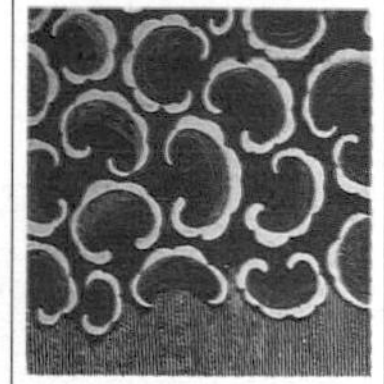

It is said that the artist was specially commissioned to paint it, so that when the rains finally *did* come the children of the royal household would not be frightened by it. A touching folk saying of the region goes, "Through snake bite, accident, lightning or the sword death may strike us; but let it not strike us by denying us rain."

Ganga Niwas.

FORT MUSEUM. Ganga Niwas, a great pink sandstone hall, its walls entirely carved with delicate tracery and scroll-work, was Maharaja Ganga Singh's contribution to Junagarh Palace in the early 20th century. Once used as the Diwan-i-Am ("Hall of Public Audience"), it now houses part of the fort museum. Here you can see an exotic array of antique Rajput weaponry, from jade-handled daggers to ivory inlaid muskets. Also, unexpectedly, you'll discover a World War One biplane in here! Other interesting items in the museum collection are an eclectic collection of royal costumes, *hookahs*, bric-à-brac, carpets, jewelry and the drums donated by Jambhoji (below), the saint who predicted that Rao Bika's dynasty would rule for only 450 years. There is a collection of personal memorabilia of the redoubtable Maharaja Ganga Singh, from old photographs of him with various great international statesmen with whom he rubbed shoulders, to an amusing soup spoon specially designed to accommodate his enormous upturned mustache. The museum also contains some beautiful examples of miniatures from the Bikaner school, as well as illuminated Sanskrit and Persian manuscripts.

THE GENERAL'S ARMOR
The armor of Raja Anup Singh (reigned 1674–98) is in the fort museum. A great renaissance man, he was, in addition to being a superb general, a mathematician, astronomer, scholar, and patron of the arts and music.

LALLGARH PALACE

Lallgarh Palace (top) and old prints of its dining room (bottom left) and smoking room (bottom right).

Around the turn of the 20th century, Maharaja Ganga Singh decided that it was time to move out of Junagarh Fort and build a modern palace that more clearly reflected the progressive new character of his kingdom. The result was the impressive Lallgarh Palace (in purple-pink sandstone again, like most of Bikaner's buildings). It took twenty-four years to complete, from 1902 to 1926. Designed by Sir Swinton Jacob ▲ *134*, and considered by many to be his greatest masterpiece, the opulent Lallgarh Palace draws its inspiration largely from the Rajput tradition, with virtually no trace of a Mughal influence. Its façade, like a Rajput fort, has almost no decorative features, except its topping of arrayed cupolas. The inside of the palace is

Bikaner miniatures reflect an exquisite marriage between the traditions of 16th-century Jain art and Mughal art.

centered around two courtyards and has a wealth of carved pillars, ornamental friezes, delicate stonework lattices and arcaded balconies. The cloistered courtyard of Laxmi Vilas, for instance, is considered to be a little architectural gem. In the grand expanses of Maharaja Ganga Singh's Durbar Hall, one can imagine how matters of great international import must have once been discussed here in remote little Bikaner. While the details of Lallgarh Palace are entirely Rajput, there is a strong touch of the Renaissance in the way it has been laid out, with its colonnades and corridors. As you wander through it, you can see its old halls, suites, billiard room and smoking room, all largely unchanged from the days of Maharaja Ganga Singh, with their Bohemian chandeliers and hunting trophies on the walls (some of them souvenirs from a hunting trip to Bavaria). There is a banquet hall that can seat up to four hundred people, and in one corner, a huge indoor swimming pool (now dry). The palace also has a significant collection of rare Sanskrit manuscripts, which in fact is one of the finest collections of ancient Sanskrit manuscripts in the world. It is open to research scholars. Many of these manuscripts were brought back from the Deccan by Raja Anup Singh, who led the Mughal armies against Golconda and Bijapur in the 17th century. A great patron of the arts and music, it is said that he came back from his south Indian campaign laden with, instead of booty, an enormous collection of sacred manuscripts and idols that he had saved, all of which are now here in Bikaner. The royal family still lives in a wing of Lallgarh Palace, but the rest of it has now been converted into a charming hotel.

Bikaner Museum. In Lallgarh Palace is a fascinating little museum, filled with the sundry possessions of the later maharajas (which give you a vivid glimpse of their lifestyle): everything from a 1921 model Simplex movie projector to the British tin soldiers that some little Bikaner prince used to play with once.

Swinging maidens
This exotic lacquered wooden swing, used to celebrate Krishna, is ornamented with carvings of maidens on its supporting columns. They were ingeniously connected with the swing's mechanism, so that as you gently swung on it, the maidens would automatically "dance" for you.

Antique Rajput weaponry from the Fort Museum.

Rhinoceros-hide shield (right), and sword belonging to Raja Man Singh I of Jaipur (left).

Weapons, not surprisingly, played an important part in the lives of the martial Rajputs. Of Maharao Umed Singh of Bundi (reigned 1771–1819), for instance, it is said that he habitually carried "a matchlock, a lance, a sword, a dagger and their appurtenances of knives, pouches and priming horn; he had a battle-axe, a javelin, a tomahawk, a discus, bow and quiver of arrows". Colonel Tod noted that the keeper of the armory was regarded as one of a prince's most confidential officers.

DEVOTED TO ARMS
Colonel Tod, in *Annals and Antiquities of Rajasthan*, describes how the Rajputs worshiped their arms: "The devotion of the Rajput is still paid to his arms...He swears by the steel and prostrates himself before his defensive buckler, his sword, or his dagger."

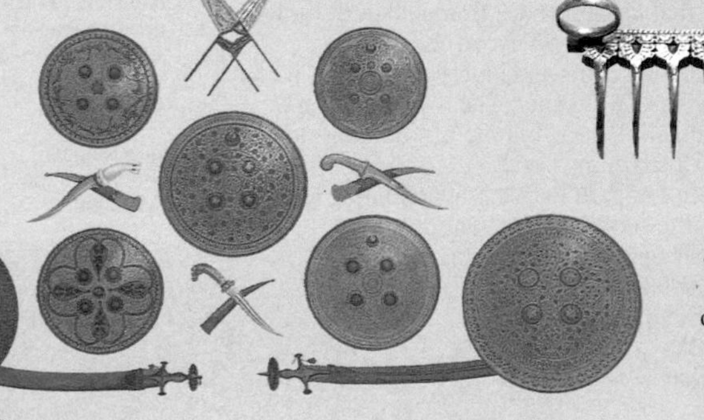

WAGH NAKH
Wagh nakh was an apt name for this strange and gruesome weapon. Literally meaning "tiger's claws", it was slipped unobtrusively over one's fingers and used to maul one's opponent in close combat.

VARIETY OF SHIELDS
Rajput shields were made from a variety of materials: wood, steel, bamboo, crocodile hide or rhino hide. The latter was by far the favorite, as it was believed to offer a warrior the greatest protection.

ANCIENT WEAPON
Rajput warriors often used a heavy mace in battle. This weapon has an ancient tradition that goes back to Lord Bhima, the great warrior in the Hindu epic, the *Mahabharata*.

CURVED FAVORITE
The Rajputs used a wide variety of different types of sabres. But their favorite was the *sirohi*, with its light, narrow, slightly curved blade, formed like that of a Damascus sword.

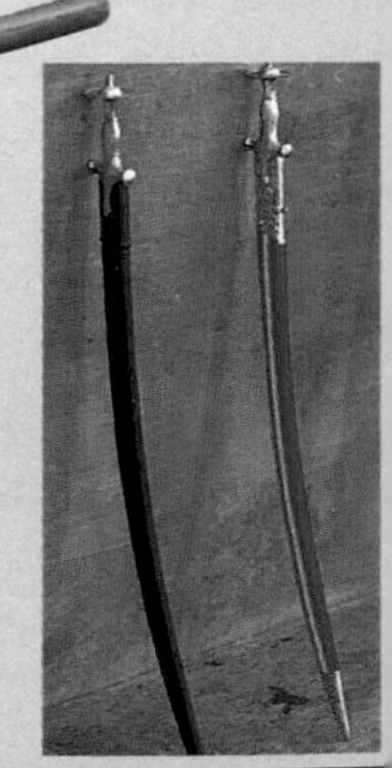

"No prince or chief is without his *sileh khana*, or armoury, where he passes hours in viewing and arranging his arms..."

Colonel Tod, *Annals and Antiquities of Rajasthan*, 1829

Exquisite swords
Rajput swords were superbly tempered and often exquisitely ornamented. They covered a wide variety of types, from the long sword for cut-and-thrust to the heavy double-edged *khandu*.

Weighty armor
Rajput warriors wore suits of armor so heavy that you wonder at the strength of the man who could fight from underneath it all. For instance, Maharana Pratap of Udaipur's armor, along with his weapons, weighed a total of 165 pounds.

Raja Anup Singh's armor
Raja Anup Singh's 17th-century armor must have seen action on numerous battlefields, from Kabul in the north to Golconda in the south. It was worn with an unusually shaped rhino-hide helmet.

Daggered fist
A *katar* was the traditional broad-bladed dagger worn over the fist. Sometimes it was designed with little pistols projecting from the sides of its handle, which could be fired by squeezing the handle.

LEGEND OF A DESERT TREE
The *khejri* (*Prosopis cineraria*) is one of the few trees that flourishes in the hostile conditions of the desert ■ 30. According to legend, Raja Gaj Singh of Bikaner, on a campaign in the Deccan with Emperor Aurangzeb's armies, came upon a *khejri* tree and began to weep, as it reminded him of his own distant kingdom. The Emperor gave him leave to go home for six months, but asked that his cousin, Raja Zorawar Singh of Khimsar, another Rajput general, stand guarantee for his return. When Raja Gaj Singh did not return in time, Raja Zorawar Singh promptly gave up three-quarters of his own kingdom of Khimsar to honor his promise to the Emperor.

HAVELIS

During medieval times, Bikaner became a haven for rich traders and bankers who felt safe here, in the desert, from the turmoil that frequently swept across north India. Several of them left their families – and their wealth – in Bikaner, as they plied their business elsewhere (paying handsomely, by the way, for the protection). That is the origin of the town's beautiful old *havelis* ● *86* or mansions, which date back to the 18th century. These handsome sandstone buildings, often multi-storied, have ornately carved lattice screens, balconies and balustrades. The windows, made from solid wood, bound with iron bands, contrast graphically with the delicacy of the carved purple sandstone. Inside, hidden away from the outside world, the descendants of those wealthy traders' families continue to live, as they have for centuries. The *havelis* of Bikaner are clustered together in the narrow lanes of the old walled city. Rampuria Haveli and Kothari Haveli are among the most impressive.

SANDESHWAR TEMPLE

There are two very interesting Jain temples here, the Sandeshwar and Bhandeshwar temples, said to have been built by two wealthy merchant brothers in the 14th century. Sandeshwar Temple is a minor masterpiece. Dedicated to the Jain *tirthankara* (saint), Neminath, its interiors are ablaze with enamel and gold-leaf frescos and leafwork scrollery. The ceiling is vaulted, arched and ornately decorated. At one end is a statue of Neminath meditating on a lotus pedestal, beneath which are rows of wonderful marble statues of other Jain saints.

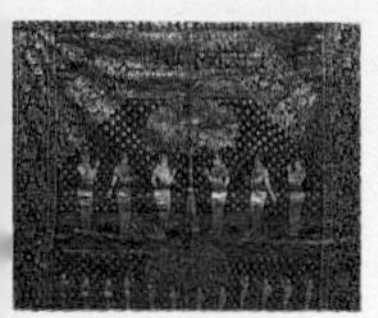

If a promise of marriage had been broken or in order to avoid widowhood, considered to bring bad luck, young girls were sometimes betrothed to trees, a *khejra* for example (left), until they could be properly married.

BHANDESHWAR TEMPLE

Dedicated to the Jain saint, Parashvanath, this temple has interestingly carved wooden columns decorated with motifs of dancing maidens. In the center lies the sanctum, which is covered with mirrorwork and gilt and houses a fine marble statue of the saint. In the temple's circular *mandapa,* or hall, you will find some superb frescos depicting processions, court scenes and battles. The red sandstone galleries and porches were later additions in the 17th century. There are several other fascinating temples in Bikaner, but if you don't have time for all of them, at least take a look at the impressive Rattan Bihari Temple opposite Junagarh Fort.

CAMEL FARM

The camels of Bikaner played a major role in the history of the kingdom, contributing greatly to its economy, as well as its defense, over the centuries. The camel breeding farm (below), set amid rolling sand dunes, was formed in 1960 to produce superior strains of camels. One of the efforts at the farm, interestingly, is to breed camels with longer, thicker eyelashes, which offer greater protection in sandstorms! Bikaner's camels have traditionally been renowned for their heavy load-carrying capacity (while Jaisalmer's camels are known for their speed). The camel farm breeds camels both for domestic haulage as well as, even today, for military use. The Indian army still boasts a crack Camel Corps, indispensable for desert warfare ▲ *194, 204*. It traces its origins back to the Ganga Risala regiment, raised by Maharaja Ganga Singh in the late 19th century. The regiment's temperamental beasts were so superbly trained that a member of a visiting Viceroy's party to Bikaner in the 1920s, on seeing a guard of honor, noted that the camels were "immoveable, as if carved out of gray granite." Incidentally, Maharaja Ganga Singh, shrewd showman that he was, used to arrange dramatic military tattoos featuring legions of camel warriors dressed in black chain-mail armor in order to impress his important guests.

THIRST QUENCHER
Traveling through the desert, you frequently see people selling melons by the roadside as thirst quenchers. Colonel Tod, writing in the 1820s, remarked on "the superior magnitude of the water melons of the desert", adding that "one is sufficient to allay the thirst both of a horse and his rider." Emperor Babur, the first Mughal, had called India an uncivilized country because, among other things, it had no melons. He is reputed to have introduced these, along with the Mughal gardens ▲ *314*.

SNAKE DEITY
All around Bikaner, as well as other parts of Rajasthan, you see the sacred slabs of Gogaji, a popular folk deity, often represented by a coiling snake with a hood. He is supposed to offer immunity against snake bites – important in this snake-infested desert region. His main shrine is in the nearby village of Gogamedi, where he is believed to reveal himself to his devotees each year, astride his blue horse, on three nights in the monsoon month of Bhadon.

Camel breeding farm (left).

▲ Bikaner Camel Corps

The Camel Corps is even advertised on cigarette packs.

The Bikaner Camel Corps had its early beginnings in 1465 when Rao Bika, the founder, led a corps of three hundred *sowars*, or camel riders, to conquer the adjoining territories. Subsequently, in the 19th century, during the reign of Ganga Singh, the Bikaner *durbar* offered to raise a camel corps of five hundred Rathor Rajputs as Imperial Service troops for the British Army ▲ *194*. The unit, known as the Ganga Risala after the name of the ruler, served in the Boxer Rebellion in 1900, the Somaliland Campaign from 1902 to 1904, and the two World Wars. After India gained independence, the regiment was effective in the desert areas during India's border disputes with Pakistan between 1965 and 1971.

The Officer and his camel
The tall, proud Rajput soldier is dressed resplendently in his white uniform and red and gold turban, while his camel is caparisoned in bright colors. According to a popular story, there was an attempt to introduce shoes for the camels as part of their uniform to protect their soft, padded feet from being damaged by the tarred roads which they had to traverse. The camels sat down en masse on the road, obstinately refusing to move till the shoes were discarded – a clear case of mutiny.

"Ships of the desert"
When Rao Bikaji in the 15th century started to deploy camels for his army, the best specimens of the *sowari*, or riding camels, were from the districts of Jaisalmer and Bikaner. Even today they are used by the Indian post for delivering mail in the remote desert regions.

Military review of the Bikaner Camel Corps, the pride of Bikaner State Forces.

Ganga Risala
Situated in the desert and near the international border, Bikaner had to maintain a well-trained and sizeable army. The Ganga Risala consisted of six units which looked after specific functions. When it was first set up, British officers were appointed to supervise the training and equipping of the units.

Ganga-Jaisalmer Risala
In 1951, the Ganga Risala amalgamated with the Jaisalmer Camel Corps to become the Ganga-Jaisalmer Risala. It was redesignated as the 13th Battalion of the Grenadiers in the Indian Army on March 4, 1955. The corps is stationed at Bikaner as part of the Border Security Force (left), a paramilitary force which patrols India's borders from the icy Himalayan passes to the desert in the west.

Ceremonial parade
The Camel Corps officiates on special occasions during peacetime. It forms part of the ceremonial parade in New Delhi on Republic Day. Its officers also excel in mounted sports such as camel polo.

RAT LEGEND
According to legend, Karni Mata once attempted to bring a dead child back to life. However, she failed because Yama, the god of death, explained to her that the child had already been reincarnated on earth. Angrily, Karni Mata proclaimed that nobody from her tribe would ever fall into the hands of Yama. Instead, when they died they would temporarily inhabit the body of a rat before being reborn into the tribe.

Karni Mata Temple.

KARNI MATA'S VICTORY
The heavy chased silver doors of the Karni Mata Temple depict the patron goddess, calm and composed after her victory over Mahishasura, the great buffalo-demon (whose head is seen at the end of her trident) while her rodent followers leap about her in glee.

DEVIKUND

The royal cenotaphs of Bikaner (above), beautifully carved in sandstone and marble and grouped around a large pool, are located 5 miles outside Bikaner. The cenotaphs are carved with the symbol of the sun, for the dynasty is *suryavanshi* ("of the family of the sun"). The cenotaphs of the ranis, including those who had performed *sati*, are signified by lotus flowers or footmarks to mark. The cenotaphs of the children, touchingly, bear hollowed cups, supposedly to hold milk for the child. It was once prophesied, apparently, that all the maharajas of Bikaner would be cremated within this complex at Devikund. Uncannily, with the cremation of the last ruling maharaja, Sadul Singh, in 1950, the complex was full.

GAJNER

The old royal hunting lodge of Gajner, 20 miles west of Bikaner, was the venue of Maharaja Ganga Singh's legendary *shikar* parties. The lodge itself, a sprawling deep-pink affair, ornamented with delicate lattice screens and cupolas, is set in lush gardens by the side of a picturesque lake (above). A member of a viceregal party that was once entertained here later reminisced, "You can't imagine the beauty, it was like 'Arabian Nights' in the desert." Incidentally, for all his huntsmanship, Maharaja Ganga Singh was also a dedicated wildlife conservationist. He enforced strict laws to prevent hunting out of season and made sure that the animals were well looked after. He even had slabs of rock salt tied to the trees on one occasion, when it was learned that a certain species of deer was suffering from a salt deficiency. Today Gajner is a good place to see blackbuck, *chinkara*, *chital*, *sambar*, wild boar, and bustard. The maharaja still uses the lodge for weekends, but most of it, like Lallgarh Palace, has been converted into a hotel.

KOLAYAT

Beyond Gajner, in the middle of the desert, is a large lake and the temple complex of Kolayat, associated with a famous ancient sage, Kapil Muni. There are several marble temples, pavilions and bathing ghats here, where pilgrims and holy men take a dip in the waters.

"The lake [at Gajner] has closed over that wonderful pink palace, compelled by some light-hearted... magician."
Yvonne Fitzroy, *Courts and Camps of India, 1926*

DESHNOKE

KARNI MATA TEMPLE. Located 19 miles south of Bikaner, Karni Mata Temple is one of the strangest in India ● *46*. Karni Mata is the patron goddess of the maharajas of Bikaner ▲ *193*. The temple is populated by hundreds of sacred rats – quite harmless, incidentally – who are fed on the offerings of the devotees. The temple itself is superbly carved in white marble, with lavishly decorated gateways, pavilions, columns, and balconies. Its heavy chased silver gates are particularly admirable.

KALIBANGAN

The pre-historic ruined town of Kalibangan lies 175 miles north of Bikaner, but the journey is worth making. Kalibangan was a city of the Harappan civilization that flourished between 3500 and 4500 years ago ● *32*. In fact, it was a sister city to the great Indus Valley cities of Mohenjodaro and Harappa, designed on basically the same plan, and almost as large. Kalibangan literally means "Black Bangles", from the numerous fragments of weather-stained terracotta bangles that were found strewn all over the excavation site. The excavations here reveal the portrait of an amazingly sophisticated urban lifestyle. The town was built around a central acropolis, with a fine system of streets that intersected at right angles, and an advanced drainage system. The houses were made of kiln-fired bricks and had bathrooms with terracotta water pipes and even faucets. Other finds range from a sophisticated system of weights and measures to a charming array of children's toys, including a delightful whistle shaped in the form of a bird. Subsequent excavations nearby have unearthed relics of an even more ancient culture, simply dubbed "pre-Harappan", which goes back five thousand years in time.

Shiva temple in Kolayat.

ROYAL HUNTING PARTY
The itineraries of visiting English dignitaries and monarchs in India were often arranged to fit in a hunt with Maharaja Ganga Singh at Gajner, usually over Christmas. They would hunt blackbuck at 50 miles per hour from open-roof Rolls Royces in the desert. Or, more frequently, they would hunt imperial sandgrouse at Gajner Lake. The birds swept down to the lake, as an English guest once wrote, "not in the hundreds, but in the thousands. Not for half an hour, but for three hours on and ... in perfect military formation." An invitation to a grouse hunt was much coveted and Maharaja Ganga Singh was sometimes referred to as "The Maharaja by the Grouse of God".

The flag of Jaisalmer flies over the fort citadel.

COAT-OF-ARMS
Jaisalmer's coat-of-arms is emblazoned with a desert fort and a naked arm holding a broken spear because, as Rudyard Kipling noted, "The legend goes that Jeysulmir was once galled by a horse with a magic spear." The hawk is a symbol of Durga, the dynasty's patron goddess. The desert antelopes below are spangled with gold coins – a tribute to Jaisalmer's wealthy Jain bankers.

DESERT MINSTRELS
The Manganiyars are wandering desert minstrels ● *79*. Historically, they had a close relationship with the Rajputs of Jaisalmer. It was the duty of the Muslim Manganiyars to entertain the Rajput before battle, as well as to stay beside him when he died, maintaining a vigil over the corpse until the ceremonies for the departed soul were over.

HISTORY

The medieval fortress town of Jaisalmer rises out of the remote deserts of Rajasthan, like a city at the very end of the world. According to mythology, after the epic battle of the *Mahabharata*, Lord Krishna and the Pandav hero, Arjuna, came here for a ceremony. Lord Krishna then prophesied that a descendant of his Yadava clan would one day establish a glorious kingdom here in the desert. Then, with his discus, he smote a rock and a sweet water spring sprang forth. In the 12th century, a Bhatti Rajput prince, Rao Jaisal, came upon the great triangular rock (where Jaisalmer now stands). Here he met a hermit, Eesul, who blessed him and learning that Rao Jaisal was descended from the Yadavas, showed him Lord Krishna's prophecy engraved on a rock. Rao Jaisal, inspired by this, decided to shift his capital here from nearby Lodurva, despite the fact that the hermit also prophesied that this new capital would be sacked two and a half times. The great fort was built in 1156, supposedly the second oldest of Rajasthan's major forts after Chittorgarh. Jaisalmer was located right on the route of the caravans from Egypt, Arabia, Persia and Central Asia carrying their spices, silks and dried fruits to the emporia of Delhi in the east, and Gujarat in the south. Thus it became an extremely prosperous town. The clanmen, the Bhatti, were marauders, known as the "wolf-packs of the desert".

THE THREE SACKINGS. In 1294, the first of the "two-and-a-half sackings" of Jaisalmer prophesied by the sage Eesul took place. When the princes of Jaisalmer ambushed and captured a treasure caravan of three thousand horses and mules belonging to Sultan Alauddin Khilji of Delhi, the Sultan launched a punitive raid on Jaisalmer and the siege is said to have lasted for eight years. Eventually, Jaisalmer fell, but not before 24,000 of its women performed *jauhar* by leaping into the flames to prevent themselves from falling into the enemy's hands. The second of the prophesied sackings took place not long after, when one of Jaisalmer's princes carried away the prize steed of Sultan Feroz Shah of Delhi. Once again the womenfolk of the fort performed *jauhar*. The third – the "half sacking" of the ancient prophecy – was the most curious of them all. In the 16th century, a neighboring Patina chieftain played a Trojan horse trick on Jaisalmer, by bringing into its fort a retinue of palanquins supposedly carrying the ladies

"A horse of wood, legs of stone
A frame of iron will alone get you to Jaisalmer."

Folk rhyme, on the inaccessibility of Jaisalmer

of his court, but filled, instead, with armed warriors. A fierce hand-to-hand battle broke out and when it seemed that the defenders were surely going to lose, the Rawal of Jaisalmer killed all his womenfolk with his own sword – since there was no time for a *jauhar*. Tragically, it turned out to have been in vain because, shortly after, reinforcements arrived and the attackers were wiped out.

END OF HOSTILITIES. In the 16th century the maharawals of Jaisalmer were attacked several times by the Mughals, but resisted defiantly. Finally, however, in the 1650's Rawal Sabal Sigh (reigned 1651–61) recognized the sovereignty of Delhi, and with the end of hostilities a new era of prosperity began for Jaisalmer. It was also an era of brilliant architectural activity during which the wealthy merchants of town, as well as the maharawals themselves, used their vast riches for building exquisite *havelis* and palaces.

BRITISH RULE. By the 19th century Jaisalmer had come under the influence of the British – one of the last of the Rajput kingdoms to sign a treaty with them. Colonel James Tod, the celebrated scholar of the Rajput civilization and author of the magnum opus, *Annals and Antiquities of Rajasthan*, was himself sent here as the British Political Agent. It is amusing to note that during this period, remote little Jaisalmer briefly figured in the arena of international geopolitics. With the then Russian Empire looking for its long sought-after access to the warm water ports of the Indian Ocean, and the threat of its invasion, the possession of Jaisalmer became, for the British, "of vital importance, by giving us the command of...the most practicable point of advance into India."

Portrait of Rao Jaisal.

GODDESS OF WAR
Bhawani, whose temple is by Bhointia Pol, is one of names of Durga, Parvati's manifestation as warrior ● *45*. The Bhatti warriors sought her blessings before riding into battle, returning to her temple to thank her for her protection on their safe return. The warriors' terrifying battle cry was "Jai Bhawani" ("Victory to Bhawani").

Painting of a battle scene on the wall of Jaisalmer Fort.

COURTESAN'S GATE
Telia, the beautiful courtesan from Jaisalmer, built an ornate gateway that led to Gadsisar Lake. But this pious and generous act was criticized by malicious people, who managed to convince the rawal never to use the gateway as this would be degrading to him. The shrewd Telia quickly installed a temple to Lord Krishna above the gate so nobody would be able to use it.

WEB OF INTRIGUE. The early century saw an era of bitter intrigue in the court of Jaisalmer between the maharawals and their powerful hereditary prime ministers, the Mehtas. Swarup Singh Mehta was beheaded by a prince of Jaisalmer when he insulted the prince over a debt owed to him. He was succeeded by his young son, Salim Singh, who had secretly sworn revenge on the Rawal's family. Salim Singh grew up to become a Borgia-like tyrant who very neatly ruined both the Rawal and the kingdom of Jaisalmer itself, and was finally stabbed to death. He was so hated by everybody that it is recorded that "since there was some fear that the (stab) wound might heal, his wife gave him poison".

JAISALMER TODAY

Jaisalmer, even today, has an exotically medieval flavor to it. Most of the town lies within the thick stone walls of the fort, 1485 feet long and 890 feet wide, and wandering through it is almost like stepping into the pages of the Arabian Nights. For eight hundred years the town flourished because of its position on the main caravan trail up through Afghanistan. According to a persistent legend, Marco Polo stopped here during his travels to China. By the 19th century, however, with the coming of the British and their new system of octroi and the opening up of ports such as Bombay, the caravan trade and,

DEPARTMENT OF NARCOTICS
Ornately crafted wood and silver boxes were used for carrying opium. The smoking of opium was historically a part of the way of life in the harsh deserts of Marwar. Warriors took a double dose before going into battle. Opium was crushed in a bowl embellished, significantly, with a cobra's hood. It was considered an insult for guests to refuse opium offered. A milder version is *bhang*, often crushed with rose petals, aniseed, and black pepper, and served in buttermilk, candies, or fried snacks. You can get *bhang* in shops licensed by a government body, interestingly named "The Department of Narcotics".

1. Jaisalmer Fort
2. City Palace
3. Salim Singh ki Haveli
4. Nathmalji ki Haveli
5. Patwon ki Haveli
6. Vyas Chhatri
7. Bara Bagh
8. Bhattiani Sati Rani
9. Gadsisar Lake

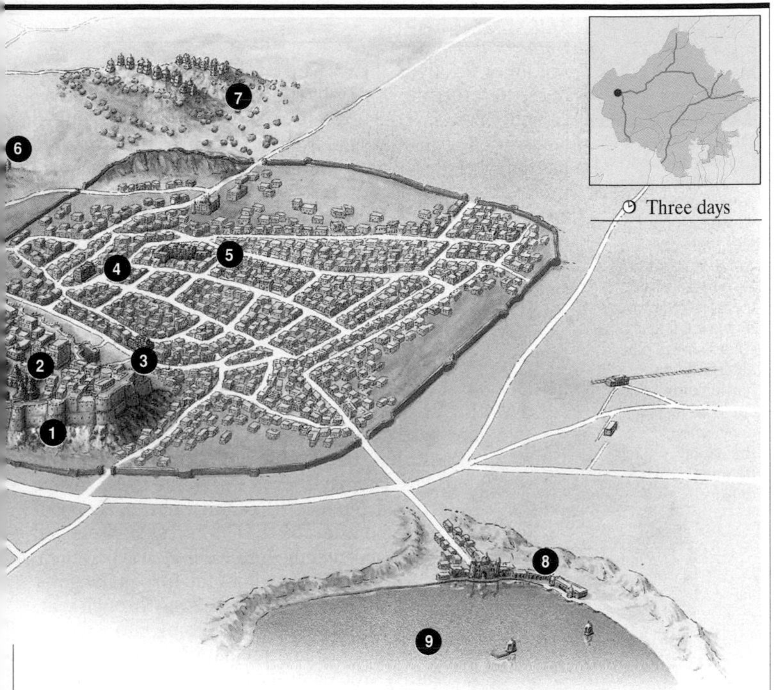

consequently, the importance of this town dwindled. In the wake of the 1965 war between India and Pakistan, the entire area became a major military base. Barely thirty-five years later, just 50 miles away, outside Pokharan ▲ *218*, the Indian Government tested a nuclear device. Today Jaisalmer's economy depends largely on the earnings of camels, sheep and cattle. But with the opening of the new Indira Gandhi Canal, the desert landscape has been transformed by agricultural use. In addition, major sources of natural gas beneath the desert sands have been exploited. Still, this region is an astonishingly arid place. Sometimes it does not rain here for five years at a time. It is said that the children, who have sometimes never seen rain, are terrified at the prospect of seeing their first shower! But the surrounding desert region has a harsh, terrible beauty about it, and going out on a camel safari is an experience not to be missed. Jaisalmer, till the very end, remained one of the kingdoms of Rajasthan that was most insulated from the outside world: there was no proper road to Jaisalmer till 1958, and it was only in 1968 that a railway line was installed. A military airport nearby is used by a few regular airlines, but Jaisalmer is still surprisingly untouched by progress and relatively inaccessible to the outside world. Best is to come around the time of the spectacular annual Desert Festival ● *81* in February, when dancers, musicians, puppeteers and other performers (including fire-walkers and sword swallowers) congregate here from all over Rajasthan. An ironic footnote: a splendid new desert fort was built at Mohangarh near Jaisalmer, as late as 1940.

Emporium of the East
Jaisalmer's bazaars are evocative of the days of the medieval camel caravans when the region was a trading emporium for splendid carpets from Herat, scimitars from Damascus, stallions from Arabia and wines from Shiraz."

Old cannon at Jaisalmer Fort.

JAISALMER FORT

Jaisalmer Fort looks like a giant child's sandcastle, or the set of the desert castle in a Hollywood epic production of *Beau Geste*. In fact, it is the ultimate in desert forts, dominating the landscape for miles around from the top of Trikuta Hill, as it has for more than eight hundred years. One of the fascinating things about the fort is its color: its massive sandstone walls are a tawny lion color during the day, turning to a magical honey-gold as the sun sets. When Satyajit Ray, the celebrated Indian film director, saw it, he was inspired to make a film called *Sonar Kila* (The Golden Fort), a charming fantasy about a treasure guarded by a peacock. The fort stands on a triangular hill 250 feet high, enclosed by a thick, crenelated wall over 30 feet high and reinforced with ninety-nine bastions, most of which were built in the mid-17th century ● *90*. Remarkably, these walls used no mortar at all. They were made entirely from huge, intricately interlocking blocks of stone. At one time the town of Jaisalmer lay entirely within the fort walls but sometime in the 17th century, part of the town moved outside, on the leeward side, protected by the hill and the fort itself. However, much of the town still lives within the fort, making it a kind of living museum. Walking through it at night, especially, is like stepping into a time machine and going straight back to the 14th century. You enter the fort up a steep incline paved with enormous flagstones, through a series of four huge gates, passing along the way a second fort wall running parallel to the outer one, and rising to half its height. Reaching the innermost gate, Hawa Pol ("Gate of the Winds"), so named because of the beautiful breezes it catches, you enter the spacious Chauhata Square. This is the heart of the fort complex. In front are the palaces of the maharawals. Toward the left

HURLING STONES
Colonel Tod, who was the British Political Agent in Jaisalmer, wrote that the fort had "very few cannons mounted". Its defenses were therefore reinforced by having huge, round stones placed all around its battlements, which could be hurled down upon the enemy in times of siege.

Hawa Pol.

WEATHER FORECAST
This curious device atop the fort was used to forecast the weather in Jaisalmer. Each year on a day in April, a flag would be planted in its center, and the direction in which it blew was believed to determine the weather for the year. If it blew to the west, for instance, it meant a good monsoon, but if it blew to the north it indicated famine.

Jaisalmer Fort.

A hive of activity within Jaisalmer Fort (below).

Turban worn in the Jaisalmeri style.

is a flight of marble steps topped by a white marble throne, where the maharawal used to sit, listening to petitions or reviewing his troops. This was also the place, by the way, where the womenfolk performed *jauhar*; it was here that they leapt into the flames en masse. By the side of the square is Rao Jaisal's well where the sage Eesul is supposed to have shown Rao Jaisal the prophecy of Lord Krishna carved on a rock ▲ *208*.

Jaisalmer Palace

As you enter the palace, you find it is actually a maze of interconnecting palaces, the oldest of which is Juna Mahal dating back to the early 16th century. Rang Mahal, built in the 18th century, is especially interesting, with its richly frescoed walls (look for the scenes of old Jaisalmer, as well as of Jaipur and Udaipur) and the superbly carved stone screen that you assume is a dark wooden lattice turns out to be cut from solid stone! Equally interesting is the slightly older Sarvottam Vilas, with its blue tiles and glass mosaics. You will also come across amusing little touches here in the palace, such as the ornate 19th-century American street lamp you suddenly discover up on the citadel, made, according to the signature, by the Pan American Light Company of Warren Street, New York. It is incongruously positioned right beside a medieval weather forecasting device and the fluttering royal Jaisalmer banner.

Jain temples. Also within the fort are some old Jain temples, dating back to the 12th century. The most interesting are the temples of Rishabhdev and Chandraprabhu. Rishabhdev Temple ● *48* has a splendidly carved *torana* archway over its entrance, and a striking group of *tirthankara* images, with jeweled eyes that sparkle in the dark. Next door is Sambhavnatha Temple. It has a fabulous library in the basement, reputed to contain some of India's oldest and rarest palm-leaf manuscripts, dating back to the 11th century.

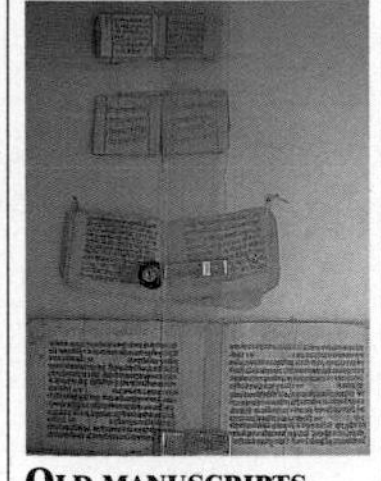

Old manuscripts
Old and rare manuscripts are kept in Sambhavnath Temple's library, including what is thought to be the oldest surviving manuscript in India – an 11th-century manuscript of one of the great *rishi* (sage), Dronacharya.

Haunting handprints
Sati stones mark all the queens of a fort who have performed *sati*, immolating themselves on their husband's funeral pyres. Before leaving her dead husband's home for the last time the widow would traditionally leave a scarlet handprint on the gatepost as a symbol of protection for the house she was about to leave.

One of the remarkable things about Jaisalmer is the *havelis* or mansions built by its wealthy merchants and nobles in the 19th century. They are famed for their exquisitely carved sandstone façades – a feat of stone-carving unmatched anywhere else in India, not even by the intricate marble screens at Agra's Taj Mahal.

PATWON KI HAVELI

The largest and most elaborate of these *havelis* is Patwon ki Haveli ("Mansion of the Brocade Merchants") (left), built in 1805 by Guman Chand Patwa, a merchant and banker, who is said to have had three hundred trading centers between Afghanistan and China. Built for his five sons, this ornate five-storied complex took fifty years to complete. It stands in the privacy of a little cul-de-sac, behind a lofty arched gateway. Its entire frontage is beautifully carved, with its sixty latticed balconies looking as if they have been created from sandalwood rather than from stone. Inside are the remnants of some fine old murals.

TORANAS
Traditionally, every home in Jaisalmer has an auspicious *torana* over the archway of the main door. They are put up over a bride's home, and never taken down. The bridegroom, when he first enters the house on horseback, will not be admitted unless he has touched the *torana* with his sword.

NATHMALJI KI HAVELI

Even more beautifully carved is Nathmalji ki Haveli (below), built by a Prime Minister of Jaisalmer as late as 1885. Its façade is a riot of ornamentation: flowers, birds, elephants, soldiers, as well as a bicycle and a steam engine! It was apparently carved by two brothers, Hathu and Lallu, each of whom completed one side of the *haveli*. You can see how the whole looks perfectly harmonious but that the right and left side differ in their details. Also, extraordinarily, the building was carved out of boulders – not dressed stone – and you can see the raw boulder faces in the fascinating rooms inside.

Façade of Patwon ki Haveli.

SALIM SINGH KI HAVELI

The third of the great *havelis* is the one built by the cruel scheming Prime Minister, Salim Singh, in 1815 (left). What makes it unique is the way it is narrow at the base, but suddenly flares out its cantilevered upper story. The *haveli* has a beautiful arched roof, capped with blue cupolas and superbly carved details. Do not miss its elegant peacock brackets. It is said that the Machiavellian Salim Singh slowly became more powerful than the maharawals themselves, and was once planning to build a passage from the upper story of this *haveli* to connect directly to the maharawal's palace, but the maharawal finally managed to scotch the idea.

BAZAARS

Wandering through the narrow alleys and bazaars of Jaisalmer, you are transported back to the time when this was the place where the products of India and China were exchanged for those of Persia, Arabia, Africa, and Europe, when "chintz, dried fruit, opium, silks, arms and salts" were traded for "elephant's teeth, dates, sandalwood, spices and coffee." A good place to start is Manak Chowk ("The Ruby Square"), the main market square, with its ancient water trough, where the town's animals are still watered. Across the road are stalls selling everything from traditional candies (the bright yellow little balls of *ghotua* are a specialty of Jaisalmer) to hardware, blankets, water containers, and desert supplies. As you walk through the narrow winding lanes, you pass by camels, desert gypsies, wandering cattle and children playing with primitive little handmade wooden toys. Jaisalmer is also a great place to shop for chunky rustic silver jewelry. There are dozens of different types of jewelry designed for different parts of the female body: forehead, nose, ears, fingers, waist, ankles, toes, even an ornament called a *chupara* for the teeth! Other things to look for are colorful embroidery and mirrorwork, brightly colored tie-and-dye fabrics, rugged looking goat-skin *mojri* slippers, traditional shawls, rugs, and woodcarving.

SADDLED FOR COMFORT
To soften an uncomfortable camel ride, a typical Jaisalmer camel saddle is specially designed with several layers. The first is a layer of wool followed by four layers of cotton and a layer of cloth, often elaborately embroidered. Over this is placed a wooden seat, embellished with engraved copper and brass and attached to a leather cushion. A well-crafted saddle can cost up to one sixth of the price of a camel.

DELICATE CARVINGS
The *silavats* (stone carvers) of Jaisalmer are known for their incredibly delicate carving. The celebrated film director Satyajit Ray wrote of a sandstone tea cup he was once shown by the Maharawal on a visit to the palace, which was carved so finely that it actually floated when placed in water! He added, "It was like magic, and we all but applauded."

Handicrafts being sold in an alley off Patwon ki Haveli (left).

Vyas Chhatri.

LARANI SATI BATTHINNI

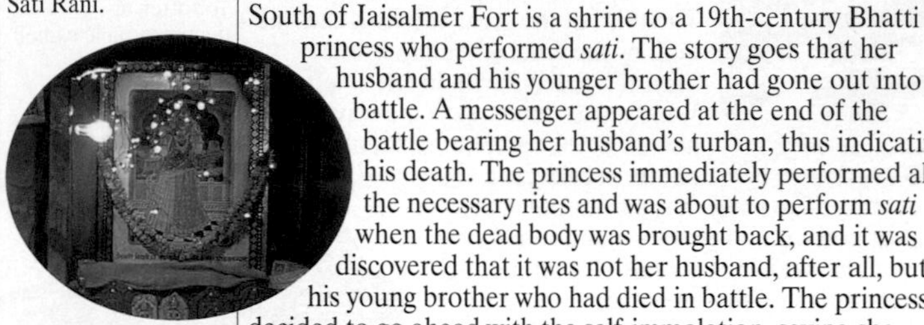
Shrine to the Bhatti princess at Bhattiani Sati Rani.

South of Jaisalmer Fort is a shrine to a 19th-century Bhatti princess who performed *sati*. The story goes that her husband and his younger brother had gone out into battle. A messenger appeared at the end of the battle bearing her husband's turban, thus indicating his death. The princess immediately performed all the necessary rites and was about to perform *sati* when the dead body was brought back, and it was discovered that it was not her husband, after all, but his young brother who had died in battle. The princess decided to go ahead with the self-immolation, saying she would become a *mahasati* – one who performs *sati* not for her husband but for her son, for the young prince was like a son to her. The keepers of this Hindu shrine are, interestingly, Muslim Manganiyars, who sing romantic ballads in praise of the dead princess and light the lamp before her memorial tablet.

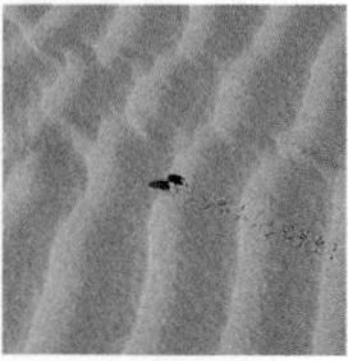

DUNG BEETLE
The dung beetle of the desert is a remarkable insect known to roll balls of dung much larger than itself. It is designed like a high-tech flying machine with wings that swing out for take-off from under an armored shield!

BARA BAGH

Situated 4 miles away in the desert is Bara Bagh ("The Great Garden") with its clusters of hauntingly beautiful cupolaed marble cenotaphs of the maharawals of Jaisalmer, set on an incline by the water of the Jait Bund. Do not miss the fine carving on the ceilings. Closer to town lies another complex of graceful marble cenotaphs, almost as impressive, belonging to the Brahmins of Jaisalmer, called Vyas Chhatri.

AMARSAGAR

Lying 4 miles west of Jaisalmer is a small lake with a 17th-century sandstone pleasure palace built by Rawal Amar Singh, its courtyard once laid with large, formal gardens. Beside the palace are pavilions and broad ghats or steps that lead down to the water of the lake. Take a look at the animal heads carved into the stone by the lake: there are also three

DESERT GYPSIES
The Kalbeliyas are gypsies from the deserts near Jaisalmer who are known for their music, dances ● 79 and snake charmers' skills. One branch of the Kalbeliyas is believed to have wandered westward over the centuries and mingled with the gypsies of Europe. There is a startling resemblance, significantly between the dances and music of Spain and those of the Kalbeliyas.

fine Jain temples, with beautifully screened walls and carved balconies, and some good examples of old step-wells.

LODURVA

The ancient Bhatti capital of Lodurva lies 5 miles beyond Amarsagar. You can still see traces of the ruins of the city in the desert, but the one monument that is intact is the Jain Temple of Parshvanatha. Rebuilt in the 17th century, its ornate *torana* archway (right) is perhaps the finest example of its kind in Rajasthan. Inside the temple is a Kalpavriksha, a representation of the Celestial Tree, with its carved copper leaves, believed to have the power to bestow any favor asked of it by a devotee. This temple, it is said, is connected by a secret underground passage to Sambhavnath Temple in Jaisalmer Fort 9 miles away. Nearby is the bed of the River Kak that has now run dry. Legend associates it with the star-crossed lovers, Prince Mahendru of Amarkot and the beautiful Princess Moomal who lived on the banks of the River Kak. Separated by a tragic misunderstanding they were reunited too late; weakened by their travails they died in each other's arms. That day the River Kak, they say, dried up in sadness and has not flowed since. Nearby are the ruins of a building that is said to have been Moomal's palace.

Jain temple at Lodarva (above).

AKAL AND KANDIALA

The Fossil Park of Akal lies 10 miles southeast of Jaisalmer. The petrified fossils of a forest of great trees that grew here 180 million years ago lie in the red, rocky terrain that now glitters with mica. At Kandiala not far away are fossils of a different kind – fossilized rocks from a probably older but undated past, when this desert was actually part of the ocean bed (as you can tell from the tiny sea shells embedded in the rocks).

SHRINE OF BHAIRONJI
Bhairon, a folk manifestation of Lord Shiva, is believed to have lived in Jaisalmer. His main shrine is at Bara Bagh, but his wayside images depicting him with his legendary dog are popularly worshiped all over Rajasthan, particularly by childless women who make offerings to him of their *kanchlis* (corsets) in the hope of becoming fertile.

The great Indian bustard.

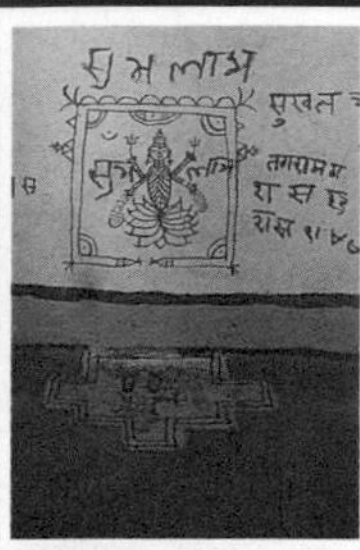

FLOOR AND WALL MOTIFS
The desert huts of Jaisalmer and Barmer are known for the fascinating, elaborate *mandana,* decorations on their floor and walls. These are considered auspicious, and as the saying goes, "It does not matter if your son remains unmarried but your courtyard floor should never be left unadorned." Drawn by the women with white lime paste, or red earth, the floor patterns are usually geometric while the wall patterns are usually animated ▲ *236.* Of the numerous traditional motifs, each has its own name and special significance. Different motifs are associated with different festivals and rituals. Thus the *feenia* (candy) motif is associated with the Makar Sankranti festival, the *paglia* (footprint) motif denotes a birth in the family, and so on.

SAMM

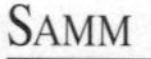

The sand dunes at Samm, 26 miles west of Jaisalmer, have an awesome beauty about them (below). The silken smooth sands are sculpted into huge, rippled hummocks by the wind. Sunrise over the dunes is spectacular. These active sand dunes can be as treacherous as they are scenic. In summer, lifted by the desert winds, they eerily disappear and reappear several yards away within a matter of a few minutes. A particularly interesting way to get to Samm is to go on a camel safari. A popular safari covering Samm and various desert villages, ruins and temples takes three nights. Sleeping overnight under a desert starscape is an unforgettable experience.

DESERT NATIONAL PARK

Located 27 miles west of Jaisalmer, Desert National Park ■ *24* contains a number of species of fauna and flora, quite remarkable for a desert region. In fact much of this 1280-square-mile park consists not of rolling sand dunes but scrubland with its own characteristic trees and flowers. In its arid grasslands you can see the *chinkara*, blackbuck, *nilgai*, wolf, and desert cat. There is also a wide range of birdlife, including the spotted eagle, tawny eagle, kestrel and lanner falcon, sandgrouse, desert courser and of course the rare desert bird known as the great Indian bustard.

POKHARAN

This interesting little garrison town at the very gates of Jaisalmer was the outpost of the rival kingdom of Jodhpur. It has a little fort and some beautiful sandstone *chhatris* or cenotaphs. The sandstone here is a deep beetroot red. Just outside this medieval fortress town is the site where India tested its nuclear device in 1974 and 1998. This links back curiously to a legend from the *Ramayana*, according to which Lord

Pokharan Fort museum.

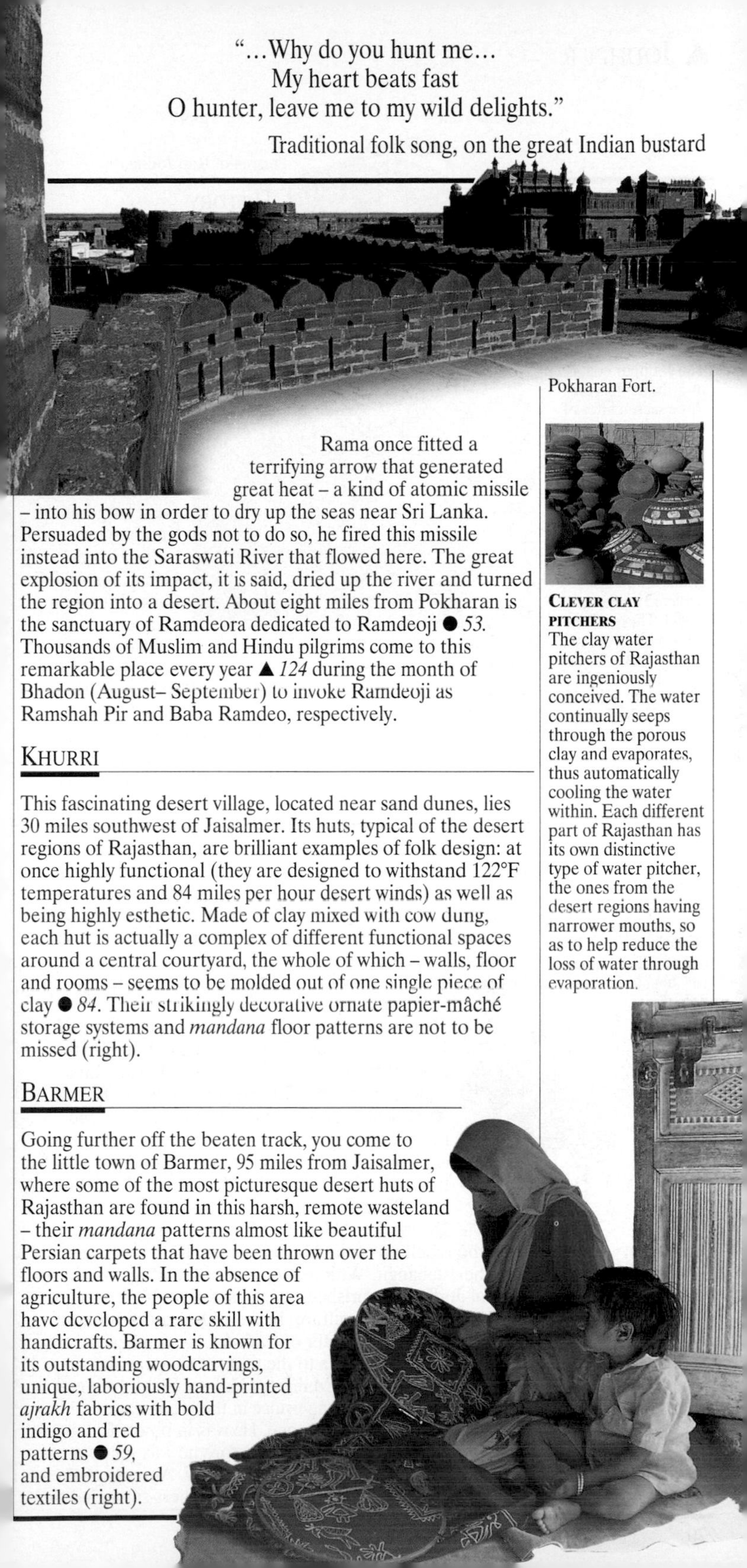

"...Why do you hunt me...
My heart beats fast
O hunter, leave me to my wild delights."

Traditional folk song, on the great Indian bustard

Pokharan Fort.

Rama once fitted a terrifying arrow that generated great heat – a kind of atomic missile – into his bow in order to dry up the seas near Sri Lanka. Persuaded by the gods not to do so, he fired this missile instead into the Saraswati River that flowed here. The great explosion of its impact, it is said, dried up the river and turned the region into a desert. About eight miles from Pokharan is the sanctuary of Ramdeora dedicated to Ramdeoji ● *53*. Thousands of Muslim and Hindu pilgrims come to this remarkable place every year ▲ *124* during the month of Bhadon (August– September) to invoke Ramdeoji as Ramshah Pir and Baba Ramdeo, respectively.

CLEVER CLAY PITCHERS
The clay water pitchers of Rajasthan are ingeniously conceived. The water continually seeps through the porous clay and evaporates, thus automatically cooling the water within. Each different part of Rajasthan has its own distinctive type of water pitcher, the ones from the desert regions having narrower mouths, so as to help reduce the loss of water through evaporation.

KHURRI

This fascinating desert village, located near sand dunes, lies 30 miles southwest of Jaisalmer. Its huts, typical of the desert regions of Rajasthan, are brilliant examples of folk design: at once highly functional (they are designed to withstand 122°F temperatures and 84 miles per hour desert winds) as well as being highly esthetic. Made of clay mixed with cow dung, each hut is actually a complex of different functional spaces around a central courtyard, the whole of which – walls, floor and rooms – seems to be molded out of one single piece of clay ● *84*. Their strikingly decorative ornate papier-mâché storage systems and *mandana* floor patterns are not to be missed (right).

BARMER

Going further off the beaten track, you come to the little town of Barmer, 95 miles from Jaisalmer, where some of the most picturesque desert huts of Rajasthan are found in this harsh, remote wasteland – their *mandana* patterns almost like beautiful Persian carpets that have been thrown over the floors and walls. In the absence of agriculture, the people of this area have developed a rare skill with handicrafts. Barmer is known for its outstanding woodcarvings, unique, laboriously hand-printed *ajrakh* fabrics with bold indigo and red patterns ● *59*, and embroidered textiles (right).

Portrait of Rao Jodha.

COAT-OF-ARMS
The Jodhpur coat-of-arms depicts the three sacred kites of the goddess Durga and the Rathor clan's battle cry, "*Ran banka Rathor*", which means "Rathor, invincible in battle". What is interesting is the grains of millet depicted on the shield. They represent the words of Sher Shah, Sultan of Delhi, who having very narrowly defeated the Jodhpur armies, ruefully commented, "For just a handful of millet, I nearly lost all of Hindustan."

JODHPUR LANCERS
The Jodhpur Lancers were a crack regiment raised in the late 19th century. They sailed to China in 1899 to help the British put down the Boxer Rebellion. The first time they went on a cavalry charge, they gallantly (and foolhardily) went in with their lances reversed, until their commander, Sir Pratap Singh, had the honor of drawing first blood. They fought alongside the Cossacks and are said to have been slightly disdainful of the latter's inferior standards of horsemanship.

HISTORY

The kingdom of Jodhpur was ruled by the powerful Rathor clan. The Rathors trace their ancestry back to Lord Rama, the hero of the epic *Ramayana,* and, through him, to the sun god himself. In AD 470, Nayan Pal, a Rathor prince, established himself as the ruler of the great kingdom of Kannauj in central India. However, by 1192 Kannauj fell to the Muslim invader, Mohammed Ghori. Rao Siyaji, an heir to the throne, escaped with the traditional *panchranga* ("five-colored") flag of the Rathors and marched into the deserts of Rajasthan with his followers to set up a new kingdom there. By the 15th century the Rathors ruled all of Marwar, with their capital at Mandore. Shortly after, they went to war with the maharanas of Mewar over the accession to the throne of Chittorgarh. The conflict was successfully resolved in 1459. Rao Jodha, the ruler of Marwar, abandoned his old capital and built a new fort on the rocky cliffs of what is now Jodhpur. Unfortunately, the legend goes, in the process he had to displace a hermit who was meditating at the site, and the hermit placed a curse on his descendants, saying henceforth they would be plagued by famine every year. Rao Jodha later placated the holy man, but the curse could not be withdrawn completely – which, they say, is the reason why, even today, there is a drought in Jodhpur every three or four years.

MEWAR AND THE MUGHALS. Rao Ganga Singh of Jodhpur (reigned 1516–32) fought alongside the army of the great warrior king of Mewar, Rana Sanga, against the first Mughal emperor, Babur ● *36*. But over the next half century or so, the rulers of Jodhpur allied themselves with Babur's grandson, Akbar. Several rulers of Jodhpur became trusted lieutenants of the Mughals, such as Raja Sur, who conquered Gujarat and much of the Deccan for Akbar, and Raja Gaj Singh, who put down the rebellion of the Mughal prince, Khurram, against his father, Jahangir. With the support of the Mughals, the court of Jodhpur flourished and the kingdom became a great center of the arts and culture. In the 17th century Jodhpur became a flourishing center of trade for the camel caravans moving from Central Asia to the ports of Gujarat and vice versa. In 1657, however, Maharaja Jaswant Singh (reigned 1638–78) backed the wrong prince in the great war of succession to the Mughal throne. He was in power for almost twenty-five years with Aurangzeb before he was sent out to the frontier as viceroy in Afghanistan ● *37*. Aurangzeb then tried to seize his infant son, but loyal retainers smuggled the

Seal of Jodhpur.

little prince out of his clutches, hidden, they say, in a basket of sweets.

POLITICAL STRIFE. The kingdom of Jodhpur then formed a triple alliance with Udaipur and Jaipur, which together threw off the Mughal yoke. As a result, the maharajas of Jodhpur finally regained the privilege of marrying Udaipur princesses – something they had forfeited when they had allied themselves with the Mughals. A condition of these marriages, however, was that the sons born of the Udaipur princesses would be first in line to the Jodhpur throne. This soon led to considerable jealousy. Nearly a century of turmoil followed, culminating in Jodhpur falling under the influence of, first, the Marathas, and then, in 1818, the British. The state of affairs was such that a young Rathor prince, when asked where Jodhpur was, simply pointed to the sheath of his dagger and said, "Inside here".

SIR PRATAP SINGH. In the 1870's, a remarkable man came to the fore in Jodhpur: Sir Pratap Singh (left) ● *114*. A son of the Maharaja of Jodhpur, he himself ruled a small neighboring kingdom called Idar, but abdicated to become Regent of Jodhpur, which he ruled, in effect, for nearly fifty years. Sir Pratap Singh was a great warrior and the epitome of Rajput chivalry. He became an intimate friend of three British sovereigns. At Queen Victoria's *durbar* he is said to have presented her not with mere jewels, like everyone else, but with his own sword, his most valuable possession as a Rajput warrior. Sir Pratap Singh laid the foundation of a modern state in Jodhpur, which Maharaja Umaid Singh (reigned 1918–47) built upon ▲ *223*. The kingdom of Jodhpur was not merely the largest of the Rajput states, but also one of the most progressive. In 1949, after the independence of India, it was merged into the newly created state of Rajasthan ● *39*.

AND THEN CAME JODHPURS...
Sir Pratap Singh was the inventor of "jodhpurs", or riding breeches, as we know them today. Since he virtually lived on horseback, he gradually evolved this item of clothing with the help of his tailor to meet his own riding needs. It all began, apparently, when he got tired of the way his traditional Rajput riding pyjamas would get frayed on the inside of the knees, as he rode. He later went on to invent ankle-length jodhpur boots and the *achkan* (close-collared jacket) – which came to be adopted as the semi-formal dress of the Jodhpur court.

FISH-SHAPED IMPERIAL STANDARD
The *Mahi Maratib* was the fish-shaped imperial standard that the Mughal emperors granted only to their most trusted allies. It was granted to Raja Ajit Singh of Jodhpur.

City of Jodhpur c. 1900.

◷ Three days

PIONEER AIR ROUTE
Jodhpur's airport, surprisingly, was one of the first international airports to be set up, in the early 1930's, on the original air route from Europe to the Far East. It served KLM and Imperial Airways, the two pioneer airlines on this route (between whom there was considerable rivalry). Later came Air France, en route to French Indochina.

THE BLUE CITY
If Jaipur is the "Pink City", Jodhpur may be called the "Blue City" from the characteristic pale indigo color of its traditional homes. Originally, the color signified the home of a Jodhpuri Brahmin. The story goes that centuries ago, the Brahmins of the town painted their homes thus, because they had discovered that the color wards off mosquitoes.

The blue houses of Jodhpur.

JODHPUR TODAY

Jodhpur is today the second largest city of Rajasthan, with a population of 1.3 million. It is a major military base and an important center of research in arid-zone agriculture. Yet, in many ways, it has not changed all that much from the old fortified town that was built under the protective cover of the brooding Mehrangarh Fort. The 15th-century town walls are still there, punctuated by massive gates; and the old quarter of Jodhpur is a fascinating place, with its narrow jumble of lanes, its *havelis* and its fine medieval water tanks. Take a walk through its lanes, starting from the old Fateh Pol ("Victory Gate"), past the 15th-century Jaita Bera tank, through the colorful little lane of Jaisalmeriyon ki Gali, past the beautiful Talati ka Mahal, a palace-turned-hospital, and ending,

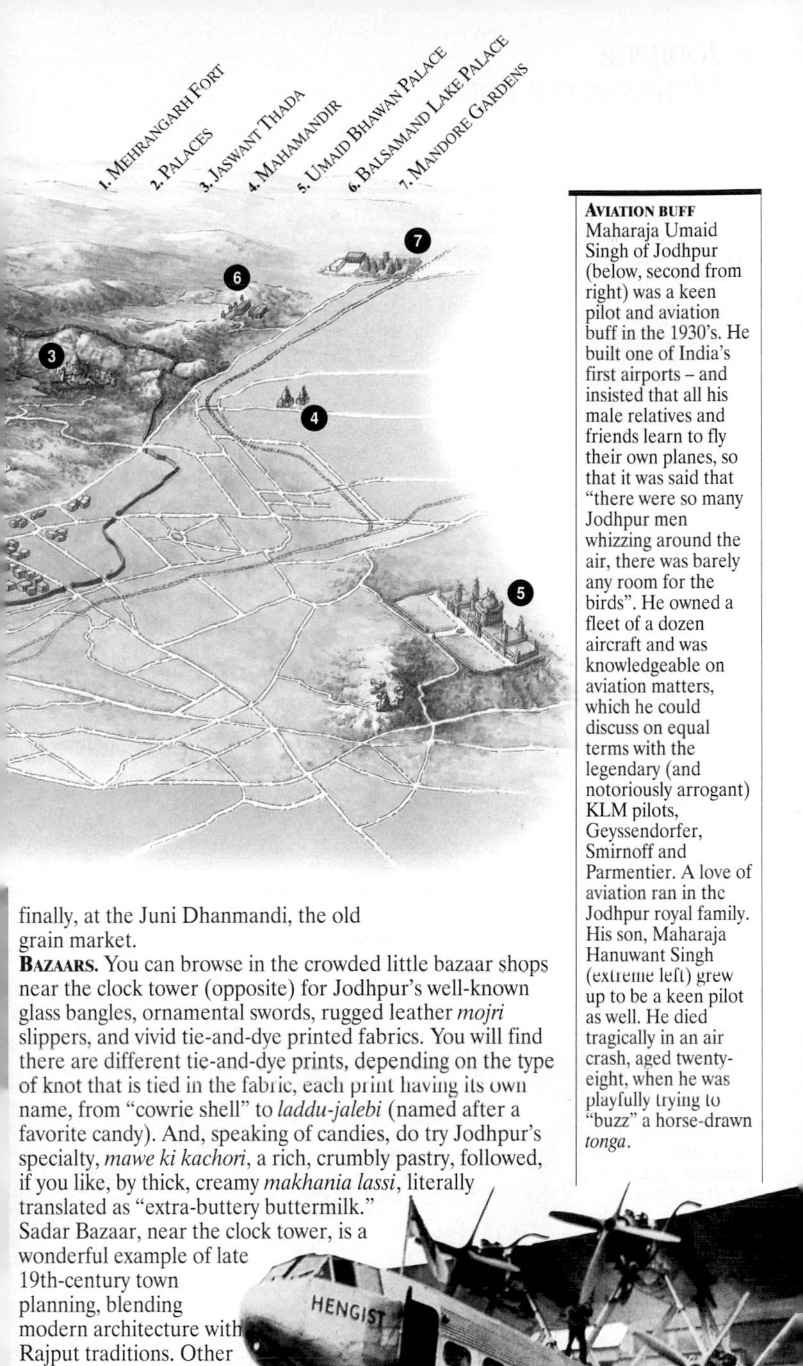

finally, at the Juni Dhanmandi, the old grain market.

Bazaars. You can browse in the crowded little bazaar shops near the clock tower (opposite) for Jodhpur's well-known glass bangles, ornamental swords, rugged leather *mojri* slippers, and vivid tie-and-dye printed fabrics. You will find there are different tie-and-dye prints, depending on the type of knot that is tied in the fabric, each print having its own name, from "cowrie shell" to *laddu-jalebi* (named after a favorite candy). And, speaking of candies, do try Jodhpur's specialty, *mawe ki kachori*, a rich, crumbly pastry, followed, if you like, by thick, creamy *makhania lassi*, literally translated as "extra-buttery buttermilk." Sadar Bazaar, near the clock tower, is a wonderful example of late 19th-century town planning, blending modern architecture with Rajput traditions. Other fine examples of this style are Jodhpur's old public buildings, such as the old railway station, the High Court, the old hospital and the Air Force Mess, which used to be a hotel, built by Maharaja Umaid Singh for the early air travelers who used to touch down here in the 1930's, en route to Batavia (Jakarta), Australia and French Indochina.

Aviation buff
Maharaja Umaid Singh of Jodhpur (below, second from right) was a keen pilot and aviation buff in the 1930's. He built one of India's first airports – and insisted that all his male relatives and friends learn to fly their own planes, so that it was said that "there were so many Jodhpur men whizzing around the air, there was barely any room for the birds". He owned a fleet of a dozen aircraft and was knowledgeable on aviation matters, which he could discuss on equal terms with the legendary (and notoriously arrogant) KLM pilots, Geyssendorfer, Smirnoff and Parmentier. A love of aviation ran in the Jodhpur royal family. His son, Maharaja Hanuwant Singh (extreme left) grew up to be a keen pilot as well. He died tragically in an air crash, aged twenty-eight, when he was playfully trying to "buzz" a horse-drawn *tonga*.

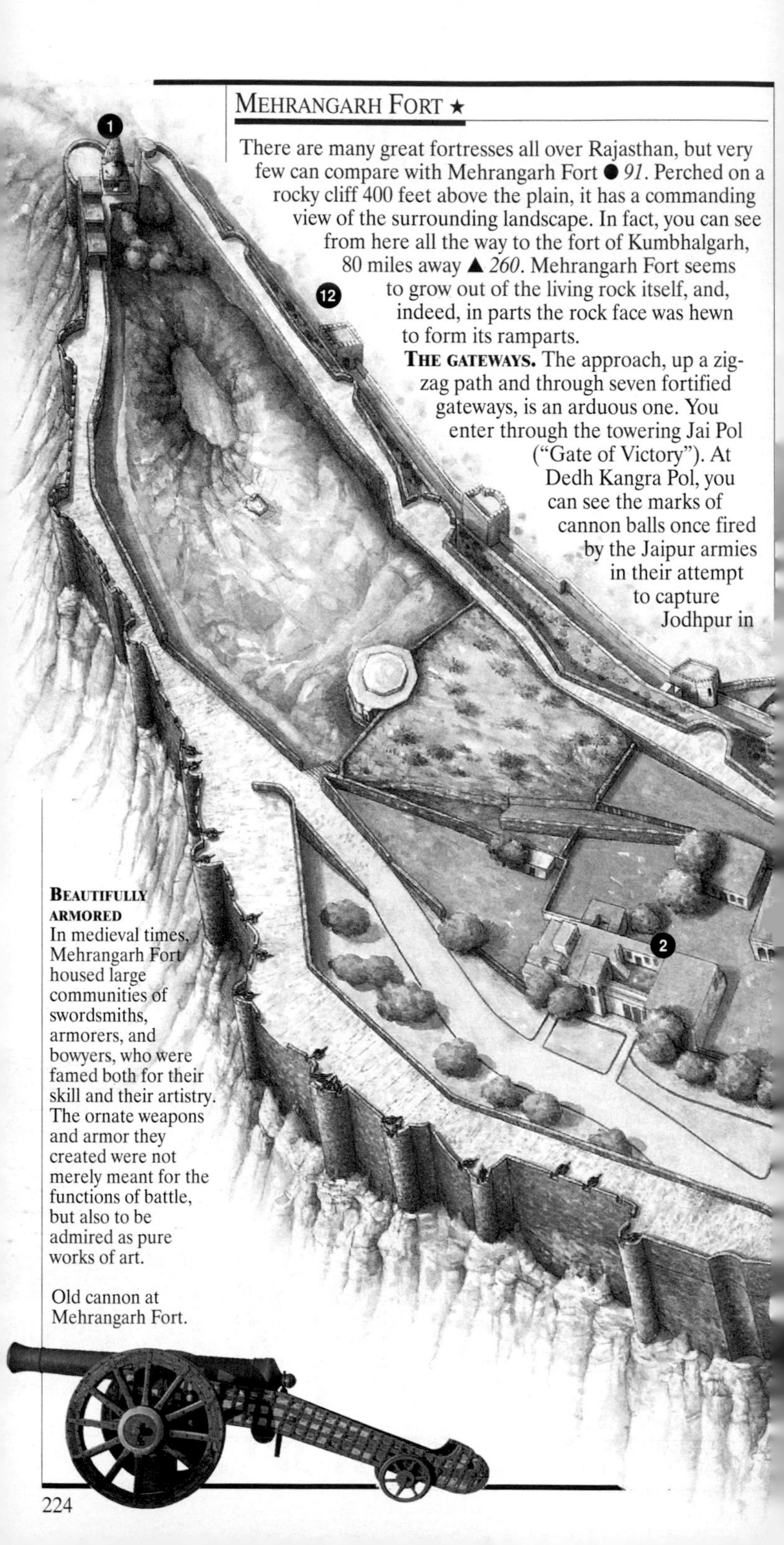

MEHRANGARH FORT ★

There are many great fortresses all over Rajasthan, but very few can compare with Mehrangarh Fort ● *91*. Perched on a rocky cliff 400 feet above the plain, it has a commanding view of the surrounding landscape. In fact, you can see from here all the way to the fort of Kumbhalgarh, 80 miles away ▲ *260*. Mehrangarh Fort seems to grow out of the living rock itself, and, indeed, in parts the rock face was hewn to form its ramparts.

THE GATEWAYS. The approach, up a zig-zag path and through seven fortified gateways, is an arduous one. You enter through the towering Jai Pol ("Gate of Victory"). At Dedh Kangra Pol, you can see the marks of cannon balls once fired by the Jaipur armies in their attempt to capture Jodhpur in

BEAUTIFULLY ARMORED
In medieval times, Mehrangarh Fort housed large communities of swordsmiths, armorers, and bowyers, who were famed both for their skill and their artistry. The ornate weapons and armor they created were not merely meant for the functions of battle, but also to be admired as pure works of art.

Old cannon at Mehrangarh Fort.

"...he who walks through it loses sense of being among buildings. It is as though he walked through mountain-gorges... "

Rudyard Kipling, *Letters of Marque*, 1899

Fort ramparts.

1807. After Dedh Kangra Pol, there is a sharp U-turn to thwart would-be attackers, and finally you come to Loha Pol, the 15th-century "Iron Gate", beside which you can see the handprints of fifteen royal *satis*, Jodhpur ranis who immolated themselves on the funeral pyres of their dead husbands. On the fort ramparts, which are 130 feet high in places, you can see a battery of fine medieval cannons. Some of these cannons were spoils of war, won in battles against the rival kingdoms of Gujarat and Jalore.

The Fort. The fort itself is divided broadly into three areas: the outer court, with its old stables and kitchens; the *durbar* hall, reception rooms and maharajas' palaces; and, finally, the *zenana*, or queens' palaces. This palace complex, constructed around a series of interconnecting courtyards and adorned with breathtakingly carved sandstone filigree work, was first built in 1459 and added to, over the centuries, by successive generations of maharajas. It is one of the most impressive palace complexes in Rajasthan. On your right, as you enter, is the white marble coronation throne, where every ruler of Jodhpur has been crowned since the 15th century.

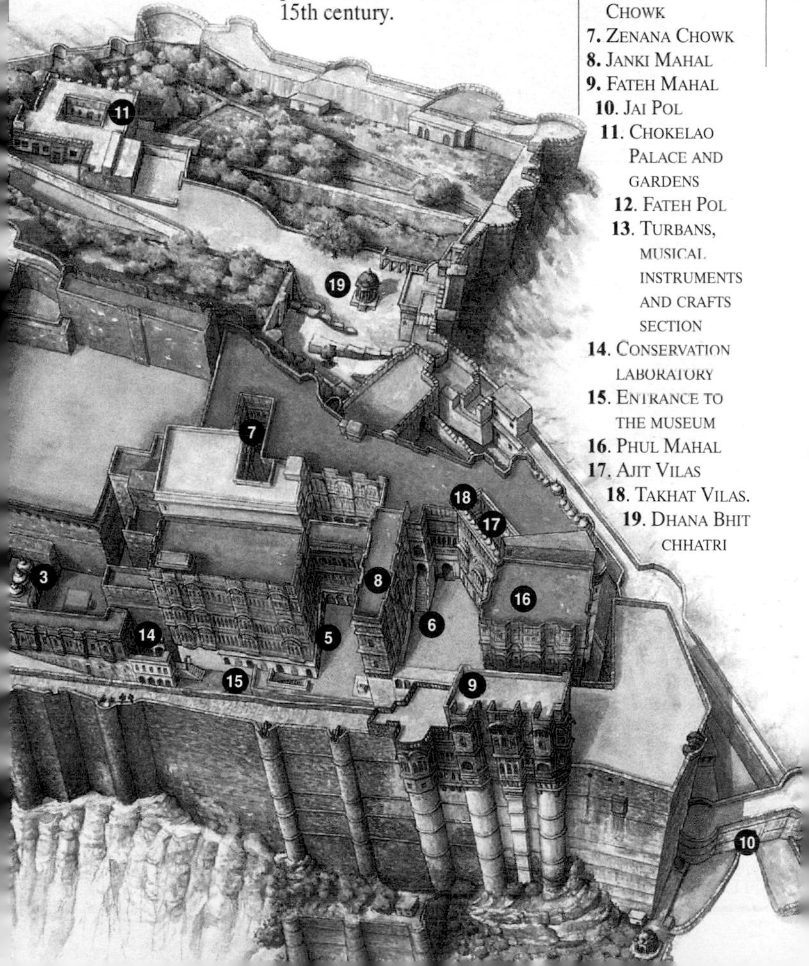

1. Chamunda Temple
2 Salim Kot
3. Nagnechiji Temple
4. Murli Manoharji Temple
5. Shriggar Chowk (Durbar)
6. Daulat Khana Chowk
7. Zenana Chowk
8. Janki Mahal
9. Fateh Mahal
10. Jai Pol
11. Chokelao Palace and Gardens
12. Fateh Pol
13. Turbans, musical instruments and crafts section
14. Conservation laboratory
15. Entrance to the museum
16. Phul Mahal
17. Ajit Vilas
18. Takhat Vilas.
19. Dhana Bhit chhatri

Façade of the palace apartments.

Mirrored walls in the fort-palace.

Palanquin in Fort Museum.

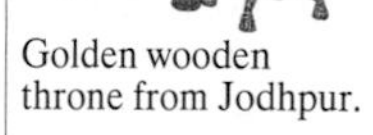

Golden wooden throne from Jodhpur.

HANGING LACE
A unique feature of the Mehrangarh Palace is the profusion of delicately latticed, overhanging *jharokhas* (balconies), which give what the celebrated architectural historian G.H.R. Tillotson has described as "the appearance of a piece of hanging lace".

FORT MUSEUM. This is one of the finest museums in Rajasthan and certainly the best laid out. In the palanquin section of the fort museum, you can see an interesting collection of old royal palanquins, including the elaborate domed gilt *mahadola* palanquin, which was won in battle from the Governor of Gujarat in 1730 ▲ *220*. Next comes the *howdah* section, with perhaps one of the finest collections of ornate elephant *howdahs* in the world. The most beautiful of these elephant seats, in engraved silver, was presented to Jaswant Singh by the Mughal emperor Shah Jahan ▲ *220*.

MAAN VILAS. Maan Vilas has one of the finest collections of weapons in India: everything from medieval mortars shaped like crocodiles to shields decorated with semi-precious stones. The swords here are particularly noteworthy (right). They range from exquisite damascened Mughal swords (including the sword of Emperor Akbar ● *36* himself) to Rao Jodha's enormous *khanda* (sabre with a straight blade), weighing over seven pounds.

UMAID VILAS. As you pass into Umaid Vilas,

"...the splendour of a Palace that might have been built by Titans and coloured by the morning sun."

Rudyard Kipling, *Letters of Marque*, 1899

you will see an excellent collection of miniature paintings from all the major schools of Rajasthan, but mainly, obviously, from Jodhpur itself. The early Jodhpur miniatures were strongly influenced by Jain art, but by the 18th century, because of Jodhpur's close links with the Delhi court, a marked Mughal influence began to manifest itself. Two particularly interesting paintings here, incidentally, are one portraying a maharaja playing *holi* with his queens, splashing each other with ceremonial colors, and one depicting a maharaja and his queens playing polo together.

TAKHAT MAHAL. Takhat Mahal is a huge royal bedchamber, with exquisitely lacquered walls depicting scenes of dancing girls and legendary lovers. (You might wonder about the glittering colored globes hanging from the fine beamed ceilings, but then you'll realize that they're just Christmas decorations that someone, curiously, decided to add to the decor in the 1930's!) This section of the museum, currently closed because of renovation work and due to reopen soon, will probably be dedicated to radio and television.

PHOOL MAHAL. Going up the stairs you come to Phool Mahal ("Flower Palace"), which is perhaps even more impressive than Moti Mahal. Built in the 18th century as a Hall of Private Audience, it has magnificently painted walls depicting the various musical *ragas* (classical Indian patterns of melody and rhythm) and their changing moods. If you look closely, you might detect a faint European influence in these 19th-century murals.

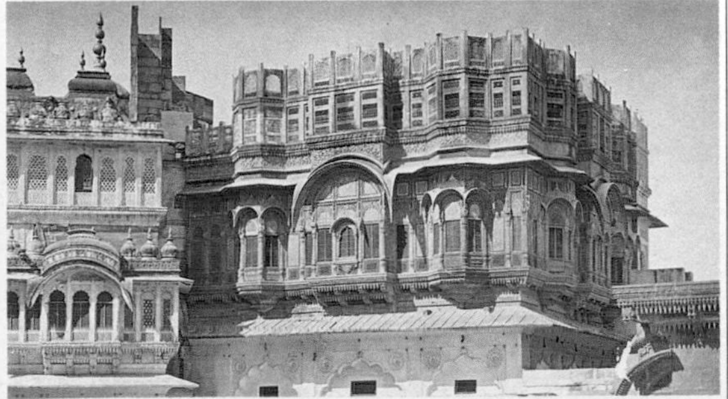

Lithograph of Mehrangarh Fort.

ROYAL CRADLE

The present Maharaja of Jodhpur once slept in a quixotic cradle, which ran on electricity and was automatically rocked by the arms of the figurines on either side, while ornately carved fairies – and the infant's father – looked down on him protectively. It was a gift to the little prince from Jodhpur's Public Works Department, and was inscribed "with profound loyalty".

Stained-glass windows of the royal bedroom in a palace.

NOT KING-SIZED

A feature of many Rajput palaces is the fact that the maharajas' apartments always occupied a much smaller area than the ranis' apartments. The reason is that, in medieval times, the maharaja spent most of the year out on his military campaigns, so the permanent residents of the palace were mainly the womenfolk.

Singhar Chowk, the courtyard of the palace complex.

SHOEING THE MISTRESS
The pearl shoes of Angoori Bai, a favorite mistress of Raja Gaj Singh (reigned 1620–38), played an interesting little role in altering the course of Jodhpur's history in the 17th century. Raja Gaj Singh's ambitious younger son, Jaswant Singh, presented these shoes to Angoori Bai, kneeling humbly to shoe her feet himself. In return, Angoori Bai persuaded his father to name Jaswant Singh as his successor in place of the rightful successor, the valiant and chivalrous Amar Singh.

SARDAR VILAS. In Sardar Vilas there are some classic examples of Jodhpur's celebrated traditional woodwork, including an array of doors in a variety of styles, superbly carved, lacquered, ornamented with gilt and inlaid with ivory.

KHAB KA MAHAL AND JHANKI MAHAL. Through Khab ka Mahal, which once housed the Prime Minister's office, and an old conference room for Rathor's nobles, you come to Jhanki Mahal ("Palace of the Glimpses"). This palace is named for its exquisitely carved sandstone lattice windows, through which princesses and noble ladies would view the world outside without themselves being seen. The stone latticework here is so fine, it actually resembles lace. There are nearly 250 different latticework patterns used all over the palace complex, each of which has its own name, such as *chaubla*, or checkerboard, and *chaufulia*, an elaborate, four-petalled flower pattern. On the walls of Jhanki Mahal, you can see old mirrors, in which generation after generation of beautiful Jodhpur ranis must have admired themselves. Here there is also a fascinating display of royal infants' cradles, which range from the exotic (do not miss the splendidly mirrored cradle with the peacock motifs) to the idiosyncratic.

MOTI MAHAL. Moti Mahal ("Pearl Palace") is a throne room built in the late 16th century. Judging from its magnificence and size, it was originally conceived as a Hall of Public Audience. Its ceiling is gorgeously embellished with mirror-work and gilt. (It is said that nearly 80 pounds of gold was used here!) Its walls are lustrously polished, and decorated with a triple band of ornate niches in which lamps once flickered, reflecting off the polished walls. At the far end is an octagonal silver throne, a rare and priceless heirloom dating back to the 17th century. A museum houses a very interesting collection of over a hundred different types of turbans from the different parts of Rajasthan, including a strange hunting turban with a visor and backflap, as well as traditional musical instruments and pottery.

JASWANT THADA. On the way down from the fort, on your left, is Jaswant Thada, the graceful marble cenotaph of Maharaja Jaswant Singh II (reigned 1873–95) and those of the other maharajas of Jodhpur who died in this century. Wives and concubines committed *sati* on Jaswanti funeral pyre. The cenotaphs of earlier maharajas and maharanis are at Mandore ▲ *232*.

Jaswant Thada.

UMAID BHAWAN PALACE

The gigantic Umaid Bhawan Palace has the distinction of having been one of the largest private residences in the world ● *88*. It has 347 rooms and used over 2.5 million cubic feet of sandstone and marble! But what is probably even more remarkable is the reason it was built in the first place: there was a major famine in Jodhpur in the early 1920's, and the construction of this enormous palace was one of the public works projects devised to offer employment to the people of the kingdom. It took fifteen years to complete. The palace was designed by a British architect, H.V. Lanchester, who was an admirer of Lutyens, the designer of New Delhi, and in both the style and the scale of the Umaid Bhawan you can see a reflection of Delhi's Viceregal Lodge (now Rashtrapati Bhawan). The interior of the palace was decorated in the Beaux Arts and Art Deco styles. And it incorporated everything from two theaters and an indoor swimming pool to its own central air-cooling plant. Unfortunately, however, not everything went according to plan. The furniture for the palace, ordered from Maples of London, was lost twice – the first time when the ship carrying it to India got torpedoed during World War II, and the second time when the company's warehouses in London were bombed by the Luftwaffe. If you think the palace's entrance hall with its sweeping marble staircases and wildlife trophies is impressive, just wait till you come to the Central Hall, under the dome, 198 feet high.

PUPPET SHOW
The finest puppeteers of Rajasthan are the Barlai Bhatts, originally from the Jodhpur area. A favorite theme of their puppet shows is the bravery of the Rathor prince, Amar Singh, who was killed after single-handedly slaying five Mughal noblemen. Another popular theme of the puppeteers is the comic drama of the washerman and his shrew of a wife in their ongoing marital battle.

MELTING INTO CORNERS
When Umaid Bhawan Palace's gigantic dome was being built, a young Jodhpur engineer thought up an ingenious way to install the cornerstones without damaging them. He first positioned huge blocks of ice in the corners and then placed the cornerstones on top of them. As the ice slowly melted, the cornerstones settled perfectly – and flawlessly – into place.

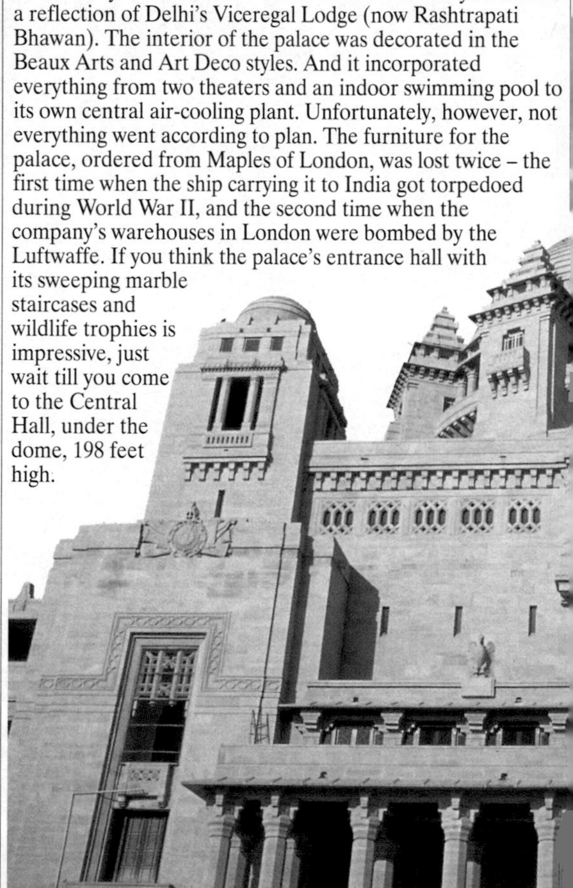

Umaid Bhawan Palace.

"In a few hundred years – probably much sooner – it [Umaid Bhawan] will have become one of the great Indian ruins, like Fatehpur Sikri or Mandu."

Ruth Prawer Jhabvala, *Autobiography of a Princess*, 1975

(Old-timers in the palace will tell you of a banquet held here in the 1940's – a sit-down affair for a thousand people.) The reception room is worth seeing, with its murals by a refugee Polish artist, which can only be termed "Ashokan Art Deco"! Wander around the spacious old billiard room, the maharaja's personal office, now a lounge, and try to take a look at some of the suites – the Maharaja suite, for instance, where the black marble Art Deco bathroom speaks volumes of the old princely lifestyle. There is also an excellent little museum here of some of the royal family's possessions. The present Maharaja now lives on the first floor of the palace, while the rest of the palace has been turned into a luxury hotel.

MAHAMANDIR

The great Shiva temple of Mahamandir, dedicated to the legendary yogi Jalandarnath (one of the founders of Hatha Yoga), was built by Raja Man Singh (1803–1843) as a mark of respect for his guru Devnath. The latter, a distant disciple of Jalandarnath, had helped the maharaja recover his throne and had a great influence over him. The temple was the first structure in Jodhpur to be built outside the city walls. It had to be surrounded by its own fortified ramparts, an indication of how insecure life was in Rajasthan in the early 19th century. Mahamandir is notable for its profusion of finely carved pillars, one hundred in all, and it is an excellent example of the architectural and artistic impulses of Jodhpur during the reign of Raja Man Singh, himself an esthete, scholar and patron of the arts.

ROYAL RAILWAY SALOON
A luxury train called the "Palace on Wheels", which takes you through Rajasthan, has been ranked by travel writers as one of "The World's Ten Best Railway Journeys". However, the old saloons of the Maharaja of Jodhpur (above) are now "parked" at the Umaid Bhawan Palace. Carefully maintaining their original 1930's charm, they are being converted into suites, a dining car and lounge, and guests can stay on board!

TREND-SETTING TURBAN
Each region of Rajasthan takes great pride in its own distinctive way of tying a turban. The people of Jodhpur, however, claim that the Jodhpuri turban is superior to all the rest, pointing to the fact that it has been adopted by trend-setters all over Rajasthan, from Bikaner to Jaipur.

Cenotaphs of Jodhpur's rulers.

LEAVING HIS MARK
Colonel Tod, who came to Mandore in 1820, admitted to scrawling graffiti on the statue of Pabuji and his steed Kesar Kalami ("Black Caesar"). He confessed: "Inscribing my name at the foot of Black Caesar [I] bade adieu to the ancient Mandor."

Hall dedicated to heroes and gods, Mandore (right).

MANDORE

Mandore, located about 5 miles north of Jodhpur, was the former capital of the maharajas of Marwar, but was later abandoned for the security of Mehrangarh Fort. Here you will find the *dewals,* or cenotaphs, of Jodhpur's former rulers. Unlike the usual *chhatri*-shaped cenotaphs typical of Rajasthan, they are built along the lines of a Hindu temple, four stories high, with fine columns and an elegant spire, all in red sandstone. The most impressive is the *dewal* of Maharaja Ajit Singh (reigned 1725–1750). These cenotaphs are set in beautiful landscaped gardens. Nearby is the Hall of Heroes (also called "The Shrine of the Three Hundred Million Gods"), dedicated to various deities and fabled Rajput folk heroes, whose statues (each one astride his steed) are carved out of rock and painted in bright colors. Next door is a small temple dedicated to Behru, with two huge statues framing an effigy of Ganesh ● *47* (above). And as you climb up the hill, you come to the ruined city of Mandore, with the old summer palace of Abhai Singh ▲ *227*.

VILLAGE DURRIES
The villages around Jodhpur are famed for their *durries* ● *68*. Woven on quaint, primitive looms by family members, the *durries* are known the world over for their beautiful simplicity.

Bishnoi farm

BALSAMAND

This pretty lakeside pleasure palace of the maharajas, 4 miles from Jodhpur, is a small oasis in the desert. Set by the side of an artificial lake created in the 12th century, measuring nearly half a mile long, the palace itself was built in the late 19th century, during the time when the lake was being enlarged. The red sandstone façade is richly carved with traditional Hindu motifs, but the interiors are clearly European, with a strong Italian influence. Around the palace is a pleasant garden and a small bird sanctuary.

BISHNOI FARMS

All around Jodhpur lie the picturesque farms of the Bishnoi community. They are worth seeing,

"It was more quiet and empty and lonely than any other place I know on earth...I thought the cenotaphs themselves resembled vultures."

Ruth Prawer Jhabvala, *Autobiography of a Princess*, 1975

not just for their folk architecture – an ingenious marriage of the functional and the esthetic – but also for a close look at the Bishnois' fascinating way of life. Both a rural community and a religious sect, the Bishnois follow the teachings of Jambha, a 15th-century master. Abstemious and vegetarian, they continue to protect black antilopes ■ *25*, and green trees such as the famous *khejra* ■ *30*, ▲ *203*. They do not live in villages, but in isolated farms, so the best way to visit these farms and meet the Bishnois is by hiring a guide.

OSIYAN ★

The temple complex of Osiyan lies 40 miles northwest of Jodhpur. Once a great religious center, its ruins today present one of the finest depictions anywhere of how Indian temple architecture evolved between the 8th and 12th centuries. There are altogether sixteen Jain and Hindu temples here. Start with the oldest, the small Sun Temple III (early 8th century), remarkable for its carved doorway, and considered one of the most impressive in India. Its vestibule is also worth seeing, with its fine carved ceiling and its frieze of Lord Krishna. The temples especially worth visiting are (in order) the Harihara Temple I, the Harihara Temple III, the Sun Temple II, and the Sachiya Mata Temple.

HARIHARA TEMPLES. The Harihara Temple I (mid-8th century) is noteworthy for its delicate cornice frieze depicting the Krishna-lila legends. But the most beautiful of all the temples at Osiyan is the Harihara Temple III (early 9th century). In fact, it is one of the finest examples of how the ancient Indian builders married architectural grace with sculptural exuberance. Don't miss the exquisite doorway and columns of the sanctum, and the highly ornamented dome-like ceiling. The richly carved outer walls of the sanctuary are also worth seeing.

SUN TEMPLE AND SACHIYA MATA TEMPLE. The Sun Temple II (8th century) is interesting mainly for its curiously Grecian-looking porch columns. The Sachiya Mata Temple (11th to 12th centuries), still in use as a temple, is notable mainly for its imposing multi-turreted spire.

Sachiya Mata Temple (top); Mahavira Temple (above); stairway in Sachiya Mata Temple (below).

▲ Expression of Piety
Mahavira Temple, Osiyan

Although now a nondescript little town in the middle of an arid expanse, Osiyan was from the 8th to the 11th centuries an important commercial, cultural, and religious center. During that time, a group of Hindu and Jain temples were built at this site. Of great stylistic significance, this group includes handsome examples of the earliest structural temples built in western India. The Mahavira Temple of the Jains is the best preserved at Osiyan because the Jains carefully conserved their temples through repairs and renovations. For the Jains, Osiyan has special significance because it is associated with the origin of the Oswal Jain community of merchants.

Figure in a niche
Many temples of western India feature the eight *dik-palas* (guardians of the cardinal directions) on their exterior wall facing their particular direction. These figures are usually accompanied by their animal vehicles. In this temple, the *dik-palas* are placed in niches framed by pilasters and surmounted by a trellis roof which echoes the style of the spire and the domical roof of the temple.

Pillars
The pillars in the temple are decorated with auspicious vase and foliage motifs popular in Indian religious architecture. The delicate and elaborate treatment of the motifs contrasts superbly with the plain surface of the pillars.

Mahavira Temple.

Temple spire
Built of sandstone, the temple complex stands on a vast terrace. As was the prevalent practice, all the various components of the temple are united in one structure along its longitudinal axis. The spire was rebuilt in the 11th century to replace the original one that had collapsed.

Chapels
In the enclosure of the temple are seven *devakulikas* (chapels), each with its shrine chamber and portico (above). Each of the chapels with its decorative moldings and carvings is an architectural masterpiece. Unlike the later Jain temples of the region, the number of chapels here does not correspond to any established convention because the style is still in its emergent stages. Chapels along the enclosure walls became an essential characteristic of Jain temple-complexes in the centuries that followed. Generally they assumed the form of simple cells joined together with a common colonnaded corridor.

Strut figures on ceiling.

Ceiling
Elaborately conceived and decorated, the ceiling (above) consists of a succession of receding concentric courses with delicately embellished lace-like scalloped motifs and a hanging pendant. The most striking feature of this arrangement is the radial struts portraying standing female dancers and musicians in an aureole, often formed by the foliage of trees.

Folk motifs.

Decorative art has been used in Rajasthan to offset the starkness of the desert. Everything in daily use is painted or decorated, from the walls of houses to pots, pitchers, musical instruments, animal carts, and even the animals themselves, thus making Rajasthan a treasure trove of traditional art. As the anthropologist, Verrier Elwin, says, "God put the tool in the wood-carver's hand. He gave the brush to the village woman."

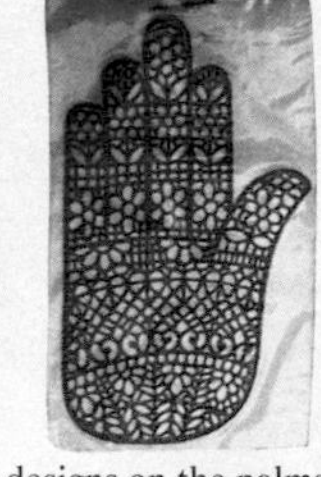

MANDANA
Wall paintings are usually executed with a small piece of cloth wrapped around the fingers. The designs can be symbolic, geometrical, or floral. Before each festival, the walls are "painted" with a mixture of cow dung and mud, and then adorned with new designs.

MEHENDI
Mehendi, the art of henna decoration, is commonly practiced in Rajasthan. Traditionally, the art involved forming hand patterns by rolling henna paste between thumb and index finger and forming the strands into *jali* designs on the palms. The less adept used matchsticks or polythene cones as brushes. The henna pattern is allowed to dry for some hours, then the henna scraped off. The pattern remains on the hand for two to three days.

A GRAND BEAUTY
Any animal which provides a livelihood is treated with great respect. The *mahout's* (elephant keeper's) family will bathe the elephant and then decorate it, either by themselves or by engaging a painter.

PROTECTIVE DÉCOR
Mandana designs are made out of rice paste or lime. Laid outside the entrance, they were supposed to keep evil forces out of the house.

CLAY FIGURES
Clay is molded into toys in the shape of human or animal figures. The link between ritual and play is intimate. The same figures serve a dual purpose, as toys and as votive offerings. A clay doll could be dressed up in red and worshiped as Gangaur or Parvati. Animal figures are sometimes found at tribal shrines as votive offerings.

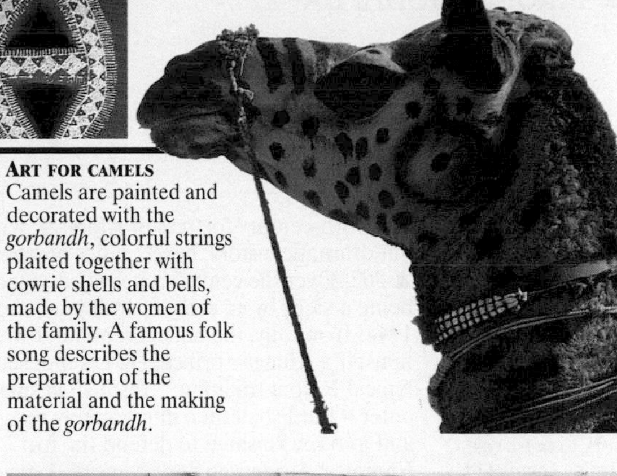

Art for camels
Camels are painted and decorated with the *gorbandh*, colorful strings plaited together with cowrie shells and bells, made by the women of the family. A famous folk song describes the preparation of the material and the making of the *gorbandh*.

Wall paintings of deities
Since most forms of traditional art have religious themes as their subject, it is not unusual to see images of deities (above) painted on the walls of houses.

Paintings around doorways
The white walls around the doorways are often decorated with figures of elephants and horses, symbols of strength and longevity.

Decorated houses
Following a 5000-year-old tradition, Rajasthani women decorate the walls of their houses ● *85*. The role of decoration for its own sake results in many geometric and abstract patterns. Specific areas are decorated, especially the entrance. The intricacy and beauty of the decorative detail denotes the wealth and status of the owner. A decorated house is considered auspicious, whereas absence of decoration indicates misfortune. Houses are not painted for a year when a death occurs.

CURE FOR SNAKE BITES
Tejaji is a folk deity, originally from Nagaur, who is believed to offer a miraculous snakebite cure. The legend goes that a snake was about to bite Tejaji, but he pleaded that he had some urgent work to finish first. Having completed the work, true to his word, Tejaji returned and offered himself to the snake. The snake duly bit and killed him, but it proclaimed that henceforth anyone chanting Tejaji's name would be cured of snakebite. Today there are Tejaji shrines all over Rajasthan which, indeed, report some miraculous cases of recovery from snakebites.

Medieval cooling system.

KHIMSAR

The 15th-century fortress of Khimsar, with its long-forgotten but dramatic history, lies 37 miles northeast of Jodhpur ▲ *202*. Over the centuries it was besieged five times – the last being a siege by an army of Jodhpur as recently as April 4, 1944! Ironically, the tank commander who led this attack was himself a Khimsar prince. He is supposed to have said, in the typical Rajput tradition, "Yes, I shall smash open the fort and enter – but I shall then immediately resign my commission and join my kinsmen to defend the fort." The fort, where Emperor Aurangzeb once came and stayed as a guest, has been converted to a hotel. It serves as a wonderful base for visits to the surrounding Bishnoi villages and for wildlife safaris.

NAGAUR

The historic, fortified town of Nagaur lies 84 miles north of Jodhpur. The mighty Nagaur Fort (right) was originally built in the 4th century, but most of what you see today dates from the 12th century onward. Set on a hill surrounded by the desert, it has two massive concentric walls, the inner one being 30 feet thick at the base! Inside are the ruins of its beautiful palaces, once set in formal gardens, where Emperor Akbar built an elaborate system of fountains. Three of the palaces are particularly worth seeing: Badal Mahal, Sheesh Mahal and Hadi Rani Mahal. All three have exquisite 18th-century frescos, painted by artists brought back from south India by Raja Bakhta Singh of Jodhpur (reigned 1751–52) after his Deccan campaigns. Hadi Rani Mahal has a particularly interesting frescoed ceiling. There is also a fascinating medieval air-cooling system in one of the palaces and an ornate old *hammam*, or bath. Unfortunately, the fort was turned into an army barracks during the 1950's and many of the frescos were vandalized. Nagaur is also known for its puppeteers and colorful annual cattle fair ● *82*.

Fresco of Krishna and the *gopis* on palace wall within Nagaur Fort.

The south

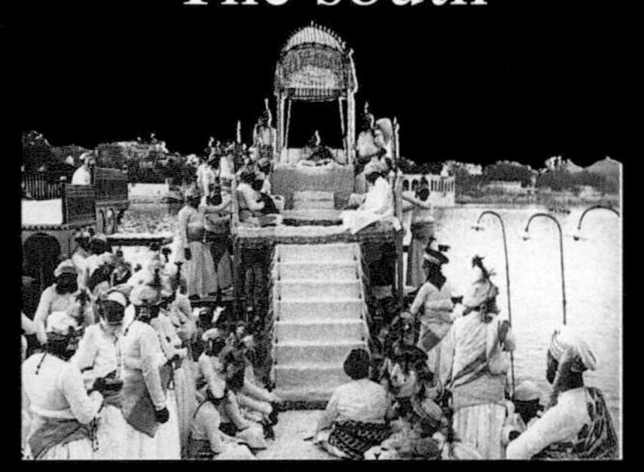

240 Udaipur
252 The Raj
254 Around Udaipur
264 Dharna Vihara
268 Mount Abu
272 Jain temples
274 Nakki Lake to Sirohi
276 Chittorgarh

◷ Nine days

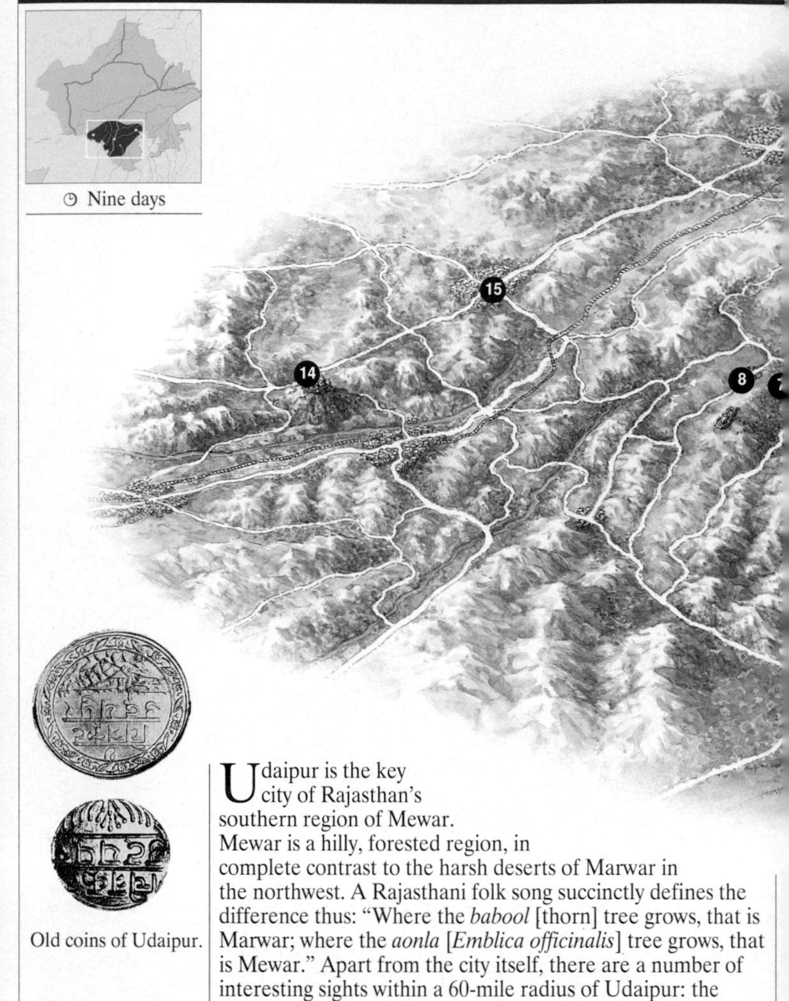

Old coins of Udaipur.

BHIL ARCHERY SKILLS
The Bhil tribesmen of Rajasthan, especially those from Udaipur, are famed for their deadly archery skills. The epic *Mahabharata* speaks of a Bhil called Eklavya who was the only man alive who could beat the legendary warrior, Arjuna, at archery. Ultimately, Eklavya, in sacrifice for his guru, destroyed his own archery skills in deference to Arjuna by chopping off his right thumb.

Udaipur is the key city of Rajasthan's southern region of Mewar. Mewar is a hilly, forested region, in complete contrast to the harsh deserts of Marwar in the northwest. A Rajasthani folk song succinctly defines the difference thus: "Where the *babool* [thorn] tree grows, that is Marwar; where the *aonla* [*Emblica officinalis*] tree grows, that is Mewar." Apart from the city itself, there are a number of interesting sights within a 60-mile radius of Udaipur: the temples of Eklingji, Nathdwara and Ranakpur, the fort of Kumbhalgarh and Jaisamand Lake. Further away are the great fort of Chittorgarh, the spectacular temples of Mount Abu and the splendid palaces of Dungarpur.

HISTORY

Of all the kingdoms of Rajasthan, the kingdom of Mewar (or Udaipur) was considered of prime importance, and its ruler acknowledged as being the most senior of all the Rajput kings ● *34*. This is because the Sisodia dynasty of Mewar was probably the oldest dynasty in the world, tracing its origins directly back through seventy-six generations to its founder, Guhil, who came to power in AD 566. However, it is not the antiquity of their lineage alone for which the Sisodias were respected, but also for the fierce zeal with which they upheld their independence and their Rajput values through the centuries. Of all the Rajput kingdoms, Mewar was the only

1. Udaipur 2. Eklingji 3. Nagda 4. Nathdwara 5. Rajsamand 6. Kankroli 7. Kumbhalgarh 8. Ghanerao 9. Ranakpur 10. Jagat 11. Rishabdev 12. Jaisamand 13. Dungarpur 14. Mount Abu 15. Sirohi 16. Chittorgarh

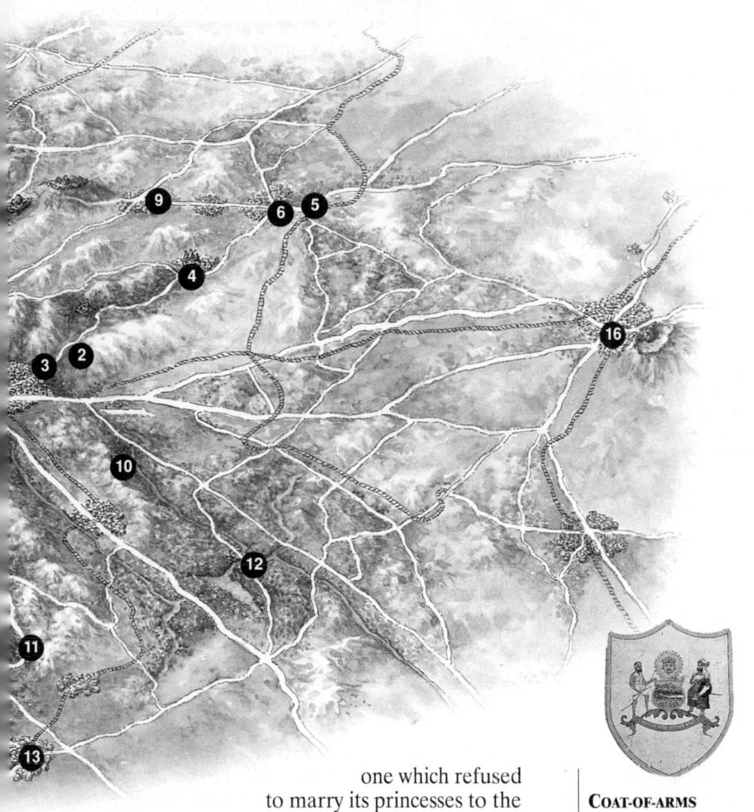

one which refused to marry its princesses to the Mughal emperors and acquire all the political advantages that accrued. The Sisodias were also staunch defenders of the Hindu faith. In fact, the dynasty's name comes from the word *sisa*, or lead, for the legend goes that a certain prince of the line was unwittingly made to eat a piece of beef. When he later discovered this, he chose to atone for his sin by swallowing molten lead. In AD 734, Bappa Rawal, the first of the great Sisodia kings, came to the throne. It was Bappa Rawal who moved his capital to the strategic hilltop fortress of Chittorgarh, which was to remain the capital of Mewar for the next eight hundred years.

Coat-of-arms
Udaipur's royal coat-of-arms depicts a blazing sun, from which its maharanas claimed direct descent. The central shield is flanked by a Rajput warrior and a Bhil archer, indicating the important role that the Bhil tribesmen played in the history of Mewar. From time immemorial, at the coronation of each maharana, a Bhil chieftain would cut his own thumb, apply a *tika* (auspicious mark) of his blood on the maharana's forehead and then lead him by the arm to his new throne.

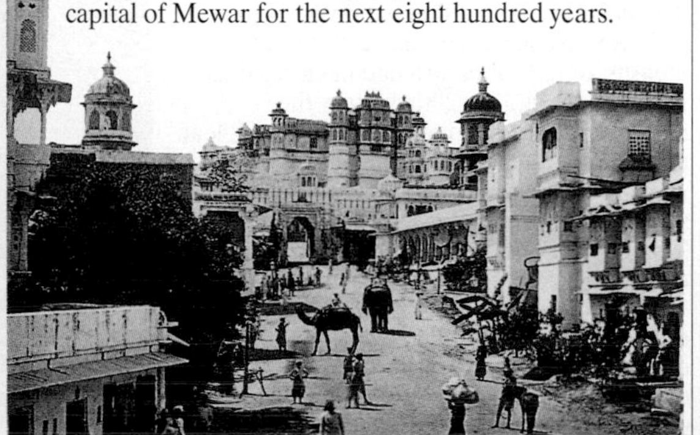

Street scene, Udaipur.

THREE SISODIA KINGS

The most glorious and eventful years of Mewar's history were probably in the 15th and 16th centuries, or more particularly, during the reign of three great Sisodia kings, Rana Kumbha, Rana Sanga and Maharana Pratap.

RANA KUMBHA. Rana Kumbha (reigned 1433–68) was a remarkably versatile man: a brilliant general, poet and musician. He built Mewar up to a position of unassailable military strength by building a chain of thirty-two forts that girdled the kingdom. But, perhaps more important, he was a patron of the arts to rival Lorenzo de Medici, and he made Chittorgarh a dazzling cultural center whose fame spread right across Hindustan.

RANA SANGA. Rana Sanga (reigned 1509–27) was a fearless warrior and a man of great chivalry and honor ● *34*. But his reign was marked by a series of continual battles, in the course of which he is said to have lost one arm and one eye, been crippled in one leg and received eighty-four different wounds on his body. The last of his battles was against the Mughal invader, Babur, in 1527. Deserted by one of his own generals, Rana Sanga was wounded in the battle and died shortly after.

MAHARANA PRATAP. Over the next half-century, most of the other Rajput rulers allowed themselves to be wooed over by the Mughals; Mewar alone held out. In 1567 Emperor Akbar decided to teach it a lesson: he attacked Chittorgarh and razed it to the ground. Five years later Maharana Pratap (reigned 1572–97) came to rule Mewar – a king without a capital. He continued to defy Akbar, and in 1576, confronted the imperial armies at Haldighati ● *36*. The battle ended in a stalemate and Maharana Pratap and his followers withdrew to the craggy hills of Mewar, from where they continued to harry the Mughals through guerilla warfare for the next twenty years. Maharana Pratap made his descendants vow that they would not sleep on beds, nor live in palaces, nor eat off metal utensils, until Chittorgarh had been regained. In fact, right into the 20th century the maharanas of Mewar continued to place a leaf platter under their regular utensils and a reed mat under their beds in symbolic continuance of this vow. When news of Maharana Pratap's death reached Emperor Akbar in 1597, it is said that the Emperor's eyes filled with tears, and he ordered his court poet to compose a poem in honor of his gallant foe.

BATTLE OF HALDIGHATI
The Battle of Haldighati in 1576, one of the most famous in Indian history, pitted the forces of Mewar against those of the Mughals ● *36*. It is interesting to note that the armies of Mewar were led by a Muslim general, Hakim Khan Suri, while the Mughal armies were led by a Rajput general, Raja Man Singh I of Jaipur.

VALIANT HERO
Maharana Pratap of Mewar is one of the greatest heroes in Rajput history. Single-handedly, for a quarter of a century, he defied the Mughal Emperor, Akbar, living in the wilderness and fighting a series of guerilla battles.

"There is not a pass in the alpine Aravalli that is not sanctified by some deed of [Maharana] Pratap – some brilliant victory, or oftener, more glorious defeat."

Colonel Tod, *Annals and Antiquities of Rajasthan*, 1829

Founding of Udaipur

One day in 1559 Rana Udai Singh II (reigned 1537–72) was out hunting on the banks of a lake when he came across a hermit meditating. The hermit blessed the young prince and advised him that this very spot would be an auspicious site for him to build a new city. After the fall of Chittorgarh to the Mughal army of Emperor Akbar, Rana Udai Singh II, needing a new capital, followed the advice he had received years before. Thus the city of Udaipur was born, watered by the beautiful Pichola Lake and guarded by hills on all four sides. It could not have been more fortunately sited.

Cultural renaissance. In the early 17th century, after decades of continuous battling with the Mughals, Rana Amar Singh (reigned 1597–1620) finally negotiated a treaty of peace with Emperor Jahangir under one condition: that his descendants would never be under an obligation to appear personally at the Mughal court. This new era of peace saw a great renaissance of the arts in Udaipur, with the building of a series of beautiful palaces along the lake front and the blossoming of the Mewar school of painting. In the early 18th century, with the disintegration of the Mughal Empire, the maharanas, with their new independence, began to set up a splendid court. The unemployed artists of Delhi found a welcome haven under its patronage.

British rule. Shortly after, a period of strife began, with internal dissensions, followed by incursions of the Maratha armies. In 1818 the Rana of Udaipur finally signed a treaty accepting the paramountcy of the British.

Courtly procession (below top). Maharana Bhim Singh receiving Colonel Tod at the Mewar court (below bottom).

Mewar school of miniatures

The Mewar school of miniatures is the oldest in Rajasthan, dating back to the 15th century. The paintings are unique in their liveliness, both through the way they depict human figures and in their brilliant primary colors: scarlets, golden yellows and lapis lazuli. Of all the miniature schools of Rajasthan, the Mewar school remained, for reasons political as well as artistic, the one that was least influenced by the Mughals. The paintings are incredibly intricate in their details, often having being painted with just a single hair plucked from the throat of a squirrel.

Durbar of the Maharana of Udaipur, late 19th century.

1. CITY PALACE
2. LAKE PALACE
3. JAG MANDIR
4. BHARATIYA LOK KALA MANDAL
5. SAHELIYON KI BARI
6. SHIV NIWAS

A PIECE OF VENICE
Udaipur today is one of the most picturesque cities in India, set as it is on three beautiful lakes and surrounded by an amphitheater of hills. In fact, Lord Northbrook, the 19th-century British viceroy, described it thus: "Take a lake about the size of Orta, with lower hills and of a lighter colour; put the walls of Verona on the lower hills with a fort or two, add islands smaller than those on Lake Maggiore, covered with marble pleasure palaces and domes… Pile up half a dozen French châteaux on the side and end with a piece of Venice."

UDAIPUR TODAY

Udaipur is a city with a population of 300,000. It is a road and rail junction, and an agricultural market town with a sprinkling of industries, ranging from handicrafts to chemicals. But more than this, it is perhaps one of the most romantic and picturesque cities in Rajasthan, with its lakes, hills and splendid palaces. The old city, once surrounded by fortified walls, like any medieval Rajput town, has five great gates: Hathi Pol ("Elephant Gate"), Suraj Pol ("Sun Gate"), Chand Pol ("Moon Gate"), Kishan Pol ("Gate of Kishan") and Delhi Gate. At one time the gates were shut each night. Today they serve as popular landmarks. Udaipur's streets are narrow and twisting, and the traditional old, whitewashed houses are painted over with brightly colored folk murals of elephants, horsemen or peacocks – auspicious motifs, usually painted on the occasion of festivals or weddings ▲ *236*.

BAZAARS. Udaipur has some fascinating bazaars. Start at Jagdish Temple and wander through Bara Bazaar, turning left at Suraj Pol into Bapu Bazaar. You will discover a vivid sprawl of little shops selling the tie-and-dye fabrics for which the city is famed, particularly the *laharia* (or wave-patterned) ones ● *58*, which are, perhaps naturally, associated with this city of lakes. Other good buys are Udaipur's brightly colored folk toys, *pichhvais* ● *67* and enamel jewelry ● *62* from nearby Nathdwara, copies of the celebrated miniature paintings of the Mewar School, terracottas from Molela ● *72*, chunky silver jewelry, lacquer-work curios, embroidered textiles, antiques and ornamental swords (a 19th-century European traveler once remarked that Udaipur's main industry seemed to be sword-making, and everybody above the age of twelve carried a sword). Until not so long ago, you

"I stood in ecstasy gazing on the sublime panorama
spread out at my feet...it resembled
one of the fairy cities in the Arabian Nights."

Louis Rousselet, *India and its Native Princes*, 1878

could also buy what must surely have been one of the world's most strangely named products: a soft drink named Pee Cola, now, alas, withdrawn from the market.

AYURVEDA CENTER. One of Udaipur's lesser-known claims to fame is that it is an important center of *ayurveda* – the three-thousand-year-old Hindu system of medicine which is founded on a belief in the holistic relationship between man and the cosmos, and which is thought to have inspired the ancient Greek system of medicine. There is an ayurvedic hospital, an ayurvedic research center, and an ayurvedic college here.

Old city gate.

The City Palace (above) is a blend of stern Rajput military architecture on the outside and lavish Mughal-inspired decorative art on the inside ● *89*. Set on a hill overlooking Pichola Lake, it is a sprawling edifice made up of at least four separate, interconnecting palaces, built over a period of nearly three centuries. The entire palace is oriented to face the east, aptly, perhaps, for a dynasty which claimed descent from the sun. The earliest parts of the palace are reminiscent of the architectural style of Chittorgarh, but subsequent additions show an interesting evolution of style, although this is sometimes disguised by later remodeling. You enter the palace through two great gates, Bari Pol and Tripolia Pol, and carved *torana* archways. The maharanas used to be weighed here, the equivalent in gold then being distributed in charity. Through Ganesh Deori, dedicated to the god of fortune, with its kitschy Japanese tiles, you come to Raj Angan, built in 1559, the oldest part of the palace. Legend says this was the very spot where Rana Udai Singh II met the sage who suggested this location for his new capital ▲ *243*, and that the first thing he built was the Dhuni Mata Temple you see here.

UNUSED CHAIR
The special chair of Maharana Fateh Singh (reigned 1884–1930), from the great *durbar* held for King George V in Delhi in 1913, is on display at the City Palace Museum. Just as his ancestors refused to attend the *durbars* of the Mughal emperors, Maharana Fateh Singh also refused to attend the *durbar* of the King of England, although he went to Delhi. He was probably the only one of India's 562 rajas and maharajas who didn't sit on the chair.

Elephant fight in Udaipur, early 20th century.

Lithograph of City Palace.

BARI MAHAL. Climbing a flight of steep steps you come to Bari Mahal, a delightful garden, nearly 90 feet above the ground. Around the garden is a marble courtyard with a square, central pool and fluted, balustered columns, reminiscent of the Mughal style. This was a royal playground once. Old miniature paintings portray the maharanas at play with the ladies of their court, sprinkling them with colored water during Holi. Looking down from here you can see the courtyard below, where Udaipur's great elephant fights were once staged, the last one being as recently as the 1950's.

A miniature of Bari Mahal. The garden is actually the summit of a small hill completely enclosed within the palace's high walls.

DILKHUSH MAHAL. Beyond this lies Dilkhush Mahal ("Palace of Joy"), originally built in the 1620's, with two splendid chambers, Kanch ki Burj ("Turret of Glass") and Chitran ki Burj ("Painted Turret"). Kanch ki Burj is a 19th-century Sheesh Mahal, with elaborate gray and red mirror-work walls and ceilings, set off by a carved ivory door. Chitran ki Burj is a little 18th-century masterpiece, its walls covered with frescos of hunting scenes, festivals and court life in princely Udaipur. There is a tragic story connected with this chamber: it was once the bedchamber of a beautiful sixteen-year-old Mewar princess who was being ardently sought by the raja of Jaipur and the Rao of Jodhpur. Since agreeing to marriage with either one would mean provoking a bloody war with the other, she chose to commit suicide here, by drinking a cup of poppy extract. Take a look also at the curious little glass portrait of Rana Karan Singh (reigned 1620–28) on one of the walls: his costume suddenly turns color from blue to gold, depending on the angle from which you look at it.

TURRET OF GLASS Kanch ki Burj ("Turret of Glass") was perhaps a 19th-century development of the traditional Sheesh Mahal concept. What makes it unusual is the fact that not only did it have mirror-worked walls and ceilings, but it also had a decorative glass floor.

CHINI CHITRASHALA. Next you see the 18th-century Chini Chitrashala ("Porcelain Painted Gallery") (above), with its striking blue Dutch inlaid tile work, an amusing European influence that suddenly appears to compete with the Rajput and Mughal styles of the rest of the palace. Don't miss the detail of Joseph and Mary with the infant Jesus on their flight into Egypt.

European-influenced Dutch tile inlays at Chini Chitrashala.

Moti Mahal.

PALACE BUILDINGS. Moti Mahal ("Pearl Palace"), built in 1620, is another Sheesh Mahal in the City Palace. Its walls are decorated with plates of mirror-work and colored glass, creating a magical interplay of reflections. Beside it is Bhim Vilas, a small prayer room, with fine murals depicting episodes from the legends of Lord Krishna and Radha. Across the courtyard is Priyatam Niwas, the simple little apartment where Maharana Bhopal Singh (reigned 1930–55) (below) used to live, right up to 1955. You can see some of his memorabilia here, including, touchingly, his wheelchair. He was paralysed from the waist down, but nevertheless was an expert hunter, going out on *shikar* strapped onto his horse ● *39*. Below these apartments is the grand Mor Chowk ("Peacock Courtyard"), its wall covered with a dramatic mosaic relief of dancing peacocks. It is one of the more celebrated features of the City Palace, though severely criticized by the famous scholar of Rajput architecture, G.H.R. Tillotson, as having "execrable glass mosaics…added in the late 19th century." Nearby is another well-known feature of the palace, Surya Gokhra ("Sun Window"),

Relief of peacock at the Mor Chowk.

OCTOPUSSY
One of the more unusual moments in Shiv Niwas's colorful history was when it was used as a location for the shooting of the James Bond film, *Octopussy*.

from where, apparently, the maharanas – descendants of the sun god himself – would show themselves to the people in times of misfortune, to reassure them that the sun was still shining on Mewar. Manak Mahal ("Ruby Palace") was built in 1620 as a dining room. It has walls inlaid with ornate mirror-work and colored glass. (Try striking a match and see how the myriad tiny convex mirrors pick up dozens of pinpoints of light.) Inside it are the amusing mosaics of 18th-century Englishmen being served wine by Rajput maidens.

PALACE MUSEUM. The palace museum contains a wonderful collection of old Rajput weaponry. One of the weapons looks like an ordinary sword, but is actually a traditional two-swords-in-one scabbard (which you would draw simultaneously, so that you have one sword in each hand). Somewhat more wicked-looking are the old maces. But what is positively gruesome is an arrow with a large crescent-shaped arrowhead – the idea being to aim for the victim's throat and thus neatly slice off his head. Other historic pieces include Maharana Pratap's suit of armor and the war bugle and drums of Rana Sanga.

SHIV NIWAS AND FATEH PRAKASH PALACES. Later additions that have been built just south of the main City Palace complex are Shiv Niwas and Fateh Prakash. Both were originally intended to be guest houses for the personal guests of the maharanas, but have now been turned into hotels. Shiv Niwas is built around a large, impressive semi-circular courtyard. Its interiors are decorated with mosaics, mirror-work and enamel, as would befit Rajasthan's premier dynasty. One of its suites, until recently, was furnished with a set of solid crystal furniture. The palace has played host, over the years, to celebrities ranging from Jackie Onassis to Queen Elizabeth II. It is said that when Maharana Bhagwat Singh was escorting the latter, he naturally gave her precedence, but she apparently demurred, saying "Please lead the way. You come from a much older family than I do." The smaller Fateh Prakash has some of the most exquisite Mewar miniature paintings from the Maharana's private collection.

An old photograph of the City Palace, with Shiv Niwas on the right.

Courtyard of City Palace (left).

FAKE TRUNK
In the palace museum, you will see the battle armor worn by Maharana Pratap's famous horse, Chetak. It has an unusual feature: a fake elephant trunk. This was specially designed so that in battle the enemy horses would mistake it for an elephant and would hesitate to attack.

Belgian glass crystal furniture at Fateh Prakash.

CURSE OF THE TIGHTROPE WALKER
Natani ka Chabutra ("Platform of the Lady Acrobat") in Pichola Lake commemorates a 19th-century acrobat to whom the maharana, half in jest, promised half his kingdom if she could cross Pichola Lake on a tightrope. She accepted the challenge, and had almost completed the feat when a shrewd courtier cut the rope, and the poor girl drowned in the lake. She apparently cursed the maharana, saying that his line would never again have any direct heirs. Strangely, after that, six out of the next seven maharanas were adopted heirs.

The banquet hall's ceiling in Jag Niwas.

PICHOLA LAKE

Perhaps the best way to see Udaipur is by boat on Pichola Lake, preferably at sunset, sailing past its picturesque ghats and palaces. Pichola Lake was originally created in the 15th century by a Banjara grain merchant, who built a small dam here in order to allow his grain carts to cross over during the monsoon. As you sail up toward the north of the city, you pass slowly by its various sights: first, the old hillside hunting box of the maharanas and the remnants of the old fortified walls; the City Palace, with its high towers and turrets; the lakeside *havelis* of the old city, with their cupolaed balconies reflected in the waters of the lake, and the high, triple-arched Gangaur Ghat (above right), where women bathe and wash their clothes and where the colorful Gangaur festival is celebrated each year in spring. Finally, past the lakeside temples, you come to the island palaces of Jag Niwas and Jag Mandir.

JAG NIWAS ★

Jag Niwas, better known as the Lake Palace (below), seems to float, as if by magic, on the waters of Pichola Lake. Built in 1746, this pleasure palace has a romantic history. The story goes that the young prince, Jagat Singh, asked his father for permission to go with the ladies of his court to the nearby Jag Mandir. His father, the Rana, refused, saying that if the prince wanted to spend his time so frivolously he should build his own pleasure palace. In a fit of pique the prince did precisely that. The palace he created covers an area of nearly four acres. It is a dreamlike confection of white marble that has been called "one of the most romantic creations of man" and was designed to catch

"If the Venetian owned the Pichola [Lake] he might say with justice, 'See it and die.'"
Rudyard Kipling, *Letters of Marque*, 1899

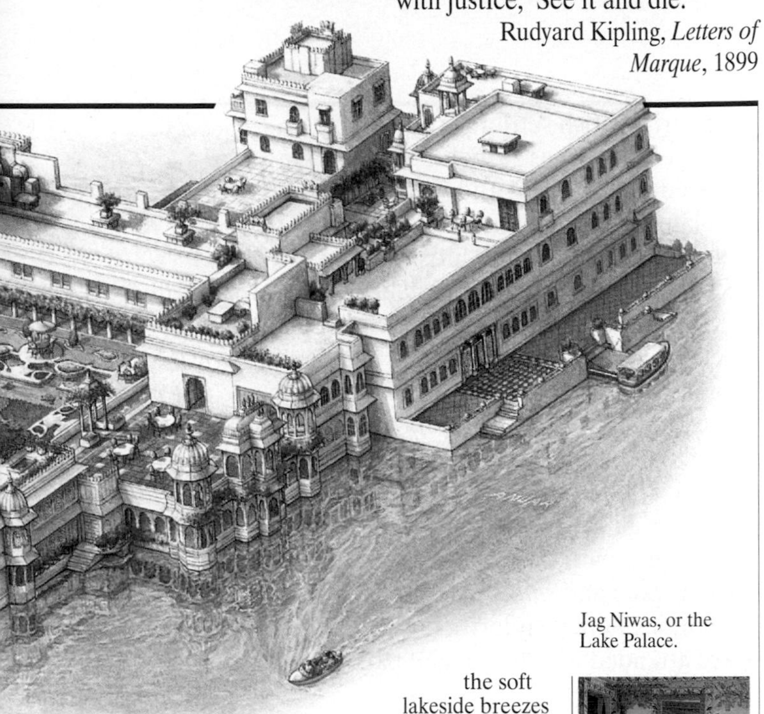

Jag Niwas, or the Lake Palace.

the soft lakeside breezes that waft through the elegant courtyards, cupolaed pavilions and fountained gardens. Its apartments are elaborately decorated with cusped arches, beautiful wall paintings, mirror-work, inlaid stones and stained glass. Colonel Tod, writing about life in the palace in the 19th century, says, "Here they listened to the tale of the bard and slept off their noonday opiate amidst the cool breezes of the lake, wafting delicious odors from myriads of lotus flowers which covered the surface of the waters." Today the Lake Palace is a hotel, perhaps one of the most romantic in the world. It has hosted a whole who's who of international celebrities.

Sajjan Niwas, a guest room in Jag Niwas.

JAG MANDIR

This older water palace, built in 1620 by Karan Singh, played an important role in Udaipur's history. The Mughal prince, Khurram, exiled by his father, Emperor Jahangir, chose to seek refuge here ● *37*. Jag Mandir owes its name to Jagat Singh, Khurram's son, who was announced as the new Emperor Shah Jahan upon his father's death in 1627, and transformed the palace quite considerably. His close relationship with the Mewar led to an important new era of peace, prosperity and architectural renaissance in Udaipur ▲ *243*. The apartment where Shah Jahan lived is a small curiosity, its lower floor designed in the Hindu tradition and its upper floor in the Mughal tradition. Jag Mandir saw another dramatic episode enacted during the Sepoy Mutiny in 1857 ● *38*, when it sheltered the British families who had fled from nearby Neemuch. The Rana of Mewar chivalrously lodged them here, after taking the precaution of destroying all the town's boats so that the angry rebels would not be able to get to the island.

Jag Mandir as portrayed in a miniature (above) and a lithograph (below).

The early British settlers in India, often referred to as Nabobs, married local women and emulated local customs and lifestyles. But after the Uprising of 1857, the British sought to establish their own identity as rulers and formed their own enclaves. Although Princely Rajasthan and British India were two different worlds, they were bound together by treaties and *sanads* (grants) between *gaddi* (Rajput throne) and Crown. Political Agents, Residents, Governor-Generals and British royalty were lavishly entertained with banquets and sports such as fishing, polo and *shikars* (hunting parties). The maharajas were wonderful hosts and these visits were attended with pomp and pageantry.

GUN SALUTES
The British instituted complicated systems of precedence and protocol, rewarding princes who toed the line with impressive titles and gun salutes. Maharaja Ganga Singh of Bikaner (above, extreme right), for instance, was entitled to a seventeen-gun salute. Known for the sandgrouse shoots he held in Bikaner ▲ *194*, he kept close personal ties with British royalty. He is shown here with King George V.

ROYAL RECEPTION
The Maharaja of Jaipur sends off his British guest at a railway station, c. 1902. Some rajas went to great lengths to satisfy the predilections of their more important British guests. Even the most fleeting visits could cause a total disruption to the smooth running of the state, prompting a flurry of road-building and spring-cleaning.

FINAL GATHERING
Lord and Lady Mountbatten stand in the center of this group photograph (right) taken during the last gathering of Indian princes at the Silver Jubilee celebrations of the Maharaja of Jaipur in 1948. Many princes felt let down by Mountbatten when he partitioned the country and cajoled them into acceding to India or Pakistan ● *39*.

POLITICAL AGENTS
British Political Agents, responsible for relations between the Indian Princely States and the British rulers, were appointed to the states of Udaipur, Jaipur, Jodhpur, Bharatpur, and Kota. The photograph above shows British officers and their guests waiting for the Viceroy outside the railway station at Bikaner.

RAJ LIFESTYLE
The British lived like mini-potentates in spacious bungalows, served by a battery of servants including cooks, bearers, ayahs, maids, sweepers, and gardeners. They were members of exclusive clubs and moved to the hills during the heat of summer. Their lifestyle reflected the might of Empire and reaffirmed the belief that Britannia ruled the waves.

Saheliyon ki Bari.

RURAL LIVING
Just outside Udaipur is Shilpagram, an interesting "living ethnographic museum". You can get a glimpse into the lifestyle of the rural folk of Rajasthan (and other parts of western India) by visiting the village huts, and watching the craftsmen and folk musicians perform their everyday tasks.

NEO-CLASSICAL ARCHITECTURE
This beautiful temple, dedicated to Vishnu, was built by the maharaja Jagat Singh I (1628–1652). Its classical architecture is a prime example of the Renaissance that took place in the late 15th century.

Jagdish Mandir

SAHELIYON KI BARI

These beautiful gardens (literally, "Gardens of the Maids of Honor") were laid out in the mid-18th century for a retinue of forty-eight young ladies-in-waiting who were sent to Udaipur as part of a princess's dowry. The gardens have beautiful lawns, lotus pools, marble pavilions, and marble elephant-shaped fountains. Once the site for royal picnics, the gardens are now a somewhat neglected public park.

JAGDISH MANDIR

Dedicated to Lord Vishnu, Jagdish Mandir was built in the classical Hindu style in the mid-17th century. The temple's bold *shikhara*, or pagoda, 79 feet high, is covered with carved friezes of dancers, musicians, elephants, and horsemen. Its archway is also impressive. Be sure not to miss the small shrine opposite the temple entrance, which houses an excellent bronze statue of Garuda, the mythical bird which is the vehicle of Lord Vishnu.

BHARATIYA LOK KALA MANDAL

Bharatiya Lok Kala Mandal has been doing admirable work over the past forty years, recording Rajasthani folklore and music and supporting the traditional folk arts. A collection of Rajasthani folk art – costumes,

Garuda statue at Jagdish Mandir.

musical instruments, paintings, folk deities, masks, dolls, and weapons – can be seen here. The puppet collection is particularly interesting.

Sajjangarh

High on a hilltop just outside Udaipur lies this dramatic 18th-century palace (below), with a breathtaking view of the Mewar countryside. On a clear day, it is said, you can see the fortress of Chittorgarh from here, so it naturally held a very special place in the hearts of the maharanas. Originally intended to be a towering five-story astronomical center, it was later abandoned and used as a monsoon palace and hunting lodge. Today entry into the building itself is restricted because it has been taken over for governmental use, but the view alone makes a visit worthwhile. At night it is gaudily lit up in pink and green, causing it to be described as "tutti-frutti" by Udaipur's inhabitants.

Ahar

This ancient capital of the Sisodias, en route from the airport, lies 2 miles east of Udaipur. It used to be the capital of the clan until Bappa Rawal founded Chittorgarh in the 8th century. There is a fine complex of royal cenotaphs here, built around the sacred tank of Gangabhar Kund (below). In all, nineteen maharanas of Mewar were cremated here, along with their ranis. Their cenotaphs were built of white marble and resemble small, graceful, colonnaded temples, each one bearing an image of Eklingji and of the maharana and his wives. The most impressive of them is the cenotaph of Rana Amar Singh (reigned 1597–1620), with its four-faced image in the center and a beautiful carved frieze depicting the *sati* of his ranis. Another beautiful cenotaph is that of Rana Sangram Singh (reigned 1710–34), with its fifty-six pillared portico and its octagonal dome. Nearby are two carved 10th-century temples dedicated to the saints Mirabai and Adinatha. There is also an archeological museum here, containing excavated specimens of an ancient civilization discovered in the vicinity, dating back three thousand years: shards of pottery ■ *20*, terracotta toys and a large earthenware grain storage pot. There are also a number of stone sculptures here from later periods, including an impressive 10th-century Surya, or sun-god image. The excavations around Ahar are of great archeological and historical interest.

Door to history
A *kavadh* (above) is a fascinating little "mobile temple", typical of Mewar. Made of brightly lacquered wood, it has several doors, which can be opened, one after the other, to display the incidents from the lives of various Hindu gods and goddesses. The *kavadh* of Lord Rama, for instance, tells the story of not only the epic *Ramayana*, but also of various popular deities and saints. The commentary is chanted by a traditional balladeer, called a Kavadia Bhat, who points to the unfolding narrative with a peacock feather. When the story is completed, the final door of the *kavadh* is opened to reveal Lord Rama and his queen, Sita, in all their splendor.

Rustic toys
Udaipur is known for its rustic folk toys. Made of brightly painted wood, these usually take the form of miniature figures or household items, such as kitchen utensils, children's cradles or miniature fruits. These toys play an important role in the lives of the local community of craftsmen, and a girl who is adept with a lathe is highly sought after as a prospective bride.

HANDMADE TERRACOTTAS
Molela, near Nathdwara, is known for its unique terracotta folk art ● *72*. These terracottas, depicting various local deities and legendary heroes, have a charming rustic beauty about them. They are dexterously made by hand, using only the most primitive of tools – no molds – and painted in bright colors. With traditions going back two thousand years, this is, unfortunately, a dying art, practiced today only by about twenty families in Molela.

EKLINGJI TEMPLE

This temple, actually a complex of 108 small temples (right), lies in a remote, hilly gorge 14 miles north of Udaipur. Eklingji, an incarnation of Lord Shiva, was the tutelary deity of the maharanas of Mewar. This temple is said to have been built in the 8th century by Bappa Rawal, the first of the great Sisodia kings, and rebuilt in the 15th century. The main temple is of an unusual design: built of marble, it has a clustered, curved tower and a *mandapa* (pillared hall) roofed with a pyramid of miniature architectural motifs. Inside is the main four-faced Eklingji image, carved in black marble. Outside the main sanctuary is a large statue of Bappa Rawal standing beside Nandi, Lord Shiva's bull. According to legend, Allaudin Khilji, Sultan of Delhi, attacked the temple in the late 13th century and struck this Nandi idol with his mace. Out of its hollow interior a swarm of angry bees emerged and attacked the Sultan, forcing him to call off his attack.

NAGDA

SAS AND BAHU TEMPLES. The 10th-century Sas and Bahu temples (literally, "Temples of the Mother-in-law and Daughter-in-law"), dedicated to Lord Vishnu, and known for their beautiful carvings, are situated by the side of a lake, two-and-a-half miles from Eklingji.

Sas Temple.

Details of carvings in Sas Temple (right and below).

Sas Temple (the larger of the two) has a richly carved porch. On its walls are elaborate friezes with scenes from the *Ramayana* and depictions of trysting lovers, as well as images of the Hindu trinity of Brahma, Shiva and Vishnu. The dome, too, has some wonderful carvings, although they are not in a very good condition today. The sanctuary itself, in contrast to the porch and *mandapa*, is simple and unadorned. Bahu Temple has a beautifully carved *torana* archway in front of it (right). Apparently the image of the presiding (Vishnu) deity was swung from the archway, to the singing of hymns, on ceremonial occasions. The basic scheme of the temple is similar to that of Sas Temple next door, although on a smaller scale. The portico, however, is open. The columns are richly carved and the octagonal ceiling is decorated with eight female figurines.

NATHDWARA

The important pilgrim center of Nathdwara, with its temple of Shrinathji or Lord Krishna, lies 30 miles north of Udaipur. According to legend, the temple's image of Shrinathji was originally located in Mathura, in a sanctuary established by Vishnu follower Vallabha, founder of the Pushtimarg sect in the 16th century. However, in 1691, fearing an attack on the temple by the fanatical Mughal Emperor, Aurangzeb, it was decided that the image should be smuggled away to a safer place. When the carriage carrying the image arrived at Nathdwara, its wheels got stuck in the sands and could not be moved. Taking this as a message from Lord Krishna, the guardians of the image decided to build a new temple on the spot. The temple itself is architecturally very simple. The Shrinathji image, carved in black marble, has the quality of a mysterious and powerful monolith, with wide hypnotic eyes and one hand held up, as if to support a mountain. It is treated with great ritual and ceremony: its clothes and jewelry are changed six times a day between *puja* (prayer) services, when it is presented before the devotees in the various different aspects of Lord Krishna. The temple is open only to Hindus. Outside the temple are colorful bazaars, where you can find Nathdwara's famed *pichhvai* paintings ● *67* and *minakari* jewelry.

RELIGIOUS PICHHVAIS

The *pichhvai* paintings of Nathdwara are a unique art form that evolved at Shrinathji Temple in Nathdwara ● *67*. They were originally created as a cloth backdrop to be hung behind the temple's idol (the word *pichhvai* literally means "at the back"). The paintings depict different episodes from Lord Krishna's life, and are changed regularly to create different moods, depending on the occasion or ritual. The *pichhvai* paintings of the 19th century were exquisite works of art, created with great passion and reflecting a symbolic imagery of their own. Swirling ink-blue clouds, for example, represent Lord Krishna, with his dark complexion; dancing peacocks again symbolize Lord Krishna, while cows symbolize devotees yearning for the god.

Carved façade of Dayal Shah Mandir (below).

BRAINWAVE FOR IRRIGATION
The "Persian wheel" that you see all over Mewar were an ingenious medieval invention ■ *23*. A large loop of water-containers is placed above a well and connected to a yoked bull (or camel) with a simple mechanical device. As the bull is driven around in a circle, the water containers are dipped into the well, brought up and emptied into a water channel, which then provides a steady stream of water for irrigating the farmer's fields.

RAJSAMAND AND KANKROLI

The royal lake of Rajsamand, with the village of Kankroli on its shores, lies about 40 miles north of Udaipur. This large, artificial lake was constructed in the 1660's. By the lake stands Nauchowki ("Nine Pavilions"). An elegant stepped embankment goes right down to the water's edge, punctuated by gracefully carved *torana* archways and marble pavilions. The entire complex was built by Rana Raj Singh I (reigned 1652–80) to commemorate an act of defiance against Emperor Aurangzeb. When Aurangzeb proposed marriage to Princess Charumati, a Rajput princess of Kishangarh, she could not refuse, so she turned to Raj Singh I to save her. The Rana gallantly married her himself.

TEMPLES. Nearby are two interesting temples, the 16th-century temple of Dwarakadhish or Lord Krishna, and a large Jain temple built by Dayal Shah. The latter has some exquisite marble carvings, almost as intricate and delicate as the ones at the Dilwara temples at Mount Abu ● *94* ▲ *270*. The other interesting feature of Rajsamand is Raj Prashasti, a history of Mewar in verse, whose 1017 stanzas were carved on twenty-seven slabs of stone in the 17th century. It is believed to be the longest literary work ever carved in stone.

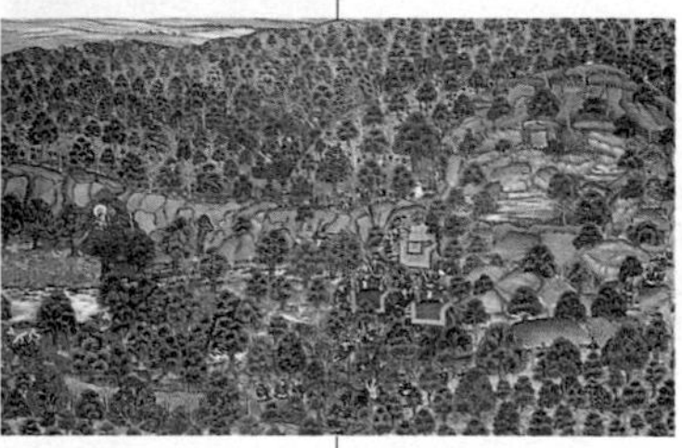

SUMMER HUNTING PARTIES
The forests around Jaisamand were once the scene of the maharanas' hunting parties in summer. These were elaborate, highly organized expeditions. Signalers, positioned on the hilltops, would first signal the locations of the panther or wild boar. The strategy would then be worked out: whether to go in with beaters, elephants or lancers. The maharana decided which of his guests would have the honor of shooting which animal. Now, of course, there is a game sanctuary in these forests.

JAGAT

AMBIKA MATA TEMPLE. Located 35 miles southeast of Udaipur is the village of Jagat and the 10th-century temple of Ambika Mata. The temple is small, but elaborately carved. The porch outside has friezes and a carved panel of a dancing Ganesha. A decorated gateway leads into the towered sanctuary. Inside are images of Durga, the goddess of war, attended by sensuous maidens in seductive postures. On the walls are more carvings: musicians, sages and amorous couples, reminiscent of the erotic carvings of Khajuraho.

RISHABDEV

The 15th-century temple of Lord Rishabdev, 25 miles south of Udaipur, is an

Carvings in Ambika Mata Temple.

important center of pilgrimage for both Jains and Hindus ● *48*. The Jains consider the deity to be one of the twenty-four *tirthankaras* of Jainism, while the Hindus consider him to be one of the ten incarnations of Lord Vishnu. This is a fascinating temple, with a black marble image of Rishabdev, smeared with saffron by the devotees. Each pilgrim can wash off the saffron paste applied by the previous pilgrim and anoint it afresh. On ceremonial occasions the image is dressed in an extravagant diamond-studded garment which was presented to the temple by the maharanas of Mewar.

JAISAMAND

Jaisamand, a vast artificial lake 32 miles southeast of Udaipur, was created by Raja Jai Singh in 1691. With an area of 13 square miles, it was the largest artificial lake in the world, until superseded by the lake that was formed by the Aswan Dam in Egypt. This is an exceptionally picturesque place, surrounded by wooded hills. On the banks of the lake are vast marble steps descending to the water, embellished with pretty domed pavilions and sculpted elephants. On either end is a small water palace, and in the center a temple dedicated to Lord Shiva. The forests around Jaisamand were once hunting grounds of the maharanas of Mewar, where they came to shoot panthers and wild boars in summer. Now the entire area has, of course, been turned into a game sanctuary. Here you can see *chitals*, *chinkaras*, wild boars, panthers and crocodiles, as well as a wide variety of birds, including several migratory species drawn to this huge lake.

THE CHITAL AND THE LANGUR MONKEY

The *chital*, or spotted deer, which can be seen at Jaisamand, is considered one of the most beautiful species of deer in the world ■ *25*. It has a curious, symbiotic relationship with the black-faced rhesus monkey. *Chitals* have often been seen with a langur monkey astride their backs, in the manner of a rider.

Terraced embankment of the lake at Jaisamand.

Lithograph of Kumbhalgarh Fort (opposite).

KUMBHALGARH FORT

Of the thirty-two forts that the great warrior king, Rana Kumbha (reigned 1433–68), built all over Mewar, the most spectacular was Kumbhalgarh. In many ways, in fact, it is even more impressive than the Mewar citadel of Chittorgarh itself. Built high in the hills west of Chittorgarh in the mid-15th century, Kumbhalgarh was called the "eye of Mewar" because of its strategic position in relation to the kingdom's aggressive neighbors in Gujarat and Marwar. It was impregnable, having withstood several attacks from the armies of Gujarat, Malwa and the Mughals. Even Emperor Akbar, after the conquest of Chittorgarh, could not get beyond Kumbhalgarh's mighty second gate. Actually, an ancient fortress had existed on this site ever since the 3rd century, but Rana Kumbha won it over from the local Mer ruler, constructing its fortifications anew, with massive walls, rounded bastions, tall watchtowers and secret passages, designed in accordance with the ancient Hindu treatise, *Vastu Shastra*. The outer wall encloses an area of 32 square miles, and the fort is said to have once contained 252 palaces.

THE GREAT WALL
The massive ramparts of Kumbhalgarh run for 2½ miles along the rugged Aravalli hillsides, and are wide enough for eight horsemen to ride abreast on top of them. They have been compared in their conception, by some, to the Great Wall of China.

FORT GATES. You approach the fort through thick forests and ravines and enter through the first of seven strongly fortified gates, Arait Pol, from whose watchtower mirrored signals could be flashed up to the citadel. The other gates continue to throw up barriers to would-be invaders, one after the other, all the way up the hill. The second gate, Hulla Pol ("Gate of Disturbance") was named such because the invading Mughal forces had reached up to here after the fall of Chittorgarh. You can still see the marks of their old cannon balls on this gate. Bhairon Pol bears a stone tablet inscribed with an order for the exile of a treacherous 19th-century prime minister. Paghra Pol ("Stirrup Gate") (right) was where the Mewar cavalry would amass before riding out into battle. Topkhana Pol ("Cannon Gate") housed an artillery emplacement, as well as, it is said, a secret passage out of the fort. As you

"[It] rises, like the crown of the Hindu cybele, tier above tier of battlements to the summit, which is crowned with the Badal Mahal, or 'cloud-palace' of the Ranas."

Colonel Tod, *Annals and Antiquities of Rajasthan*, 1829

climb the steep ramp that leads up the hill to the citadel, you can almost hear the clatter of horses' hooves on these cobbled stones. Finally you come to the innermost gate, Nimbu Pol ("Gate of the Lemon Trees"). Nearby is a shrine to the original chieftain from whom Raja Kumbha won over this fort. According to a gory and fanciful legend, the chieftain, refusing to go on living after his defeat, had his head cut off at the bottom of the hill, and yet his body continued to walk up to this point, where it finally fell. There are small shrines that supposedly mark both these points.

BADAL MAHAL. At the citadel lies Badal Mahal ("Cloud Palace"), with its beautiful apartments painted with delicate pastel-colored murals in the 19th century. In these chambers you can see an ingenious "air-conditioning" system, with a series of ducts that draw cool air into the rooms and ventilate them from the bottom, rather than from the top, as convention might dictate. Two other curiosities to see are the quaint toilets and the royal bedchamber with its (presumably erotic) echo effects! The view from Badal Mahal of the surrounding countryside is stunning. There is a romantic story about how Rana Kumbha once carried away a beautiful Jalore princess from her betrothed, a prince of Marwar, and brought her here to Kumbhalgarh. It is said the dejected Marwar prince would sit at night in his palace at Mandore, over 72 miles away, and watch the lights in the towers of Kumbhalgarh, knowing that there was no way he could storm the mighty fortress and win his princess back.

OTHER BUILDINGS. Apart from the palace, there are various other buildings that are worth seeing. Near Ram Pol, for instance, is the beautiful three-storied Vedi building, with its massive columns and sculpted parapet, where the consecration of the fort was celebrated in 1458. There are also some fine old temples here: the Kumbhaswami, Mahadeo, and Nilkanth temples are just some of the 365 temples that the fort is said to have once contained. And, of course, there is the cenotaph of Rana Kumbha, who was murdered here by his own son, known to history only as Hathiaro ("The Murderer").

GARRISON FORTS
Around each of the major forts of Rajputana were several little garrison forts, which were commanded by the chieftains of the ruler, and which acted as the first line of defense in case of invasion. One of the garrison forts around Kumbhalgarh was the one at Ghanerao, with a late 16th-century palace beside it. The palace is now a charming little hotel.

Wall painting at Badal Mahal.

Neelkanth Temple.

Vedi building.

LORD PARSHVA
According to a Jain legend, Prince Parshva once saved a snake from being killed by the evil Kamatha. Years later, Kamatha, reborn as a heavenly being through his penances, saw Parshva deep in meditation, and whipped up a terrible storm to kill him. Despite the rising storm waters that threatened to drown him, Parshva continued to meditate serenely. The snake whom he had saved years earlier, now reborn as the Lord of the Snakes, came to his rescue, coiling his body below Parshva, thereby raising him above the water's level. Spreading his thousand hoods over Parshva's head, the snake shielded him from the cyclonic winds ▲ *265*.

RANAKPUR

Deep in the forest, 56 miles north of Udaipur, is the huge 15th-century Adinatha Temple at Ranakpur ● *94*. It is the largest and most complex Jain temple in India, with twenty-nine halls covering 4,320 square yards. Holding up its domes and spires are 420 ornately carved pillars. The temple was built by a wealthy Jain merchant, Dharna Sah. According to legend, one night he dreamed of a celestial vehicle. Enchanted by this vision, he vowed to make it a reality and invited architects from all over India to present designs. Finally, a sculptor named Depa produced a design that perfectly captured Dharna Sah's vision. The construction of the main shrine took fifty years.

DESIGN. The temple is one of the five great holy places of the Jain sect. Dedicated to the first *tirthankara*, Adinatha ● *49*, it has twenty-nine rooms supported by more than 1,400 pillars over a surface of 3,937 square yards. It is so complex in form and overwhelming in scale that at first it leaves you quite bewildered. But, as you walk through its chambers, the pattern gradually emerges. It takes an unusual form, as Indian temples go, for it rejects the traditional longitudinal plan in favor of a cruciform plan, with four separate entrances, one on each side. Each of these leads, through a series of columned halls, to the central court and cruciform sanctum chamber with its four-faced Adinatha image. The temple is enclosed on all four sides by rows of chapels (eighty-six in all), and is topped by twenty domes and five spires.

STONE CARVINGS. What makes the Adinatha Temple truly remarkable, of course, is the fact that all these grand architectural elements are completely covered with carvings, so profuse and so intricate that they resemble lace-work, rather than stone-carving ▲ *264*. The ceiling panels are decorated with geometric patterns and scrollery; the domes are embellished with ornate concentric friezes

Adinatha Temple (right) and Jain pilgrims entering the temple (above).

Interior of Adinatha Temple.

and descending pendants; the brackets supporting the domes are designed with dancing goddesses. And when you study the richly carved pillars, you will realize that each one of them is carved with a different pattern from the rest. Look out also for one of the columns facing the sanctum, on which there is a small panel depicting a man with his hands joined. This is supposed to be Dharna Sah, the man who built this temple, while the figure next to him is Depa, his sculptor and architect. The temple is also remarkable for its spatial complexity. The pillared *mandapas* (halls) around the sanctum and the surrounding colonnades regularly open up to create large, octagonal areas which are double or even triple-storied and which are ornamented with corbeled domes and delicate balconies. Architectural scholars have been uniformly eloquent in their praise of the temple. Fischer wrote of the "unending vistas of the columns, interrupted at intervals by open courts, each compartment covered with carving of a most intricate character, and the whole illuminated by light that is thrown from pavement to pillar, and from pillar to screen to penetrate into all parts." In the temple courtyard is a tree that is believed to be over four hundred years old, having been planted at the time the temple was built.

OTHER TEMPLES. There are two other temples nearby, a 15th-century Jain Parshvanatha temple, remarkable especially for its ornately pierced stone windows, and another 15th-century Hindu Surya temple. Ranakpur is named after Rana Kumbha ▲ *242*, whom Dharna Sah approached when he had the vision of his great temple, to ask for the land for its construction. Rana Kumbha apparently agreed on condition that the temple be named after him.

LIGHT AND SHADOW
The temple of Ranakpur is held up by a forest of 1444 carved pillars. One of the remarkable things about the temple is the wonderful play of shadow and light, as the sun's rays shift through the day, changing the pillars' color from gold to pale blue.

NEMI'S RENUNCIATION
Nemi, one of the great Jain *tirthankaras*, was riding to his marriage ceremony when he heard the piteous cries of the animals being slaughtered for his wedding feast. Deeply saddened, Nemi immediately renounced the world and its pleasures, and, leaving his young bride-to-be, embarked on the life of an ascetic.

▲ HYMN IN MARBLE DHARNA VIHARA, RANAKPUR

On the curve of a boulder-strewn river, in a tiny enclave within the forested Aravalli hills, lies the sacred site of Ranakpur. There, Dharna Sah, a minister of the Rana of Mewar, sought permission to construct a Jain temple. The Rana desired that with the temple, a small township should also be built. Accordingly, a settlement was created on the western slopes of the hills and was named Ranakpur, in honor of the Rana. Apparently, in the 15th century, several temples were constructed at the site, of which four survive. One of them, the Sun Temple, is believed to have been built by Rana Kumbha. Of the remaining three Jain temples, the *chaumukh* (with four entrances) temple of Adinatha, completed in AD 1439 by Dharna Sah, is the most imposing, a veritable hymn in stone and marble.

PILLARED HALL Though conforming to the prevailing architectural tenets, the temple is exceptional because of its compact plan, pillared vistas, soaring domes, and open courts. The pillars are not conceived in one single piece, but as a series of drums of varying heights and receding diameter. They are placed one upon another to form an elegant tapering shaft. The temple has more than 1400 pillars, each of which, interestingly, displays a different decorative design.

CELESTIAL FIGURES The plain exterior of the temple gives no indication of the richly embellished interior. Inside the main shrine, the four images of Adinatha face the four directions respectively. The basement is decorated with moldings, and the projections and recessions of the central portion are enlivened with figures of celestial beings, the guardians of the eight cardinal directions, and various divinities. The stylistic rendering has lost its earlier spontaneity and tends to be mechanical.

CEILING
It is not clear exactly when the town of Ranakpur was abandoned after the Muslims desecrated the temples. The ruined Adinatha Temple became a hiding place for dacoits and wild animals. At the end of the 19th century, the site was cleared and fortified. The renovation of the Adinatha Temple was entrusted to the descendants of Depa, the original architect of the temple. Depa's family had been practicing the art of temple architecture as a living tradition for centuries, and only the discerning eye can easily differentiate between the original and renovated elements in the reconstructed ceilings and pillars.

PLAQUE OF PARSHVA
This plaque, approximately 3 feet in diameter, is a later addition to the temple. Placed against the wall of the southern side shrine in the row of chapels, it depicts Parshva, the twenty-third *tirthankara*, a historical figure who lived in the 8th or 7th century BC. On either side of Parshva is a Jina, and an attendant. A cobra protects the three Jinas with his thousand hoods. This common motif of Jain iconography has been treated very innovatively.

PILLARS
The carved patterns on the pillars reveal a preference for floral, vegetal, and scroll motifs over depictions of human figures.

Spine of the Temple of Adinatha.

Udai Villas.

TROPHY ROOM
Most of the maharajas of Rajasthan were expert *shikaris* or huntsmen and had splendid collections of hunting trophies. But the trophy room in Dungarpur Palace is said to house one of the finest collections of such trophies in all of Asia.

DUNGARPUR

Situated 69 miles south of Udaipur, the town of Dungarpur was the capital of a kingdom of the same name. The rulers of Dungarpur were Sisodias, who branched away from the main line of Mewar in the 12th century. There are various stories behind this, but the most colorful one tells of a misunderstanding between the eldest prince of Mewar and his father, the Rana. The prince was getting married, and the bride's family sent him the customary ceremonial coconut. By mistake the coconut was accepted by the prince's father. The prince thereupon got angry and said, "Since you accepted the coconut, you marry the girl. I will leave Chittorgarh forever." He rode south with his followers to found the kingdom of Dungarpur, while his younger brother succeeded to the throne of Mewar (thus making Dungarpur the senior branch of the Sisodias). The region surrounding Dungarpur was an inhospitable place known, apparently, for five things: water, rocks, thorns, thieves, and foul language. Here, on an enormous rock, the town of Dungarpur was founded. Juna Mahal and Udai Vilas palaces in Dungarpur represent some of the finest examples of art and architecture in existence in Rajasthan today.

Durbar hall in Juna Mahal.

JUNA MAHAL. Juna Mahal rises above the town in a fierce, medieval jumble of white battlements, turrets, and watchtowers. In complete contrast to this warlike exterior, the apartments within the palace are sumptuously covered with paintings, inlay work and ornamentation. Its walls and ceilings are alive with scenes from Dungarpur's history and portraits of bygone princes, all dating from the 16th to the 18th centuries. What's more, since the palace is so remote – and has been unused since the 18th century – Juna Mahal's art work is far better preserved than any other palace in Rajasthan.

UDAI VILAS. Another nearby palace, Udai Vilas, was built in the late 18th century. This, too, is equally interesting, for in the middle of its courtyard rises an extraordinarily ornate carved

HIS WEIGHT IN GOLD
A carved stone arch in Dungarpur's Udai Vilas was supposedly part of an elaborate weighing device. The reigning maharawal was balanced on it, and his weight would determine the amount of silver or gold that was to be distributed to the populace as charity.

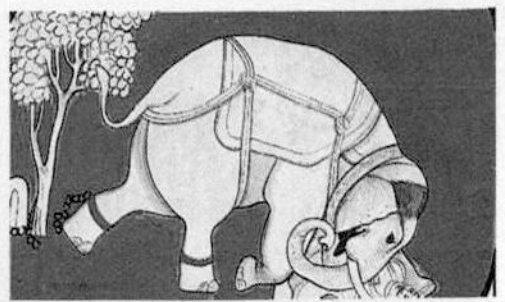

pleasure pavilion. Its lower level is a mass of intricate friezes, columns and arches, but the second story is even more ornate, with decorative brackets, unusually sculpted figurines and extravagantly carved pillars. Above this is a terrace with a profusion of kiosks, canopies, and balustrades. Inside, the apartment walls are created in inlaid marble, as at the Taj Mahal. The palace is one of the most exuberant and fantastical examples of Rajput architecture.

Five examples of frescos in Juna Mahal are shown above. The erotic painting below is also from Juna Mahal.

Deolia

The town of Deolia, about 100 miles southeast of Udaipur, is off the usual beaten tourist track. But if you are adventurous it is worth visiting for the brilliant wall paintings in its ruined palace. The palace was built in the 16th century, and one can imagine that it must have had a glorious past, but it now lies neglected and crumbling. Inside, especially in the royal bedchamber and the large *durbar* hall, are some truly exquisite wall paintings, which appear to have been painted in the early 19th century. Do not miss the rich crimson glass paintings embellished with gilt on the vaulted ceiling of one of the chambers, nor the frieze of wall paintings appearing like an endless row of framed miniatures. A predominant theme here is Lord Krishna as the great lover. Several of the paintings are charmingly erotic, like the ones in the bedchamber. These paintings are similar in style to the highly intricate style of the Mewar school ▲ *243*. This is not surprising, as the royal family of Deolia was an offshoot of the Sisodias of Mewar, with whom, over the centuries, it had a love-hate relationship. Deolia is also famed for its splendid Partabgarh *thewa* enamel-work on glass.

Family secret
An exquisite and unusual (but unfortunately dying) art of Rajasthan is the *thewa* work of Deolia. A silver wire frame is covered with delicately patterned gold leaf and then sunk into a softened layer of green or crimson enamel or glass. This is then used as a plaque or an ornamental box top. Common design themes are religious and court scenes. There is only one family left in Deolia who knows the secret of this craft, and they guard it jealously. Not even the daughters, it is said, are taught the secret, as they will one day marry and leave the family.

Lake at Mount Abu.

THOU SHALT NOT KILL
The Jain religion teaches that all living beings possess a soul, and must therefore be treated on a par with human beings ● *48*. Not only will a Jain never consciously kill any animal or insect, but devout Jains actually wear a cloth to cover their mouths in order to avoid accidentally killing insects by inhaling them.

HISTORY

Mount Abu was the site of a little colonial hill station, set, surprisingly, in the middle of this desert state. "A sort of Simla of Rajputana," as somebody once called it. It has a fascinating history that goes back, layer by layer, into deepest antiquity and has long been considered a holy spot by both Hindus and Jains. Once the tranquil hilltop retreat of meditating *rishis,* or holy men, it is supposed to have been home to no less than 330 million different gods and goddesses. To the Rajputs, however, this was a Mount Olympus, the scene of the great *agni-kunda* (sacred fire pit) of ancient times, out of which thirty-six Rajput warrior clans were born ● *32*. The legend goes that snake-like demons were ravaging this region, so the Brahmins perform an elaborate fire rite. In response to their prayers, Rajput warriors emerged from the fire, vanquished the demons and saved the land. Historians say the story is an allegory: the "demons" were actually the Indo-Scythian invaders of the 6th century; the ritual was an elaborate purification ceremony by which various lesser castes were given the exalted status of warriors and thereby inducted into the defending armies.

PILGRIMAGE CENTER. By the 11th century, Mount Abu had become an important Jain center of pilgrimage. Over the next two centuries, some of India's most spectacular marble temples were built here. In the 15th century these hills were conquered by Rana Kumbha of Mewar (who built a fortress here ▲ *274*).

HILL STATION. In the early 19th century, Mount Abu was developed into its present form as a hill station, where the British from the hot, dusty

BORN OF FIRE
Many ruling clans of Rajasthan traced their descent directly back either to the sun or the moon. But certain clans traced their origins to a great fire ceremony performed here at Mount Abu in ancient times, out of which thirty-six clans of warriors are said to have been born. These "fire-born" Rajputs consider themselves superior to all the others, since they were born not of woman, but out of the sacred fire itself. And among the fire-born Rajputs themselves, the Hara Chauhans (who ruled the kingdoms of Bundi and Kota) were considered to be supreme ● *35* ▲ *290*.

plains of Rajasthan could seek refuge during the summer months, amid the eucalyptus trees and oleanders. Charming English countryside cottages were built around Nakki Lake. As time passed it became a British enclave, the official summer capital to which the Chief Commissioner for Rajputana would shift his officc from Ajmer for two months each year. With the emergence of an administrative center, most of the major Rajput maharajas, too, built palaces here (some of which have now been converted into hotels). There was crickct and golf at the Rajputana Club and considerable intrigue at the British Residency. The maharajas used the opportunities Mount Abu offered for casual encounters with the Chief Commissioner for political ends, since approaching him here was much more discreet than public visits to Ajmer.

The gothic-style palace built by Maharaja Jai Singh of Alwar. The palace has some interesting anecdotes associated with it. On one occasion, the story goes, when a fellow maharaja was hosting a dinner to which he had pointedly not been invited, Maharaja Jai Singh bought up all the food supplies for miles around, forcing the dinner to be canceled. He then added insult to injury by inviting everybody to his place instead.

MOUNT ABU TODAY

While the surrounding hills, with their waterfalls and bamboo and eucalyptus groves, are still extremely charming, Mount Abu has become an overcrowded and somewhat gaudy little town. If you can imagine an Indian version of Las Vegas and Disney World rolled into one, this would probably be it. Still, its bazaars are fascinating as a living museum of contemporary Indian kitsch. The temples of Dilwara, of course, simply have to be seen ● *94* ▲ *270*. Some of the old palaces make interesting viewing, such as Bikaner Palace, where Maharaja Ganga Singh used to come every year with a retinue of four hundred people, and the gothic towered palace of the bizarre Maharaja Jai Singh of Alwar ▲ *173*.

Interior of Jain temple.

Temples at Dilwara.

POETIC BEAUTIES
The marble *nayikas* (maidens) that adorn the Dilwara temples are not just ethereally beautiful in form, but they are often presented in a highly poetic context. One of them, for instance, is depicted as having just emerged wet from her bath. The droplets of water falling from her long hair are being drunk by a swan sitting by her feet!

Situated 2 miles north of Mount Abu, these breathtakingly beautiful carved Jain temples date back to the 11th and 13th centuries ● *94*. They are among the finest temples India has to offer, so intricately and delicately wrought that they look as though they had been carved out of ivory, rather than marble. They are an absolute must-see for any traveler in Rajasthan, considered by many experts to be superior to the Taj Mahal.

VIMALA-VASAHI TEMPLE ★

Built in AD 1030 by Vimala Shah, a minister of Gujarat, to atone for his earthly sins, the temple is said to have involved a work force of 2700 men, and taken a total of fourteen years to complete. The cost at that time is supposed to have been over US$6 million! From the outside the temple is deceptively austere, but as you enter through the ornate doorway, the beauty of the marble carvings is simply overwhelming. The temple is a classic example of Jain architecture, with a central shrine, a colonnaded hall and an ambulatory passage around it, with fifty-two small shrines against the surrounding wall, each one containing the image of a Jain *tirthankara*. The inner sanctum houses the image of Adinatha, the great Jain saint. The real beauty of the temple, of course, lies in its profuse and intricate decorations. The columns are carved with figures and friezes of scrollwork. The domes and vaults of the ceilings are corbeled and embellished with row upon row of musicians, dancers, warriors and elephants, set around beautiful medallions decorated with lotus-blossom motifs. Each of the canopies of the roof is said to have been carved by two workers, one on either side, and yet they match perfectly in the center. The large dome of the open *ranga mandapa* (main hall) is an especially impressive feature of the temple, with roof brackets carved in the form of seductive maidens, and a clustered lotus pendant. Take a look also at the splendid carved panels in the aisles, depicting figures from Jain, as well as Hindu, mythology. In the porch

Interior of Vimala Vasahi Temple at Dilwara.

TWO MONK SECTS
Jain monks are divided into two sects: Svetambaras, the "white-robed", and Digambaras, the "sky-clad" (naked) ascetics ● *48*. One can recognize which of the two groups a *tirthankara* statue represents by looking at its eyes. Wide open, enameled eyes mark a *Svetambara*, while closed eyes indicate a *Digambara*.

there is a marble figure seated on a horse, believed to be the builder, Vimala Shah.

LUNA-VASAHI TEMPLE ★

Built in AD 1232 by two wealthy brothers, Luna-Vasahi Temple is similar in form to Vimala-Vasahi Temple, but smaller. Its carved ornamentation is even richer, denser and more delicate – resembling paper cut-outs more than marble. In some places, in fact, the marble is carved so finely that it is actually translucent! The doorways of the temple are framed by ornate pediments and pilasters; the columns are magnificently carved; and the ceiling is ablaze with mythological figures, processions of horsemen, elephants and dancers. The carvings on the corners of the ceilings in the fourth, fifth and sixth cells are exceptional. Other features worth taking a closer look at are the caparisoned elephants in the elephant chamber and the magnificent image of Lord Adinatha seated in a triple-storied marble tower with Jain devotees on its four sides. However, the greatest masterpiece in the entire Dilwara complex is the *ranga mandapa* of the Luna-Vasahi, and, more specifically, its ceiling. From its center hangs a clustered marble pendant of unsurpassed richness and delicacy (someone described it as a "cluster of crystal drops", which sounds overly poetic, but under the circumstances, entirely appropriate). On a nearby frieze are sixty-eight maidens caught in different dance poses on the petals of a lotus, and on a raised platform above is an arrangement of nine canopies with more examples of superbly intricate carving. The two *gokhadas*, or filigreed marble niches, containing Jain idols and images of the goddess Lakshmi, are also worth taking a closer look at. There are two other temples in the complex, dedicated to Parshvanatha and Adinatha. The former is notable for its columned *mandapa* (hall), and the latter for its carved pillars and its massive brass idol.

PAINSTAKING REWARD
The marble pendant that descends from the ceiling of Luna-Vasahi Temple's main hall is so delicately carved that it simply takes one's breath away. It is said that this astonishing delicacy of carving was achieved by offering the artisans the weight of their marble shavings in gold: the more finely they carved, the more they earned.

▲ FILIGREED SPLENDOR JAIN TEMPLES, DILWARA

Detail of marble carving in a ceiling panel.

On the summit of the lofty mountain of Mount Abu are two magnificent Jain temples built in marble. The earlier of the two, completed in AD 1030, the Vimala-Vasahi, dedicated to Lord Adinatha, was commissioned by Vimala, the Commander-in-Chief of Bhimadeva I, the ruler of Gujarat. The other, enshrining the image of Lord Neminatha, was constructed two hundred years later in AD 1232 by the Minister, Tejpala, the brother of Vastupala. Both Tejpala and Vastupala were famous for having constructed more than fifty Jain shrines. Tejpala built the Luna-Vasahi temple for the spiritual welfare of his wife and his son, Lavanyasimha, after whom the temple was named.

INTERIOR OF VIMALA-VASAHI TEMPLE
Scenes from Jain myths, gods and goddesses, portrayals of *Tirthankaras*, and monks with devotees are carved in relief on every possible surface – door frames, pillars, niches, ceilings, and arches. The exquisite workmanship heightens the translucency and shell-like delicacy of the carvings, which owe their fragile beauty not to the process of chiseling but to the painstaking technique of thinning the marble into the incredible shapes by gently scraping it.

KALPAVALLI MEDALLION
The architectural vocabulary of the region included ornamental renderings of flowers and creepers. The motif of the *kalpavalli*, a filigreed scroll in varied and replicated forms was prevalent. In the 15th century, it is encountered again on a ceiling in the Jain temple of Adinatha at Ranakpur.

Arches
In the interior of the temples at Mount Abu, a dramatic accent is added by the intricately sculpted arches connecting the pillars. They are of two varieties – the wave, with its regular undulations, and the caterpillar, with its exaggerated curves. The latter variety, preferred in the temples of Gujarat, occurs in the Vimala-Vasahi Temple, adding to the richness of its interior.

Divinities
The portrayal of Yakshini Chakreshwari, the attendant deity of Adinatha, is an integral part of the scheme of figural sculptures of the temple. The figures have broad faces, sharp facial features, and narrow waists, in keeping with prevailing esthetic norms. The plastic grace of the earlier expression at Osiyan gradually yielded to greater stylization and stiffness at Mount Abu.

Ceiling pendant
Of incomparable beauty are the ornamental pendants hanging from the decorated domical ceiling of the temples at Mount Abu. The patterns of the ceilings in the corridor and vestibules are variations on certain geometrical and floral motifs that have been integral to the architectural tradition of the region. Often, however, the inventive genius of the sculptor creates a different pattern of light and shade by carving the motif at varying depths and in different arrangements.

Damascened swords The kingdom of Sirohi, near Mount Abu, has traditionally been famous for its damascened swords. These slender, slightly curved swords were the favorites of the Rajputs. They were called *sirohis*, after the town itself. The sword-makers would first chase the motif on the steel with a sharp chisel. Then fine gold or silver wire would be painstakingly hammered into the groove. The hammering was so skillfully done that the wire actually became welded to the steel surface. After the hammering process, the slight spreading of the inlaid wire would be carefully scraped away by the sword-maker, just as a jeweler would do. The mark of a good *sirohi* sword is that if you run your finger along its flat surface, the wire and steel would form a single, perfectly smooth surface.

Sketch of Gomukh Temple (right); a deity in the temple (below).

Nakki Lake

The name of this lake (right) has a curious origin. The word *nakki* means fingernails, reflecting the belief that the lake was clawed out of the earth by the fingernails of the gods. It is a pretty lake, surrounded by wooded hills, which, as in many Indian hill stations, was the focal point of the entire town. Boating is a popular pastime here, and a walk along the banks is quite pleasant. From here you can see the strange rock formation called "Toad's Rock", one of many fascinating rock formations sculpted by the forces of nature in the area. Southwest of the lake is Sunset Point, with its lovely view of the surrounding hills. From here you can see the sun set spectacularly between two rocky peaks.

Gomukh Temple

Located about 2 miles from Mount Abu, this is the site of the ancient *agnikunda*, where the great fire rite is said to have been carried out by the Brahmins. Gomukh Temple contains images of Lord Rama and Lord Krishna, both of whom are considered to have been incarnations of Vishnu, "The Preserver" of the Hindu trinity. The name "Gomukh" literally means "cow's face", referring to a spring here which flows through a rock carved in the shape of a cow's mouth. The spring water, said to have sacred, purifying properties, is taken home by pilgrims.

Achalgarh Fort

The ruins of this 15th-century fort, built by the warrior king, Rana Kumbha, who conquered Mount Abu from its Chauhan rulers ▲ *268*, lie 5 miles from Mount Abu. This was one of a girdle of thirty-two forts that he constructed all over Mewar in order to secure the kingdom against invaders. From its crumbling battlements there is a superb view of the surrounding plains. Nearby are the remains of several ancient temples. Of these, the most interesting is the 15th-century temple of Lord Shiva, where you are shown what is said to be Lord Shiva's toenail. It is unusual for a Shiva temple, as it does not have a characteristic *Shivalinga*; instead there is a deep pit that is believed to lead straight down into the underworld. The peak of Guru Shikhar, the highest point in Rajasthan, at an altitude of 5,676 feet, lies 2 1/2 miles beyond Achalgarh. There are more dramatic views of the surrounding countryside from here, of wooded hills, waterfalls and the plains.

Plains near Achalgarh Fort.

SIROHI

The little town of Sirohi, once the capital of the Deora Chauhan clan of Rajputs, is situated down on the plains, 36 miles from Mount Abu. Founded in 1347, after the clan had been driven south by the Muslim invaders, Sirohi, protected by the surrounding Aravalli hills, was able to retain its independence in the face of attacks by the Mughals, the Marathas and the Rathors of Marwar. An indication of the volatility of those times is the fact that the 16th- century ruler, Rao Sultan Singh, fought fifty-two battles in the fifty-one years of his reign! Sirohi, a fascinating little town, rather off the usual beaten tourist track, is known for its fine ornamental swords and daggers. Kesar Vilas Palace has some fine gesso ornamentation in gold and white, reminiscent of Junagarh Fort in Bikaner and the City Palace in Jaipur. It is the private property of the Maharao, but if you are lucky, you may be able to obtain permission to see it. There are also some 17th-century frescos in Sirohi Fort and the 1621 *chhatri* of Rao Raj Singh in the nearby fortified hill temple of Sarneshwar Mahadev. One of Sirohi's claims to fame, incidentally, was that it was the very last Rajput kingdom to sign a treaty of "perpetual friendship" with the British: while all the other kingdoms signed treaties between 1817 and 1818, Sirohi held out until 1823.

Achalgarh Fort.

SON OF THE HIMALAYAS
According to legend, Mount Abu is the "Son of the Himalayans". The nearby peak of Guru Shikhar is, in fact, the highest peak between the Himalayas in the north and the Nilgiri Hills in southern India. Mount Abu takes its name from Arbuda, a goddess from a metaphysical story about the fall of a sacred cow into an abyss.

Throne in Sirohi Palace (above).

The town of Sirohi has twenty-eight temples on one street, which they consider a world record (left).

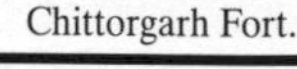

Chittorgarh Fort.

Chittorgarh, the awe-inspiring hill fort built on a massive rock 3 miles long and 495 feet high, lies 72 miles northeast of Udaipur. It was said that this fort was the key to all of Rajputana, and any conqueror who had ambitions on Rajputana had to first wrest control of it. It is considered by many to be the finest medieval Hindu fort in existence. But more than that, it is cloaked in legends of valor, chivalry and glorious death and occupies a preeminent position in the Rajput psyche. Chittorgarh was built in the 8th century by Bappa Rawal (reigned AD 734–53), the first of the great Sisodia rulers (although legend traces it all the way back to Bhima, the mighty warrior of the epic *Mahabharata*). Between then and 1567 it fell victim to three bloody sieges, each one ending in glorious defeat and *jauhar*, the mass self-sacrifice of its womenfolk in a sacred fire.

THE SIEGES OF CHITTORGARH. The first great siege was in 1303, at the hands of Alauddin Khilji, Sultan of Delhi. It is said that the Sultan had heard of the legendary beauty of Rani Padmini, the wife of the then Rana, and requested that he be allowed to gaze at her face, just once. It was finally agreed that although this would not be permitted directly, he would be allowed to see her reflection in the waters of a pool, which in turn would be reflected in a mirror. Having seen her beauty, and being completely smitten by it, the Sultan ambushed and captured the Rana and demanded the hand of

A PRINCESS'S HYMNS
Mirabai, the celebrated 16th-century poet, singer and saint, was a Rajput princess who lived at Chittorgarh. The daughter-in-law of the great warrior king, Rana Sangha, she was an ardent devotee of Lord Krishna, in praise of whom she composed and sang her hymns. It was scandalous in those distant times for a rani to profess her love for anyone but her husband, even if it was a god. There was much intrigue in the court against her, but she stood firm in her devotion, ultimately leaving her family to follow the trail of Lord Krishna to Brindavan and Dwarka. Her hymns are widely sung all over India today.

Mughal miniature portraying the siege of Chittorgarh by Akbar's forces in 1567.

"I gazed until the sun's last beam fell on the 'ringlet of Chittor', illuminating its grey and grief-worn aspect, like a lambent gleam lighting up the face of sorrow."

Colonel Tod, *Annals and Antiquities of Rajasthan*, 1829

Rani Padmini in ransom. The Rajputs agreed and sent a procession of palanquins to Alauddin's camp, ostensibly carrying the Rani and her ladies, but in fact filled with armed warriors. The Rana was rescued, but a massive battle ensued, in which 50,000 Rajput warriors were slain, and Rani Padmini, along with the rest of the womenfolk, threw herself into the flames rather than fall into the hands of the enemy. The *jauhar* was repeated a second time in 1535 when Sultan Bahadur Shah of Gujarat captured Chittorgarh. On this occasion, it is recorded that 32,000 warriors fell on the battlefield and 13,000 womenfolk died in the *jauhar*. The third and final sack of Chittorgarh took place in 1567, at the hands of no other than the Mughal Emperor Akbar. Two young Rajput chieftains, Jaimal and Patta, both in their teens, led the fortress's defense. Both died fighting valiantly, the former with his mother and wife fighting beside him. And, once again, a great *jauhar* was called, and the womenfolk hurled themselves into the flames. It is said that Akbar, on returning to his capital after the fall of Chittorgarh, had statues erected to commemorate the valiant young chieftains, Jaimal and Patta. The ascent to the fort is by a tortuous, winding road, defended by seven fortified gateways. Bhairon Pol was where Jaimal fell, while the innermost, Ram Pol, was where Patta fell. Both these sites are marked by cenotaphs.

RANA KUMBHA'S PALACE. Past the crenelated, loopholed fort wall, you come to the oldest palace of Chittorgarh, Rana Kumbha's palace, with its beautiful series of cantilevered, canopied balconies and a stepped outer wall. Beneath its courtyard is an underground passage leading to the chamber where Rani Padmini is said to have performed *jauhar*. Opposite this palace lies Kunwar Pade ka Mahal ("Crown Prince's Palace"), a wonderful example of early Rajput architecture. Just beyond lies the imposing temple of Vraj-ji, built by Rana Kumbha, and, nearby, the temple of Mirabai, the celebrated 16th-century poet-saint.

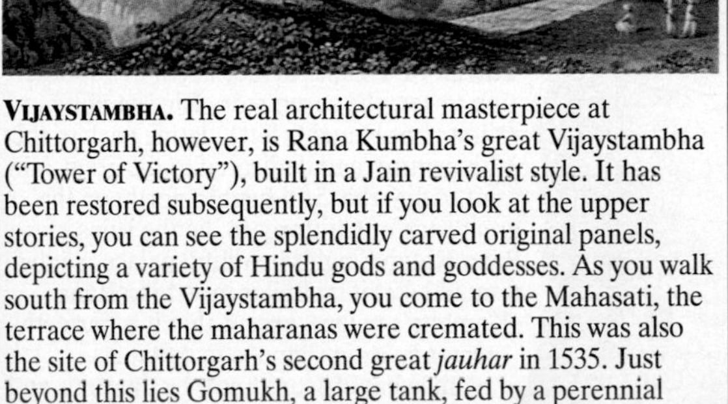

VIJAYSTAMBHA. The real architectural masterpiece at Chittorgarh, however, is Rana Kumbha's great Vijaystambha ("Tower of Victory"), built in a Jain revivalist style. It has been restored subsequently, but if you look at the upper stories, you can see the splendidly carved original panels, depicting a variety of Hindu gods and goddesses. As you walk south from the Vijaystambha, you come to the Mahasati, the terrace where the maharanas were cremated. This was also the site of Chittorgarh's second great *jauhar* in 1535. Just beyond this lies Gomukh, a large tank, fed by a perennial spring through a rock carved with the face of a cow.

TOWER OF VICTORY
Vijaystambha, ("Tower of Victory") is an extraordinary structure, visible from the plains below for miles around. Built by Rana Kumbha to celebrate a great victory over the Sultan of Malwa in 1440, the nine-storied structure is profusely carved with images of gods and goddesses. Lithograph of Vijaystambha (below left).

Spring water flows from a "cow's mouth" in Gomukh tank.

Kalika Mata Temple (left);
Patta's palace (right).

NOMADIC BLACKSMITHS
The Gadholia Lohars, whom you see all over Rajasthan today, are a caste of nomadic blacksmiths who trace their origins back to Chittorgarh. The legend goes that after the fall of Chittorgarh in 1567, they vowed that they would not cease to wander until the fortress was reconquered. They have never given up their nomadic ways.

PALACES OF PATTA AND JAIMAL. South of the Gomukh tank are the ruins of a row of great mansions, including those of the heroes who defended Chittorgarh, Patta and Jaimal. These two palaces were among the last of the monuments to be built in the fort before it was destroyed in 1567. Patta's palace echoes the style of the palace of Rana Kumbha and Kunwar Pade ka Mahal, with a stepped wall in the case of the former, and rich decorations in the case of the latter. If you look closely, you can see the ornamented blue tiles that once adorned many of the buildings here. Jaimal's palace, on the other hand, is solid and austere, but displays the perfect symmetry of plan that can be traced back to even the oldest Rajput palaces. Nearby is the Bundi Chief's palace, with its beautiful old pool, lined with bathing terraces, and beyond it lie the ruins of Chittorgarh's old Pearl Market.

KALIKA MATA TEMPLE. Toward the south end of the fort is Kalika Mata Temple, originally dedicated to Surya, the sun god. It dates back to the 8th century, making it the oldest structure in the fort.

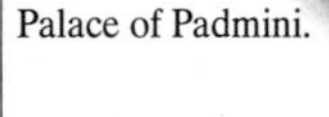
Palace of Padmini.

PADMINI'S PALACE. Still further south, beyond Chonda's Palace, lies the palace of Rani Padmini ▲ *118*. According to legend, she is said to have been a Sri Lankan princess, so fair and delicate that when she drank water, you could see it pass through her throat! The original palace was a beautiful water palace, a forerunner of the later Jag Mandir and Jag Niwas in Udaipur ▲ *250*. What you see today, however, is a 19th-century recreation that bears little resemblance to the original. However, you are shown a mirror on the wall of an adjacent building and invited to simulate for yourself how Alauddin Khilji must have gazed on the reflection of Rani Padmini in the waters behind him. As you turn north again, and continue along the eastern ramparts, you come to Suraj Pol. Look down on the plains below from here: this is where Akbar's forces are said to have camped during their final campaign for Chittorgarh.

DIFFERENT ROLES
While Emperor Akbar was responsible for the destruction of Chittorgarh, his father, Humayun, ironically, played a defensive role in its history. In 1535 Rani Karnavati of Chittorgarh, under siege from the Sultan of Gujarat, sent Humayun a *rakhi*, the traditional ornamented wristlet that a sister presents to her brother, and asked for his assistance. Humayun rushed here from Bengal. He defeated the Sultan of Gujarat and expelled him from Chittorgarh.

TOWER OF FAME. Further north lies another fine tower, the seven-story Kirtistambha ("Tower of Fame") (left), dating back to the 12th century and dedicated to the great Jain saint, Adinatha. Still further north, on the great rock of Chittorgarh, lie the ruins of Rana Ratan Singh's beautiful palace. Set by a small lake, it is similar in style to Rana Kumbha's palace, except that it is perfectly rectangular in shape, a fact that is somewhat obscured now by the ruins and subsequent alterations.

The southeast

280 Kota
284 Around Kota
290 Bundi
292 Garh Palace
296 Around Bundi

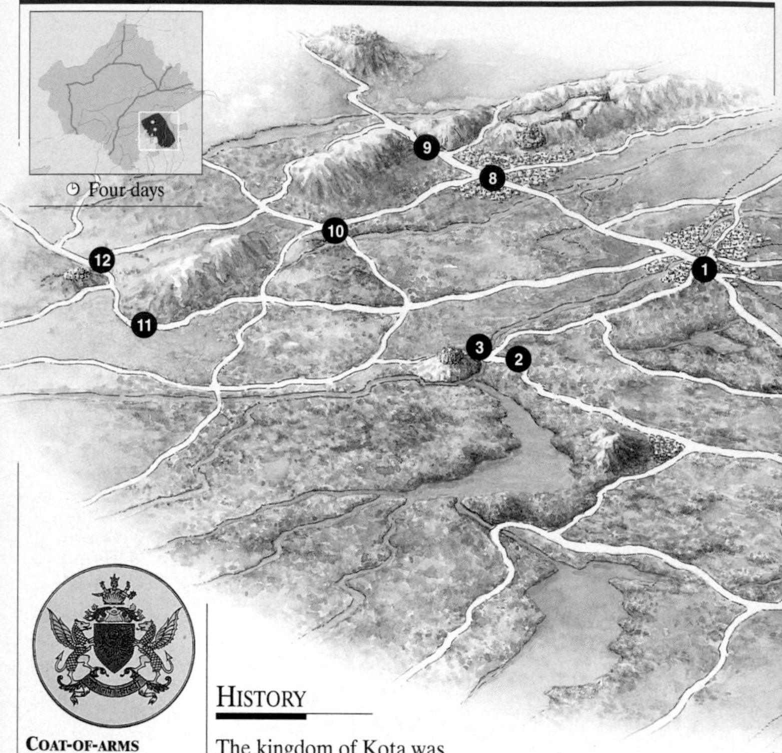

COAT-OF-ARMS
Kota's royal coat-of-arms shows the great mythological bird, Garuda, the mount of Lord Vishnu, set within a central shield. This is topped by a warrior emerging from the flames, symbolizing the emergence of the ruling family from the great sacred fire at Mount Abu, out of which it is said to have been born ▲ *269*. The winged gryphons flanking the shield seem to have a curiously European touch, thought up by the British heraldry experts who were commissioned to devise coats-of-arms for all the Rajput states.

HISTORY

The kingdom of Kota was carved out of Bundi in 1579 by a ruler of Bundi as a gift for a favorite younger prince, Rao Madho Singh, who is said to have proven himself as a successful and courageous general at the tender age of fourteen. This great martial tradition continued down the family: fighting on behalf of the ageing Mughal emperor, Shah Jahan, against the usurper prince, Aurangzeb, five of Rao Madho Singh's sons died on the battlefield. The sixth, who narrowly survived, lived on to count no less than fifty wounds on his body, acquired during the course of a long and eventful military career. Kota has a complex history, with great swings of fortune, unlike its sister kingdom of Bundi, hidden away behind its rampart of hills. Menaced over the centuries by various Mughal rulers, the maharajas of Jaipur and Mewar, the Maratha warlords,

Country seat of the Kota princes (right).

An artist's impression of the city of Kota.

and even sometimes their own cousins in Bundi, the rulers of Kota developed a keenly honed instinct for diplomacy. One result was a treaty with the Marathas in the 18th century to keep the Kachhawaha rulers of Jaipur at bay.

ZALIM SINGH'S LEADERSHIP. It was around this time that Kota produced one of the most fascinating characters of modern Rajput history: Zalim Singh, a statesman and diplomat who has been referred to as the "Talleyrand of North India" and the "Machiavelli of Rajwarra." Starting out as a general of the Kota armies, he became Regent of the kingdom when the ruler died, leaving an infant son on the throne. He then set about manipulating the kingdom's belligerent neighbors, parleying with them and shrewdly setting one against the other. Meanwhile, he also reorganized the kingdom completely, setting up a modern administration, adopting European weapons and tactics for its armies and creating a comprehensive revenue system that taxed everything from widows to brooms. In doing all this, he certainly was not without personal ambition – the result of which was that there were numerous attempts on his life, including a memorable one when he was set up by a rani and attacked by a band of armed ladies in the *purdah* palace.

KOTA AND THE BRITISH. In 1817, under Zalim Singh's leadership, Kota became one of the first of the Rajput states to sign a treaty with the British, in return for which Zalim Singh extracted an agreement that the kingdom would be divided, and a separate kingdom carved out of it for his own descendants. The result was the new kingdom of Jhalawar, formed in 1838. The rulers of Kota had their little revenge on the British: during the great Uprising of 1857, Kota was one of the few states of Rajputana where the Indian troops rebelled, discreetly aided, it is said, by the ruler.

Zalim Singh is famed for the legendary gardens he laid out at Kota. Almost defying the laws of nature, he grew a variety of exotic fruits here, "where even grass could not grow": coconuts and palmyras from Malabar, apples and quinces from Kabul, oranges from Bengal and the famed "golden plantains" from the Deccan. He also, incidentally, invited weavers from Kashmir to settle here in Kota, weaving shawls to rival the finest that Kashmir could produce.

KOTA MINIATURES
The celebrated miniature paintings of the Kota school frequently depict the kingdom's jungle-covered hills and flowing rivers, combining these with scenes of hunting (which was a passion of its maharajas). The Kota school was an offshoot of the Bundi school; it is often difficult to distinguish between the two.

SOLAR CLOCK
The sun clock in the Kota Palace Museum incorporated a miniature cannon, which was automatically fired by the sun's rays precisely at noon each day. This signaled the firing of a regular cannon that would indicate the time to the townspeople. Made by the old British firm of Lawrence and Mayo in Bombay, the sun clock was carefully calibrated, so that you could adjust it according to your latitude for perfect accuracy.

City Palace.

KOTA TODAY

Kota today is a complete contrast to its neighboring town, Bundi, only 14 miles away, which seems to be still caught in a medieval time warp. Kota is one of Rajasthan's premier industrial and commercial centers, with a major hydro-electric plant, an atomic power station, as well as various manufacturing industries, ranging from precision instruments to synthetic fibers. Unfortunately, the city has paid a price for this – losing a great deal of its olden-day character. However, it has some interesting palaces and old Indo-Victorian public buildings, such as the Herbert College, Curzon Wylie Memorial, and Crossthwaite Institute. But even more interesting, perhaps, is the fact that it is the key to a fascinating and largely undiscovered region of Rajasthan, studded with forts, temples, pleasure palaces and opportunities for wildlife safaris.

CITY PALACE

Built from 1625 onward, Kota's City Palace reflects the city's stormy history – its exterior marrying rugged bastions and ramparts with delicate cupolas and balustrades. Basically Rajput in form, it also reflects the close connections the kingdom had with the Mughals in its graceful Mughal-style design elements. The palace is a rambling complex of suites and apartments built by different rulers at different times. You enter through the 17th-century Hathi Pol ("Elephant Gate"), typical of the Hadauti region of southwest Rajasthan in design, with its bracketed elephants forming an archway with their raised trunks. Inside lies the grand Raj Mahal, with ornate medieval glass and mirror inlay-work covering its walls and ceilings. There are also some fine 18th-century frescos here, mainly depicting scenes from the legends of Lord Krishna. Adjoining this is a gallery with a fine collection of period Rajput weaponry, including Prithviraj Chauhan's historic scimitar and a fascinating array of old firearms, many of them superbly inlaid with gold and ivory. Beyond this lies another gallery with old family photographs from the Maharaja's personal albums, depicting the princely lifestyle of the 19th century. Still further beyond lies an art gallery with some interesting examples of *Kotah Kalaam* miniature paintings. (Look, for instance, for the amusing scene of the holy man being entertained by

> "The appearance of Kotah is very imposing, and impresses the mind with a more lively notion of wealth and activity than most cities in India."
>
> Colonel Tod, *Annals and Antiquities of Rajasthan*, 1829

devoted ladies of the court.) Across the courtyard outside is Akhade ka Mahal ("The Palace of the Wrestling Arena"), where there is a collection of treasures and memorabilia of the maharajas, from an elephant *howdah* and ivory palanquin to a mysterious-looking 17th-century astronomical device. Bhim Mahal, on the first floor, has some superb friezes of Rajput miniature paintings covering its walls, set off by beautiful ebony and ivory inlaid doors. Climbing up the stairs you come to Bada Mahal and Chhatar Mahal, with more exquisite paintings, ornate glass inlay and frescos. However, you need an extra ticket to visit these rooms in the personal palace of the maharaja. In the ornate Hawa Mahal ("Palace of the Winds") is the Government Museum, with some excellent stone carvings and antiquities.

LETHAL WEAPON
Yet another of the strange and bloodthirsty weapons of the Rajputs, these *bhujtrans* in the Kota Palace Museum are shaped rather like knuckle-dusters, but with three lethal daggers in place of mere studs.

BRIJRAJ BHAWAN

Another interesting palace, now converted into a hotel and therefore accessible to travelers, is Brijraj Bhawan. Built in 1840, high above the banks of the River Chambal, this white-pillared colonial building was once the British Residency and is said to be haunted by the ghost (apparently benign) of the Resident, Major Charles Burton, who was killed here during the Uprising of 1857.

UMAID BHAWAN

Umaid Bhawan Palace, designed by Sir Swinton Jacob ▲ *134* and built in 1904, is a charming creation in beige stone that seems more Edwardian than Rajput, with features such as a billiard room, tennis courts and a beautiful English-style garden, well known for its beautiful herbaceous borders. It is now the personal residence of the maharaja.

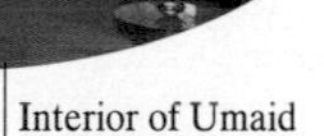

Interior of Umaid Bhawan Palace.

JAGMANDIR

Jagmandir is a graceful 18th-century pleasure palace built on the waters of Kishor Sagar Lake, along the lines of Udaipur's Jag Niwas Palace. Colonel Tod described it as "a little fairy islet with its light Saracenic summer abode". A trifle neglected today, it makes a picturesque sight reflected in the lake's waters. Nearby, on the shore, are the splendid old royal cenotaphs, also, alas, in a state of neglect.

Ivory palanquin.

Jagmandir.

Kansuan Temple.

KOTA DORIA
Kota is known for its gossamer-fine Kota Doria fabrics, woven with a cotton warp and silk weft, and often embellished with delicate floral motifs. The fabrics have an interesting history behind them. The weavers were brought here from faraway Mysore in the 17th century by the then Rao of Kota, who discovered them during his military campaigns in south India. Incidentally, the handicraft still flourishes here, while it has died out in its original home in Mysore. The fabric is also called Kota-Masuria, recalling its ancestry.

Weaving the fine Kota Doria fabric.

Temple ruins at Baroli (above). Ghateshwara Temple (center).

KANSUAN TEMPLE

This ancient Shiva temple, with an inscription dating back to AD 738, lies 6 miles from Kota. Within a walled enclosure is the main temple and various smaller shrines, pavilions and *Shivalingas*. It must have been an extremely beautiful temple once, but is now in a somewhat weathered condition.

BAROLI TEMPLES

The ruins of this superb 9th–12th century temple complex (left), one of the finest of its kind in Rajasthan, picturesquely sited in a forest, are located 34 miles southwest of Kota. Colonel Tod, visiting the Baroli Temples in 1820, was so impressed that he proceeded to devote eleven entire pages of his book, *Annals and Antiquities of Rajasthan,* to the wonders he saw there. The principal temple of the complex is Ghateshwara Temple (center), with its richly ornamented porch, ceilings and pillars, the latter exquisitely carved with images of celestial nymphs. The *shikhara,* or pagoda, is profusely and delicately embellished, and there are some elegant sculptures set around the walls: a dancing Shiva; Shiva slaying the demon, Andhaka; and Chamunda (one of the forms of the Great Goddess, wearing a necklace made up of skulls). By the sanctum doorway is another dancing Shiva, this one surrounded by Brahma, Vishnu and various other mythological figures.
Do not miss the temple's wonderfully carved *torana* archway. Two other temples within the complex that are especially interesting are the 10th-century Trimurti and Mahishasuramardini temples. Near the former are the carved columns of an old gateway, decorated with graceful maidens, devotees and flowers. In Mahishasuramardini Temple, do take a close look at the curved pagoda, with its intricately etched motifs, almost like a fine screen. There is also a picturesque little Shiva temple nearby, set inside a pool of water.

"To describe its [the Baroli Temples'] stupendous and diversified architecture is impossible...The carving on the capital of each column would require pages of explanation."

Colonel Tod, *Annals and Antiquities of Rajasthan*, 1829

Bhensrorgarh Fort

Colonel Tod wrote in the 1820's, "The Castle of Bhainsror is most romantically situated upon the extreme point of a ridge." The ridge itself is composed of solid rock, 230 feet high, just a few miles beyond Baroli. Protected by the River Chambal on two sides, this 14th-century fort was once one of the most powerful in Rajasthan – it was never captured. It is worth seeing on your way back from Baroli to Kota.

Bhensrorgarh Fort.

Darrah Wildlife Sanctuary

Darrah, once the private hunting grounds of the maharajas of Kota – and the place where many of the splendid hunt scenes in the Kota miniature paintings were set – is situated 35 miles south of Kota. Spread over an area of 106 square miles, these forests were once thick with everything from tigers to rhinoceros. Today neither the wildlife nor the forests themselves are as rich as they used to be, but Darrah is still worth visiting. You can view animals such as the leopard, sloth bear, *chinkara* and wolf, from the old hunting boxes of the maharajas. The word *darrah* literally means a "pass", and these forests were once a place of great strategic importance, opening up the hills of Hadauti to the plains of Malwa in the east. They were also the scene of several battles between the Rajputs, the Marathas and, later, the British. Another very pretty, and almost totally undiscovered, little sanctuary 30 miles southeast of Kota is Sorsan. It is a naturalist's paradise, with its rich species of birdlife, and reputedly the best place in India to view the endangered great Indian bustard ■ 27.

Within the Shiva Temple at Ramgarh are some very interesting erotic sculptures (above), reminiscent of those at Khajuraho.

Ramgarh

Located 40 miles north of Kota, Ramgarh is known for its fine 10th-century temple ruins, accessible only by jeep and therefore somewhat off the beaten track. Here, in the middle of the wilderness, is a Shiva temple, carved in rich mauve-brown stone, with superbly ornamented columns. Nearby are several other ruins, notably Kishnai Mata Temple, sited on a hilltop. There's also a ruined medieval palace by the side of the hill.

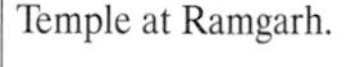

Temple at Ramgarh.

Garh Palace, Jhalawar.

COAT-OF-ARMS
The Jhalawar coat-of-arms depicts Hanuman, the great monkey-god of the epic *Ramayana,* on the central shield. The shield is flanked by a horse and a lion. A trident is positioned over the shield to represent the Goddess Durga.

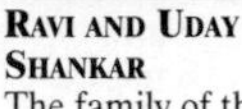

RAVI AND UDAY SHANKAR
The family of the celebrated *sitar* maestro, Ravi Shankar, is from Jhalawar. Originally from the distant state of Bengal, they moved to Jhalawar, where Ravi Shankar's father was the Prime Minister. His old family bungalow is still here.
The legendary oriental dancer, Uday Shankar (Ravi Shankar's elder brother), who grew up in Jhalawar, danced at the Natyashala long before he was discovered by Anna Pavlova in Europe, with whom he later danced.

JHALAWAR

Jhalawar, 54 miles south of Kota, is a fascinating little Rajput town, all the more interesting because it is relatively undiscovered, and therefore quite unspoiled. It also lies in one of the most scenic parts of Rajasthan, and the drive from Kota, through the Darrah forest, is in itself a part of the experience. Jhalawar (literally "Place of the Jhala Clan") was the principality specially set up for that remarkable 19th-century statesman, Zalim Singh, in 1838, on the understanding that it would be ruled by his descendants ▲ *281*. Zalim Singh encouraged the wealthiest people of the region to settle here and set up an amazingly modern, well-planned town. It was, in fact, the first town anywhere in India to have its own municipality. Progressive a man as he was, he also had, back in those feudal days, a charter of rights of the city inscribed on a stone pillar, which made Colonel Tod observe that it had elements of "that commercial greatness which made the free cities of Europe the instruments of general liberty." As a result the town soon became "the grand commercial mart of Upper Malwa", absorbing all the trade of the surrounding region. Most of this trade, by the way, was opium, the region being one of the world's greatest opium-producing areas in the 19th century and the main source of the opium supplied to China. It also became a great cultural center, a focus of music, the theater, and the arts under the patronage of its highly cultured rulers, and actually boasted one of the finest Western-style opera houses in India.

JHALAWAR TODAY. Jhalawar is a sleepy little town which belies the highly progressive spirit of its 19th-century beginnings. Visiting the old Garh Palace of the maharajas is a slightly bizarre experience, for its marvelously frescoed 1840's halls and chambers have now been converted into government offices, and you

Interior of Surya Temple, Jhalrapatan (center).

wander from office to office, peeping past conferring officials at the gloriously decorated walls and ceilings. The Deputy Superintendent's office with its glass paintings and mirrored ceilings is perhaps the only one of its kind in Rajasthan. Valiant efforts are being made by conservationists to preserve the frescos. Within the palace walls is Bhawani Natya Shala, the old theater, built along the lines of the opera houses that Maharaja Bhawani Singh (reigned 1899–1929) had seen in Europe, fitted with a remarkable acoustic system. Nearby is the Government Museum with some very good old sculptures from the 8th-century ruined township of Chandravati nearby. The oldest exhibit here is a stone inscription, dating back to the 5th century.

Opera theater in palace, Jhalawar.

JHALRAPATAN

Adjoining Jhalawar is the ancient walled town of Jhalrapatan (or, picturesquely, "The Town of the Temple Bells"). It was once a temple town with no less than 108 temples. The finest of them is the 11th-century Surya Temple, with its ornately carved 10-foot high curved dome, surrounded by miniature tower-like motifs of different sizes. The temple is reminiscent of the famous Surya Temple at Konarak. It used to house a spectacular gold image of the sun god, said to have been the finest in India, but this was carried away by dacoits who plundered the temple in 1857. There are some fine carvings on the *torana* archway and the columns, which are worth taking a close look at. What is also interesting is the quaint, lithographed European-style tiles of Lord Vishnu and Lord Krishna on either side of the sanctum. Nearby are three other ancient Hindu temples and a fascinating 11th-century Jain temple. At the Jain temple, take a look at the curious painted frieze of murals on a wall in one of the corners, graphically specifying the punishments in the hereafter for various lapses in behavior. The bazaars of Jhalrapatan are especially interesting to wander through, with their colorful hodge-podge of little shops, temples and old houses.

Surya Temple, Jhalrapatan (left), and detail of sculpture from the temple (above).

PRITHVI VILAS
Originally built as a garden-house in the mid-19th century, the Prithvi Vilas was expanded at the turn of the century to accommodate the personal library of Maharaja Bhawani Singh. Its collection of European books is today considered one of the finest in Rajasthan and contains many hand-painted manuscripts and first editions.

Chandravati Temples: doorway (right) and a view of the temple grounds (below).

PROTECTED BY WATER AND JUNGLE
According to the ancient Sanskrit texts, there were basically six types of forts: *dhanva durg* (protected by desert), *giri durg* (protected by mountains), *mahi durg* (protected by mud walls), *nara durg* (protected by men), *jala durg* (protected by water) and *vana durg* (protected by jungle). Obviously, in the largely desert area of Rajasthan, the last two types of forts are the most uncommon. However, Gagron Fort is an example of both a *jala durg* and a *vana durg*, having been protected both by the river that forms its natural moat and the thick forest that once grew here.

CHANDRAVATI TEMPLES

Just outside Jhalawar are the ruins of the ancient temple town of Chandravati ("The Province of the Moon"), one of India's most ancient towns. Here you can see, by the banks of a stream, a group of temples dating back to the 6th century. Chandramauleshwar Temple, in particular, is an outstanding example of ancient temple art, with its ornately carved pillars and gateways. It was described by Cunningham, the well-known 19th-century archeologist, as one of the finest of its kind in India. Chandravati was once one of India's most important centers of dance and music. The temples here, with their traditional temple dancers, contributed greatly to the evolution of classical Indian dance forms.

Gagron Fort.

Life-sized Ganesha in old temple at Kakuni.

Gagron Fort

The splendid Gagron Fort, a rare example of a *jala durg* (a fort protected by water) in Rajasthan, lies 6 miles from Jhalawar. Spectacularly located at the confluence of two rivers and set against a backdrop of hills, this fort has had a long and turbulent 1200-year history, having gone through fourteen major battles and three acts of *jauhar*, when the womenfolk immolated themselves in the sacred fire rather than fall into the hands of the enemy. Sultan Alauddin Khilji of Delhi is said to have besieged it – unsuccessfully – for eleven years. Captured ultimately by the Mughal emperor Akbar in 1561, it was ceded to the Maharaja of Kota in 1715 by the Mughals. The interiors of the fort are now in ruins, overgrown with weeds, but you can still see the remains of the township that was located inside here, with its barracks, stables, gunpowder magazine, and beautiful palace complex. Wandering through the palace, you can see the remains of its beautiful sculptures, ornately carved walls, canopied balconies and even the hooks in the ceilings used to hang fans.

Parrot's tongue
Gagron is famed for its "Ram Tota" parrots. Much sought after, as they are reputed to be the finest talking parrots in India.

Temple ruins.

Kakuni

The ancient ruins of Kakuni, a majestic group of temples dating back to the 8th century, are scattered in the wilderness 40 miles east of Jhalawar. Here, you can see an enormous, life-sized idol of Lord Ganesha, the elephant-headed god of fortune, and the impressive 8th-century *Shivalinga*, the phallic symbol of Lord Shiva. Evidence shows that this was once an important town, a major center of trade and religion. Nearby, across the river, lie the ruins of Bhimgarh Fort, also worth visiting.

Mango orchards
According to a local legend, during Sultan Alauddin Khilji's eleven-year siege of Gagron Fort, his soldiers ate a ration of mangos. It is said that the mango seeds they threw away gave birth to the noted mango orchards of this area.

Shergarh Fort

This splendid medieval fort, 33 miles east of Jhalawar, is another fine example of a *jala durg* or water fort. Built on the banks of the river Parwan, it was renamed after Sher Shah, the 16th-century Afghan ruler of Delhi. However, evidence shows that its history goes back much earlier, to the 10th century, when there was a major center of Shiva worship here. Subsequently Jain religious influences played an important role. Take a look at the fort walls, which have interesting statues and icons from different periods of history embedded in them. Later Shergarh became an important frontier fort of the Kota kingdom, the first line of defence against its belligerent neighbors in Malwa.

An old painting of Bundi town, dominated by the imposing Taragarh Fort.

History

The rulers of the kingdom of Bundi were Hara Chauhans, one of the four clans of warriors said to belong to the legendary *Agnikula*, or "Fire Lineage", having been born from the sacred fire of a ceremony conducted by the Brahmins on top of Mount Abu ▲ *269*. Together with the Paramara, the Pratihara and the Solanki, they were considered superior to all of the other Rajput clans. Originally, the Hara Chauhans ruled Ajmer, but after being defeated by Muhammad Ghori, in 1192, they drifted down to Mewar. One of the great Hara chieftains in the 14th century was Rao Dewa, of whom it is said that he possessed a magnificent horse, so swift that it could cross a stream "without wetting its hooves". The Sultan of Delhi coveted the horse and tried to imprison Rao Dewa, but the latter escaped, shouting out "There are three things you must never ask of a Rajput: his horse, his mistress and his sword." It was this spirit of pride perhaps that led Rao Dewa out of Mewar into the rocky hills of the Chambal Valley, where in 1342, he founded the kingdom of Haravati ("The Province of the Haras"), with its capital at Bundi. Here the Haras ruled, largely protected from the influences of the outside world by the hill country around them.

Bundi and the Mughals. When the Mughal emperor Akbar began his policy of winning over the allegiance of the Rajputs in the mid-16th century, he guaranteed Rao Suran of Bundi religious freedom and regal privileges for his descendants. Subsequently, the rulers of Bundi became one of the Mughals' closest allies in Hindustan. In fact, it is said that in two battles on behalf of the Mughal emperors in the 17th century, the Bundi armies lost twelve royal princes and the head of every single Hara clan. One of the great rulers of Bundi in the 17th century was Rao Chhatar Sal, who served the Mughals with such distinction that Emperor Shah Jahan

The town of Bundi.

Coat-of-arms
Bundi's royal coat-of-arms depicts a Hara Chauhan warrior emerging from the flames of the sacred *agni-kunda* fire pit. On either side of the shield are bulls, representing *dharma*, or piety. It is topped by a diagonal *katar* or dagger, which, according to Rudyard Kipling, was "in commemoration of the defeat of an Imperial Prince who rebelled against the Delhi Throne in the days of Jehangir".

Fatal encounter
An ancient prophecy made by a dying *sati* foretold that if a maharao of Bundi and a maharana of Mewar should ever meet at the annual Aheria (Bundi's ritual spring hunt), one of the two would surely die. Over the next three centuries, it is said, such a meeting took place four times, and on each of the four occasions, one of the two princes ended up being slain by the other.

A step-well inside Taragarh Fort.

made him the Governor of the imperial city of Delhi, a rare privilege for a Rajput. He was a loyal ally, and when the usurper prince, Aurangzeb, tried to woo him over in his battle for the throne, Rao Chhatar Sal refused, even in the face of the greatest of temptations. He was killed fighting Aurangzeb at the head of a *gole*, a terrifying battle formation invented by the Bundi armies, whereby they formed a tight circle, bristling with spears and swords, and rushed at the enemy "like an angry porcupine". It was a highly effective tactic in its time, but became a suicidal exercise with the introduction of artillery. And yet the Bundi armies defiantly persisted with it. Apart from fighting on behalf of their Mughal allies, the rulers of Bundi were continually at war with their powerful and somewhat overbearing Rajput neighbors: the maharanas of Mewar could never forget that Bundi had originally been carved out of Mewar's territories and therefore constantly attempted to subjugate it. Later the maharajas of the increasingly powerful kingdom of Amber tried repeatedly to annex Bundi's territories, leading Rao Umed Singh to lament that the kingdom he inherited was nothing more than "a heap of cotton".

Bundi and the British. In 1818 Bundi succumbed to the British and signed a treaty with them, like all the other Rajput kingdoms. However, despite this fact, the maharaos of Bundi steadfastly refused to admit any British influence in their state.

City of wells
Bundi has been known as a "city of wells", with over fifty beautifully designed old step-wells and tanks. One of the finest examples is Sabirna-dha-ka-Kund, a deep 17th-century step-well, whose marvelous geometry gave the maximum number of people access to the water, regardless of erratic annual fluctuations in the water level.

Portrait of Maharao Raja Sir Raghubir Singh Bahadur of Bundi, a colorful man who paid special attention to traditional regalia and ceremony.

Bundi today

Remote as it is in its hilly terrain, Bundi continues to be a place where life is largely untouched by the outside world. In fact, even today, Bundi is one place in Rajasthan that has a delightfully medieval flavor – visiting it is like stepping into some kind of time warp. The town nestles at the foot of a large rocky hill, dominated by Taragarh Fort and Garh Palace. It is a town of numerous ornate step-wells dating back to the 17th century. The tiny, winding lanes of its bazaars are among the most fascinating you will find anywhere in Rajasthan.

Cityscape as seen from the Fort.

Thunderous! The Bhim Burj bastion was built to house Bundi's famous 16th-century cannon, Garbh Gunjam, one of the largest, most feared artillery pieces of medieval Rajputana. Its sound was so terrifying that, legend says, it used to cause pregnant women to lose their unborn children.

Garh Palace

Garh Palace is not a single palace but actually a whole complex of different palaces, built by different rulers at different times. Hugging the steep hillside, the complex looks, if viewed from above, like a checkerboard. The most impressive of all the palaces, however, is Chhattar Mahal, built by Rao Chhattar Sal in 1660. Rao Chhattar Sal was a veteran of fifty-two battles and a man of unbending pride. It is perhaps characteristic of the man, therefore, that despite his closeness to the Mughal emperors, he allowed no Mughal influence to dilute the proud Rajput style of his palace. The material he used was not the sandstone that was favored by the Mughals (and by other Rajput princes), but the green serpentine from Bundi's own quarries. Nor did Rao Chhattar Sal use the arches and columns typical of the Mughal style of architecture; instead he retained the traditional Rajput style, with its characteristic lotus-flower spandrels, recurrent elephant motifs, richly ornamented brackets and a profusion of drooping, arcuated roofs, kiosks, and pavilions. A steep ramp takes you up through two towering gates, Hazari Pol ("The Gate of the One Thousand") and Hathi Pol ("Elephant Gate"). Hathi Pol is topped with two enormous elephants with raised trunks, once apparently cast from brass, but later replaced by plaster elephants painted in bright yellows, reds, and blues. Through Hathi Pol you come to a small, rough courtyard faced by an arched arcade and stables. (It is very clear that this palace was a warrior's retreat, and not some luxurious Mughal-style court.) Here you will find the Diwan-i-Am ("Hall of Public Audience"), with a white marble throne set

Garh Palace.

"The Palace of Boondi, even in broad daylight, is such a Palace that men build for themselves in uneasy dreams – the work of goblins rather than of men."

Rudyard Kipling, *Letters of Marque*, 1899

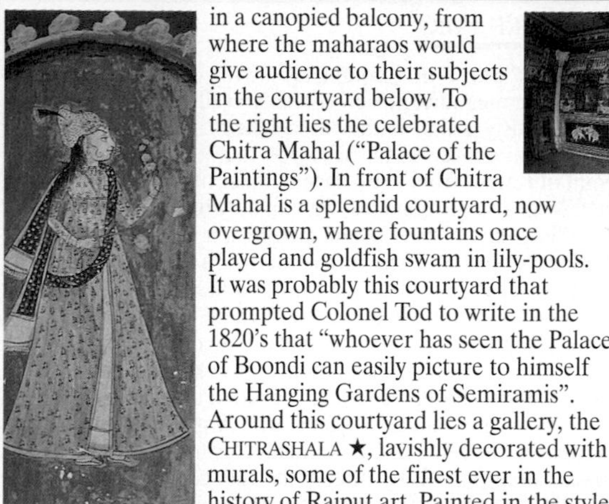

in a canopied balcony, from where the maharaos would give audience to their subjects in the courtyard below. To the right lies the celebrated Chitra Mahal ("Palace of the Paintings"). In front of Chitra Mahal is a splendid courtyard, now overgrown, where fountains once played and goldfish swam in lily-pools. It was probably this courtyard that prompted Colonel Tod to write in the 1820's that "whoever has seen the Palace of Boondi can easily picture to himself the Hanging Gardens of Semiramis". Around this courtyard lies a gallery, the CHITRASHALA ★, lavishly decorated with murals, some of the finest ever in the history of Rajput art. Painted in the style of the Bundi school of miniatures, these murals are executed in the characteristic shades of blue, green, and maroon (above). They cover a wide range of subjects: on the maroon dados are depicted a series of elephant fights; higher up are scenes from the legends of Lord Krishna, battle scenes, lovers' trysts, and scenes of Garh Palace as it was during the 19th century, including an interesting panel on Chitra Mahal itself. (Be sure you look inside the inner chamber of the gallery, with its murals in glowing colors, untouched by the effects of sunlight and rain over the centuries.) Garh Palace had had a dark and tangled history, and there are numerous chilling legends associated with it, like that of Hada Rani, who beheaded herself and had her head sent to her husband on the eve of battle, so that he would not be distracted by thoughts of her while fighting the enemy.

A BEEHIVE OF ACTIVITY

When Rudyard Kipling visited Bundi's Garh Palace, he saw some of the later frescos being painted. He noted that there was a great deal of activity and noise there, like "a broken beescomb, with the whole hive busily at work". The results are

fine examples of wall paintings in the distinctive Bundi style, with subjects ranging from palace life to scenes of Lord Krishna and the *gopis*.

"The *coup d'œil* of the castellated Palace of Boondi, from whichever side you approach it, is perhaps the most striking in India."
Colonel Tod, *Annals and Antiquities of Rajasthan*, 1829

Walls of fort.

MISSING TREASURE
According to an old legend, there is a secret treasure hidden inside Taragarh Fort that each ruler was allowed to visit just once in his lifetime. The treasure was guarded over the centuries by a family of loyal Pathan retainers. Unfortunately, the last of the old Pathans died during World War Two, taking the secret of the treasure with him. When the young Maharao Bahadur Singh returned from Burma, where he was serving during the War, he launched a major treasure hunt within the fort, but nothing was found. The treasure must still be there somewhere.

TARAGARH FORT

Taragarh ("Star Fort") dominates the top of a steep, craggy hill, with a magnificent view of the Aravalli hills on one side and the dusty plains on the other. Like many other Rajput forts, it was conceived in such a way that it provided a final point of retreat from the palace in times of siege. The two, in fact, form a single complex, with an outwork of the fort wall encircling the palace wall and providing it with a formidable double fortification. The fort's outer walls are, in many places, over 10 feet thick and run for miles along the hillsides. Yet, as Rao Umaid Singh once said, these walls "are not required against an equal foe, and are no defence against a superior foe…Bundi's best defence is always its hills." You enter the fort through a strongly fortified main gate to find that it is roughly square in shape, with large bastions at each corner (below). The fort is dominated by a huge masonry tower called Bhim Burj, built in the 16th century to house Bundi's legendary cannon, the Garbh Gunjam (which roughly translates as "The Thunder that Echoes in the Womb") ▲ *292*. It was one of the most powerful – and dreaded – artillery pieces in all of Rajputana. Its sound was so loud that a deep pit was provided alongside the emplacement, into which its gun crew had to jump after lighting its fuse, in order to protect their eardrums! Today there is not much else left standing within the fort, apart from the old water tank that provided the garrison's water supply and Rani Mahal, with its fading murals and stained-glass windows. But most interesting of all are the tales of the secret underground passages that are said to have once honeycombed the entire hillside, leading to the palace, the town below and the neighboring hills, to provide a variety of escape routes for the fort's defenders. These secrets, alas, are now lost forever.

The steep ramps of Taragarh Fort down which the water gushes during the annual flooding ▲ *297*.

It has been estimated that there are approximately one thousand different styles and types of turban in Rajasthan.

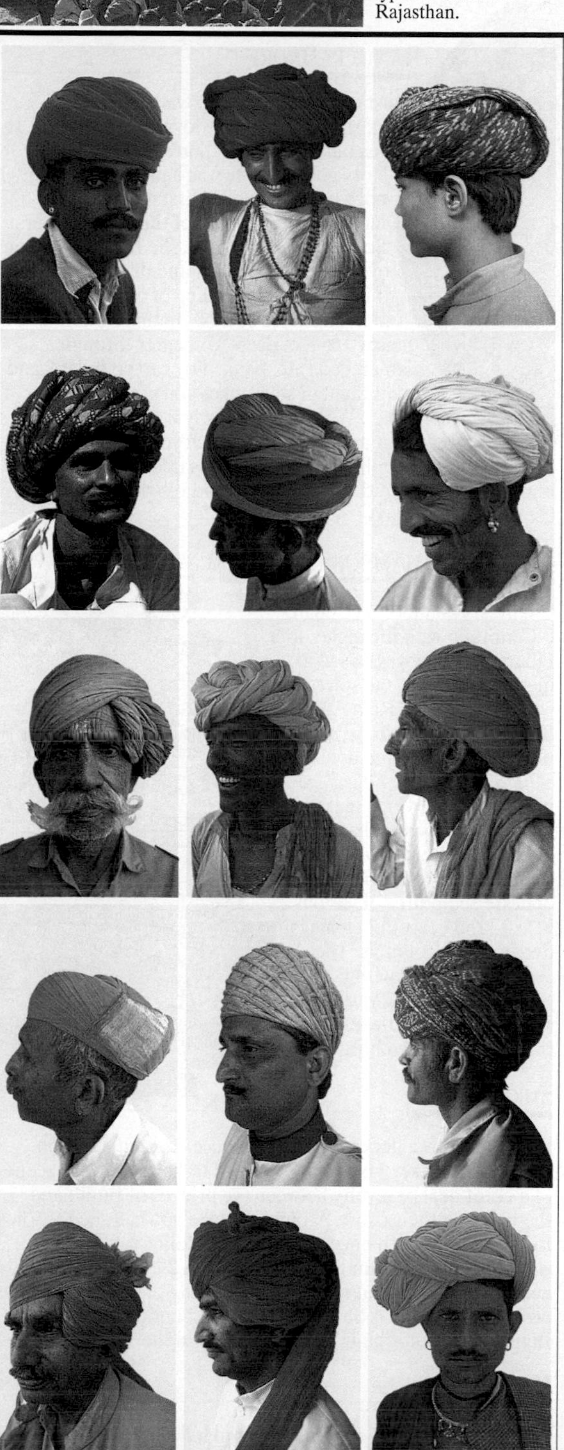

WHAT THE TURBAN REVEALS

A *safa* (turban) is much more than a just an item of headgear to protect the wearer from the sun's heat. By its shape, color, and size it tells you a great deal about the man, such as where he comes from, what he does for a living, and his position in society. A *safa* is about 30 feet long and about 4 feet wide. It was traditionally considered an essential part of a man's clothing, and to appear in public without one was a sign of grossly bad behavior. The color, pattern, and style of tying a turban vary according to community, region, and even district. Thus it is said that the dialect of men's turbans changes every 12 miles in Rajasthan. *Safa*-tying is considered a fine art. Men who have mastered it take great pride in the fact. Some colors and patterns are seasonal, such as the white *falguniya* turban with a red border that is worn in spring. Others signify family circumstances; for instance, the dotted *chunri* pattern or bright colors signify a marriage or the birth of a child. On the other hand, colors like dark blue, maroon, or khaki signify a death in the family. Wearing the wrong type of turban under the wrong circumstances can make you an object of ridicule.

RANIJI KI BAORI

Just outside the old city walls is Raniji ki Baori, one of Bundi's loveliest step-wells. It was built by Rani Nathavati in 1699. The story goes that she was a junior rani who bore her husband his first male heir, incurring the jealousy of the senior rani. So, very diplomatically, she handed her son over to the senior rani and devoted the rest of her life to the building of wells and to other charitable causes. Raniji ki Baori is nearly 165 feet deep. You enter through a high arched gate, flanked by carved pillars, and a broad flight of steps takes you down to the water level. What is particularly noteworthy is the ornate *torana* archway under which you pass, with its frieze of carved elephants. A well such as this was an important center of the town's social and religious life in the olden days.

Raniji ki Baori.

CHAURASI KHAMBON KI CHHATRI

Chaurasi Khambon ki Chhatri ("Cenotaph with the eighty-four Pillars") (right) was raised in memory of Deva, the son of the wet nurse of Rao Raja Anirudh Singh, in 1683. Built on a high platform, this unique double *chhatri* has a large *Shivalinga* in the center – which makes it both a temple as well as a cenotaph. The sides of the plinth are covered with delicate sculptures of various beasts, and beautiful etchings decorate the columns. The ceiling is covered with paintings depicting various subjects, from battle scenes to traditional fish symbols.

BUNDI MINIATURES
Bundi miniature paintings are considered to be among the finest in Rajasthan ● *65*. Reaching their zenith in the 18th century, they are known for their brilliant colors, their elegant sense of design and their masterful technique. Favorite subjects were court and hunting scenes and episodes from the Radha and Krishna mythology. But what is most fascinating is the depictions of sensuous Bundi maidens, bathing, pining for absent lovers, flirting, or sometimes indulging in more wine than is good for them.

SUKH MAHAL

Sukh Mahal is a delicate pleasure palace, built in 1773, on Sukh Sagar Lake, which was supposed to have been the scene of a great deal of revelry between the princes of Bundi and the ladies of their court. Around the lake you can see the low forested hills which once teemed with wildlife, and which were the scene of Bundi's great Aheria ▲ *290*, the celebrated annual boar hunt that heralded the coming of spring. Further down the lakeside is Shikar Burj, an old hunting lodge of Bundi's maharaos built by Umaid Singh in the 18th century.

KESAR BAGH

On the other side of the lake from Sukh Mahal lie the old cenotaphs – sixty-six of them – commemorating Bundi's

Kesar Bagh (left); Sukh Niwas (right).

kings, queens and princes. The garden is now overgrown with weeds, but the cenotaphs are beautiful, many of them with elegantly carved marble ceilings, decorative friezes and elephants, and topped with a characteristic *Shivalinga*. They span, between them, a period of two-and-a-half centuries, from 1581 to 1821.

Bazaars

In the tiny, twisting lanes of Sadar Bazaar and Chaumukh Bazaar (left) at the base of Taragarh Hill, you will discover one of the quaintest bazaars in Rajasthan today, virtually untouched by the outside influences that creep into the larger towns. Some of the shops – as you can tell from looking at their architecture and crumbling masonry – date back to the 17th century. You can browse in them for items such as silver jewelry or brightly colored turbans.

Bijoliyan Temples

On the road to Chittorgarh are the ruins of three temples rising out of a field, just outside the fortified walls of Bijoliyan. This, sadly, is all that remains of a complex of over one hundred temples built here from the 11th century onward. The finest of these is the 13th-century Undeshwar Temple, with its curving pagoda covered with bands of beautifully carved stone motifs. It represents a tradition of ancient Hindu architecture, according to which surface decoration was just as important as structural form. The unusual feature of this temple is that the inner sanctum is submerged in water, out of which you can see a *Shivalinga* emerge. Nearby is the Mandakini Kund temple tank and two other temples, including a lovely, old Ganesha temple, which has the unusual feature of four elevated *chhatris* surrounding its main pagoda. There is also a fine image of Ganesha guarding the entrance. In the surrounding fields you can see the ruins of other old temples. This was the site of a great cultural center of the Chauhan kingdom, and inscriptions found in the temples, dating back to 1170, give us the first ever historical mention of the city of Delhi.

Palace sojourn
Sukh Niwas ("Palace of Bliss") was the summer palace where Rudyard Kipling stayed when he visited Bundi in the late 19th century. While he was there, he wrote about some of the later frescos he saw being painted on the walls of Chitrashala in Bundi's Garh Palace.

Annual flood
Bundi is an old-fashioned little town that follows its own quaint, centuries-old traditions. One of these is the annual ritual of flooding the streets. At a given signal, the entire town takes cover, and the tank in Taragarh Fort is emptied. The tank's waters then rush down the hill, flooding the town's little lanes and paralyzing it, until the water finally drains away, hours, or even days, later.

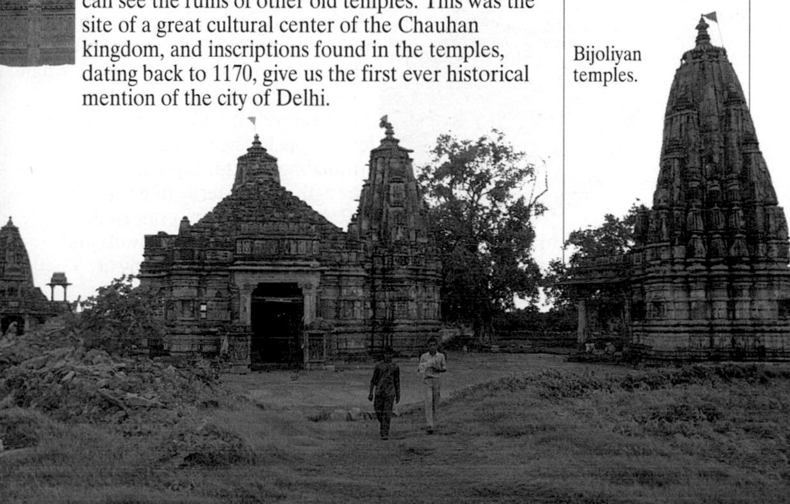

Bijoliyan temples.

Temples of Menal.

GOLD ARROWHEAD
Mandalgarh is an ancient Solanki fort lying 20 miles south of Menal. Rebuilt by Rana Kumbha of Mewar, it became one of the most important of his chain of thirty-two forts, because of its strategic location at the gates of Mewar. Captured by Emperor Akbar during his campaign against Chittorgarh, it was later recaptured by the maharanas of Mewar in 1706. The fort has an interesting legend behind it. According to Colonel Tod, a local Bhil named Mandu, while sharpening his arrow on a stone, suddenly found that his arrowhead had turned to gold. He immediately took the *paras patthar* (philosopher's stone) to his chieftain, who used the resultant wealth to build this fine fort, which he named Mandalgarh after the fortunate Bhil.

MENAL

In the middle of beautifully wooded ravines, 10 miles from Bijoliyan, is a gorge of the Menal River, and the ruins of what used to be a 12th-century mountain retreat of the great raja, Prithviraj Chauhan ● *35, 55*. On the banks of the river are the ruins of an ancient palace, and nearby, a complex of beautiful temples. You enter the complex through a handsome double-story gateway carved with images of Bhairava and Ganesha. In the courtyard is an imposing Shiva temple, a wonderful example of the western Indian temple style, but also incorporating central Indian elements, such as the meshed bands in the middle of its pagoda and tiers of miniature tower-like motifs on either side. On the walls are graceful carvings of Shiva and Parvati in various aspects, as well as of dancers, attendants, musicians and animals, including, halfway up the tower, a curious mythical lion. Opposite the Shiva temple lie the ruins of several other smaller temples, one of which has a beautifully carved double *torana* archway.

HINDOLI FORT

The long-forgotten 15th-century hill fort of Hindoli (left) lies 9 miles northwest of Bundi. Described by Professor Herman Goetz as "a gem of early Rajput architecture", it is visited by only very few people today. Set among low hills surrounding a picturesque lake, it has all the strength and austerity of design of classical Rajput architecture prior to the ornamental influences of the Muslims. Yet, its walls and apartments are notable for their perfect harmony of proportion. With its strategic location on the frontier guarding Bundi from powerful Mewar, Hindoli had a dramatic history, changing hands several times over the centuries. For a while it was occupied by Maharana Pratap of Mewar (who added to its fortifications) but finally, in 1659, it was won back by Rao Bhao Singh of Bundi. As Professor Goetz wrote, "in the dust of these ruins there still lives the breath of the Golden Age of early Rajput civilization".

Bharatpur to Karauli

300 Bharatpur
304 Ranthambhor
308 Birds of Bharatpur
310 Around Bharatpur

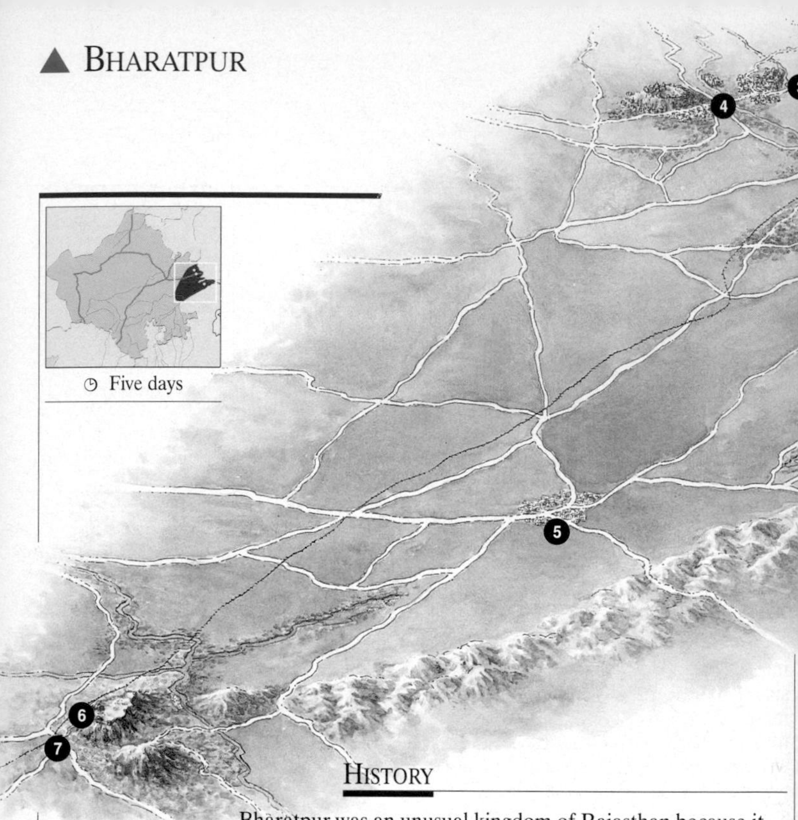

◷ Five days

HISTORY

Bharatpur was an unusual kingdom of Rajasthan because it was the only one that was ruled by a dynasty of Jats – peasant sons of the soil – rather than Rajputs ● *35*. Under its aggressive rulers, the kingdom of Bharatpur became a major military and political force in the 18th and 19th centuries, its armies sweeping the plains of northern India, virtually lords and masters of all they surveyed. However, the history of Bharatpur goes back far, far earlier, to the great ancient kingdom of Matsyadesh that flourished here around the 5th century BC. There are several fine archeological remains of this civilization which you can see in the Bharatpur Museum.

17TH AND 18TH CENTURIES. The region came to the fore in the late 17th century when a powerful Jat village headman named Churaman rose up against the Mughals. His armies ranged the countryside, raiding and pillaging, until finally in 1721, the Mughals came down with a heavy hand, killed Churaman and smashed the Jat strongholds. The Jats, however, were not to be put down. Under Badan Singh, they rose up again, and by 1750 their marauding armies controlled a wide expanse of territory, almost from Delhi to Agra, until their ruler was finally, fearfully, recognized by the Mughal emperor and given the hereditary title of Raja. Raja Badan Singh's son, Raja Surajmal, consolidated all this power and used the enormous wealth that his armies had acquired for him to good effect: he built numerous forts and palaces across his kingdom, including the exquisite pleasure palace complex in Deeg ▲ *310* and the great fort of Bharatpur, said to have been one of the mightiest ever built in Indian history ▲ *302*. By the 1760s, with the Mughal Empire in tatters, Raja Surajmal began to get even more ambitious, regularly raiding the imperial cities of Delhi and Agra and carrying away a vast amount of booty. He actually dismantled entire Mughal palaces and brought them back with him to Bharatpur, and, on one particularly brazen occasion, even plundered the very

COAT-OF-ARMS
The Bharatpur coat-of-arms depicts a shield flanked by a lion and an elephant, the symbol of royalty. The shield itself bears a bull, symbolizing piety, and a pair of crossed *katars* or daggers. All this is topped by the representation of a fort flying the banner of Hanuman, the great monkey god of the epic *Ramayana*. The motto beneath says "Shri Gokulendurjati". Jats being of peasant stock, the maharajas of Bharatpur were never completely accepted by the other Rajput princes of Rajasthan despite all their efforts to assert their royal status.

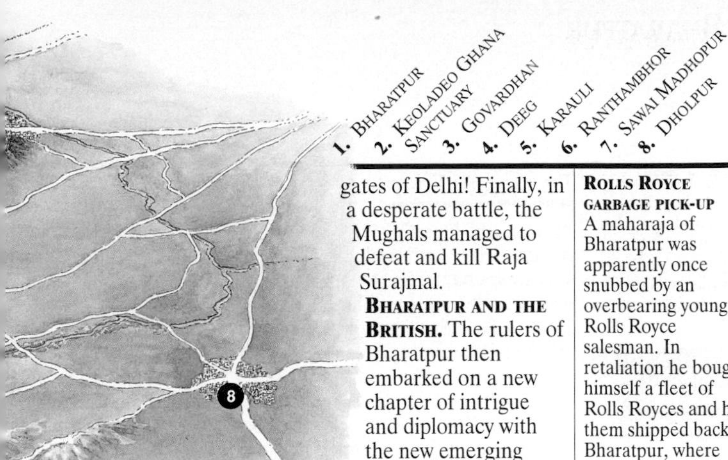

gates of Delhi! Finally, in a desperate battle, the Mughals managed to defeat and kill Raja Surajmal.

Bharatpur and the British. The rulers of Bharatpur then embarked on a new chapter of intrigue and diplomacy with the new emerging powers in India, the Marathas and the East India Company. This culminated in British attacks on Bharatpur Fort in the early 19th century. The attackers, to their great surprise, were repulsed and defeated. Finally, in 1818, Bharatpur entered into a treaty with the British, one of the very first states in Rajasthan to do so. Bharatpur's most important role in the pages of Indian history, however, was an episode that was written – by default – in the 1820's. For it was here that the British, involved in a succession struggle to the Bharatpur throne, first developed the Doctrine of Paramountcy over the princes, which ultimately led to their becoming the supreme political power in India ● *35*.

Bird-lands. In the years that followed, the maharajas of Bharatpur became known mainly for one thing: the bird-lands they carefully developed in the marshes just outside Bharatpur and the spectacular duck shoots – perhaps among the most famous in the world – that they hosted for visiting British dignitaries (and fellow maharajas) ▲ *306, 308*. These splendid bird-lands have now been converted into a remarkable little national park, considered to be one of the wonders of the natural world. Bharatpur as a town is not overly attractive, but it is a useful jumping-off point for a region that is rich and quite undiscovered, a region dotted with the old forts and palaces of the Jat kings. Deeg, with its pleasure palaces, is, of course, almost as much of a "must-see" as Agra's Taj Mahal, but there are also other interesting places such as Dholpur, Karauli, Govardhan and Bayana, for which Bharatpur is a convenient springboard.

Rolls Royce garbage pick-up

A maharaja of Bharatpur was apparently once snubbed by an overbearing young Rolls Royce salesman. In retaliation he bought himself a fleet of Rolls Royces and had them shipped back to Bharatpur, where they were put to use as municipal garbage collection vehicles!

Residence of the British Political Agent in Bharatpur, circa 1900.

General view of Bharatpur.

Ashtadhati Gateway, Lohagarh Fort.

Lohagarh Fort was protected by deep moats, and according to legend, would fall "only when a crocodile swallowed up all the water of the moat".

THE UNDOING OF A GENERAL
Bharatpur's Lohagarh Fort proved to be the undoing of Lord Lake (above), until then, one of the most successful British generals. His armies decimated in the bloody siege of Bharatpur, Lord Lake disappeared into obscurity, paving the way for an up-and-coming young officer named Arthur Wellesley, later to become famous as Duke of Wellington. Wellesley ultimately managed to capture Bharatpur, but not before it had given him some anxious moments.

LOHAGARH FORT

"Lohagarh" literally means "Iron Fort", and it was an apt name, for it was virtually impregnable. Built by Raja Surajmal in the mid-18th century, its defense systems are said to have been inspired by a description given in the epic, *Ramayana*. It had two formidable concentric ramparts, made of beaten earth and rubble, each surrounded by a moat 149 feet wide and 60 feet deep. The outer wall, about 7 miles long, took eight years to construct. What's more, being a *mahi durg*, or "mud fort", as described in the ancient Sanskrit scriptures, Lohagarh's thick walls were able to absorb even the most furious of artillery barrages. The cannon balls would simply sink into the mud walls, to be collected later and used against the enemy. As a result, the fort had stood up to several attacks by the Mughal armies, and no less than four attacks by the British, before it finally fell. The fort's outer ramparts were demolished by the British after the Treaty of 1818, but the inner battlements remain, punctuated by two massive towers commemorating two great victories of the Bharatpur armies: the first tower, Jawahar Burj, marking Raja Surajmal's storming of Delhi in 1764, and the second, Fateh Burj, commemorating the rout of Lord Lake's British armies, when the attackers were repulsed, leaving three thousand men dead in the battlefield. At Jawahar Burj, do not miss the iron "Victory Column", bearing the inscriptions of the genealogy of the Jat kings. There are two imposing gates to the fort: in the north is the historic Ashtadhati Gate, with its huge, rounded bastions and war elephants painted on either side, and in the south, Loha Gate. Both of these were torn down from the walls of the imperial capital of Delhi and brought back by the victorious Jat armies in an act of supreme military arrogance.

PALACES AND MUSEUM. Within Lohagarh Fort is a complex of three palaces: Khas Mahal, Kamra Palace and Raja Badan Singh's Palace, built by successive generations of Bharatpur's rulers – and set around a small, but elegant, old Mughal garden (above). Khas Mahal, built by Raja Balwant Singh (reigned 1826–53), houses the royal apartments, which reflect the simple lifestyle of the Jat rulers. Its chambers are small, with ornate pierced stone windows and patterned marble tiled floors. In the corners are octagonal chambers with domed ceilings and delicately painted walls. On the lower floor is an interesting *hammam*, or sunken bath house. Raja Badan Singh's Palace, adjacent to Khas Mahal, has an imposing sandstone *durbar* hall, with finely carved walls, pillars and archways, and a beautiful alcove set into the far wall, from where the Raja himself would hold court. Today this palace houses part of Bharatpur's Archeological Museum, with Kamra Palace next door housing the other half. The museum has some carvings dating back to the second century and terracotta toys from the first century, excavated at the village of Noh, just a few miles east of here. Some of the carvings worth taking a closer look at are the 7th-century image of Shiva and Parvati, the 11th-century image of the Jain saint, Parshvanatha, and the 10th-century Ganesha. However, the prized piece here is the unique 2nd-century red sandstone *Shivalinga* (above).

GOLBAGH PALACE

Built in the early 1900's, this fascinating palace drew its inspiration freely from a variety of sources, ranging from the pleasure palaces of Deeg to the Art Nouveau salons of Europe. Set in Mughal gardens, it is a riot of lotus arches, ornate balconies, canopies, and delicate latticework screens. Take a close look at some of the latticed windows and you will see the curious influence of the Art Nouveau style that was so fashionable at the time. Once the home of Maharaja Kishan Singh, the palace has now been converted into a hotel, after the royal family moved in to Moti Mahal Palace next door.

HAVE GATE WILL TRAVEL
Ashtadhati ("Eight-Metal") Gate of Lohagarh Fort has a history behind it. It is said to have originally been the gate of Chittorgarh Fort, but was carried away by Sultan Alauddin Khilji of Delhi. In 1764 it was torn down from the walls of the Mughal capital of Delhi and brought back in triumph to Bharatpur.

Raja Badan Singh's palace.

FAMILY HISTORY ON COLUMN
The Vijay Stambha, ("Victory Column"), erected inside the Fort by the maharajas of Bharatpur, has engravings tracing their family history back, generation by generation, to the Hindu god, Lord Krishna himself.

CATCHING PREY
The tiger has developed a high degree of cunning to overcome the highly evolved self-preservation systems of all its prey species. When attacking its prey it creeps up as if in slow-motion, often taking up to fifteen minutes to cover about 165 feet. Then, pausing cautiously for a long while – perhaps two to three minutes – it leaps upon the unsuspecting beast with lightning speed. However, it gives man, the craftiest of predators, a very wide berth indeed.

PROJECT TIGER
In the late 1960's it was realized that the tiger was on its way to extinction – with only two thousand of these magnificent beasts still surviving. As a result, Project Tiger ▲ *176* was launched in 1972 – an ambitious project based on the premise that the species could be saved only by the total conservation of its habitat, based on an ecosystem approach. It is considered to be one of Asia's most important conservation efforts.

Gray partridge, Ranthambhor National Park.

RANTHAMBHOR FORT

Of all the forts in Rajasthan, one of the most dramatic is the mysterious jungle-fort of Ranthambhor (below). Set high on a rock cliff, its ruined battlements loom over the dense surrounding foliage. It is one of the finest examples of the ancient Hindu concept of a *vana-durg*, or a fort protected by a jungle. Built in AD 944, this fort has had a bloody and complex history. In 1192 it was taken over by the Chauhans, who had been forced out of their own strongholds in Ajmer and Delhi. In the late 13th century it went through a glorious epoch, during the reign of Raja Hamir Dev, but was sacked by Sultan Alauddin Khilji in 1303. Regained by the Rajputs, it was once again lost in 1569, this time to the Mughal emperor Akbar, who, after a 37-day artillery barrage, finally took it through an audacious bluff. Disguising himself as an ordinary mace-bearer, he entered the fort with one of his Rajput generals, and in a bewilderingly rapid sequence of events, was placed upon its throne. You enter the fort through a narrow, fortified defile in the jungle, via a steep, serpentine ramp. Here you can see the four massive gateways that any attacking army would have to break through, defended by elephant spikes, massive chains and tricky zig-zag configurations. By the way, do not miss the enigmatic ancient Ranthambhor monolith by the side of the third gate. The fourth gate is at the head of a steep flight of stairs: a thick bastion, reinforced by a turret. From here a long vaulted tunnel takes you into the fort itself. The interiors of the fort now lie in splendid ruin. You can see two small, old temples here and the remains of a fine tank. From the battlements there is a great view of the surrounding forests, and a sheer drop of over 200 feet.

Lawns of Sawai Madhopur Lodge, the royal hunting lodge of the Maharaja of Jaipur in the 1930's.

RANTHAMBHOR NATIONAL PARK

This must certainly be one of the most picturesque game reserves in the world, the entire forest being dominated by the silent, ruined battlements of Ranthambhor Fort. Seeing a tiger roaming over these ruins, as one often does here, is a moment of eerie beauty. The park has a core area of 158 square miles, and is one of the parks covered by Project Tiger ▲ *176*, a conservation project. Ranthambhor is noted for its tigers, who are not merely nocturnal, but frequently seen during the day, often stalking their prey in full view of visitors. As a result of such sightings, Ranthambhor has become a favorite place for wildlife buffs and professional wildlife photographers. Its tiger population, which had dropped to just fourteen in 1973, has now grown to about forty. The park also has a large population of panthers. Their habitat does not overlap with that of the tigers: they keep to the outer areas. Other predators here are the caracal, hyena, jackal and jungle cat. Marsh crocodiles can also be seen basking by the banks of the lakes. There are various species of deer, such as the *sambar*, *chital*, *chinkara,* and *nilgai*. Ranthambhor is also known for its rich birdlife, drawn here by the wide variety of flora and the lakes. Some of its many species of birds are the great Indian horned owl, various species of eagle, painted and white-necked stork, spoonbill, partridge and quail. Another interesting feature of the park, incidentally, is a huge banyan tree – supposedly one of the world's largest – near the graceful Jogi Mahal water palace.

PRIVATE GAME RESERVE

Ranthambhor was once the private game reserve of the maharajas of Jaipur, who used to bring their personal guests here for tiger shoots ▲ *176*. Royal hunts have a tradition that goes back to at least the 12th century. Historical records show that Prithviraj Chauhan, the last Hindu raja of Delhi, was an enthusiastic hunter, so much so that his hunting activities in other rajas' territories frequently led to war!

Animals grazing at Ranthambhor National Park (left). *Sambar* (above) can be seen at the park.

▲ Bharatpur
Keoladeo Ghana Sanctuary

Duck-shoot ritual
The maharajas of Bharatpur developed the marshlands of Ghana into a hunting reserve ▲ *301*. Their great duck shoots were a major event on the sporting calendar of old Imperial India, and the British pro-consuls and generals used to vie for invitations. Each duck shoot took months to arrange and allotting the shooting butts was said to be "as tricky an exercise as making the seating arrangements at a formal banquet". The firing would begin at the sound of a bugle call and ended strictly at the sound of a second bugle call hours later.

Just outside Bharatpur lies this small, but amazingly rich, bird sanctuary, considered to be one of the world's outstanding heronries ▲ *308*. Covering an area of just 12 square miles, it is an interlocking ecosystem of woodlands, swamps, wet prairies and dry savannah, home to over 370 varieties of birds, of which more than 115 are migrants flying in from Central Asia, Siberia and western China during the winter months. Perhaps no other bird sanctuary in the world offers so many different species within so small a compass, creating a uniquely rewarding bird-watching experience. The park, originally called Ghana, which means "dense", takes its name from the ancient temple of Keoladeo, or Lord Shiva, that you will find inside it. It was painstakingly created in the 19th century out of the arid surrounding scrubland by diverting the waters of a nearby canal and creating a series of dykes and dams. The new ecosystem that emerged became an ideal habitat for birds of all kinds. It is perhaps surprising that so many birds continue to flock here, given the park's rather bloody history: from 1902 to 1947, this was the site of some of the most extravagant duck shoots the world has known. The most notorious one was in November 1938, when the British Viceroy, Lord Linlithgow (right), and his party massacred 4273 ducks and geese. It was recorded that the Viceroy himself had two loaders to help him reload, and his guns got so hot that they had to be cooled down by sloshing them regularly with water. The Maharaja of Bharatpur used Rolls Royces, which he converted into shooting brakes, to transport his guests within Ghana. Today motor vehicles are forbidden. One has to travel either by boat, bicycle or cycle-rickshaw.

Storks and cranes. The highlight of the park is perhaps its storks and cranes. Most famous of all is the nearly extinct Siberian crane that flies in each winter from Siberia ■ *27*. It stands up to 4½ feet tall and has a wing span of over 6 feet. It has been called the "lily of birds", for as an ornithologist once noted, "It is the most elegant of birds and, stand in what position it may, its head, neck and body presents a series of the most graceful and harmonious curves." Being the wintering ground of this rare species, Keoladeo has been included among the World Heritage sites. About thirty Siberian cranes visit Keoladeo each year, although for unknown reasons not a single bird arrived in the winter of 1994. The birds in Keoladeo are often enormous in size: the

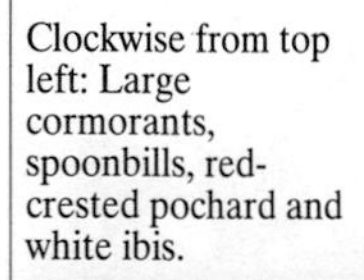

Clockwise from top left: Large cormorants, spoonbills, red-crested pochard and white ibis.

Graylag geese (left) and nesting painted stork (right).

White-breasted kingfisher.

tallest bird in North America, for instance, the great blue heron, approximately 4½ feet tall, would be completely dwarfed by birds here such as the greater adjutant stork and the black-necked stork, which are up to 6 feet tall, about the height of a man. Keoladeo is also Asia's largest breeding ground of the painted stork.

Other species. Other notable species of birds found here are the openbill stork (below), spoonbill, white ibis, heron, egret, cormorant and several species of splendid, brilliantly colored kingfisher. Among the migrant species are the steppe eagle (one of the largest species of eagle), peregrine falcon, marsh harrier, graylag geese, plover, sandpiper and rosy pelican. In addition, there are larger numbers of gadwal, shoveler, wigeon, whistling and common teal. Keoladeo is also famed for its ducks: in winter they sometimes completely cover the sky, and when they suddenly rise from the lake, as a wildlife writer once noted, "they make a noise like thunder." The park also has some interesting species of animals such as the *sambar*, *chital*, blackbuck, wild boar, and various species of wild cat and large rock python, found especially near Python Point.

Till death do us part

The sarus crane is celebrated in Indian mythology for its fidelity: it mates with the same partner for a lifetime ■ *28*. Its mating dance – a magnificent aerial ballet – is an unforgettable sight.

Winter's flight

The Siberian crane, one of the world's rarest birds ■ *27*, migrates here in winter from the frozen tundras of south Siberia – a journey of two months. Incredibly, it flies 3900 miles to this tiny patch of marshlands, just 12 square miles in size.

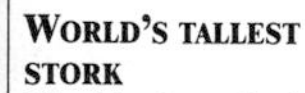

World's tallest stork

The black-necked stork, seen in Keoladeo in large numbers, is the world's tallest stork, standing up to 6 feet tall. Its dramatic black and white wings span up to 8 feet.

"A LIVING SOUP"
Bharatpur's wetland habitat has been graphically described as "a living soup", and it is the birds' specialized and differentiated feeding habits that allow the "soup" to go around.

Keoladeo Ghana in Bharatpur, where thousands of migratory waterfowl arrive every winter, is part of the Indo-gangetic plains of India where waterbirds nest in thousands during the monsoon ▲ *306*. Created in the late 19th century by the maharaja of Bharatpur to bring the pleasures of wildfowl hunting to his doorstep, the reserve came into being by the simple act of diverting water from a nearby irrigation canal. The lowlands holding the monsoon flood water have been an ageless avian paradise, and were where the maharaja of Bharatpur hosted duck shoots for British luminaries (above).

SNAKE BIRD
The snake bird, or darter, hunts for fish with its spring-like neck, which acts as a "javelin" at short distance. As its feathers lack waterproofing, the bird is commonly seen drying itself with wings spread.

LISTING THE BIG SHOTS
At the entrance of the sanctuary, a veritable who's who lists the big shots of the 1930's with details of the shoot.

DATE	ON THE OCCASION OF THE VISIT OF	BAC
1902 1st DEC.	1st SHOOT H.E. VICEROY LORD CURZON H.E. C-IN-C LORD KITCHENER	540
1903 9th FEB	2nd SHOOT H.R.H. THE DUKE OF CANNAUGHT	780
1903 14th DEC	1st SHOOT H.E. VICEROY LORD CURZON	2049
1907 15th NOV	1st SHOOT HON'BLE Mr E. COLVIN A.G.G.	1750
1908 30th NOV	1st SHOOT HON'BLE COL. PINNEY A.G.C.	2141
1908 12th NOV	2nd SHOOT	1086

These waters, rich in microbes, insects, fish, frogs, and reptiles, provide food for the nesting waterbirds. Nests are built with strong and elastic material from acacia trees ■ *30* and the soft lining is from algae and water plants.

Bar-headed Goose
Once India's most common goose – the 19th-century naturalist, A. O. Hume, counted over ten thousand in 1877 along a single 10-mile stretch – this snow-white bird with black markings has dwindled to under one thousand in recent winters.

A winter's tale
Aristotle speculated about where the swallows went in winter. Today, scientific studies on the accuracy, regularity, velocity, and altitude of the birds' migratory flight are carried out.

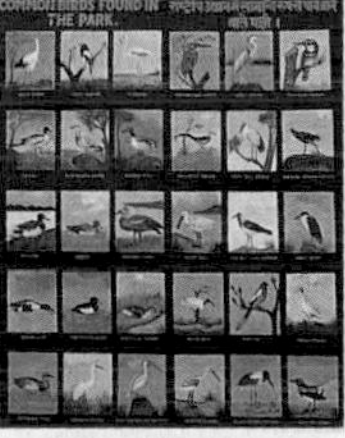

Birds' habitat
Keoladeo Ghana Sanctuary is home to over 370 varieties of birds from over fifty families, of which some 120 species nest here.

Painted Storks
The painted stork is symbolic of Keoladeo Ghana, where it nests in colonies of thousands on tree tops. It visits the sanctuary between July and October during the monsoon to breed.

SIDDHARTHA
The pleasure palace complex at Deeg was the exotic setting for the shooting of Conrad Rook's film, *Siddhartha*, based on Herman Hesse's celebrated novel.

DEEG

Deeg, with its exquisite complex of pleasure palaces (above), lies 22 miles north of Bharatpur. Created in pale yellow sandstone and set around large, formal Mughal gardens, these palaces are architectural gems, considered by some to be second only to Agra's Taj Mahal in their beauty and symmetry. The palaces were laid out in the mid-1700's by Raja Badan Singh and, later, Raja Surajmal, as an idyllic place of refuge from the battles in which they were constantly engaged. In creating them, the Bharatpur rulers freely sought inspiration from the architectural traditions of the Mughals. Ironically, they succeeded brilliantly in this endeavor, at a time when Mughal architecture was becoming a sad parody of itself. The main pavilion of the complex is Gopal Bhawan, built by the banks of a large tank in 1763. It is an elegant piece of architecture, and fascinatingly designed: what appears to be a two-storied structure actually has four stories that descend gracefully down to the waters of the tank. This is where the Bharatpur royal family lived until 1951. Inside you can still see their furniture and some of their objets d'art. Gopal Bhawan is flanked by two beautiful little pavilions named Sawan and Bhadon, named after the two months of the monsoon. With their drooping *bangaldar* eaves perfectly mirrored in the still waters of the tank, they were designed to look like house boats, rather than buildings. To the east lie the beautiful Mughal gardens, interspersed with pools, water channels and five hundred fountains, which are still turned on once a year – although without the rainbow colors that used to play in them during the days of the maharajas ▲ *312*. South of the gardens lies Kishan Bhawan, another beautiful, yellow sandstone pavilion with splendidly carved archways, covered with rich arabesque motifs. Inside, it is embellished with carved motifs of flowers and peacocks, with an alcoved balcony set into its wall, where the maharaja used to sit. The dining room with a low horseshoe-shaped marble table was used for Indian meals partaken in silver *thalis* while sitting on the floor. The open end of the table was

SITE PLAN

TEMPLE
RAM BHAWAN
SINGH POL
NAND BHAWAN
TEMPLE
RANI GARDEN
GOPAL SAGAR
RUP SAGAR
GOPAL BHAWAN
KESAV BHAWAN
SURAJ BHAWAN
KISHAN BHAWAN
SHEESH MAHAL
SURAJ GATE
TANK
PURANA MAHAL
HARDEV BHAWAN

FAKING A MONSOON
In Keshav Mahal (above), huge stone balls in the ceiling would be rolled by channels of running water to create the sound of thunder, and the water released through outlets above the arches fell like sheets of rain all around the pavilion.

Badal Mahal.

"The apartments we occupied were unique...paved with fine marble, in which bouquets of flowers are represented by onyx, lapis lazuli and agate..."

Louis Rousselet, *India and its Native Princes*, 1878

used for service. There are two other very interesting pavilions set around the gardens, Keshav Bhawan and Nand Bhawan. Keshav Bhawan, an open, columned summer pavilion, is particularly charming. To the far south of the complex is the beautiful, white marbled, verandahed Suraj Mahal pavilion, with its delicate mosaic inlay work in semi-precious stones. It bears a particularly close resemblance to the Mughal architecture of Shah Jahan's times – which is not surprising, for it is actually made from several pillaged Mughal buildings brought back by the Jats from Delhi and reassembled here. As a result, when you look closely, you will notice how its marble slabs are not perfectly matched. An interesting architectural feature of the palace complex is the projecting double cornices which give the buildings a striking appearance, and creating a subtle balance of shadow and light. The complex, incidentally, is only half-finished. Raja Surajmal was planning to build a mirror image of it on the other side when he was killed in battle. Near the palace complex is Deeg Fort, which is also worth a visit.

A royal carriage at Deeg, circa 1902.

Govardhan

The small sacred town of Govardhan is located 9 miles east of Deeg. Associated with legends of the Hindu deity, Lord Krishna, who is said to have lived in these parts, it is an important place of pilgrimage. In its narrow winding lanes you can feel the pulse of the real India. Harideva Temple, built in the 16th century, is particularly worth a visit. The impressive cenotaph of Raja Surajmal, 2 miles north of here, has some fascinating frescos of scenes from the Raja's life under its dome. Near Harideva Temple is another interesting complex of cenotaphs of the Bharatpur maharajas, which are also notable for their frescoed ceilings. Their curved cornices and multiple domes and pavilions are typical architectural features of northeastern Rajasthan.

Frescos at a cenotaph in Govardhan.

Shielded from cyclone
According to legend, Lord Krishna once protected the people of Braj from a cosmic cyclone hurled at them by Lord Indra, the god of the rain. To shield them from the rain and floods, Krishna lifted Mount Giriraj, near Govardhan, on the tip of his little finger and held it aloft for seven days and nights, like an umbrella, until the cyclone finally died out, and Indra apologized at the feet of Krishna – a subject much represented in Indian art.

BABUR'S GARDEN
Just outside Dholpur lie the remains of a splendid Mughal garden laid out in 1529 by the first Mughal emperor, Babur. Lost for centuries, it was rediscovered in 1978 by Elizabeth Moynihan, the wife of the then United States Ambassador to India. Using Babur's autobiography as a guide, she followed a trail of clues from Uzbekistan to Dholpur. The gardens have long since vanished, but there are still traces of the beautiful old lotus pools hewn from the living rock, around which the gardens were laid.

DHOLPUR

Situated 66 miles southeast of Bharatpur is the town of Dholpur, once the capital of a little kingdom of the same name. Dholpur was founded in the 11th century by Raja Dholan Deo, and its rulers were vassals of the Hindu rajas of Delhi. One of them, Palun Singh, died leading the troops of the last great Hindu raja of Delhi, Prithviraj Chauhan ● *35, 55*, into battle in AD 1175. This region saw several historic battles, including a decisive one in 1658 between the Mughal heir, Dara Shukoh, and his younger brother, Aurangzeb, the usurper who became emperor ● *36*. Dholpur is an interesting town to visit, particularly because it is far from the usual tourist track and is quite undiscovered. It is famed for its pink sandstone quarries, whose stone was specially selected by Lutyens for the building of the new city of Delhi in the early part of this century. Dholpur Palace, a splendid early 19th-century sandstone edifice, is worth seeing, particularly for its extensive use of Art Deco English tiles that cover the walls of each room from floor to ceiling. See also the 16th-century mausoleum of Sadiq Khan (now converted into a school).

BARI

Bari, 18 miles southwest of Dholpur, has an elegant 17th-century lakeside pleasure palace built by Emperor Shah Jahan. Nearby, there is also an interesting 13th-century fortress and two wildlife sanctuaries, Vana Vihar and Ram Sagar.

KARAULI

The picturesque old fortified town of Karauli, about 76 miles southwest of Bharatpur, was founded in 1348. Its richly ornamented 18th-century City Palace is worth visiting for its orange sandstone cupolas, its elaborate stucco-work details and its impressive *durbar* hall. There are also some interesting frescos inside, which you should not miss. The Maharaja of Karauli has converted his country palace into a heritage hotel which can be used as a base to discover some fascinating old temples, as well as a game sanctuary with wonderful opportunities for jeep safaris.

Karauli's coat-of-arms (right).

Practical information

314 Getting there
316 Local transport
318 Getting aro
322 Useful w
324 How
326

ADDRESSES

→ **HIGH COMMISSION OF INDIA (UK)**
India House
London WC2B 4NA
Tel. 020 7836 8484
www.hcilondon.org

→ **EMBASSY OF INDIA (US)**
2107 Massachusetts Ave., Washington D.C. 20008
Tel. (202) 939 7000
www.indianembassy.org

→ **CONSULATE GENERAL OF INDIA (US)**
– 3 East 64th St.
New York, NY 10021
Tel. (212) 774 0600
www.indiacgny.org
– 540 Arguello Blvd.
San Francisco, CA 94118
Tel. (415) 668 0662
www.indianconsulate-sf.org

→ **GOVERNMENT OF INDIA TOURIST OFFICES**
– 7 Cork Street
London W1X 2LW
Tel. 020 7437 3677
www.indiatouristoffice.org
– 1270 Av. of the Americas, Suite 1808
New York, NY 10020
Tel. (212) 586 4901
– 3550 Wilshire Blvd.
Room 204, Los Angeles, CA. 90010
Tel. (213) 380 8855
www.tourindia.com

BUDGET

→ **ACCOMMODATION (DOUBLE ROOM)**
Cheap
Basic amenities
100 to 450 INR
Average
Comfortable
450 to 1,500 INR
Expensive
From international comfort to the luxury of palaces
1,500 to 7,000 INR
See also Accommodation ◆ *318*

→ **MEALS**
35 INR in a cheap eating place
200 INR in a good restaurant
400 INR in a large hotel

MIN. AND MAX. TEMPERATURES IN FAHRENHEIT			
	JAIPUR	JODHPUR	UDAIPUR
APR.–JUNE	79–102	79–106	75–102
JUL.–SEP.	75–88	77–95	74–88
OCT.–NOV.	55–88	59–88	55–86
DEC.–MAR.	50–79	54–82	52–81
RAINFALL IN INCHES			
	JAIPUR	JODHPUR	UDAIPUR
APR.–JUNE	1	½	1¼
JUL.–SEP.	6	4	6½
OCT.–NOV.	⅓	⅙	¼
DEC.–MAR.	⅓	⅕	⅙

CLIMATE

→ **APRIL–JUNE**
The heat in April is still bearable, but avoid traveling during May and June when the temperatures are at their highest. During that period, it is best to go out in the morning or in the late afternoon.

→ **JULY–SEPTEMBER**
Monsoon season. The heat gradually goes down and the rains bring a welcome coolness. However, the level of humidity rises; 95% of the annual rainfall occurs during the monsoon. Unpredictable torrential rains make roads impassable. However, in July and August the landscape offers a stunning display of colors.

→ **OCTOBER–MARCH**
Following the monsoon, in Oct.–Nov., the temperature goes up again. "Winter" (Jan.–Mar.) is the most pleasant season, with very little rain and temperatures that do not exceed 82°F. (See table above.)

FORMALITIES

→ **VISA**
Compulsory.
A tourist visa is valid for six months from the date of issue. Check with the High Commission or the nearest General Consulate for opening hours, requirements and cost.
Warning
Consular authorities normally take two or three days to issue a visa, but they may take longer during the holidays due to shorter working hours. Make sure you apply for your visa well in advance.

→ **EXTENSION OF VISAS**
Visas may be extended by 15 days at the Foreigners' Registration Office in Delhi:
Tel. (011) 331 9781
in Jaipur:
Opposite the City Palace museum
Tel. (0141) 669 391
Open Mon.–Fri. 10am–1.30pm and 2–5pm.

→ **DECLARATION OF FOREIGN CURRENCIES**
From $1,000.

HEALTH

→ **VACCINATIONS**
Compulsory
Yellow fever for people coming from high-risk areas
Recommended
Diphtheria–Tetanus
Poliomyelitis
Hepatitis A and B
Typhoid
Rabies

→ **ANTI-MALARIA TREATMENT**
Essential

→ **FIRST-AID KIT**
General
Antibiotics, pain killers, antidiarrhea and antihistamine tablets, one or two syringes, water-purifying tablets
Mosquitos
Repellent and sting relief creams, a mosquito net previously soaked in a repellent lotion (available from pharmacies).
Wear long-sleeved garments and trousers in the evening.

HEALTH INSURANCE

You are advised to purchase personal health insurance before departure. Ask your travel agents to make the necessary arrangements, or check whether insurance is included in the services offered by your credit card company. In general, this kind of insurance covers both local medical or hospital treatment and repatriation.

MONEY

→ **MONETARY UNIT**
The Indian rupee (INR)
£1 = around 67 INR
$1 = around 47 INR
The US$ is the foreign currency that is most readily exchanged. It can also be used as local currency.

→ **CREDIT CARDS**
There are few autotellers, but credit cards can be used in large hotels and restaurants, as well as in some stores. The most commonly accepted cards are Visa, Mastercard and American Express.

→ **TRAVELER'S CHECKS**
Get US$ traveler's checks.
Warning
Bureaux de change and banks do not necessarily have an

agreement with all issuers of traveler's checks. The most commonly accepted checks are those issued by American Express and Thomas Cook.

TELEPHONE

→ FROM THE UK AND US TO RAJASTHAN
00 + 91 + city code (omitting the 0) + number you wish to call
See the list of city codes ◆ *321*

TIME DIFFERENCE

Rajasthan is 5½ hours ahead of London and 10½ hours ahead of New York in winter, and 4½ and 9½ hours respectively in summer.

TRAVEL

→ UK/US TO DELHI

■ Air India
UK:
Tel. 020 7495 7950
US:
Tel. (212) 407 1379
www.airindia.com

■ British Airways (UK)
Tel. 08457 222 111
www.britishairways.com

■ KLM (UK)
Tel. 08705 074 074
www.klmuk.com

■ Northwest Orient/ KLM (US)
Tel. 1-800-447-4747
www.nwa.com

■ Singapore Airlines
UK:
Tel. 0870 608 88 86
US:
Tel. 1 800 742-3333
www.singaporeair.com
Check with airlines for details of flights and fares.

→ DELHI AIRPORT–CITY CENTER (10 MILES)

■ By bus
– DELHI TRANSPORT CORPORATION
Non-air-conditioned shuttle (Airport bus)
– EATS (EX-SERVICEMEN'S AIRLINK TRANSPORT SERVICE)
The two companies run services to Connaught Place and to the bus terminal ISBT (*Inter State Bus Terminus*).

■ By prepaid taxi
Go to the Prepaid Taxis desk in order to book and settle your fare in advance. Keep the receipt and hand it to the driver upon reaching your destination.

■ Information
International terminal
Tel. (011) 565 20 50 or 548 26 21
National terminal
Tel. (011) 566 51 21

→ DELHI–RAJASTHAN

■ By air
Indian Airlines operate flights between Delhi and the major cities in Rajasthan: Jaipur, Jodhpur, Jaisalmer and Udaipur. Domestic flights leave from Palam terminal (6 miles from the Indira Gandhi international terminal). Shuttle buses link the two terminals.
FARES (APPROXIMATE)
Delhi–Jaipur: £38/$55
Delhi–Udaipur and Delhi–Jodhpur: £73/$105
INFORMATION
Indian Airlines
Tel (011) 462 05 66
http://indian-airlines.nic.in

■ By train
Cheaper and reasonably reliable.
– DELHI–JAIPUR
Shatabdi Express
Comfortable air-conditioned train. Duration: 4½ hours.
Garib Nawab Express
Duration: 5 hours. Also serves Ajmer, Chittorgarh and Udaipur.
– DELHI–JODHPUR
Delhi–Jodhpur Express
Stops at Alwar and Jaipur.
– DELHI–BIKANER
Stops at Churu in the Shekhavati.
– DELHI–BHARATPUR AND KOTA
On the Delhi–Bombay line.
– DELHI–MOUNT ABU
On the Delhi–Ahmedabad line, via Jaipur and Ajmer.
Warning
Always reconfirm with the station of departure.

■ Stations for trains to Rajasthan
– DELHI MAIN STATION
Near the Red Fort, 3¾ miles from Connaught Place.
– DELHI SERAI ROHILLA STATION
Old Delhi, 2¾ miles northwest of Connaught Place.
– NEW DELHI STATION
Less than ¾ of a mile north of Connaught Place.
Tip
A ticket office reserved for foreigners is located on the second floor of New Delhi Station and in the IRCA Building, Chelmsford Road, Paharganj. It saves waiting in long queues and guarantees tickets as a number of seats is allocated to foreign visitors.

■ By bus
Slower, not as comfortable and not necessarily cheaper. Links major cities in Rajasthan. An express bus to Jaipur (5½ hours) leaves from Bikaner House on Pandara Road.
INFORMATION
Rajasthan Roadways
Tel. (011) 296 12 46 or 338 34 69
ISBT (Interstate Bus Terminus)
4½ miles from the city center, Kashmir Gate, north of Delhi Serai Rohilla Station.
Tel. (011) 296 88 36

■ Car
Delhi–Jaipur on Expressway no. 8. Duration: around 5½ hours.
See also Car rental ◆ *317*

TRAVEL AGENT

Award-winning UK-based travel company Western & Oriental organizes unique journeys to Rajasthan.
Tel. (+44) 20 7313 6600
info@westernoriental.com

WHAT TO PACK

→ CLOTHING
No shorts or vests but long-sleeved garments, trousers and skirts to cover arms and legs. A sweater for cool evenings. Waterproof jacket for the monsoon season. Hat for protection from the sun, and headscarf to visit mosques, mausoleums and Sikh sanctuaries.

→ DOCUMENTS
International driving license. International vaccination book.

→ DON'T FORGET
Sun hat and cream. Padlocks to lock your bedroom door in some small hotels and for your bags when traveling by train. A torch as there are many power cuts.

→ FILMS FOR CAMERAS
Make sure you take enough rolls with you as the quality of those on sale locally may vary. Color films can easily be found, but films for slides are sold only in large cities.

WHEN TO GO?

October to March is the best and most popular time for tourists. Blue skies guaranteed.
See also Festivals and Celebrations ◆ *319*

◆ LOCAL TRANSPORT

AIR TRAVEL
Indian Airlines operate regular direct flights between Jaipur, Jodhpur, Jaisalmer. The flight from Jaisalmer to Udaipur is not direct.

→ DURATION AND FARES
Jaipur–Jodhpur
40 mins, £60/$85
Jaipur–Udaipur
40 mins, £60/$85
Jaipur–Jaisalmer
1 hr 10mins, £90/$130
Jodhpur–Udaipur
40 mins, £60/$85
JODHPUR–JAISALMER
1 hr 50 mins, £90/$130
Note
There is a 25% discount for 12- to 30-year-olds

→ INFORMATION
Indian Airlines
Nehru Place, Tonk Road, Jaipur
Tel. (0141) 515 324
At Jaipur airport:
Tel. (0141) 721 333

BICYCLES
Bicycles are an ideal means of transport for visiting small towns and the surrounding areas. They can be hired near stations and from some hotels.
Rates
Around 2 INR/hr, 5 INR/day

BUSES
→ STATE BUSES (RSTC)
■ Standard buses
These buses are quite slow, with many stops, and tend to be crowded (passengers also travel on the roof!). They serve major cities and villages.
■ Express buses
Faster, but it is essential to reserve one's seat in advance at bus terminals to avoid having to stand all the way.
■ "Deluxe" buses
"Deluxe" buses are more spacious, and some even have reclining seats. Reservations are compulsory. Some of these buses operate by night.

→ PRIVATE BUSES
Private buses are "deluxe" buses for tourists, but the quality may vary from one company to another. These buses tend to offer the same kind of comfort and speed as state "deluxe" buses, but at much higher prices.

CAR RENTAL
→ SELF-DRIVE
This is still quite rare and is offered by only a few agencies.

→ WITH DRIVER
Service offered by agencies, hotels and the RTDC (Rajasthan Tourism Development Corporation) office in every city.
Tip
Make sure the driver's meals and overnight stay are included in the contract.

→ DRIVING IN INDIA
■ State of the roads
On the whole the roads in India are quite poor. They are made worse by the heavy rains during the monsoon season.
■ Traffic
Drive on the left.
■ Prudence
Driving is a rather perilous activity. The driving code is not always respected, and pedestrians and cyclists are rather unpredictable.
Warning
You are strongly advised not to drive at night. The horn is used more readily than the indicators when turning off streets, and heavy goods vehicles are always right!

RICKSHAWS
Typically Indian means of transport in city centers and surrounding areas. Can be found everywhere.
■ Cycle rickshaws
Tricycle with two seats behind the rickshaw driver.
■ Autorickshaws,
Motorized tricycle with two seats behind the rickshaw driver.
Warning
The meter – when there is one! – in autorickshaws is not always switched on. Be sure to fix the price of your journey before boarding.

SAFARIS
Organized by hotels, travel agents and the RTDC.

→ AROUND JAISALMER
On camel's back or by Jeep.
■ Duration
Half-a-day to 4 days
■ Where?
To explore the Thar desert (sand dunes at Samm, royal cenotaphs, Jain and Hindu temples, small isolated villages). If you decide to go for more than a day, you can sleep overnight in tents or under the desert starscape.

→ AROUND JODHPUR
By Jeep, on camels or horseback.
■ Duration
Usually half-a-day
■ Where?
Visit to Bishnoi villages, craftsmen's shops and animal reserves. The price of Rajasthani meals is also included.

→ AROUND PUSHKAR
By jeep, on camels or horseback
■ Duration
3 to 4 days
■ Where?
Idwa, Bharunda, Govindgarh and Pushkar. Overnight stay in small forts or in tents. Visits to traditional villages.

→ AROUND UDAIPUR
On horseback.
■ Duration
7 to 10 days
■ Specialist tour
Pratap Country Inn, where *marwari* race horses are bred.
■ Where?
Ranakpur, Eklingji, Nagda. Crossing the Aravalli mountains to the Kumbhalgarh fort. Overnight stay in small forts or luxury tents.

→ ELEPHANT SAFARIS
Reservations recommended
– JAIPUR VISION
Tel. and fax (0141) 62 21 85

TAXIS

→ SHORT JOURNEYS
The meter is usually obsolete and the driver must be able to produce a table of rates to work out the correct fare.
Warning
Those taxi drivers who do have a meter often refuse to switch it on and prefer to fix the fare beforehand.

→ DAY HIRE
Minimum journey of 155 to 190 miles, with overnight supplement. Ideal to visit out-of-the-way places. Good value for a group of persons, especially if the car runs on diesel.

TRAINS

→ TYPES OF TRAINS
■ **Passenger trains**
The slowest.
■ **Mail trains**
Faster, with fewer stops.
■ **Super-fast trains**
The fastest and most reliable trains. Serve only major stations.

→ CLASSES
Not all trains have the same classes.
■ **Air-conditioned first class**
Seats and sleepers. Very comfortable.
■ **Standard first class**
Seats can be turned into sleeping berths. Compartments can be locked.
■ **Air-conditioned second class**
Seats or sleeping berths are separated from the corridor by a curtain (these are to be avoided if possible). It is preferable to use those in closed compartments.
■ **Standard second class**
Similar to the previous class but without air conditioning and always crowded.

→ RESERVATIONS
At the station (ticket office for foreigners) or at travel agents. A number of seats are allocated to foreign visitors on every train, but it is always best to reserve in advance for long-distance journeys.

→ FINDING ONE'S SEAT
Tickets show the car and compartment or seat numbers. Signs on the platforms or cars indicate the passengers' names and seat numbers. For a small charge, a coolie will lead you safely through the crowd to your seat.

→ TIMES
A comprehensive timetable, *Trains at a glance*, is available in all stations.
■ **Cost**
25 INR

→ INDRAIL PASS
7- to 90-day unlimited travel pass on sale at the main stations and at RTDC agencies.

→ PALACE ON WHEELS
Formerly used by maharajahs, this luxury train includes a library, a bar, a bureau de change, conference rooms, as well as restaurants that serve Indian, Continental and Chinese cuisine. Each compartment offers every comfort and is attended by its own staff. The arrangement of all meals taken at leading hotels and guided tours are included in the package.
■ **Journey**
One-week trip though Rajasthan, with most journeys taking place at night. You can also buy a single destination ticket.
■ **Stops**
Jaipur, Jaisalmer, Jodhpur, Sawai Madhopur, Chittorgarh, Udaipur, Bharatpur, Agra, Fatehpur-Sikri.
■ **Times**
Sep.–Apr.
Departure Wed. from Delhi. Returning to Delhi the following Wed.
■ **Fares per person per day**
Per person per night: £338/$485 (Oct.–Mar) and £275/$395 (Apr.–Sep.)
Per person per night (twin): £244/$350 (Oct.–Mar.) and £205/$295 (Apr.–Sep.)
Per person per night (triple): £198/£285 (Oct.–Mar.) and £167/£240 (Apr.–Mar.)
■ **Information**
– RTDC
Jaipur
Tel. (0141) 203 531
Fax (0141) 201 045
www.palaceonwheels.net
– Palace on Wheels
New Delhi
Tel. (011) 338 18 84
Fax (011) 338 28 23

→ ROYAL ORIENT
Jointly operated by the Tourism Corporation of Gujarat and Indian Railways, the *Royal Orient* offers yet another journey back in time. It has 13 coaches with every comfort and equipped with a lounge, a mini-bar and a kitchenette.
■ **Journey**
One-week trip through Rajasthan.
■ **Stops**
Udaipur, Chittorgarh, and Jaipur, traveling through neighboring regions (Palitana, Sasangir, Ahmedabad and Junagadh).
■ **Times**
Sep.–Apr.
Departure Wed. from Delhi station, returning to the same station the following Wed.
■ **Fares per person per day**
Per person per night: £140/$200 (Oct.–Mar.) and £104/$150 (Apr.–Sep.)
Per person per night (twin): £243/$350 (Oct.–Mar.) and £183/$263 (Apr.–Sep.)
Per person per night (triple): £122/$175 (Oct.–Mar.) and £92/$132 (Apr.–Mar.)
■ **Information**
A-6, State Emporia Building
Baba Kharak Singh Marg
New Delhi
Tel. (011) 373 40 15
Fax (011) 373 24 82

WARNING
All telephone numbers have changed as the result of the recent modernization of the Indian telephone system. Further changes are expected.

ACCOMMODATION

During the peak season, and depending on the type of hotel selected, it is better to book in advance. However, it is usually quite easy to book a room on the spot.

→ PALACES AT REASONABLE PRICES
Many maharajah palaces have been turned into hotels. They may appear to be expensive, but they are cheap by Western standards. Some rooms cost as much as a one-star hotel in Europe.
Note
For a few rupees the hotel's dhobi, *or washerman, collects clothes for washing every day and returns them clean in the evening. Don't hesitate to use his services (do not use for clothes that require special attention).*

→ FIVE-STAR HOTELS
The Welcomgroup and the Taj Group are the two leading chains in India operating five-star hotels. These hotels offer high-quality accommodation and service often comparable with those of five-star hotels around the world.
Heritage Hotels are palaces converted into hotels. Some are professionally managed and the owners personally see to it that the guests are provided with the best service.
www.indianheritagehotels.com

→ MID-RANGE HOTELS
Some of these hotels can be good, while others provide only essential services.

■ **Tourist Bungalows or RTDC hotels**
Minimum amenities: rooms (some with air-conditioning), or beds in a dormitory. Most places have a bar and a restaurant.
RTDC RESERVATION CENTER
Swagatam Hotel
Station Road
Jaipur
Tel. (141) 20 35 31 or 20 25 86
Fax (141) 20 10 45

→ PAYING GUEST ACCOMMODATION
Another alternative is to live in a home listed under the paying guest scheme of Rajasthan Tourism. You get a room with an attached bathroom with hot water. Home-cooked meals upon request. Check with the tourist office in Jaipur ◆ *318*.

→ CHEAP HOTELS
For those on the tightest of budgets. Expect the worst!

ADDRESSES

→ BRITISH HIGH COMMISSION
Shantipath, Chanakyapuri, Delhi 110021
Tel. (011) 687 21 61
Fax (011) 687 00 62
www.ukinindia.org

→ EMBASSY OF THE UNITED STATES
Shantipath, Chanakyapuri, Delhi 110021
Tel. (011) 419 80 00
Fax (011) 419 00 17

→ TOURIST OFFICES
■ **Delhi**
88 Janpath
Tel. (011) 332 00 08
■ **Jaipur**
– RAJASTHAN TOURISM DEVELOPMENT CORPORATION (RTDC)
Railway station, platform no. 1
Tel. (0141) 315 714
– TOURIST RECEPTION CENTRE
MI Road
Tel. (0141) 365 256
Open Mon.–Sat. 10am–5pm
■ **Jaisalmer**
Tourist Reception Centre
Gadi Sagar Road
Tel. (02992) 524 06
Open Mon.–Sat. 10am–5pm
■ **Jodhpur**
– TOURIST RECEPTION CENTRE
Next door to Hotel Ghoomar (RTDC), High Court Road
Tel. (0291) 545 083
Open Mon.–Sat. 8am–7pm
– INTERNATIONAL TOURIST BUREAU
Railway station
Tel. (0291) 439 052
■ **Udaipur**
Tourist Reception Centre
Fateh Memorial Building, near Surajpol
Tel. (0294) 411 535
Open Mon.–Sat. 10am–1.30pm and 2–5pm

BARGAINING

Bargaining is normal practice just about everywhere (markets, etc.), except in pharmacies or in places that display the *Fixed Price* or *Government of Rajasthan* signs.
Warning
The Approved by the Rajasthan Government *sign has no meaning!*

ELECTRICITY

230–240 V
■ **Power cuts**
A frequent, if not a daily occurrence.

ETIQUETTE

→ PHOTOS
Always ask for permission before taking photographs of people. Hindu and Muslim women cover their faces in public. It is forbidden to take

photographs of strategic places (bridges, stations, airports, etc.). If you have any doubts, ask a local resident or the police.

→ ACCESS TO HOLY PLACES
See Places to visit ◆ *341*

→ RIGHT HAND
Use only the right hand when eating, greeting or handing something to someone.

FESTIVALS AND CELEBRATIONS

→ FAIRS AND FESTIVALS
Dates of festivals follow the lunar calendar and vary every year.
See the above table.

Events	2002	2003
BIKANER FESTIVAL	JAN. 27–28	JAN. 17–18
NAGAUR FAIR	FEB. 19–22	FEB. 8–11
DESERT FESTIVAL	FEB. 25–27	FEB. 14–16
ELEPHANT FESTIVAL	MAR. 28	MAR. 17
GANGAUR FAIR	APR. 15–16	APR. 4–5
MEWAR FESTIVAL	APR. 15–16	APR. 4–5
TEEJ FESTIVAL	AUG. 11–12	AUG. 1–2
RAMDEORA FAIR	SEP. 15–16	SEP. 4–5
MARWAR FESTIVAL	OCT. 19–20	OCT. 8–9
PUSHKAR FAIR	NOV. 16–19	NOV. 5–8
KOLAYAT FAIR	NOV. 15–25	NOV. 4–14
SUMMER FESTIVAL	JUN. 1–3	JUN. 1–3
CHANDRABHAGA	NOV. 18–20	NOV. 7–9

→ SHOWS
All major towns have theaters or townhalls available for performances brought in by cultural organizations in the form of plays, classical and folk shows, as well as entertainment shows with movie personalities and other celebrities. The best way to keep in touch is through the local tourist office.

■ **Panghat Theater**
Rambagh Palace
Jaipur
Tel. (0141) 38 19 19
The Bird's repertory of performers from all Rajasthan is directed by Himmat Singh, who also designed this picturesque theater under the trees. Performances here are highly recommended during the tourist season (from October until April). Dinner is included in the price of the ticket.

■ **Jawahar Kala Kendra**
Jawahar Lal Nehru Marg, Jaipur
Tel. (0141) 63 00 51
This cultural complex comprises two theaters and a village arena. Performances representing the arts of Rajasthan and sometimes those of other states in India and even foreign countries, are organized all year round.

■ **Shilpagram** ▲ *254*.
Rani Road, near Lake Fateh Sagar, 1¾ miles from Udaipur
This center has recently gained popularity as a performance venue since local artists and craftsmen gather here to demonstrate their skills.

■ **Bharatiya Lok Kala Mandal**
Chetak Circle, Udaipur
Center founded in 1952. Hosts puppet shows and folk dances, and even houses a museum of folklore. Its company has performed in major cities around the world.
Puppets: 6–6.30pm
Dance: 6.30–7pm
– MEERA KALA MANDIR
Hiran Magari, Udaipur
Traditional folk dances.

■ **Hotels**
Throughout Rajasthan, hotels vie with each other in putting on a variety of shows every evening with the available local talent (dancers, musicians, snake charmers, etc.). This is often an opportunity to see authentic, traditional performances which may be as good as any put on by theaters. Some places have paid shows, while others arrange a dinner-cum-free-cultural-show. It is customary to give the performers a tip. Artists are also available for personalized performance should any tourist so desire.

FOOD

Do not eat uncooked vegetables, undercooked meat or fruit that you cannot peel. Beware of fresh fruit juices sold on the street as they are almost always mixed with water. Ask the vendor to use water from your own bottle.

Advice
Eat local food as it is well adapted to the living conditions. Wash your hands regularly, especially before meals.
See also How to read a menu ◆ *324*

HEALTH

→ PHARMACIES
Indicated by a red cross. If you're following a particular treatment, bring your prescription with you with the names and details of the medicines you need in order to obtain equivalent medicines if yours are not available in India. Don't forget to check the expiry dates of medicines.

→ DOCTORS
In case of illness, go and see a private doctor (in a private surgery or in a clinic) who will recommend a private hospital.

→ EMERGENCIES
For transport in an emergency anywhere in Rajasthan, contact the local agent of *Europe Assistance*, Dr Chandra Sen Galundia.
Tel. (mobile): 982 906 1040

INTERNET

There are cybercafés and computer bureaux (especially in leading hotels) in Jaipur and Udaipur, and in a growing number of smaller towns.
www.cybercaptive.com
Lists the addresses of cybercafés around the world.

MONEY

→ INDIAN CURRENCY
1 rupee (1 INR) = 100 paises
■ **Notes**
The Indian currency is available in notes of 500, 100, 50, 20, 10 and 5 rupees.
Advice
Notes have a longer life than in Western countries. Beware of damaged, torn or patched-up bills as they are not always accepted. Check those given to you when changing money. Some banks are willing to change them.
■ **Coins**
There are coins of 1, 2 and 5 rupees, as well as coins of 25 and 50 paises.

→ EXCHANGE RATES
£1 = around 67 INR
$1 = around 47 INR

→ CHANGING MONEY
You can change money at banks (branches of the *State Bank of India* can be found in most towns) and at official bureaux. See also Opening times ◆ *320*
Warning
Indian currency cannot be imported nor exported. Keep all exchange receipts to change back remainder rupees.

→ AUTOTELLERS
There is a 24-hour autoteller at the HDFC bank
D–54 Siddhi Vinayak

Asok Marg,
C-Scheme
Jaipur 302001.

MOVIES

→ CHOOSING A MOVIE
Indians are passionate movie-goers and, as such, can offer the best advice about what to see, what theaters to go to and how to get there.

→ TICKETS
There are two queues at movie theaters: one for women and the other for men. When buying a ticket, ask for a seat in the dress circle (around £0.85/$1.25). The stalls are often taken by storm as the seats there are cheaper, albeit not as comfortable. The audience tends to be quite emotional. If the movie theater displays a "sold-out" sign, don't hesitate to talk to the manager who always keeps a few tickets aside for the more persistent customers.

NEWSPAPERS

→ LOCAL NEWSPAPERS
Several English-language newspapers are on sale in bookstores, at newspaper stands and from street vendors. Among them are the national daily *The Times of India* and its local edition the *Indian Express,* and the local daily *Rajasthan Patrika*.

OPENING TIMES

→ BANKS
In general Mon.–Fri. 10am–1pm, Sat. 10am–noon. Some, such as The State Bank of India and The Rajasthan Bank, are also open 3pm–6pm. Some branches in leading hotels open until 8.30pm.

→ STORES
Mon.–Sat. 10am–6pm. Some close at lunchtime.

POST OFFICE

→ OFFICES
■ **General Post Office (GPO)**
Poste restante service available. Open Mon.–Fri. 10am–7pm, Sat. 10am–noon. Branches in every town. Open Mon.–Fri. 10am–5pm, Sat. 10am–noon.
■ **Postal services (RMS) in the main station**
Open daily 10am–8pm
■ **Hotels**
Some have mail boxes and sell stamps and postcards.

→ POSTAL ORDERS
Available until 3pm on weekdays and 1pm on Sat.

→ RATES
■ **Local rate**
2 INR for a letter
■ **International rates**
15 INR for a letter and 8 INR for a postcard

→ INTERNATIONAL NEWSPAPERS
Found only in major towns

SOUVENIRS

→ TEXTILES ● *56, 58*
The most beautiful textiles come from Sanganer, Bagru and Barmer. You can observe the craftsmen at work in their shops before making any purchases.
■ **Anokhi**
Tilak Marg
Embroidered and mirror-work textiles (*shishadar*) are Jaipur's specialty.
■ **Mohit Art and Crafts**
Jorawar Singh Gate, opposite the National Institute of Ayurved, Amber Rd
■ **Handloom House, Khadi Ghar and Rajasthali**
MI Road
Advice
Don't worry if you haven't had the chance to purchase souvenirs in any of the places listed above. Any bazaar in Rajasthan is a shopper's paradise.

→ CARPETS AND DURRIES ● *68*
Saraf Carpets and Textiles
Khawasji ka Bagh
Outside Zorawar Singh Gate, Amer Road, Jaipur
Tel. (0141) 63 50 70

→ JOOTIS ● *69*
These leather sandals can be found everywhere, particularly in Jodhpur.

→ MINIATURE PAINTINGS
As you wander the streets, especially in Udaipur, you can see the painters at work.

■ Lakshmi Arts
232 A Soniyion Ka Rasta Kishan Pole Bazaar
Jaipur
Tel. (0141) 31 25 74
Picturesque boutique in an old merchant's house in the heart of the old city, with typical *haveli* decoration.

→ BLUE POTTERY OF JAIPUR ● *72*

■ Kripal Singh Shekhawat
B-18 A Shiv Marg
Bani Park, Jaipur
Tel. (0141) 201 127
One of the longest established craftsmen. Some fine pieces can be found here.

■ Dhola Maru – The Art Gallery
71 Gupta Gardens, Amer Road, Jaipur
Tel. (0141) 63 67 14
Also stocks a range of attractive miniature paintings and has a welcoming demonstration workshop. Honest prices and quality guaranty.

→ JEWELRY ● *62*

■ Precious stones
In the small streets behind the market (Johari Bazaar, Haldion ka Rasta and Gopalji ka Rasta) are the artisans who cut and polish the stones. There are no fixed prices for these gemstones.

■ Silver jewelry
Silver jewelry abounds in Jaipur, Pushkar and Jaisalmer. Silver is sold at a per-gram rate or on the percentage of silver, in which case a hallmark in the form of a three-digit number indicates the silver content (999 is the maximum).

→ SHOPPING ADVICE

■ Rajasthali
Rajasthali are state government's outlets found in the major towns. They offer a range of crafts at fixed prices. Even if you shop in other places, visit Rajasthali to get an idea of the price range and quality of workmanship.

■ Prices
Craft shops other than state outlets sometimes charge much higher prices. Don't hesitate to bargain to bring these prices down. If there's a guide or rickshaw driver with you, bear in mind that he is entitled to a commission. When paying by credit card, make sure you get a bill and receipt.

TAXES
There is tax on food, drinks, services and accommodation in restaurants and hotels (6%, 10% or more according to the price). This is added to the total amount on your bill.

TELEPHONE

→ CALLS WITHIN INDIA

■ In the same town
Just dial the number

■ From one town to another
Dial the area code preceded by 0 + the number you need

→ CALLS TO UK
00 44 + the number you need, omitting the initial 0

→ CALLS TO THE US
00 1 + state code + number

→ INTERNATIONAL INQUIRIES AND COLLECT CALLS
186

→ WHERE TO MAKE CALLS

■ From STD/ISD call centers
These are private shops:
STD: national lines,
ISD: international lines

■ Rates
Around 60 INR per min.

■ From hotels
Directly or through the operator

→ MAIN AREA CODES IN RAJASTHAN	
Ajmer	0145
Alwar	0144
Bharatpur	05644
Bikaner	0151
Bundi	0747
Chittorgarh	01472
Jaipur	0141
Jaisalmer	02992
Jodhpur	0291
Kota	0744
Mandawa	01592
Mont Abu	02974
Nawalgarh	01594
Pushkar	0145
Sawai Madhopur	07462
Udaipur	0294

TIPPING
This is not a must as in some parts of the world. However, service personnel such as waiters or hotel staff do expect a tip, which can be up to 10%. Always keep a few rupees handy for any small services you may receive on the street.

TOBACCO
Bidis, mini cigarettes made up of a rolled-up tobacco leaf, are very strong and acrid. Indians hold them between the little and third fingers with the hand closed, and inhale the smoke through the space between the thumb and index finger.

WATER
Never drink tap water. Don't use ice cubes, except in major hotels where they are made with filtered water. Mineral water can easily be found, but make sure the top of the bottle is still sealed. If no mineral water is available, use water-purifying tablets for the water provided in jars by hotels. Never drink running water, which almost always comes from reservoirs.

◆ USEFUL WORDS AND EXPRESSIONS

PRONUNCIATION

The Hindi words listed here have been transcribed according to the following phonetic rules:
double vowel = long vowel
ai = e as in bed
au = o of love
c = ch of Churchill
e = e of mermaid
g = hard g, as in get
j = j as in jeans
k = c as in cat
n = preceding vowel is nasal
tc = sound somewhere between ch and j
u = oo, long or short, as in book or pool, tool

General rules
– some letters are not pronounced,
– all underlined characters are pronounced from the back of the throat,
– breathe in strongly when pronouncing h at the beginning of a word or next to a vowel.

EMERGENCIES

Hospital : aspataal
Pharmacy: davaaiyon kii dukaan
Police station: thaanaa / kotwalii
I'd like to see a doctor: mujhe kisii doktar se milnaa hai

FOOD

Bowl: katorii
Breakfast: naashtaa
Can you bring the bill, please?: bil laao
Chair: kursii
Cheap restaurant: dhaabaa
Cup: pyaalii
Dinner : shaam (soir) ou raat (nuit) kaa khaanaa **Do you have a table?** koii mez milegii?
Flask: ghiiyaa
Food: khaane-piine kaa saamaan
Fork: kaantaa
Glass: gilaas
Knife: churii
Lunch: dophar kaa khaanaa
Meal: bhojan
Menu: menu
(Everything is served at the same time on a tray, there are no words for starter, main dish or dessert.)
Napkin: ruumaal
Non-vegetarian restaurant: mansaahaarii
Plate: plet
Restaurant: restaurant / bhojanaaly
Vegetarian restaurant: shaakaahaarii
Table: mez

TASTE

Bitter: karvaa
Bland: phiikaa
Cold: thandaa
Delicious: svaadist
Dry: suukhaa
Honey: shahad
Hot (heat): garam
Hot / Spicy: masaaledaar
Liquid: rasedaar
Salty: namkiin
Salt: namak
Sour: khattaa
Sugar: shakkar / ciinii
Sweet (adj.) : miithaa
Taste: svaad
Too salty: khaaraa
Very spicy: catpataa

CEREALS AND PULSES

Barley: jau
Cereal: anaaj
Chickpea: canna
Chickpea flour: besan
Corn (US)/ Wheat (UK): gehuun
Corn (US) / Maize (UK) : makkii
Ear of corn (US) / Ear of maize (UK) : bhauttaa
Indian bread : rotii
Maize-based Indian bread: makkii kii rotii
Millet-based Indian bread: bajre kii rotii
Split lentils: daal
Millet: bajra
Unleavened bread: capaatii
Potato: aaluu
Rice: caaval / bhaat
Semolina: suujii
Things in batter: pakoraa
Wheat flour : maidaa
Wholewheat: aataa

FRUIT

Almond: baadaam
Apple: sev
Banana: kelaa
Coconut: naariyal
Date: khajuur
Dried fruit: suukhaa mevaa
Fig: anjiir
Guava: amruud
Grapes: anguur
Lemon: niimbuu
Mango: aam
Melon: kharbuuzaa
Olive: jaituun
Orange: santaraa / naarangii
Papaya: papiitaa
Peach: aaruu
Pear: naag / naashpaatii
Pineapple: anannaas
Pistachio nut: pistaa
Pomegranate: anaar
Raisins: kishmish
Tamarind: imlii
Tomato: tamaatar
Walnut: akhrot
Watermelon: tarbuuz / matiiraa

VEGETABLES

Vegetables : sabzii / tarkaarii
Aubergine: baingan
Bean: lobiyaa / cavlaa
Carrot: gaajar
Cauliflower: phuul gobhii
Courgette/Zucchini: taroii
Cucumber: kakrii / khiiraa
Garlic: lahsun
Green bean: sem kii phalii
Green vegetable: harii sabzii
Onion: pyaaz
Peas: matar
Pepper: shimlaa mirc
Pumpkin / Squash: kohlaa
Radish: muulii
Salad: salaad
Spinach: paalak
Turnip : shalgam

DRINKS

Beer: biiyar
Black tea (without milk): binaa duuch kii caay
Bottled water: botal kaa paanii
Coffee: kofii
Condensed milk: khoyaa
Drinking water: piine kaa paanii
Fresh lemonade: shikanjii
Fruit juice : phal kaa ras
Juice: ras
Milk: duudh
Syrup : sharbat
Tea: caay
Water: paanii
Western wine: vilaaytii sharaab
Wine: sharaab

MEAT AND FISH

Chicken: murgii / murg
Fish: machlii
Lamb: bher kaa bacaa
Meat: gosht
Mutton: bher
Pork: suuar

DAIRY PRODUCTS

Butter: makkhan
Cheese: paniir
Eggs: andaa
Plain yoghurt: dahii

GETTING AROUND

Backyard: tchauk
Bus stop: bus stop / bus stand
Close / Near: nazdiik / paas
Crossing: cauraahaa
Crossroads : tchauk
Desert: registaan
East : puurab
Far: duur
Fort: kilaa
Garden: baag / bagiicaa
Gate: darwaazaa
Go straight on: siidhe jaaiye
Go that way: udhar se jaaiye
Here: yahaan
How far is Udaipur? Udaipur kitnii duur hai ?
In which direction is Udaipur? Udaipur kidhar hai?
Lake: taalaab
Left : baaiin or
Market: baazaar
Mountain: pahaar
Museum: museum
North: uttar
Over there: vahaan
Palace: mahal
Right: daaiin or
Road: sarak
South: daksin
Square: tchauk
Street / Avenue : maarg
Temple : mandir
The bus to Udaipur: Udaipur kii bus
The train to Udaipur: Udaipur kii gaarii / rail
Town: shahar
Valley: ghaatii
Village: gaanv
Way: raastaa
(to ask the way to ...)
West : pashcim

GREETINGS

Hello: namaste
See you soon: phir milenge
Good-bye: namaste
Good night: shubh raatri
Have a good trip: shubh yaatraa
Please: meharbaanii karke / kripyaa
Thank you: danyavaad *(The use of thank you is not as common as in English. Say it only at the end of a conversation. Gestures, intonation and a slight bow of the head are other ways of expressing thanks.)*
Do you speak English? kyaa aap angrezii bolte hain?
I don't speak Hindi : mujhe hindi nahiin aatii
What it is? yah kyaa hai?
What is your name? aapkaa naam kyaa hai?
My name is Saraswati : meraa naam Saraswati hai
Where do you live? aap kahaan rahte hain?
I live in India: main Bhaarat men rahtaa huun
I am American/ English: main amerkan/angrazi huun
Come and visit, this is my address: mujhse milne aaiye, ye meraa pataa hai
Come in / Come: aaiye
Sit down: baithiye
Pleased to meet you: aapse milkar khushii huii
How are you? aap kaise hain?
I'm fine: main thiik huun
Do ...? / Which ...? / What ...? kyaa?
What time is it? kitne baje hain?
A pack of cigarettes, please: kripiyaa ek paiket sigret diijiye
Where are the toilets? batrum kaahan hai?

A lot: bahut
Because: kyonki
First: pahle
Good / All right: acchaa / thiik hai
Hotel: hotal (also means restaurant)
How: kaise
I: main
India: bhaarat / Hindustaan
Laundry: laundrii
Laundryman: dhobii
Later: baad men
Little / Not a lot: kam
No: nahiin
Now : abhii
Quickly: jaldii
Room: kamraa
Slowly : dhiire
There: vahaan
They: ve
Toilets : batrum
We: ham
When? kab?
Where: kahaan
Who? kaun?
Why? kyon?
Yes: haan
You: aap / tum

MONEY

Bank: bank
Credit cards: credit cards
Money: paisaa
Traveler's checks: traveller's cheques
I would like to change dollars / pounds?: mujhe dollars / pounds badaalne hain
Do you take (accept)...? kyaa aap... lete hain?

NUMBERS

zero: shuunya
one: ek
two: do
three: tiin
four: caar
five: paanc
six: chah
seven: saat
eight: aath
nine: nau
ten: das
eleven: gyaarah
twelve: baarah
thirteen: terah
fourteen: chaudah
fifteen: pandrah
sixteen: solah
seventeen: satrah
eighteen: athaarah
nineteen: unniis
twenty: biis
thirty: tiis
forty: caaliis
fifty: pacaas
sixty: saath
sevety: sattar
eighty: assii
ninety: nabbe
one hundred: sau
one thousand: ek hazaar
one hundred thousand: ek laakh

PLACES TO VISIT

Admission ticket: ticket
Closed: band
Film (for camera): film
Film developing: dhulai
Open: khulaa
Reduction: sastii ret
At what time does the palace open? mahal kitne baje khultaa hai?
At what time does the palace close? mahal kitne badje band hotaa hai?
Is there a guide? koii gaaiid hai?
May I take a picture?: kyaa main foto khiinc saktaa huun?

POST OFFICE

I have to call London/ New York : mujhe London/New York fon karnaa hè
I have to call this number: mujhe is nambar par fon karnaa hai
Policeman: pulisvaalaa

Letter: pattr
Post office: daak ghar
Postcard: postcard
Stamp: ticket
Telegram: taar
Telephone: phone
Where can I make a phone call? main fon kahaan se kar saktaa huun?

SHOPPING

Beautiful: sundar
Carpet: kaalin / galiicaa
Earrings: jumkaa
Enamel: miinaa
Fabric: kapraa
Gold: sonaa
Jewelry: zevar / gahne
Miniature: miniature
Money: caandii
Necklace: haar
Painting: penting
Precious stones : ratna
Prices: daam
Ring: anguuthii
Sari: saarii
Shirt: kamiiz
Shoes: juute
Shop / Store: dukaan
Skirt: ghaagra (in villages); lahangaa (in towns)
Trousers: salvaar
Black: kaalaa
Blue: niilaa
Color : rang
Green: haraa
Pink: gulaabii
Red: laal
White : safed
Yellow : piilaa

Different : alag
Large: baraa
Long: lambaa
Short: chotaa
Small: chotaa

How much is it? iske kitne paise lagenge?
It's too expensive: ye bahut mahangaa hai
Is there something cheaper? is se sastaa kuch hai kyaa?

TIME

Morning: subah
Midday: dopahar
Evening: shaam
Night: raat
Today: aaj
Tomorrow / Yesterday: kal
Day: din
Week: saptaah / haftaa
Monday: somvaar
Tuesday: mangalvaar
Wednesday: budhvaar
Thursday: guruvaar
Friday: shukravaar
Saturday: shanivaar
Sunday: ravivaar
Month: mahiinaa
Year : saal / varsh
This year: is saal
Last year: pichle saal
Next year: agle saal

TRANSPORT

Airport : hawaii adda
Bus: bus
Bus terminal: bus kaa adda
Car / Vehicle: motar gaarii / kaar
Driving license: driving license
Garage: garage
Left-luggage office: saamaan rakhne kii jagah
Luggage : saamaan
Plane: havaaii jahaaz
Porter: kulii
Station: railway station
Taxi: taxi
Ticket office: khirkii
Train: rail gari
How much is it per day? kitne paise roz lagte hain?
The car has broken down: gaarii kharaab hai

SPICES AND CONDIMENTS

Acaar: condiment
Adarak: ginger
Daanaa methii: fenugreek
Daarciinii / daalciinii: cinnamon
Dhaniyaa: coriander
Garam masala: mixed ground spices
Haldii: kurkuma
Ilaaycii: cardamom
Kaalii miirc: pepper
Kesar: saffron
Laal mirc: red chilli pepper
Laung: clove
Masala: spices
Masaaledaar: spicy
Pudiinaa: mint
Raaii: black mustard
Sarson: mustard
Tejpattaa: laurel
Tel: oil
Til: sesame
Ziiraa: cumin

A

Alu gobhi: potato- and cauliflower-based dish.
Alu ki tikiya: fried potato balls stuffed with spiced **mung**.
Alu mangori: mung bari.
Alu mughlai: potato dish with green chilli peppers and curry.
Amcur: dried green mango powder.
Arhar: yellow lentils with edible yellow skin.

B

Bapla: fried, spicy wheatflour balls.
Bari: lentils soaked in water and turned into spicy, sundried droplets which are then kept in cans.
Bari papar: bari served with fried chunks of **papar**.
Barvan parata: Indian bread made with **ghee** and filled with vegetables.
Bati: braised wheatflour balls.
Besan gatta: spicy lentil balls, fried in **ghee** and served with a spicy yoghurt sauce.
Bevecha: coconut rice cake.
Bundi ke ladu: cake made of chickpea flour droplets and syrup. Served on very special occasions such as engagements or weddings.
Butter chicken: chicken in spicy butter and curry sauce.

C

Chach: buttermilk spiced with cumin seeds and coriander.
Channa dal: spicy chickpeas.
Chapati: thin wheatflour Indian bread.
Churme ke ladu: sweet wheatflour balls with **ghee**.
Curry: a special mixture of spices used as a base for many dishes.

D

Dahi bara: deep-fried balls made of green lentil and chickpeas in a spicy yoghurt sauce, served with mint and coriander chutney.
Daliya: crushed wheat preparation.
Dalmoth: fried, spicy mixture of lentils, cashew nuts, peanuts, almonds and raisins.
Dam alu: potatos cooked in embers and served with a spicy sauce.
Dana methi: fenugreek leaves and seeds sauteed in **ghee** with mustard seed, molasses and pieces of green mango.
Dokle: spicy cubes made of chickpea flour, boiled then fried with cumin, black mustard, and green chilli peppers.
Dosa: flat bread made of rice flour and sometimes served in a coconut sauce.

F

Fini: fried wheatflour paste dipped in syrup and flavored with saffron. This sweet can also be served with hot milk if there is no syrup.

G

Gajar ka halwa: carrot **halwa** prepared with condensed milk, clarified butter and dried fruit.
Garam masala: powder made with black pepper, clove, cardamom, dried ginger, laurel leaves, cinnamon and cumin.
Gat: crushed maize which is then boiled and salted, served with milk or yoghurt.
Ghee: clarified butter.
Ghevar: wheatflour cake in the shape of a wheel, fried and covered with a layer of syrup or milk.
Gulab jamun: condensed milk balls, covered in syrup and cardamom-flavored.
Gur: molasses (boiled sugar cane). Sweet supposed to be favored by the gods and served on important occasions.

H

Halal: meat from animals killed in accordance with Muslim tradition.
Halwa: paste made of wheatflour, sugar and **ghee**, to which dried fruit is sometimes added.

J

Jalebi: fried twisted paste with syrup and sweetened saffron.
Jhatka: meat from animals killed in accordance with Hindu tradition (with one single blow).

K

Kabulii: rice- and chickpea-based dish.
Kachori: spicy wheat semolina fritters stuffed with spicy beans or lentils and flavored with clove, pepper and *alchalkhora* (scented bark of a tree).
Kadi: sauce made of spiced chickpea flour and yoghurt. Small flour and lentil fritters are sometimes added. The dish is then called **kadi pakora**.
Ker: berry of a spiky desert tree.
Ker sangri: found only in Rajasthan, this dish is made with the famous desert beans (hull of the *khejra*), with **ker**, *kumatia* (berries in the shape of buttons) and lotus stems (*bhe*). This mixture is cooked in oil with spices, and crushed dried green mango is added to it, giving the dish its slightly acid taste.
Kesar ki kulfi: saffron **kulfi**.
Kesar pilau: sweet rice.
Kesar pulav: saffron-flavored rice.
Khichari: cooked rice-and-lentil mixture.
Khir: milky rice flavored with cardamom or saffron, sometimes served with sauteed coconut, raisins, etc.
Kofta: chickpea or **mung** flour fritters mixed with vegetables or white cheese, raisins and cashew nuts.
Kofta ka salan: meatballs in curry sauce.

Kofte ki sabzi: kofta served with a spicy yoghurt or tomato sauce.
Korma: small pieces of mutton cooked with spices.
Kulfi: ice cream made with condensed milk and cardamom.

L

Ladu: sweet wheatflour or lentil balls with clarified butter and dried fruit.
Lahsuni murg tikka: chicken marinated with spices and garlic.

M

Majan: **bari** made with condensed milk, Indian hemp and sugar.
Makki ke dokle: spicy maize balls, boiled and flavored, served with **urad.**
Makki ki roti: flat Indian bread made with maize flour.
Mala dosa: pancake stuffed with vegetables and dried fruit.
Malai: boiled top of the milk.
Malai kofta: spicy wheatflour balls, sauteed in milk fat and **ghee**.
Malpue: flat wheatflour Indian bread fried and dipped in syrup.
Masala dosa: **dosa** stuffed with potato and onions.
Matar paneer: dish made of green peas with small cubes of curd cheese in curry sauce.
Mawa: whole milk boiled until it solidifies.
Mawa kachori: round wheatflour fritter, sugared and stuffed with condensed milk and dried fruits, flavored with cardamom and saffron, fried and covered with syrup.
Mishi mawa: cardamom-flavored condensed milk pudding, sometimes served with almonds and pistachio nuts.
Mulligautin: curry soup.
Mumal: flat bread or cakes made with dried fruit.
Mung: yellow lentils, with an edible green skin.
Murba: candied fruit.

N

Nan: flat, leavened, wholemeal Indian bread.

P

Pakora: salty and spicy chickpea flour fritter stuffed with vegetables and curd cheese.
Paneer: curd cheese.
Paneer butter masala: dish from the Punjab: small cubes of fried curd cheese, served with a spicy butter sauce.
Paneer ghevar: sweet balls made with milk and lemon.
Papar: flat crispy and peppery bread made with lentil flour, cumin- or clove-flavored.
Papri chat: Gujarati dish. Small flat wheatflour or lentil bread, fried and served with tamarind or spicy yoghurt. Sometimes flavored with mint, coriander leaves and green chilli pepper.
Parata: flat bread cooked in **ghee**.
Piste ki kulfi: pistachio nut **kulfi**.
Potato shop: chickpea flour and potato pancakes.
Pulav: rice cooked with spices, vegetables or meat.
Puri: fried flat wholemeal Indian bread.

R

Rab: salted, boiled maize flour dish, served with **chach** or yoghurt.
Raita: yoghurt with vegetables.
Ras malai: sweet balls made with curds, and flavored with various spices (cardamom, saffron, pistachio nuts, etc).
Rasgula: boiled white cheese balls covered with syrup.
Roghan gosht: lamb cooked in a yoghurt and tomato sauce.
Roti: flat bread made of wheatflour, maize flour, etc. Thicker than **chapati**.

S

Safed nan: white bread.
Sag roti: flat bread made of chickpea flour and spinach.
Samosa: wheatflour fritters stuffed with spicy cooked vegetables or minced meat.
Saubt: dried ginger.
Seed tukra: Sindhi dish. Sweet dish made of syrup, nutmeg, cardamom and clove.
Sevaiyan: grilled, sweetened vermicelli.
Sevaiyon ki khir: **sevaiyan** with milk.
Shahi: curry with almonds, pistachio and cashew nuts, and fresh cream.
Shami kabab: meatballs or balls made of lentils with onion stuffing.
Shati legumes: lentil dish served with flat bread.
Sheekh kabab: minced-meat kebab flavored with crushed spices.
Sonf: aniseed supposed to help the digestion.
Suji ka halwa: **halwa** made of wheat semolina.
Suji karkarias: semolina cake.

T–U

Tali saag: spiced spinach.
Tandoor: name of the oven in which *tandoori* dishes are cooked.
Tchola: chick pea.
Teri: rice cooked with spices and green peas.
Thali: metal dish or oval plate, or actual meal served on this dish.
Urad: white lentil with black skin.

DRINKS

Badam ki lassi: boiled milk made with almond and pistachio powder, with cardamom or saffron flavor.
Chach: buttermilk flavored with cumin and coriander. Can also be a savory drink.
Dahi: yoghurt, sometimes sour.
Fen: coconut or cashew nut milk.
Imli pani: spicy, sweet or savory tamarind drink.
Keri ki chach: boiled green mango drink, sweet and savory, spiced with red chilli pepper, cumin, etc.
Lassi: sweet or salty yoghurt or milk drink.
Tchaag: Tibetan beer made from rice.
Thandai: water and milk drink, with poppy seeds, and flavored with almonds, rose petals, melon and watermelon seeds and black pepper.

EAST: AJMER

HOTELS
- < £7/$10
- £7–22/$10–30
- £22–45/$30–65
- > £45/$65

Addresses are grouped into four zones:
East, page 326
North (Shekhavati), page 331
West, page 332
South, page 336
Towns are listed in alphabetical order within each zone, followed by a letter and number which correspond to the town's location on the map given at the beginning of the book. The diamond and number appearing in bold refer to the main part of the book.

A list of symbols is on page 313.

RTDC: Rajasthan Tourism Development Corporation

EAST

AJMER

F6 ▲162

→ RESTAURANTS

Bhola
Agra Gate
Sabzi Mandi
Tel. (0145) 238 44
Excellent thalis. Pure vegetarian Indian and Rajasthani food.

Honey Dew
Opposite the railway station.
Tel. (0145) 324 98
Vegetarian food. Pleasant garden.

Jai Hind
Opposite the railway station, Madar Gate, behind the clock tower.
Tel. (0145) 225 46
Has been serving tasty vegetarian dishes for almost three decades. Value for money. Pleasant surroundings.

Shish Mahal
Mansingh Hotel
Ana Sagar Road
Vaishali Nagar
Tel. (0145) 42 58 55
Excellente tandoori and Indian cuisine.

→ ACCOMMODATION

Ambassador
Ashok Marg
Tel. (0145) 52 50 95 or 42 84 79
21 rooms.

Khadim Hotel (RTDC)
Near the RPS Office
Civil Lines
Tel. (0145) 62 74 90 or 62 75 36
50 rooms, including 11 air-conditioned rooms. Dormitory.

Mansingh Hotel
Ana Sagar Road
Vaishali Nagar
Tel. (0145) 42 58 55, 42 59 56 or 42 57 02
Fax (0145) 33 08 78
112 rooms, including 50 air-conditioned double rooms. Conference hall and bar.

Prithvi Raj Hotel
Jaipur Road
Tel. (0145) 43 22 97 or 62 24 72
50 rooms, including 18 air-cooled double rooms and 2 air-conditioned rooms.

Regency Hotel
Delhi Gate
Tel. (0145) 62 02 96 or 62 24 39
56 rooms, including 7 air-conditioned double rooms, 8 ordinary double rooms, 3 suites. Conference hall.

ALWAR

H-I5 ▲ 168

→ ACCOMMODATION

Aravalli Hotel
Tel. (0144) 33 216, or 33 28 83
Fax (0144) 33 20 11
Visits and trekking in the Sariska Reserve in advance. 28 rooms.

Meenal Hotel (RTDC)
Tel. (0144) 228 52
6 rooms.

BAR

56 miles southwest of Ajmer.

→ ACCOMMODATION

Motel Bar (RTDC)
On the NH 8 between Jaipur and Jodhpur
Tel. (02937) 42 24
2 rooms.

BEHROR

H4

→ ACCOMMODATION

Rajasthan Motel Behror
On the NH 8 between Jaipur and Delhi
Tel. (01494) 200 87
10 rooms, 3 of which are air-conditioned. Restaurant.

BHANDAREJ

Approximately 37 miles east of Jaipur

→ ACCOMMODATION

Bhadrawati Palace Hotel
In the Dausa District
Tel. (01427) 83 51
Located outside the town, on the road between Agra and Jaipur. The restaurant, the Shish Mahal, serves international cuisine. 25 rooms.

LAKSHMI VILAS PALACE HOTEL

BHARATPUR

I5 ▲ 300

→ RESTAURANTS

Deepali
Park Palace Hotel
Kumher Gate
Tel. (05644) 232 22
Restaurant that serves Indian and Rajasthani cuisine. Vegetarian dishes.

Kohinoor
Near the Power House
Tel. (05644) 237 33
Open 8am–8pm
Vegetarian and non-vegetarian Indian cuisine.

Spoon Bill
Near Saras Hotel
Tel. (05644) 235 71
Open 8am–8pm
Indian, Chinese and Continental cuisine. Vegetarian and non-vegetarian dishes.

→ ACCOMMODATION

Eagle's Nest Hotel
Tel. (05644) 251 44
Campfire upon request. More expensive in high season. 12 rooms.

Forest Lodge
Keoladeo National Park
Tel. (05644) 227 22 or 227 60
Fax (05644) 228 64
More expensive in high season. 17 rooms.

Govind Niwas
Gol Bagh Road
Tel. (05644) 232 47
Set in an old colonial-style house. 6 rooms.

Lakshmi Vilas Palace Hotel
Kakaji ki Kothi
Tel. (05644) 252 59
Fax (05644) 252 59
Heritage Hotel
Hundred-year-old palace near the Keoladeao Ghana Bird Sanctuary and set in landscaped gardens. It is only one hour's drive from Agra and the Taj Mahal. 22 rooms.

Park Palace Hotel
Kumher Gate
Tel. (05644) 232 22
or 237 83
Fax (05644) 231 70
Bright, airy rooms.

Saras Hotel (RTDC)
Fatehpur Sikri Road
Tel. (05644) 237 00
25 rooms.
Dormitory.

Spoon Bill Hotel
Near Saras Hotel
Tel. (05644) 235 71
Ideal for bird lovers, who can hire bicycles and binoculars here. Books are also available on the various species living in the region. In winter evenings you can sit around a campfire.
2 rooms.

Tourist Guest House
Near Saras Circle
Tel. (05644) 254 02
Arranges bird-watching outings.
4 rooms and 2 tents.

JAIPUR

H5-6 ▲ *130*.
See also the map provided at the end of the book

→ RESTAURANTS

Aangan
Holiday Inn Jaipur
Amer Road
Tel. (0141) 63 50 00
Open noon–3.30pm, 7.30pm–11.30pm
Typical Rajasthani ambience. Serves authentic Mughal cuisine.

Angithi Maharani Palace
Station Road
Tel. (0141) 37 41 04
Barbecue in the poolside terrace garden.

Annapurna
C-20, Radha Marg
C-Scheme
Near the Raj Mandir Cinema
Tel. (0141) 36 87 59
or 37 13 05
Vegetarian Indian, Rajasthani and Gujarati specialties.

Aravalli
Jaipur Ashok Hotel
Jai Singh Circle
Bani Park
Tel. (0141) 32 00 91
or 32 00 98
Vegetarian Indian and continental cuisine.

Bhuwaneshwari
Bissau Palace Hotel
Opposite Chandpol
Tel. (0141) 30 43 71
Fax (0141) 30 46 28
Open 6am–11pm
Royal dining room with intimate atmosphere. Serves Rajasthani special dishes.

Chandralok
MI Road
Above Lakshmi Commercial Bank
Traditional Rajasthani vegetarian food.

Chandravansh Pavilion
Rajputana Palace Sheraton
Palace Road
Tel. (0141) 36 00 11
Open all day
Serves Indian (all regional cuisines), Western (French, English, Italian), and Indian and Chinese vegetarian food.

Chanakya
2AB, MI Road
Tel. (0141) 37 61 61
Open noon–11pm
Cuisine from Rajasthan and northern India. Specialities: paneer butter masala *and* malai kofta.

Copper Chimney
Tel. (0141) 37 22 75
Opposite the General Post Office
MI Road
Open 12.30–3.30pm and 6.30–11pm
An air-conditioned restaurant serving Indian and Mughal food and vegetarian dishes.

Garden Cafe
A-6, Mahaveer Marg
C-Scheme
Tel. (0141) 62 08 11
11am–11pm (summer),
10am–10pm (winter).
An open-air fast food outlet, serving South Indian food, burgers, pizzas, drinks, and ice cream. Casual décor, friendly atmosphere.

Gauri
Gangaur Hotel
Hathroi Fort Road
off MI Road
Tel. (0141) 37 16 41
Open 7am–1pm
Serves Indian and Chinese food. Air-conditioned.

Golden Sands
Sansar Chandra Rd
Tel. (0141) 37 05 31
Quality Indian food in pleasant surroundings.

Gulab Mahal
Jai Mahal Palace
Civil Lines
Jacob Road
Tel. (0141) 37 16 16
Open for lunch and dinner.
The service is elegant and refined. Managed by the Taj Group, the cuisine ranges from continental to Indian. It has the best Rajasthani thali *in town. The typical local fare includes* lahsuni murg tikka, alu mangori, *and* safed naans.

Jal Mahal
Rajputana Palace Sheraton
Palace Road
Tel. (0141) 36 00 11
Open 6.30–10am, noon–3pm, 7–11pm
Buffet restaurant.

Khasa Rasoda
Maharani Farms
Durgapura
An open-air restaurant where guests can sit on the terrace. Dinner is served by candlelight.

Lakshmi Misthan Bhandar ▲ *143*
Johari Bazaar
Tel. (0141) 56 58 44
Open 8am–10.30pm
Specializes in North Indian cuisine. Vegetarian dishes are also available. It is the largest confectioner of Indian sweets. Its most popular items include: ras malai, paneer ghevar *and* mishi mawa.

Niros Restaurant
MI Road
Tel. (0141) 37 44 93
or 37 18 74
Open 9.30–11pm
Air-conditioned restaurant. Serves Mughal, continental, and Chinese cuisine as well as tandoori and vegetarian dishes. Moderately priced.

Palms
Holiday Inn Jaipur
Amer Road
Tel. (0141) 63 50 00
Serves continental and Indian cuisine.

Shivir
Mansingh Hotel
Sansar Chander Road
Tel. (0141) 37 87 71
Fax (0141) 37 75 82
Open 12.30–3pm and 7.30–11.30pm
A rooftop restaurant in a contemporary luxury hotel. Shivir offers a pretty view of the city. An array of succulent meats and poultry dishes. Don't miss the mumal *(dessert).*

HOTELS
- ⚀ < £7/$10
- ⚁ £7–22/$10–30
- ⚂ £22–45/$30–65
- ⚃ > £45/$65

Surya Mahal
MI Road
Tel. (0141) 36 98 40
or 37 18 62
Fax (0141) 36 63 23
Multi-cuisine, including South Indian, Indian, Chinese and continental food. Also serves pizzas, snacks, and shakes. Fast and efficient service.

Zaika
Uniara Fort
near Trimurti
JN Road
Tel. (0141) 62 03 86
Located in the haveli, it serves multi-cuisine in a quiet, pleasing atmosphere.

→ ACCOMMODATION
Youth Hostel
Near the stadium
Tel. (0141) 37 33 11

Paying guest scheme
COL. O. P. DRALL
61, Hathroi Fort
Tel. (0141) 37 65 25
⚀

GHARONDA
C-14, Jyoti Marg
Bapu Nagar
Tel. (0141) 51 56 73

HEMANT GOYAL
B-119, Kabir Marg
Bani Park
Tel. (0141) 31 78 23
⚀

MADAME BHAGWATI INDRA NARAIH
C-267, Bhabha Marg
Tilak Nagar
Tel. (0141) 62 21 85
Situated near Ganesh Temple and Moti Dungri Palace. Rooms with or without bathrooms. Mrs Pandey prepares vegetarian meals herself. Cable television available.
⚀

MADAME KAMLA SINGH GAUR
24-B, Ganesh Colony
Imliwala Pathak
Jyoti Nagar
Tel. (0141) 51 38 03
⚀

M. BHUVANESHWARI KUMARI
9 Barwara Colony
Civil Lines
Tel. (0141) 38 17 96
⚀

M. S. D. KULSHRESHTHA
B-33 Sethi Colony
Tel. (0141) 60 45 70
⚁

Hotels
Achrol House
Jacob Road –
Civil Lines
Tel. (0141) 38 21 54
Heritage Hotel
This hotel is of 1930 Rajasthani vintage and is set in a large garden.
7 rooms.
⚁

Aditya Hotel
2 Bhawani Singh Road
Tel. (0141) 38 17 20
Fax (0141) 38 17 30
Rajasthani folk dance and songs on request.
24 rooms.
⚂

Arya Niwas
Sansar Chandra Road
Behind Amber Tower
Tel. (0141) 36 85 24
Fax (0141) 36 43 76
Old palace renovated in haveli style, with typical Jaipur-style façade, veranda and courtyards.
70 rooms.
⚁

Bissau Palace Hotel ▲ *145*
Opposite Chandpol
near the Saroj Cinema
Tel. (0141) 30 43 71
or 30 43 91
Fax (0141) 30 46 28
Heritage Hotel
Situated in the foothills of Tiger Fort, this is the traditional summer residence of the Rawal of Bissau. It has a private museum displaying portraits, armory, and jewelry. The restaurant serves Indian, continental, and Rajasthani specialties. Folk dances and sitar recitals are staged.
⚁

Choki Dhani
Tonk Road
Tel. (0141) 55 35 34
Fax (0141) 38 18 88
Newly built resort with multi-cuisine restaurant, swimming pool, bar, riding and in-house boating facilities.

Clark's Amer Hotel
Jawahar Lal Nehru Marg
Tel. (0141) 55 06 16
Fax (0141) 55 00 13
Close to the city and only five minutes away from the airport, the hotel is situated amid lush green surroundings.
202 rooms.
⚂

Diggi Palace
Hospital Road
Shivaji Marg
Tel. (0141) 37 30 91
Fax (0141) 37 03 59
A family-run hotel set in an 18th-century haveli, with a 30,000 square foot lawn. 45 rooms, 15 air-conditioned and the rest provided with fans and air coolers; all have running hot and cold water. Horse-riding available. Five minutes walk from the city walls.
⚁

Durg Nahargarh (RTDC)
Tel. (0141) 32 05 38
⚀

Fort Uniara
Near Trimurti
JN Road
Tel. (0141) 62 06 68
or 62 03 86
A 12-roomed haveli hotel located on the road to the airport.
⚁

Gangaur Hotel (RTDC)
MI Road
Tel. (0141) 37 16 41
or 37 16 42
63 rooms.
⚁

Holiday Inn Jaipur
Amer Road
Tel. (0141) 63 50 00
Fax (0141) 63 56 00
Hotel with traditional haveli structure – a central inner courtyard and open corridors.
72 rooms and suites.
⚂

Jai Mahal Palace Hotel
Jacob Road
Civil Lines
Tel. (0141) 37 16 16
Fax (0141) 36 52 37
Built in 1745 in typical palace fashion with high domed chhatris and cupolas and intricate latticework. The hotel is a fine blend of Mughal and Rajput styles. Most rooms have a panoramic view of the beautifully landscaped Mughal gardens.
102 rooms.
⚃

Jaipur Ashok Hotel
Jai Singh Circle
Bani Park
Tel. (0141) 20 44 94
Fax (0141) 20 49 91
In the heart of town. Rajasthani folk dance performances every evening.
99 rooms.
⚂

Jaipur Palace Hotel
Tonk Road
Tel. (0141) 51 29 61
Fax (0141) 51 29 66
A modern hotel with a palace look. Located 3 miles from the city. Serves Indian, continental and Chinese food.
59 rooms.
⚂

Karan's Guest House
D-70 Shiv Heera Path
Chomu House
C-Scheme
Tel. (0141) 38 00 81
Fax (0141) 38 28 10
Guesthouse offering deluxe comforts at a budget price.
8 rooms.

Khasa Kothi Hotel
MI Road
Tel. (0141) 37 51 51 or 37 51 55
Fax (0141) 37 40 40
Located in the heart of the city, close to the railway station and bus stand. This is a regal white mansion set among tall, century-old trees. It was the summer palace of the former Maharaja of Jaipur. Dance performances and folk songs can be arranged on request.
36 rooms with fans.

Lakshmi Vilas
Sawai Ram Singh Road
Tel. (0141) 38 15 67 or (0141) 38 15 69
22 rooms.

LMB Hotel
Johari Bazaar
Tel. (0141) 56 58 44
Fax (0141) 56 21 76
Very good restaurant with a kitsch, 1950s décor. Exceptional service.
33 rooms.

Madhuban
D-237 Behari Marg.
Bani Park
Tel. (0141) 20 00 33 or 20 54 27
Fax (0141) 20 23 44
Open all year round.
Restaurant.
Charming guest-house. Rooms decorated in local style. Garden. Fine cuisine.

JAI MAHAL PALACE HOTEL

Maharani Palace
Station Road
Tel. (0141) 20 43 78
Fax (0141) 20 21 12
Located close to the railway station, this is a modern hotel with well-furnished rooms and a rooftop swimming pool. Barbecue served in the terrace garden, and multi-cuisine restaurant.

Mandawa Haveli
Sansar Chandra Road
Reservations :
Tel. (0141) 40 60 81 or 37 52 19
Fax (0141) 40 60 82
This haveli was built in 1896 by the Mandawa family, to whom it still belongs.
28 rooms.

Mansingh Hotel
Sansar Chander Road
Tel. (0141) 37 87 71
Fax (0141) 37 75 82
A contemporary luxury hotel that caters to foreign tourists and local business groups. 8 miles from airport, 2 miles from railway station.
91 rooms.

Megh Niwas
C-9 Jai Singh Highway
Bani Park
Tel. (0141) 20 26 61 or 20 20 18
Fax (0141) 20 24 20
Small, top-quality hotel offering good food and personalized service. Puppet shows can be arranged on request. Air-cooled and air-conditioned rooms.

Narain Niwas Palace ▲ *145*
Kanota Bagh
Narain Singh Road
Tel. (0141) 56 12 91
Fax (0141) 56 10 45
Heritage Hotel
Former residence of the Kanota princes. One of the finest hotels in town. Restaurant located next to Diwan-i-Khas.
36 rooms.

Rajmahal Palace Hotel ▲ *145*
Sardar Patel Marg
Tel. (0141) 38 16 25
Fax (0141) 38 18 87 or 38 17 57
Heritage Hotel
Set amid 15 acres of lush green lawns, it was built in 1729 by Sawai Jai Singh of Jaipur for his favorite queen. From 1821, the palace functioned as the residence of the British Ambassador, and in 1956 Maharaja Sawai Man Singh II renovated and renamed this palace, which served as his residence until his death. Throughout that period, it was patronized by the "old" aristocracy – Queen Elizabeth II – as well as the "new" – Jackie Kennedy.
12 rooms.

Rajputana Palace Sheraton
Palace Road
Tel. (0141) 40 11 40
Fax (0141) 40 11 23
Welcomgroup
Modern, constructed along the lines of traditional haveli architecture.
1 presidential suite.
218 rooms.

Raj Vilas
Goner Road
Near the Agra Road
Tel. (0141) 64 01 01
Fax (0141) 64 02 02
Oberoi group
Three styles of accommodation are on offer: in the former palace, in small independent luxury cottages (with bathroom, cuisine, three rooms), or under air-conditioned tents. The old Shankar temple within the complex is currently being restored. Absolutely charming.

Rambagh Palace ▲ *144*
Bhawani Singh Road
Tel. (0141) 38 19 19
Fax (0141) 38 10 98
Set in 47 acres of fine gardens, this palace is the former residence of the Maharajah of Jaipur and one of the oldest and most prestigious palaces in India. A visit is an absolute must even if you decide not to stay.
106 rooms.

Rose Hotel
B-6 Subhash Nagar
Shopping Center
Tel. (0141) 30 54 22 or 30 60 44
Fax (0141) 30 53 28
Personalized welcome.

HOTELS
- < £7/$10
- £7–22/$10–30
- £22–45/$30–65
- > £45/$65

Saket
Opposite Udyog Bhawan,
C-Scheme
Tel. and fax
(0141) 38 17 69
Restaurant serves Indian, continental, and Chinese cuisine.
39 rooms.

Samode Haveli ▲ *145*
Gangapole Street
Tel. (0141) 470 68
Fax (0141) 60 23 70
Heritage Hotel
Situated just outside Jaipur, this is one of the most charming hotels in town. Original haveli décor of mosaics, mirrors and frescos.
22 rooms.

Swagatam Hotel (RTDC)
Station Road
Tel. (0141) 20 05 95
39 rooms.

Teej Hotel (RTDC)
Sawai Singh Highway
Tel. (0141) 20 05 95
Dormitory.
42 rooms.

The Royal Castle
A-70 Jai Ambey Nagar
Tonk Road
Tel. and fax
(0141) 55 14 25
Pleasant surroundings. Each room is decorated differently, in the style of a particular Rajasthani town.
10 rooms.

The Trident
Oberoi Group
Amber Road
Tel. (0141) 63 01 01
Fax (0141) 63 03 03
Decorated in the style of a Rajput palace, this superb hotel looks down over the Jal Mahal's lake.

Tourist Hotel (RTDC)
Opposite the main post office (GPO)
MI Road
Tel. (0141) 36 02 38
Dormitory. 40 rooms.

JAMWA RAMGARH

Approximately 27 miles east of Jaipur
→ **ACCOMMODATION**
The Ramgarh Lodge
Tel. (0141) 26 22 17
Fax (0141) 38 10 98
Situated on the shores of the famous Ramgarh Lake, 24 miles from Jaipur, this was the hunting lodge of the former rulers of Jaipur. An idyllic retreat, it gives an idea of how royalty "roughed it". Beautiful prints of hunting scenes decorate the walls of the rooms and corridors. Recreation facilities include tennis, squash, and billiards. Breakfast and either lunch or dinner included.

KANOTA

Approximately 9½ miles east of Jaipur
→ **ACCOMMODATION**
Royal Castle
Agra Road
Tel. (0141) 56 12 91
Fax (0141) 56 34 48
This 18th-century fort offers a unique opportunity to enjoy village life. The special attraction here is the library, with a collection of 10,000 rare books, manuscripts, miniature paintings, old arms, buggies, and saddlery.

KARAULI

I6 ▲ *312*
→ **ACCOMMODATION**
Bhanwar Vilas Palace
Sawai Madhopur District
Tel. (07464) 200 24
Reservations in Jaipur: Karauli House, New Sanganer Road
Sodala
Tel. (0141) 36 75 32
Fax (0141) 38 28 10
A delightful location if you want to participate in camel, horse, and Jeep safaris.
20 rooms. Tents available on request.

KESROLI

Approximately 7½ miles from Alwar
→ **RESTAURANT**
The Hill Fort
Tel. (0144) 813 12
Reservations in Delhi:
Tel. (011) 461 61 45
Fax (011) 462 11 12
Open 1–3pm and 8–10pm
Specializes in Indian and continental cuisine.

→ **ACCOMMODATION**
The Hill Fort
Tel. (0144) 823 12
Reservations in Delhi:
Tel. (011) 461 61 45
Fax (011) 462 11 12
A fort located on top of a hill, with a commanding view of the countryside. Medieval Rajasthani architecture. Basic comfort.
10 rooms.

KISHANGARH

G6 ▲ *166*
→ **ACCOMMODATION**
Phool Mahal Palace
Kishangarh
Tel. (01463) 47 405
Fax (01463) 42 001
www.royalkishangar.com
White lakeside palace. Restaurant and many activities: yoga, massage, trekking, safaris…
14 air-conditioned rooms.

Rupangarh Fort
16½ miles from Kishangarh
Tel. (01463) 20 217
Fax (01463) 42 001
15 double rooms and one suite.

MAHUWA

Approximately 37 miles west of Bharatpur
→ **ACCOMMODATION**
Motel Mahuwa (RTDC)
NH 11, Jaipur–Agra
Tel. (07461) 332 60
4 rooms. Dormitory.

Rajasthan Motel Mahuwa
NH 11 Jaipur-Agra
Tel. (07461) 332 10
Fax (07461) 331 88
6 rooms, 2 of which are air conditioned.

NIMAJ

Approximately 66 miles southwest of Ajmer
→ **ACCOMMODATION**
Jagram Durg (Fort)
Pali District
Tel. (02939) 65 22

NIMRANA

H4 ▲ *178*
→ **ACCOMMODATION**
Nimrana Fort Palace
▲ *178*
Tel. (01491) 60 07
Reservations in Delhi:
Tel. (011) 461 61 45
Fax (011) 462 11 12
Heritage Hotel
Built in 1464, Neemrana Fort Palace is Rajasthan's closest palace to New Delhi, two hours' drive away on the Delhi–Jaipur highway. The rooms in this reconstructed fort-palace are furnished with an eclectic mix of traditional Indian and colonial furniture, antiques and objets d'art.

PUSHKAR

F6 ▲ *164*
→ **RESTAURANT**
Prince's Restaurant
Hotel Pushkar Palace

Tel. (0145) 720 01
Offers a lovely view of the lake. Terrace garden. Can seat up to 50 people at a time. Serves a large variety of vegetarian cuisine.

→ **ACCOMMODATION**
Colonel's Desert Camp
Tel. (01457) 24 07
Reservations in Jaipur:
Megh Niwas
C-9 Jai Singh Highway
Bani Park
Tel. (0141) 32 26 61 or 32 10 18
Fax (0141) 32 14 20
Open Oct.–Mar.
Tents with and without bathrooms. Excellent cuisine. Dancing shows. Camel and horse safaris.

Pushkar Palace Hotel
Tel. (0145) 720 01 or 724 01
Fax (0145) 722 26
Overlooking a lake, this heritage property was built around 400 years ago by the Maharaja of Kishangarh. The royal family would come here to take a holy dip in the lake. Camel, horse and Jeep safaris. 36 rooms.

Safari Club
Office:
High Court Colony
Jodhpur
Tel. (0291) 370 23
Fax (0291) 370 23
Experience living in a tent in the midst of the desert. Particularly worthwhile during the Pushkar Fair. The camp in Pushkar operates only during the fair. Book in advance. 30 tents with attached bathrooms.

Sarovar Hotel (RTDC)
Near the lake
Tel. (0145) 720 40 or 720 74
40 rooms.

Tourist Village (RTDC)
Pushkar–Nagaur Roadd
Tel. (0145) 720 74
28 rooms.

RAMGARH

G5 ▲ *190*
→ **ACCOMMODATION**
Jheel Tourist Hotel (RTDC)
Tel. (014262) 370
10 bungalows.

RANTHAMBHOR

H-I7 ▲ *304*
→ **ACCOMMODATION**
Safari Club
Office:
High Court Colony
Jodhpur
Tel. (0291) 370 23
Fax (0291) 370 23
Permanent camp. Included in the price are meals, accommodation, the crossing of Chambal River, guided tours and showing of documentaries.

SARISKA

▲ *174* I5
→ **ACCOMMODATION**
Sariska Palace Hotel
Alwar District
Tel. (0144) 41 322
Reservations:
1/1 – B
Mohammadpur
Bhikaji Cama Place
New Delhi
Tel. (011) 61 88 861
Fax (011) 61 88 862
Built between 1892 and 1900 by Maharaja Jai Singh of Alwar as a royal hunting lodge, it is now a modern hotel etched against the backdrop of the Sariska nature reserve. The palace uses original Louis XIV and Art Deco furniture. Offers many excursions. 49 rooms.

Tiger Den Hotel (RTDC)
Jaipur Road
Alwar District
Tel. (0144) 41 342
26 rooms.

SAWAI MADHOPUR

H7
→ **ACCOMMODATION**
Ankur Resorts
Ranthambhor Road
Tel. (07462) 207 92
Fax (07462) 206 97
Rooms air-conditioned or with cooler. Special price for double room and 2 "jungle rides" (trips into Ranthambore National Park).

Castle Jhoomar Baori (RTDC)
Ranthambhor Road
Tel. (07462) 204 95
12 rooms.

Sawai Madhopur Lodge
Ranthambhor National Park Road
Tel. (07462) 205 41
Fax. (07462) 207 18
Heritage Hotel
Ideal base visiting the Ranthambhor National Park. 16 rooms. 6 tents.

Tiger Den Resort
Ranthambor Road
Tel. (07462) 52070
Fax (07462) 207 02
www.tigerdenindia.cjb.net
18 cottages. 2 air-conditioned suites.

Tiger Moon Resort
Sawai Madhopur, on the Ranthambor road
Tel. (09122) 640 63 99
Fax (09122) 640 01 28
Bungalows set in picturesque undergrowth and equipped with all mod cons. The restaurant has a fireplace for cold winter evenings. 12 rooms.

SHAHPURA

G5
→ **ACCOMMODATION**
Motel Shahpura (RTDC)
Jaipur–Delhi Road
Tel. (01422) 22 64
2 rooms.

SILISERH

H5 ▲ *174*
→ **ACCOMMODATION**
Lake Palace Hotel (RTDC) ▲ *174*
Alwar District
Tel. (0144) 229 91
A lakeside castle that is now a hotel. This former royal residence has traditional Rajput and Islamic architecture. Dormitory. 10 rooms.

NORTH (SHEKHAVATI)

BAGGAR

G4 ▲ *183*
→ **ACCOMMODATION**
Piramal Haveli ▲ *183*
Tel. (01592) 22 20
Reservations:
A–58 Niramuddin Estate, New Delhi
Tel. (011) 46 16 145 or 46 18 962
Fax (011) 46 21 112
8 rooms.

DUNDLOD

▲ *182* G4
→ **ACCOMMODATION**
Dundlod Castle ▲ *182*
Fort
Tel. (01594) 521 80
Jaipur reservations:
Tel. (0141) 21 26 11
Fax (0141) 21 12 76
Heritage Hotel
The castle houses two hotels (owned by two brothers): the more pleasant Dundlod Castle and the Dera Dundlod Kila located respectively in the residential half of the castle and in the military section. This sometimes gives rise to some confusion amongst the guests. Safaris, shows. 22 rooms.

HOTELS
- < £7/$10
- £7–22/$10–30
- £22–45/$30–65
- > £45/$65

FATEHPUR
G4 ▲ 183

→ ACCOMMODATION

Ashirwad Palace
On the NH 11:
Bikaner–Fatehpur
Tel. (01571) 306 35
Rooms air-conditioned or with air cooler.

Hotel Haveli (RTDC)
On the NH 11:
Bikaner–Fatehpur
Tel. (01571) 202 93
9 rooms.

JHUNJHUNU
G4 ▲ 183

→ ACCOMMODATION

Jamuna Resort
Near Nathji ka Teela
Tel. (01592) 328 71
4 traditional, air-conditioned bungalows.

Sangam Hotel
Opposite the bus terminal
Tel. (01592) 325 44
Fax (01592) 340 63
30 rooms.

Shiv Shekhavati Hotel
Khemi Sadi Road
Near Muni Ashram
Tel. (01592) 326 51
Folk music and dance can be arranged on request.
20 rooms and a restaurant.

MANDAWA
G4 ▲ 182

→ ACCOMMODATION

Castle Mandawa
▲ 182.
Tel. (01592) 231 24
Fax (01592) 231 71
Heritage Hotel
Chariot, camel, and horse rides are available. Jeep rides can be arranged on request. Folk dances and puppet shows.
70 rooms.

The Desert Resort
Tel. (01592) 231 51
(Castle Mandawa)
Reservations in Jaipur:
306, Anukampa Tower, Church Road
Tel. (0141) 37 41 12
Fax (0141) 37 20 84
51 cottages built as a mud-walled tourist hamlet on a sand dune overlooking the desert. Traditional frescos and local crafts give the place a special ambience.

MUKUNGARH
Approximately 5½ miles from Dundlod

→ ACCOMMODATION

Mukundgah Fort
Tel. (015945) 523 96 or 523 97
Fax (015945) 523 95
Heritage Hotel
52 rooms.

NAWALGARH
G4 ▲ 182

→ RESTAURANT

Roop Niwas Palace
Tel. (01504) 220 08
Serves fixed menus and à la carte. Vegetarian and non-vegetarian Indian and Rajasthani cuisine.

→ ACCOMMODATION

Apani Dhani
Jhunjhunu Road
Tel. (01594) 222 39
Fax (01592) 240 61
Traditional "mud/straw architecture" of Rajasthan in the middle of an ecological farm. All huts have attached organic toilets. 10 rooms with ceiling fans and coolers. Hot water available; heated by solar panels. Serves Indian and Rajasthani vegetarian food. About half a mile east of Apani Dhani.

Jangid Haveli Hotel
Behind Maur Hospital
Tel. (01594) 24 060
Fax (01594) 24 061
5 double rooms with ceiling fans and coolers. The family kitchen serves Indian and Rajasthani vegetarian food.

Roop Niwas Palace
Tel. (01594) 220 08
Heritage Hotel
Situated in the heart of Shekhavati, the hotel is a blend of European and Rajput styles of architecture. Camel and horse rides, puppet shows, folk dances, and jeep drives on request. 30 rooms with ceiling fans and air coolers.

PACHERI BADI

→ RESTAURANT

Aravali Resorts
On the Jaipur–Mandawa road, just after the Rajasthan border.
Tel. (01593) 715 01
Friendly restaurant between Narnaul (11 miles) and Singhana (9½ miles).

RATANGARH
F4

→ ACCOMMODATION

Midway Kurja
On the NH 11:
Jaipur–Bikaner
Tel. (01567) 228 73
Convenient stop between Mandawa and Bikaner. Restaurant.
2 rooms.

Motel Chinkara (RTDC)
On the NH 11:
Jaipur–Bikaner
Tel. (01567) 222 86

SAMODE
H5 ▲ 180

→ RESTAURANT

Shish Mahal ▲ 181
This is worth a visit, if just to see the stunning "Palace of Mirrors". Food is good too.

→ ACCOMMODATION

Samode Bagh
Jaipur reservations:
Tel. (0141) 60 24 07
Fax (0141) 60 23 70
Heritage Hotel
This Mughal-style garden near the palace (just under 2 miles) has 40 tents with attached bathroom.

Samode Palace ▲ 180
Tel. (0141) 913 441 23
Jaipur reservations:
Tel. (0141) 63 24 07
Fax (0141) 63 10 68
Heritage Hotel
Charming 19th-century palace 25 miles outside Jaipur on the Jaipur–Sikar route. Live Rajasthani folk music every evening, folk dances on request.
35 rooms.

WEST

BIKANER
E4 ▲ 192

→ RESTAURANTS

Amber
Station Road
Tel. (0151) 618 61
Fax (0151) 52 31 04
Moderately priced. Vegetarian Indian and Rajasthani cuisine. Try the cheese cutlets, cheese naan and shahi *vegetables.*

Annapurna
Mahatma Gandhi Rd
Tel. (0151) 276 74
South Indian and continental dishes. Enjoys an excellent reputation.

Chotu Motu
Station Road
Tel. (0151) 446 66
Local fare and Indian vegetarian dishes.

Dhola Maru
Restaurant of the Dhola Maru Hotel
Puran Singh Circle
Near Gandhi Path
Tel. (0151) 52 96 21
Vegetarian and non-vegetarian Indian and Rajasthani cuisine.

Dining Room
Lalgarh Palace
Tel. (0151) 52 21 05
Open 7–10am, 1–3pm and 7.30–10pm
Serves Indian, continental, and Rajasthani specialties.

Lakshmi Niwas
Near Lalgarh Palace
Tel. (0151) 250 20
Indian and Rajasthani specialties.

→ ACCOMMODATION

Bhanwar Niwas
Rampuria Mohalla
Tel. (0151) 52 93 23
Fax (0151) 618 80
Heritage Hotel
A luxurious hotel, whose architecture and décor are a fascinating potpourri of Indian and European styles. This haveli has beautiful public areas and 14 stunningly appointed rooms.

Dhola Maru Hotel (RTDC)
Puran Singh Circle
Near Gandhi Path
Tel. (0151) 52 96 21
27 rooms.
Dormitory.

LALGARH PALACE, BIKANER

Heritage Resort
Jaipur–Bikaner Highway
Tel. (0151) 75 22 34 or 75 26 27
Fax (0151) 20 76 74
Charming, comfortable, well-kept hotel. Restaurant and bar. Safaris by Jeep or camel.
36 rooms.

Inder Lodge
Opposite Tata Co.
GS Road
Tel. (0151) 52 48 13
20 rooms.

Karni Bhawan Palace Hotel
Tel. (0151) 52 47 01, 52 47 02, 52 47 03, 52 47 04 or 52 47 05
Fax (0151) 52 24 08
This modern residence was built by His Late Highness Dr Karni Singhji of Bikaner in Art Deco style.
15 rooms.

Lalgarh Palace ▲ *198*
Ganga Avenue Road
Tel. (0151) 52 21 05
Fax (0151) 52 22 53
Heritage Hotel
Indo-Saracenic-style palace set amid sprawling lawns.
40 rooms.
Breakfast included.

Laxmi Niwas Palace
Ganga Avenue Road
Tel. (0151) 52 52 19
Fax (0151) 20 27 77
www.lalgarthpalace.com
Heritage Hotel
In the same palace as the Lalgarth hotel. Beautiful inner courtyard, restaurant, bar.
31 rooms.

Meghsar Castle
Opposite MS Hostel
8 Gajner Road
Tel. (0151) 52 73 15
Fax (0151) 52 20 41
10 clean and spacious rooms. Excellent food.

Sagar Hotel
Lalgarh Palace
Compas
Tel. (0151) 52 06 77
Fax (0151) 20 18 77
22 rooms in a very friendly hotel. Also offers high-quality cuisine.

Thar Hotel
Hospital Road
Ambedkar Circle
Tel. (0151) 271 80
Safaris and desert treks can be arranged.
30 rooms.

DESHNOKE

E4 ▲ *207*

→ ACCOMMODATION

Y Atriki Niwas
Near Karni Mata Temple
10 rooms.

DHAMI

E4 ▲ *206*

→ ACCOMMODATION

Fort Dhami
Via Kherwa Pali District
Tel. (02935) 67 739
Fax (02935) 35 69 59
Renovated and decorated in 1985 in traditional style. Safaris on horseback or by four-by-four. Folk dancing on request.
15 rooms.

GAJNER

E4 ▲ *206*

→ ACCOMMODATION

Gajner Palace ▲ *206*
Tel. (0151) 55 063 or 55 064
Fax (0151) 522 408
Hotel, built of red sandstone, located beside a lake.
39 well-equipped rooms.

JAISALMER

B5 ▲ *209*

→ RESTAURANTS

8th July
Tel. (02992) 531 64
Located in the fort, it overlooks the main square. Offers an extensive and imaginative menu.

Fort View
Fort View Hotel
Gola Chowk
Tel. (02992) 522 14
Enjoy a meal or just a drink at this rooftop hotel restaurant. One of the most popular hotels in Jaisalmer. View of the fort from every table.

Gay Time
Gandhi Chowk
Vegetarian Indian and Rajasthani food.

Kalpana
Gandhi Chowk
Tel. (02992) 524 69
Punjabi cuisine and tandoori dishes.

Moti Mahal
Opposite Salim Singh ki Haveli
Tel. (02992) 526 77, 530 77 or 520 49
Non-vegetarian and vegetarian meals. Excellent and inexpensive.

Natraj
Opposite Salim Singh ki Haveli
Tel. (02992) 526 67
Beer bar with a terrace. High-quality Indian food.

The Trio
Mandir Palace
Gandhi Chowk
Tel. (02992) 527 33
Fax (02992) 527 78
Open 6am–midnight
Indian, Chinese, and Western cuisine. Delicious food, good service, and a very pleasant atmosphere. Offers a panoramic view of the fort. Assistance provided for camel and Jeep safaris into the heart of the Thar Desert. Live folk music.

Top Deck
Gandhi Chowk
Tel. (02992) 532 44
Restaurant with a terrace with a good

HOTELS
- < £7/$10
- £7–22/$10–30
- £22–45/$30–65
- > £45/$65

view of the fort. Varied cuisine. Reasonably priced.

→ **ACCOMMODATION**

Fort View Hotel
Gola Chowk
Tel. (02992) 522 14
Perched on a terrace. Ask for a room with a view. Basic comfort and reasonable prices.

Gorbandh Palace
1 Tourist Complex
Samm Road
Tel. (02992) 515 11
Fax (02992) 527 49
Inspired by the fort, this hotel is built of yellow sandstone. Lying a couple of miles outside the city, it is a tranquil hideaway. The only hotel in Jaisalmer with a swimming pool.
67 air-conditioned rooms.

Heritage Inn Hotel
Samm Road, BP 43
Tel. (02992) 527 69
Fax (02992) 516 38
36 rooms and 6 family suites with modern amenities.

Himmatgarh Palace Hotel
1 Ramgarh Road
Tel. (02992) 520 02
Fax (02992) 520 05
Built of the same yellow sandstone as the fort and situated opposite the Vyas Chhatris, this hotel has a spectacular view of the entire fort.
35 rooms.

Jaisal Castle Hotel
Fort
Tel. (02992) 523 62
A highly interesting place to stay within the fort. You can watch the sunrises and sunsets from the roof.
10 rooms.

Jawahar Niwas Palace
Amarsagar Road
Tel. (02992) 522 08
Fax (02992) 510 63
26 rooms.

Laughing Camel Inn
Near Hanuman Circle
Tel. (02992) 531 64
Air-cooled rooms.

JAISALMER

Moomal Hotel (RTDC)
Amar Sagar Road
Near the bus terminal
Tel. (02992) 523 92
Reservations:
RTDC Jaipur
Tel. (0141) 20 25 86
Fax (0141) 20 10 45
56 rooms.

Narayan Niwas Palace
Malka Prol
Near Ramesh Takies
Tel. (02992) 524 08
or 526 01
Fax (02992) 521 01
43 rooms, including 5 air-conditioned, and 33 air-cooled.

Pleasure Hotel
Near the Bank of Baroda
Gandhi Chowk
Tel. (02992) 52323
15 rooms, air-cooled and with ceiling fans.

Sona Hotel
Majdoor Para
Tel. and fax
(02992) 52 468
55 rooms, 2 with air-conditioning.

Suraj Hotel
Behind the Jain temple inside the fort
Tel. (02992) 530 23
Located inside the fort, the havelis, which is more than 500 years old, has retained its original paintings and carvings. It is the second highest point in the fort.
10 beds.

JHALAMAND

Approximately 6 miles from Jodhpur

→ **RESTAURANT**

Jhalamand Garh
Reservations in Jodhpur:
TGS Office
Jhalamand House
Airport Road
Tel. (0291) 740 481
Fax (0291) 741 125
Traditional and continental cuisine. Delightful garden and beautiful terrace.

→ **ACCOMMODATION**

Jhalamand Garh
Jodhpur reservations:
TGS Office
Jhalamand House
Airport Road
Tel. (0291) 74 04 81
Fax (0291) 741 125
18th-century fort. Traditional music performances. Horse, camel and Jeep safaris.

JODHPUR

E6 ▲ 220

→ **RESTAURANTS**

Balsamand Lake Palace ▲ 232
Mandore Road
Tel. (0291) 455 91
Fax (0291) 542 240
Dine on Indian and Western vegetarian and non-vegetarian cuisine in an exceptional setting. The restaurant is in the beautiful old Lake Palace.

Courtyard Restaurant
Ajit Bhawan
Palace Hotel
Opposite Circuit House
Tel. (0291) 612 410
Fax (0291) 437 774
Open 7.30–10.30pm
Exquisitely intricate latticework stone screens and turbaned men recreate the charismatic atmosphere of the legendary past with daily folk music and dance performances. Serves Indian and Rajasthani cuisine, including vegetarian food.

Kalinga
Station Road
Tel. (0291) 240 66
or 269 39
Open 7am–10pm
Serves Rajasthani, South Indian, Gujarati, continental, and Chinese food. Children's menu available.

Khamaghani
Ratanada
Polo Palace hotel
Presidency Road
Tel. (0291) 319 10
Continental, Indian and Chinese cuisine.

Marwar Hall
Umaid Bhawan
Palace Hotel
Tel. (0291) 433 316
Fax (0291) 635 373
Chinese, Indian, continental and Rajasthani cuisine. Buffet.

Midtown
Opposite the railway station
The best restaurant in town serving Chinese, Indian, and vegetarian cuisine. Dinner-show on the terrace. Reasonably priced and air-conditioned.

On the Rock
Ajit Bhawan
Palace Hotel
Opposite Circuit House

Tel. (0291) 612 410
Fax (0291) 437 774
Open 7.30–10.30pm
A garden restaurant with rocky surroundings and fountains. Serving barbecue, Indian food and tandooris. Concerts.

Reggie's Restaurant
Near the Safari Club
High Court Colony
Tel. and fax
(0291) 437 023
A rooftop restaurant with a Texas ranch-like look. Caters to foreign tourists, with lots of black-and-white photographs of Frank Sinatra, Dean Martin, Bing Crosby, and so on. Excellent tandoori or barbecue and Western cuisine from grilled chicken to baked fish.

Risala
Umaid Bhawan
Palace Hotel
Tel. (0291) 433 316
Fax (0291) 635 373
Restaurant serving Indian, Rajasthani, Chinese, and continental cuisine. Sitar performances.

The Pillars
Umaid Bhawan
Palace Hotel
Tel. (0291) 433 316
Fax (0291) 635 373
Open 6am–11pm
Open-air restaurant overlooking the lush green lawns of the palace that offers a view of the fort.

Toran
Rajputana Palace Hotel
Panch Batti Circle
Airport Road
Tel. (0291) 431 672
Fax (0291) 438 072
Open 7am–10.30pm
Serves Rajasthani, Indian, Chinese, and continental meals. Live folk music and dances on request at extra cost.

→ ACCOMMODATION

Ajit Bhawan Palace Hotel
Opposite Circuit House
Tel. (0291) 612 410
Fax (0291) 437 774
Heritage Hotel
A legendary resort with traditional palace architecture and a garden laid out in traditional Rajasthani style. Personalized hospitality provided by the late Maharaja's brother and his family. The open-air restaurant serves Indian and continental meals. Rajasthani folk music and dance every evening during dinner. Village safaris by Jeep are very popular.
50 rooms, 38 cottages, 4 suites and 5 tents.

Balsamand Lake Palace ▲ *232*
Mandore Road
Tel. (0291) 455 91
Fax (0291) 542 240
Welcomgroup
Approximately 4 miles north of Jodhpur and set within lush green gardens, this beautiful old Lake Palace has for centuries been a venue for royal parties and picnics.
30 rooms and 6 suites.

Ghoomar Hotel (RTDC)
High Court Road
Tel. (0291) 544 010
or 548 010
80 rooms, including 10 with television and air-conditioning. Dormitory. Indian and continental cuisine.

Karni Bhawan Hotel
Palace Road
Tel. (0291) 432 220
or 639 380
Fax (0291) 433 495
Heritage Hotel
The restaurant serves thali Indian meals. Folk music and dance on request at extra cost.
25 rooms, including 11 luxury.

Rajputana Palace Hotel
Panch Batti Circle
Airport Road
Tel. (0291) 43 16 72
or 43 80 59
Fax (0291) 43 80 72
Two miles from town, near to the airport. Live folk music and dance on request at extra cost.
24 rooms air-conditioned and 14 air-cooled.

Ranbanka Hotel
Opposite Circuit House
Tel. and fax
(0291) 51 01 62
In the same palace as the Ajit Bhawan Palace Hotel.
30 rooms.

Ratanada Polo Palace Hotel
Presidency Road
Tel. (0291) 43 19 10
or 43 19 11
Poolside shows arranged with Rajasthani folk music and dance on request.
62 rooms.

The Safari Club
Office: High Court Colony, Jodhpur
Tel. and fax
(0291) 43 70 23
A modern bungalow, with an old family house beside it, it is located slightly more than a mile from the railway station. The guest house is run by Reggie Singh, the grandson of Maharaj Ratan Singh, known for his polo and shikar exploits. There is an excellent rooftop restaurant. Breakfast is served on a big lawn. The only place in town playing recorded jazz, blues, reggae and rock-and-roll music, with a small dance floor. Cultural performances are occasionally held. Village safaris, horse safaris, or jungle drives available. Boat across River Chambal can be arranged.
13 spacious double rooms with attached bath, with running hot and cold water. Three of the bedrooms are air-conditioned and the rest are air-cooled.

Umaid Bhawan Palace Hotel ▲ *230*
Tel. (0291) 51 01 01
Fax (0291) 51 01 10
Welcomgroup
100 palatial rooms, overlooking lush, green lawns. The view over the blue city is breathtaking. If you cannot afford to stay at the hotel, you can still enjoy breakfast on the terrace (a supplement is charged). Folk dances every evening in season.

KHEJARLA

F6

→ ACCOMMODATION

Fort Khejarla
Tel. (02930) 583 11
Reservations in New Delhi:
Meridian holidays
45 Yoshwant Palace
Chanakyapuri
Tel. (011) 467 53 38
Fax (011) 688 29 95
Camel safaris and excursions to Bishnoi and Raika villages.

HOTELS
- < £7/$10
- £7–22/$10–30
- £22–45/$30–65
- > £45/$65

KHIMSAR

▲ 238 E5

→ RESTAURANTS
Khimsar Fort ▲ 238
Nagaur District
Tel. (01585) 623 45
Fax (01585) 622 88
Three restaurants: on the rooftop, in the 16th-century fort and near the pool. Serves Rajasthani and continental cuisine.

KHIMSAR FORT, KHIMSAR

→ ACCOMMODATION
Khimsar Fort ▲ 238
Nagaur District
Tel. (01585) 623 45
Fax (01585) 622 88
Reservations in Jaipur:
Tel. (0141) 38 23 14
Fax (0141) 38 11 50
A 16th-century fort situated about half a mile from the village center.
50 air-conditioned rooms.

LUNI

D–E7

→ ACCOMMODATION
Fort Chanwa Hotel
Jodhpur District
Tel. (0291) 842 16
Fax (0291) 324 60
Heritage Hotel
On the Luni River, which is dry for much of the year. It is owned and was restored by the uncle of the present Maharaja. The fort is carved out of the red sandstone of Jodhpur, with ornate latticework friezes and intricate jarokhas *(balcony windows). Serves Rajasthani cuisine. Camel, horse and Jeep safaris to the nearby villages.*
12 luxurious suites.

POKARAN

C5 ▲ 218

→ RESTAURANT
Fort Pokaran ▲ 218
Jaisalmer District
Tel. (02994) 222 74
The old darbar has been turned into a restaurant. Indian and Rajasthani cuisine. Refreshing desserts. Exceptional atmosphere.

→ ACCOMMODATION
Fort Pokaran
Jaisalmer District
Tel. (02994) 222 74
Fax (02994) 222 79
Reservations:
Pokaran House
Jodhpur
Tel. (0141) 306 14
Part of this 14th-century fort has been converted into a charming hotel. Camel safaris can be arranged.
10 rooms.

Motel Godavan (RTDC)
Jodhpur–Jaisalmer Highway
Tel. (29942) 222 75
2 rooms and 6 bungalows.

ROHET

E7

→ ACCOMMODATION
Rohet Garh
PWD Road
Pali District
Tel. (02932) 662 31
Reservations in Jodhpur:
Tel. (0291) 431 161
Fax (0291) 649 368
reservations@rohetgarh.com
Heritage Hotel
This traditionally decorated hotel is situated on the banks of a great lake that provides water to 50 villages. The luxuriant vegetation surrounding the lake, contrasted against the barrenness of the region, gives it the appearance of an oasis in the middle of the desert. Delicious traditional cuisine. Jeep safaris to Bishnoi farms and to villages famous for their potters and weavers. Horse and camel safaris.
25 rooms.

SAMM

A6 ▲ 218

→ ACCOMMODATION
Sam Dhani Hotel (RTDC)
Tel. (02992) 523 92
8 bungalows. Dormitory.

SARDAR SAMAND

E7

→ RESTAURANT
Sardar Samand Palace Lake Resort
Via Sojat City
Pali District
Tel. (0291) 455 91
Fax (0291) 542 240
Open 6.30am–11.30pm
Restaurant serving international cuisine. View over the lake.

→ ACCOMMODATION
Sardar Samand Palace Lake Resort
Tel. (0291) 455 91
Fax (0291) 542 240

SARDAR SAMAND PALACE LAKE RESORT

Welcomgroup
This Art Deco hunting lodge built by Maharaja Umaid Singh in 1933 is still used by the present family. It is full of atmosphere and has wonderful views of the lake and flamingos.
99 rooms.

SOUTH

BIJAIPUR

Approximately 25 miles south of Chittorgarh

→ RESTAURANT
Shakti
Castle Bijaipur
Tel. (01472) 400 99
Fax (01472) 410 42
Located in a 16th-century castle, it is a perfect setting for traditional Mewari cuisine.

→ ACCOMMODATION
Castle Bijaipur
Reservations:
Pratap Palace
Tel. (01472) 400 99
Fax (01472) 410 42
Heritage Hotel
Set amid the serene Vindhyachal ranges, this 16th-century castle is a symbol of Rajput pageantry and hospitality. Attractions in the area are camel safaris, boating on Lotus Lake, village excursions and a visit to the 12th-century Pangarh Fort.
16 rooms.

BUNDI

G-H7 ▲ 290

→ RESTAURANTS
Bundi Cafe & Crafts
Opposite the Ayurvedic Hospital
Tel. (0747) 323 22
Fax (0747) 321 42
Located in the Braj Brushanji haveli, this restaurant has a large hall with an adjoining terrace.

You can also try eating meals Indian-style, sitting on the floor. Good food. An interesting handicrafts shop.

Diamond
Tel. (0747) 226 56
Vegetarian North Indian and tandoori cuisine.

→ ACCOMMODATION
Castle Awan
Garh Awan
Tel. (01432) 85 08
Reservations:
3 Naru Path, Govind Marg, Jaipur
Tel. (0141) 56 07 31
Located 43½ miles from Bundi, in Tonk district and known for its wells, this old fort used to be a hunting lodge.

Diamond
Tel. (0747) 226 56
A 10-bed hotel. The rooms have en-suite bathrooms.

Haveli Braj Bhushanji
Opposite the Ayurvedic Hospital
Tel. (0747) 323 22
Fax (0747) 321 42
Situated below the palace, this 19th-century building has an architecture typical of its period, and some exquisite examples of wall paintings of the Bundi miniature school. There is a stunning view of the fort from the terraces.

Ishwari Niwas Palace
1 Civil Lines
Opposite Circuit House
Tel. (0747) 42 24 14
Fax (0747) 44 24 86
Old heritage mansion belonging to the Raja's family. Friendly atmosphere. Good restaurant with home-cooked meals. 18 rooms.

Vrindawati Hotel (RTDC)
Near Jait Sagar Lake
Tel. (0747) 324 73
Tents. 2 rooms.

CHITTORGARH

F8 ▲ *276*
→ RESTAURANT
Morcha
Hotel Pratap Palace
Near the post office
Tel. (01472) 400 99
Fax (01472) 410 42
Traditionally decorated, the restaurant serves delicious vegetarian and non-vegetarian Rajasthani and Mewari cuisine.

→ ACCOMMODATION
Panna Chittor Hotel (RTDC)
Near the railway station
Tel. (01472) 412 38
31 rooms. Dormitory.

Pratap Palace
Near the post office
Tel. (01472) 400 99
Fax (01472) 410 42
Centrally located and run by the same family that manages Castle Bijaipur. 12 rooms.

DEOGARH

F7
→ ACCOMMODATION
Deogarh Mahal
Deogarh Madaria
Rajsamand District
Tel. (02904) 527 77
Fax (02904) 525 55
A 17th-century palace full of charm outside the village. Typical décor and performances of tribal dances. Jeep safaris are arranged to the nearby lakes for birdwatchers. 22 rooms including 5 suites.

Gokul Vilas
Rajsamand District
Tel. (02904) 520 17
A 150-year-old guest house with just 4 rooms. Once a royal retreat of the Deogarh nobility, it is now a home to the present Rawatsahib and Ranisahiba. A paradise for birdwatchers.

Motel Deogarh (rtdc)
Udaipur–Rajsamand Road
Tel. (02904) 520 11
2 rooms.

DUNGARPUR

E9 ▲ *266*
→ ACCOMMODATION
Udai Vilas Palace
▲ *266*
Tel. (02964) 308 08
Fax (02964) 310 08
Reservations:
Curvett India Pvt. Ltd., New Delhi
Tel. (011) 684 00 37
Fax (011) 682 28 56
Located on the banks of Lake Gaibsagar, this 19th-century palace built by the Maharawals of Dungarpur is still occupied by his descendants. Art Deco furniture combines with exquisite carvings to result in an architectural marvel. Sightseeing tours are arranged. 16 rooms, including 5 suites.

GOVARDHAN VILAS

Approximately 5 miles from Udaipur
→ RESTAURANTS
Baithak
Shikarbadi Hotel
Tel. (0294) 58 32 00
Chinese and Western cuisine.

Cheetal
Shikarbadi Hotel
Tel. (0294) 58 32 00 or 58 32 04
Charming décor of antique paintings and baskets of flowers hanging from the ceiling. Indian cuisine.

→ ACCOMMODATION
Shikarbadi Hotel
On the NH 8
Tel. (0294) 58 32 00
Fax (0294) 58 48 41
A forest hunting lodge. The hotel, which faces a small lake, is near a deer park. Horse-riding, polo and shooting available. Indian, continental, and Mewari food. 25 rooms including 3 suites.

HALDIGHATI

Approximately 25 miles north of Udaipur
→ ACCOMMODATION
Chetak Rest House (RTDC)
Tel. (02953) 309 17

JHALAWAR

H8 ▲ *286*
→ ACCOMMODATION
Chandravati Hotel (RTDC)
Patan Road
Tel. (07432) 300 15
Dormitory. 6 rooms.

KOTA

H8 ▲ *280*
→ RESTAURANT
Brijraj Bhawan Palace
Civil Lines
Tel. (0744) 45 05 29
Only restaurant to be recommended in Kota. Wide range of vegetarian and non-vegetarian dishes.

→ ACCOMMODATION
Brijraj Bhawan Palace
▲ *283*
Near the PWD Office Civil Lines
Tel. (0744) 45 05 29
Fax (0744) 45 00 57
Small, peaceful palace by the river. 3 air-conditioned rooms.

Chambal Hotel (RTDC)
Near Chambal Garden
Tel. (0744) 32 65 27
Dormitory. 50 rooms.

HOTELS
< £7/$10
£7–22/$10–30
£22–45/$30–65
> £45/$65

Umed Bhawan Palace
▲ *283*
Station Road
Tel. (0744) 32 52 62 to 65
Welcomgroup
This hotel also offers a billiard room and badminton court.

KOTRI

Approximately 87 miles from Udaipur

→ ACCOMMODATION

Kotri Raola
Via Nandol
Pali District
Tel. (02934) 63 24
Reservations in Udaipur:
Ghanerao Hotels Pvd. Ltd.
2-A, New Fatehpur
Near Union Bank
Tel. (0294) 56 08 22
Ideal for those in search of peace and quiet. Jeep or horse safaris available. 6 bedrooms and 2 suites.

MONT ABU

D8 ▲ *268*

→ RESTAURANTS

Aangan
Near the tourist office
Tel. (02974) 383 05
Serves typical Gujarati vegetarian dishes.

Cloud 9
Sunrise Palace
Old Bharatpur Kothi
Tel. (02974) 35 73
Fax (02974) 37 75
Located on top of a hillock it has glass walls on three sides offering a spectacular view of the surroundings. A multi-cuisine restaurant.

Haveli
Nakki Lake
Expensive, but worth the price. Tasty Punjabi food.

Jungle Corner
Kesar Bhawan Palace
Sunset Road
Tel. (02974) 386 47
Serves excellent Gujarati (vegetarian) meals.

Madhuban
Madhuban Hotel
Near the bus stand
Tel. (02974) 388 22 or 388 33
Fax (02974) 389 00
Serves Indian, Rajasthani and Gujarati cuisine.

Madras Cafe
Near Chacha Museum
Tel. (02974) 381 68
*Wide range of ice creams, fruit juices and milk shakes. South Indian specialties (*dosa, idli, *etc.)*

UMED BHAWAN PALACE, KOTA

CONNAUGHT HOUSE, MONT ABU

MK
Nakki Lake
Good Chinese cuisine.

Sher-e-Punjab
Inside the bazaar
Tel. (02974) 383 44
Serves vegetarian, non-vegetarian and tandoori meals.

Veena
Near the taxi rank
Tel. (02974) 380 33
Open 11am–2.30pm and 7–9.30pm
Open-air restaurant serving vegetarian South Indian and Gujarati meals.

→ ACCOMMODATION

Connaught House
Rajendra Marg
Tel. (02974) 385 60
Fax (02974) 54 22 40
Reservations in Jodhpur:
Tel. (0291) 333 16 or 209 41
Fax (0291) 353 73
Heritage Hotel
A charming country cottage set in shady gardens within easy walking distance of the town of Mount Abu and the famous Nakki Lake. This was the former summer residence of the Maharaja of Jodhpur. 14 air-conditioned rooms.

Hiltone Hotel
Near the bus stand
Tel. (02974) 383 91 to 93
Fax (02974) 383 95
Modern hotel with swimming pool. The restaurant serves Indian, Gujarati, Chinese, and continental food.

Hillock Hotel
Near the tourist office
Tel. (02974) 384 63
Hotel with panoramic view. Indian, Continental and Chinese food.

Kesar Bhawan Palace
Sunset Road
Tel. (02974) 386 47
10 rooms.

Madhuban Hotel
Near the bus stand
PB 33
Tel. (02974) 388 22 or 388 33
Fax (02974) 389 00
Centrally located hotel. 14 rooms, air-cooled and equipped with ceiling fans. This hotel offers reductions of up to 50% out of season.

Savera Palace
PB 23 Sunset Road
Tel. (02974) 383 54
Fax (02974) 383 54
24 rooms.

Shikhar Hotel (RTDC)
Bus terminal
Tel. (02974) 381 44
Small individual bungalows. 8 bedrooms.

Sunrise Palace
Old Bharatpur Kothi
Tel. (02974) 387 73
Fax (02974) 387 75
On the crest of a hill, with a panoramic view. 16 rooms with attached bathrooms, 2 air-conditioned suites.

Sunset Inn
PB 24
Sunset Road
West of the town
Tel. (02974) 431 94
Fax (02974) 435 15
40 rooms of which 14 are air-conditioned.

The Palace
Bikaner House
Dilwara Road
Tel. (02974) 381 21
Fax (02974) 386 74
Heritage Hotel
A former summer palace with its own lake. A peaceful haven with a

number of facilities, including a tennis court. Reservations essential in the high season.
35 rooms.

NAGDA

▲ *256* E8

→ **ACCOMMODATION**

Heritage Resorts
Lake Bagela
Sas Bahu Temple
Udaipur District
Tel. (0294) 52 86 28
Fax (0294) 52 75 49
Reservations in Udaipur:
Tel. (0294) 41 40 76
Located amid the Aravalli Hills on the fringe of Lake Bagela, it overlooks the Nagda Temples
26 rooms.

NARLAI

Approximately 90 miles from Udaipur

→ **ACCOMMODATION**

Rawala Narlai
Via Desuri
Pali District
Tel. (02934) 824 25
Reservations in Jodhpur:
Ajit Bhawan
Tel. (0291) 43 74 10
Fax (0291) 63 77 74
Heritage Hotel
Located in a renovated 17th-century fort. Safaris in the Aravalli mountains.
12 rooms.

NATHDWARA

E8 ▲ *256*

→ **ACCOMMODATION**

Gokul hotel (RTDC)
Near Lal Bagh
Tel. (02953) 309 17
7 rooms. Dormitory.

POSHINA

Approximately 56 miles west of Udaipur

→ **ACCOMMODATION**

Darbargadh Posina
Via Khed Brahma
Sabarkanta
Tel. (02775) 833 25
Fax (02712) 237 29
Part of a 15th-century fortress with havelis dating from the 17th to 19th centuries. Period furnishings, carvings, and a pleasant setting. Antiques and handicraft shop. Can arrange safaris to neighboring hamlets and scenic spots.
6 rooms, 2 deluxe suites.

RANAKPUR

E8 ▲ *262*

→ **ACCOMMODATION**

Maharani Bagh
2½ miles before the Ranakpur temples, as you come from Jodpur
Tel. (02934) 85 105
Hotel with comfortable cottages and restaurant serving family fare, set in a beautiful, well-kept garden.

Shilpi Hotel (RTDC)
Jain Temple Road
Tel. (02934) 318 39
13 rooms. Dormitory.

RISHABDEV

▲ *259* E9

→ **ACCOMMODATION**

Hotel Gavri
Tel. (029072) 301 45
7 rooms. Dormitory.

SADRI

Approximately 62 miles north of Udaipur

→ **RESTAURANT**

Maharani Bagh Orchard
Near Ranakpur
Pali District
Tel. (02934) 37 05
Fax (02934) 37 51
Set in the middle of an orchard, this restaurant offers vegetarian and non-vegetarian dishes. A good starting point for excursions to Ranakpur and to Kumbhalgarh. Shows.

TITARDI

Approximately 4 miles from Udaipur

→ **ACCOMMODATION**

Pratap Country Inn
Jaisamand Road
Tel. (0294) 58 31 38
Fax (0294) 58 30 58
Beautiful setting. The inn organizes interesting horse safaris.

UDAIPUR

E8 ▲ *240*

→ **RESTAURANTS**

Berry's
Chetak Circle
Tel. (0294) 52 51 32
Open 7–11pm
An air-conditioned restaurant serving Indian, continental, and Chinese food. Specialties: shish kebab, shami kebab, *tomato fish, tandoori butter chicken. Vegetarian dishes and children's menu available.*

Gallery Restaurant
Fateh Prakash Palace
Palace Road
Tel. (0294) 52 84 17 or 52 84 18
An ideal spot to have a cup of afternoon tea and scones while you gaze across Lake Pichola.

Garden Restaurant
Opposite Gulab Bagh
Tel. (0294) 52 80 13
A colonial-style building with high ceilings and white columns. The palace cars were once garaged here and an old petrol pump in the forecourt bears testimony to this. Serves typical Gujarati vegetarian thalis.

Jharokha
Lake Palace Hotel
▲ *250*
PB 5
Lake Pichola
Tel. (0294) 52 79 61 to 73
Fax (0294) 52 79 74
Coffee shop open around the clock
Dinner 7.30–10pm
One Thousand and One Night *décor.*
One of the best restaurants in town.

Kumbha Palace
Bhatina Chotta
Near the Mona Lisa Hotel
Run by an English woman. Recommended for its Western dishes and pizzas. Try the home-made chocolate cake.

Oriental Palace Resorts
Subash Nagar
Tel. (0294) 41 23 60
Open around the clock
Indian, Chinese and continental cuisine.

Padmani
Lakshmi Vilas Palace Hotel
Fateh Sagar Road
Tel. (0294) 52 97 11
Fax (0294) 52 55 36
Serves Indian and continental cuisine.

Park View
Opposite the Town Hall
Tel. (0294) 52 80 98
Open 8.30am–11pm
Serves Indian, continental and Chinese cuisine. Specialties: butter chicken, paneer butter masala, *chillied chicken.*

Roof Garden Cafe
Delwara House
Opposite the Lake Palace's Main Gate
Tel. (0294) 297 48
Open 8am–10pm
An open-air rooftop restaurant offering a magnificent view of the palace. Serves Indian, continental and Chinese food. Specialties: tandoori items, chicken Hong Kong, chillied chicken.

HOTELS
- < £7/$10
- £7–22/$10–30
- £22–45/$30–65
- > £45/$65

Sai Niwas
75 Navghat Road
near the City Palace
Tel. (0294) 52 49 09
Highly recommended for its fresh food and excellent service. Local Indian cuisine.

Shilpi Village Restaurant
Shilpagram
Tel. (0294) 52 24 75
Open 11am–11pm
Open-air restaurant offering traditional Indian and Chinese cuisine. Vegetarian dishes available.

→ **ACCOMMODATION**

Anand Bhawan Hotel
Fateh Sagar Road
Tel. (0294) 52 32 56
Fax (0294) 52 32 47
Good value, excellent view. Serves Indian, continental, and Rajasthani food.
22 rooms.

Caravanserai Hotel
14 Lalghat
Tel. (0294) 52 12 52 or 41 11 03
Small, comfortable hotel located in the center near the ghat. Restaurant with a terrace overlooking Lake Pichola and the City Palace.

Fateh Prakash Palace Hotel ▲ *249*
City Palace
Tel. (0294) 52 80 16
Fax (0294) 52 80 06
Part of the City Palace complex together with the Shiv Nivas. Similar to the latter but slightly more intimate. A visit to the Crystal Gallery and Durbar Hall is a must.
6 suites and 2 deluxe rooms.

Hilltop Hotel
5 Ambavgarh
Fateh Sagar
Tel. (0294) 52 19 97, 52 19 98 or 52 19 99
Fax (0294) 52 51 06
Hotel located high above Fateh Sagar. Daily puppet shows, and folk dances on request.
55 rooms.

Jagat Niwas Palace Hotel
25 Lal Ghat
Tel. (0294) 42 01 33
Fax (0294) 52 00 23
A traditional haveli converted into a hotel. Located in the heart of town, this hotel offers a panoramic view overlooking the Lake Palace Hotel and the historical Lake Pichola.
22 rooms, including 15 with en-suite bathroom.

Kajri Hotel (rtdc)
Shastri Circle
Tel. (0294) 41 05 01
Dormitory.
53 rooms.

Lake Palace ▲ *250*
Lake Pichola
Tel. (0294) 52 79 61 to 52 79 73
Fax (0294) 52 79 74
Located in the middle of Lake Pichola. Belonging to the Historic Resort Hotels, this palace appears to be something out of a fairytale. It allows a glimpse into the princely life of the Rajputs, with all its many splendors.
81 rooms, including suites.

LAKE PALACE, UDAIPUR

Lake Pichola Hotel
Opposite Chandra Pol
Tel. (0294) 42 03 87
Fax (0294) 41 05 75
Magnificent view of the lake and its gath opposite. Live music and puppet shows on request.
25 rooms.

Lakend Hotel
Rani Road
By Lake Fateh Sagar
Tel. (0294) 41 51 00
Fax (0294) 52 38 98
Modern hotel with lake-side gardens and a panoramic view of the Aravalli range.
78 rooms.

Lakshmi Vilas Palace Hotel
Fateh Sagar Road
Tel. (0294) 52 97 11
Fax (0294) 52 55 36
Puppet shows every evening, and dancing on request.
54 rooms.

Lalghat Guest House
Behind Jagdish Temple
Tel. (0294) 52 53 01
Built on the bank of the lake, some rooms offer a view of the lake and the palace. There is a large open courtyard ideal for relaxing.
25 rooms.
Dormitory (10 beds).

Oriental Palace Resorts
Subhash Nagar
Tel. (0294) 41 23 60
Fax (0294) 41 12 38
Folk music and dances every night and puppet shows every evening.
35 rooms.

Padmini Hotel
27 Gulab Bagh Road
Tel. (0294) 41 41 91
Set in the heart of the city in peaceful surroundings. Near the famous Gulab Bagh garden.

Raj Darshan Hotel
18 Panna Dhai Marg
Tel. (0294) 52 66 01
Fax (0294) 52 45 88
Puppet shows and dances on request.
52 rooms.

Rang Niwas Palace Hotel
Rang Niwas
Lake Palace Road
Tel. (0294) 52 78 84
Fax (0294) 52 02 94
Garden, terrace and swimming pool. Good food.
22 rooms.

Sai Niwas Hotel
75 Navghat Road
Near City Palace
Tel. and fax (0294) 52 49 09
A haveli-style hotel reputed for its excellent cuisine.

Shiv Nivas Palace Hotel ▲ *249*
City Palace
Tel. (0294) 52 80 06
Heritage Hotel
The most charming hotel in Udaipur, part of the royal palace (one section is still occupied by the maharaja) with wonderful views of Lake Pichola. Visitors in search of peace and tranquility will prefer to stay here than at the Lake Palace. Beautiful swimming pool.
31 rooms, some quite reasonably priced.

The information given here serves only as a rough guide. As most places do not have an address or telephone number and opening hours may vary, we recommend that you check on the spot or that you contact local tourist offices ◆ **318** for more accurate information.

RELIGIOUS SITES		
HINDU TEMPLES Generally open very early in the morning and closed at sunset	*Take off your shoes before going in and leave them in the appointed cloakroom or with the guard, who will look after them for a few rupees. Women: proper dress compulsory (no clothing that may be considered indecent, such as shorts, short skirts; cover your shoulders). Photographs: ask permission from the priest or from the guard. If it is a protected monument (indicated by a "Protected monument" sign), video recordings are not allowed but photographs are usually permitted free of charge.*	
JAIN TEMPLES Opening times may vary according to whether the temple is in use or whether it is a protected monument. At Ranakpur, all Jain temples are open from noon until 6pm. At Jaisalmer, they are only open from 8am until noon.	*Take off your shoes before going in. Proper dress compulsory. Photographs are allowed (usually for a small charge), except of idols and inside the cella* ● ***94****. All leather items are prohibited.*	
HINDU FUNERAL SITES Usually open from sunrise to sundown	*Take off your shoes before going in. Photographs: ask for permission.*	
MUSLIM FUNERAL SITES (DARGAHS) Usually open from sunrise to sunset	*Take off your shoes before going in. Long garments covering both arms and legs compulsory. Cover your head (always carry a scarf). Photographs: ask for permission*	
MOSQUES Open from sunrise, except during prayer (5 times a day)	*Take off your shoes before going in. Long garments covering both arms and legs compulsory. Cover your head (always carry a scarf).*	
HAVELIS		
Havelis are private and often guarded. Access and times depend very much on the owners' and the guards' goodwill.	*If permission to visit and take photographs is granted, you are expected to give a tip (30 to 50 INR) to the guard or* Chaukilar.	
PALACES, FORTS AND MUSEUMS		
State museums: open daily 10am–5pm. Most of the forts and palace-museums open at 9am or 10am and close at 4.30pm or 5pm.	*There is usually a charge for photographs. Some places close during important festivals, such as Holi, and on Independence Day. Tickets are usually on sale until 4pm or 4.30pm.*	
NATURAL PARKS AND ANIMAL RESERVES		
GENERAL INFORMATION Closed or impossible to visit during the monsoon season (Jul.–Aug.). Best time to visit: Sep.–Apr. Unless otherwise indicated, open daily from sunrise to sunset.		
BHARATPUR **KEOLADEO GHANA SANCTUARY** 1¼ miles from Bharatpur. Best time to watch migratory birds: end Nov.–beg. Feb.	*There is a charge for photographs and video recordings. Guided tours are arranged on the spot (on hired bicycles, or rickshaw-bicycles with specialized drivers who know the names of the birds in several languages).*	▲ 306
RANTHAMBHOR NATIONAL PARK 8¾ miles from Sawai Madhopur	*Individual or group tours (by Jeep) are arranged by the nearby hotels. There is a charge for photographs and video recordings.*	▲ 305
DESERT NATIONAL PARK About 19 miles from Jaisalmer	*Tours, free of charge and usually by Jeep, can be arranged by hotels and by the Jaisalmer tourist office, Tel. (0292) 524 06.*	▲ 218
SARISKA TIGER RESERVE 22½ miles from Alwar	*Individual or group tours (by Jeep) are arranged by the nearby hotels. There is a charge for photographs and video recordings.*	▲ 174
STATE CAMEL BREEDING FARM 6¼ miles from Bikaner. Open Mon.–Sat. 10am–4pm. Closed on public hols.	*Free walking tour with an official guard (tip expected: 50 INR). Photographs and video recordings are not permitted.*	▲ 203

A

Aangan: Courtyard.
Aarti: The ritual of passing an oil lamp or flame in a circular movement in an act of devotion or homage.
Achakan: Traditional Indian long, formal coat.
Agarbatti: Incense.
Agnikula: Literally "Fire-born". A set of thirty-six Rajput clans who trace their ancestry not to the Sun or Moon (like the others), but to a great ancient fire rite.
Ahimsa: Non-violence.
Ajrakh: Handprinted fabric, typical of Barmer.
Angrakhi: A loose, double-breasted jacket worn by men.
Aonla: A yellow-blossomed tree typical of southern Rajasthan, which bears sour berries.
Arayish: A traditional lime plaster technique with a finish as smooth as marble.
Atmasukh: A quilted jacket. Literally "the happiness of the soul".
Attar: Traditional Indian perfume. Also spelled *ittar.*
Ayurveda: Traditional Hindu medicine.

B

Babool: Thorny tree, characteristic of the desert region of Rajasthan.
Bagh: Garden.
Bajra: Millet.
Bandhani: Tie-and-dye fabric, typical of Rajasthan. The origin of the English word "bandanna".
Bangaldhar: A style of drooping eaves found in Rajput architecture, inspired by Bengali village huts.
Baniya: Trader or moneylender caste.
Baraat: Wedding procession.
Baradari: Pavilion.
Batti: Light or lamp.
Bazaar: Market.
Bhagwan: God.
Bhajan: Hindu devotional song.
Bhakti: Devotion.
Bhala: Spear.
Bhang: Dried hemp leaves. A narcotic often mixed with drinks or food.
Bhatt: A community of bards.
Bhil: Aboriginal tribes of southern Rajasthan, known for their archery skills.
Bidi: Traditional Indian "mini-cigarette" made from rolled tobacco leaves.
Brahma: One of the Hindu Trinity, considered the god of creation.
Brahmin: Hindu priestly caste.

C

Chandravanshi: Rajput clan, believed to be descended from the moon.
Charan: A community of bards and poets, believed to have special spiritual powers.
Chhatri: Literally "umbrella", used to signify the royal cenotaphs of the Rajputs.
Chik: Reed screen to provide shade from the hot summer sun.
Chital: A species of small, graceful deer.
Chitrashala: Frescoed hall. Literally, "Hall of Paintings".
Choli: Woman's blouse.
Chowk: Public square.
Churidar: A kind of skin-tight pyjama, with horizontal folds around the ankles. Literally, "the pyjamas with bangles."

D

Dargah: Mausoleum or memorial of a Muslim saint.
Darshan: An audience or viewing, usually of a Hindu deity, royalty or important personage.
Darwaza: Door or gateway.
Desert-cooler: A kind of primitive "air-conditioner" that blows air through a moistened reed screen at high velocity.
Dev: God. Also *devata.*
Dhobi: Washerman.
Dhol: Drum.
Dhoti: Hindu man's garment comprising a long white cloth that is folded intricately around one's waist and legs.
Durrie: A flat, woven floor covering.
Diwan: Prime Minister.
Diwan-i-am: Hall of Public Audience in a medieval palace.
Diwan-i-khas: Hall of Private Audience in a medieval palace.
Durbar: Gathering of a king's court.
Durg: Sanskrit word for fort.
Durga: Hindu goddess of destruction. An incarnation of Parvati, wife of Lord Shiva. Another incarnation is Kali, goddess of death.
Dwarpala: Sentry or symbolic carvings flanking a doorway. Literally "door-keeper".

F

Fakir: Muslim mendicant.

G

Gaddi: Throne.
Galli: Alley or narrow lane.
Ganesha: Elephant-headed Hindu god of fortune.
Gaon: Village.
Gazal: Urdu poetry, usually of romantic mood.
Garh: Fort. Also *kila.*
Ghagra: Loose, pleated Indian skirt.
Ghat: Steps going down to a lake.
Ghoda: Horse.
Guru: Teacher, spiritual guide.

H

Haldi: Turmeric, a root considered to have beneficial properties.
Hammam: Medieval bath.
Hathi: Elephant.
Haveli: Mansion.
Hawa Mahal: Literally "Palace of the Winds", where royal ladies could enjoy the breeze without being seen. Also called "Hawa Ghar" (house).
Holi: Hindu festival of spring, celebrated by sprinkling colors on people.
Hookah: Hubble-bubble.
Howdah: Elephant seat.

I

Ishwar: God.
Izzat: Honor, prestige.

J

Jai: Victory.
Jali: Lattice.
Jauhar: Ritual mass immolation of women at the time of defeat, to save themselves from falling into the hands of the enemy.
Jharokha: Window of a balcony.
Ji: A suffix that is added to a person's name as a mark of respect.
Johri: Jeweler.

K

Kala: Art.
Karma: Action. Also used to signify "Fate".
Katar: Traditional Indian dagger.
Kathputli: Puppet.
Kavad: A small portable temple with brightly painted wooden panels depicting various deities.
Khamba: Pillar.
Khanda: Heavy saber.
Khazana: Treasure.
Khejri: A tree that blooms in the deserts of Rajasthan (*Prosopis cineraria*).
Khus: Scented shrub, believed to have cooling powers. Often used for making screens and awnings.
Kila (or *qila):* Fort.
Kothi: Mansion.
Krishna: Hindu god. Known for his amorous exploits in his youth; later the mentor of the Pandavas in the epic *Mahabharata.*
Kshatriya: Hindu military caste.
Kuan: Well.
Kum-kum: Red powder used by Hindus in rituals. Also worn as a dot on the forehead or in the parting of the hair by married women.
Kundan: Jewelry setting of uncut gems in gold.
Kunja: A narrow-necked earthen pitcher.
Kunwar: Prince.
Kurta or Kameez: Traditional loose Indian shirt.

L

Lakh: 100,000.
Lassi: Thick buttermilk.
Laharia: Wave-patterned fabric or turban.
Loo: Dust storm.

M

Mahabharata: Hindu epic telling of the war between the clan of the virtuous Pandavas and their cousins, the wicked Kauravas.
Mahal: Palace.
Maharaja: Literally "Great King". The rulers of most major Rajput kingdoms were called this. There were variants on this: the ruler of Mewar was a *maharana*; the rulers of Jaisalmer and Dungarpur were *maharawals*; the ruler of Bundi was a *maharao*.
Maharani: Literally "Great Queen". Wife of a maharaja.
Maharajkumar: Literally "Great Prince". Son of a maharaja.
Mandapa: Pillared hall of temple.
Mandir: Temple.
Mandana: Traditional auspicious floor or wall patterns in a Rajasthani village.
Mardana: Men's quarters in a palace.
Marg: Main road or street.
Matka: Large, round-shaped earthen pitcher.
Mehendi: Henna decorations on the palm of a woman's hand.
Mela: Village fair.
Memsahib: Lady. A term of respect.
Minakari: Enamel-work ornamentation rendered on jewelry.
Mojri: Traditional Rajput slippers with pointed, upturned "toes". Also called *jootis*.
Moochh: Mustache.
Mor: Peacock. Also called *mayoor*.

N

Nagada: Ceremonial drum.
Nawab: Muslim ruler.
Nilgai: A species of deer often considered sacred by Hindus.
Niwas: Abode.
Namaste: Traditional Hindu greeting. Said with folded hands. Also *namaskar*.

O

Odhni: A long scarf worn by women over the head, shoulders, and bosom. Also called *dupatta*.
Oont: Camel.

P

Pagari: A small turban, smaller and less flamboyant than a *safa*.
Paisa: Money.
Palki: Palanquin.
Panchayat: Village council.
Pandit: Hindu priest or scholar.
Pankha: Fan, including the hand-held variety.
Parvati: Consort of Lord Shiva.
Patwari: Leader of a village.
Phad: Traditional painting depicting the legends of the Rajasthani folk hero, Pabuji.
Pichhvai: Paintings based on the life of Lord Krishna. Typical of the area north of Udaipur. Literally, "That which hangs behind."
Pol: Gate. A variant in some places is *prole*.
Puja: Hindu religious ritual.
Pukka: Proper. Colloquially it means "definite", a promise or commitment.
Purdah: Veil or curtain. Also the practice of keeping the women secluded from the men.
Purohit: Hindu priest.
Pyjamas: Literally, "leg covering". Traditional Indian trousers, usually worn loose.

Q

Qila (or *kila*): Fort.

R

Raga: Traditional Indian melody.
Raj: Reign, sovereignty, or government.
Raja: King.
Rajkumar: Prince.
Rajkumari: Princess.
Rajput: A member of the Kshatriya community of Rajasthan. Literally, "son of a king."
Rajputana: The old name for the present state of Rajasthan. Literally, "The land of the Rajputs."
Rama: Hindu god. Hero of the epic *Ramayana*. An incarnation of Vishnu.
Ramayana: Hindu epic, whose hero is Lord Rama.
Rang Mahal: Literally, "Palace of Colours". A frescoed palace.
Rangoli: Traditional, auspicious floor patterns drawn in brightly colored powders.
Rani: Queen.
Ravanhatta: A stringed folk music instrument.
Registan: Desert.
Reti: Sand.
Razai: Quilt.
Rishi: Hindu sage.

S

Sadhu: Hindu mendicant.
Salaam: A greeting. Literally "peace".
Safa: Turban.
Sagar: Lake or pond.
Sahib: Gentleman. A term of respect for a man.
Salwar: Loose trousers worn by women.
Sambar: A species of deer.
Sansayi: Hindu hermit.
Sarangi: A stringed musical instrument.
Saraswati: Hindu goddess of learning.
Sardar: Chieftain.
Sati: The immolation of a wife on her husband's funeral pyre.
Shamiana: A large, open-sided tent.
Shastra: A Hindu scripture or text.
Sheesh mahal: Hall of mirrors.
Shehnai: Traditional Indian wind instrument, played on ceremonial occasions.
Sherwani: Knee-length coat worn by men, usually over *churidars*.
Shikar: Hunt.
Shilpa Shastra: Ancient Hindu treatise on architecture.
Shiva: One of the Hindu Trinity, considered the god of destruction.
Shivalinga: The symbol of Lord Shiva's phallus, symbolizing fertility.
Sileh Khana: Armory.
Singh: Literally "lion". Also used as a family name by Rajputs.
Sirohi: A light, curved sword favored by the Rajputs.
Sowar: Horsemen.
Surahi: Narrow-necked earthen pitcher.
Surya: Sun or sun god.
Suryavanshi: Rajput clan, believed to be descended from the sun.

T

Tabla: Small Indian drum.
Teej: Festival welcoming the monsoons.
Thakur: Chieftain or nobleman.
Thali: Large, circular stainless steel eating utensil, with small bowls known as *katoris* for curries, yogurt and sweet dishes; also refers to a set meal.
Thewa: Enamel-worked glass ornaments typical of Deolia, near Udaipur.
Tikka: Ritual anointing of the forehead with *kum-kum* or sandalwood paste.
Tirthankara: Jain saint.
Torana: Ornate archway.
Toshakhana: Treasury or wardrobe.
Tripolia: Triple arched gateway.
Trimurti: Represents the Hindu Trinity of Shiva, Vishnu, and Brahma.
Trishul: A trident, symbolic of Lord Shiva.

V

Vijay: Victory.
Vimana: Temple tower or pagoda.
Vishnu: Hindu god. One of the Hindu Trinity, considered the god of preservation.

W

Wagh: Tiger.
Waghnakh: A curious weapon shaped like a set of tiger claws and used in close combat.
Wallah: Person. A suffix used as an occupational name such as *"phool-wallah"* (flower-seller), *"akhbar-wallah"* (newspaper vendor), etc.

Y

Yagna: An elaborate Hindu ritual.

Z

Zamindar: Landlord.
Zenana: Women's quarters in a palace.

◆ NOTES

◆ BIBLIOGRAPHY

ESSENTIAL READING

◆ DAVIDSON (ROBYN): *Desert Places*, Viking, London, 1996.
◆ PALLING (BRUCE): *India: a Literary Companion*, John Murray, London, 1992.
◆ DEVI, MAHARANI (GAYATRI) AND RAMA RAU (SANTHA), *A Princess Remembers, The Memoirs of the Maharani of Jaipur*, Wiedenfield & Nicholson, London, 1976.
◆ PATNAIK (NAVEEN): *A Second Paradise: Indian Courtly Life, 1590-1947*, Sidgwick & Jackson, London, 1985.
◆ TOD (JAMES COLONEL): *Annals and Antiquities of Rajasthan*, Low Price Publications, Delhi, 1990.

ARCHITECTURE

◆ DAVIES (PHILIP): *The Penguin Guide to the Monuments of India, Vol. II, (Islamic, Rajput, European)*, Penguin Group, London, 1989.
◆ EDWARDES (MICHAEL): *Indian Temples and Palaces*, Hamlyn, London, 1969.
◆ GHURYE (G.S.):*Rajput Architecture*, Popular Prakashan, Bombay, 1968.
◆ GOETZ (HERMANN): *Rajput Art and Architecture*, Franz, Steiner, Verlag, Wiesbaden, 1978.
◆ GOETZ (HERMANN) AND CASSIRER (BRUNO): *The Art and Architecture of Bikaner*, Oxford, 1950.
◆ MITCHELL (GEORGE): *The Penguin Guide to the Monuments of India, Vol.1, (Buddhist, Jain, Hindu)*, Penguin Group, London, 1989.
◆ TILLOTSON (G.H.R.): *The Rajput Palaces*, Oxford University Press, Bombay, Calcutta, Madras, 1987.

THE ARTS

◆ AGARWALA (R.A.): *Marwar Murals*, Agam Prakashan, New Delhi, 1977.
◆ ARCHER (MILDRED) AND FALK (TOBY): *Indian Miniatures in the India Office Library*, Sotheby, Parke, Bernet, London, 1981.
◆ ARCHER (WILLIAM G.): *Indian Painting in Bundi and Kota*, Victoria and Albert Museum, London, 1959.
◆ CHANDRA (MOTI): *Mewar Painting*, Lalit Kala Akademi, New Delhi, 1955.
◆ COOMARASWAMY (ANANDA): *Rajput Painting*, Hacker Books, New York, 1975.
◆ COOPER (ILAY): *The Painted Towns of Shekhavati*, Mapin Publishing, Ahmedabad, 1994.
◆ NEERAJ (JAI SINGH): *Splendour of Rajasthani Painting*, Abhinav Publications, New Delhi, 1992.
◆ RANDHAWA (MOHINDER SINGH) AND SCHREIER (DORIS): *Kishangarh Painting*, Randhawa, Vakils, Feffer & Simon, Bombay, 1980.
◆ TOPSFIELD (ANDREW): *Paintings from Rajasthan*, National Gallery of Victoria, Melbourne, 1980.
◆ WACZIARG (FRANCIS) AND NATH (AMAN): *The Painted Walls of Shekhavati*, Croom, Helm, London, 1982.

THE CRAFTS

◆ WACZIARG (FRANCIS) AND NATH (AMAN): *Arts and Crafts of Rajasthan*, Mapin International, New York, 1987.
◆ BHISHAM (PAL H.): *Handicrafts of Rajasthan*, Asia Book Corporation, Delhi, 1984.

FICTION

◆ ACKERLEY (J.R.): *Hindoo Holiday*, Penguin 20th century Classics, London, 1994.
◆ FORSTER (E.M.): *The Hill of Devi*, Edward Arnold, London, 1953.
◆ KIPLING (RUDYARD): *Collected Stories*, Everyman's Library, London/Alfred A Knopf, New York, 1985.
◆ MEHTA (GITA): *Raj*, Jonathan Cape, London, 1989.
◆ MEHTA (RAMA): *Inside the Haveli*, Arnold Heinemann, Delhi, 1981.
◆ RICHARDSON (JANE): *Virgin Princess*, India Book Distributors, Bombay, 1992.

GENERAL

◆ ANAND (MULK RAJ): *Private Life of an Indian Prince*, Hutchinson, London, 1985.
◆ ANAND (UMA) AND ANAND (VIVEK): *Mansions of the Sun*, Al Falak Scorpion, London, 1982.
◆ AHUJA (D.R.): *Folklore of Rajasthan*, National Book Trust, New Delhi, 1980.
◆ DUBE (DINA N.): *Folk Tales of Rajasthan*, Asia Book Corporation, Delhi, 1983.
◆ ERDMAN (JOAN L.): *Patrons and Performers in Rajasthan, The Subtle Tradition*, Chanakya Publications, New Delhi, 1985.
◆ FASS (VIRGINIA): *The Forts of India*, Collins, London, 1986.
◆ FASS (VIRGINIA) AND MAHARAJA OF BARODA: *The Palaces of India*, Collins, London, 1980.
◆ FITZROY (YVONNE): *Courts and Camps of India*, Methuen, London, 1987.
◆ FRATER (ALEXANDER): *Beyond the Blue Horizon*, Penguin, London, 1987.
◆ HOLKAR (SHIVAJI RAO) AND HOLKAR (SHALINI DEVI): *Cooking of the Maharajas, The Royal Recipes of India*, Viking Press, New York, 1975.
◆ HUXLEY (ALDOUS): *Jesting Pilate, An Intellectual Holiday*, Doran, New York, 1926.
◆ IWATA (HIROKO): *Desert Villages, Life and Crafts of Gujarat and Rajasthan*, Yobisha, Tokyo, 1984.
◆ JAIN (KAILASH CHAND): *Ancient Cities and Towns of Rajasthan*, Motilal Banarsidas, Delhi, 1972.
◆ KHANGAROT (R.S.) AND NATHAWAT (P.S.): *Jaigarh, The Invincible Fort of Amber*, RBSA Publishers, Jaipur, 1990.
◆ KIPLING (RUDYARD): *Letters of Marque*, P.F. Collier & Son, New York, 1891.
◆ LOTHIAN, SIR (ARTHUR): *Kingdoms of Yesterday*, John Murray, London, 1951.
◆ MERCHANT (ISMAIL): *Hullabaloo in Old Jeypore, The Making of "The Deceivers"*, Viking, London, 1988.
◆ RUDOLPH (SUZANNA AND LLOYD): *Essays on Rajputana*, Concept Publishing, New Delhi, 1984.
◆ SCHOMER (KARINE), ERDMAN (JOAN L.), LODRICK (DERYCK O.), RUDOLPH (LLOYD I.) (EDS.): *The Idea of Rajasthan*, Manohar Publications, New Delhi, 1994.
◆ SHARMA (DASHARATH): *Lectures on Rajput History and Culture*, Motilal Banarasidass, Delhi, 1970.
◆ SHARMA (G.N): *Social Life in Medieval Rajasthan*, Laxmi Narain Agarwal, Agra, 1968.
◆ SHERRING (M.A): *Tribes and Castes of Rajasthan*, Cosmo Publications, New Delhi, 1975.
◆ SMITH (JOHN D.): *The Epic of Papuji*, Cambridge University Press, Cambridge, 1991.
◆ SUGICH (M): *Palaces of India*, Pavilion Books, London, 1992.

GEOGRAPHY

◆ MISRA, DR (V.C.): *Geography of Rajasthan*, National Book Trust, New Delhi, 1967.

HISTORY

◆ DAVENPORT (HUGH): *Trials and Triumphs of the Mewar Kingdom*, Maharana of Mewar Charitable Foundation, Udaipur, 1975.
◆ GASCOIGNE (BAMBER): *The Great Mughals*, Cape Publications, London, 1971.
◆ HALLISEY (ROBERT C.): *The Rajput Rebellion Against Aurangzeb*, University

of Missouri Press, Columbia & London, 1977.
◆ MENON (V.P.): *The Story of The Integration of the Indian States,* Longman, London, 1956.
◆ QANUNGO (K.R.): *Studies in Rajput History,* S. Chand & Co., Delhi, 1969.
◆ SARKAR (JADUMATI): *A History of Jaipur,* Longman, Hyderabad, 1984.
◆ SHARMA (DASHARATH): *Rajasthan through the Ages,* Rajasthan State Archives, Bikaner, 1966.
◆ SHARMA (G.N): *Mewar and the Mughal Emperors,* Shiv Lal & Sons, Agra, 1962.
◆ SINGH (BRIJRAJ M.K.): *The Kingdom that was Kotah,* Lalit Kala Akademi, New Delhi, 1985.
◆ SINGH (R.B.): *Origin of the Rajputs,* Sahitya Sansar Prakashan, Buxipur, 1975.
◆ SPEAR (PERCIVAL): *A History of India,* Penguin, Harmondsworth, 1965.

ROYALTY

◆ ALLEN (CHARLES) AND DWIVEDI (SHARADA): *Lives of the Indian Princes,* Century, London, 1984.
◆ BARTON, SIR (WILLIAM): *The Princes of India,* Nisbet & Co., London, 1934.
◆ CORFIELD, SIR (CONRAD): *The Princely India I knew,* George Thomas for the Indo-British Historical Society, Madras, 1975.
◆ CREWE (QUENTIN): *The Last Maharajah,* Michael Joseph, London, 1985.
◆ DASS (DIWAN JARMANI): *Maharajah,* Allied Publishers, Bombay, 1969.
◆ FITZE, SIR (KENNETH): *Twilight of the Maharajahs,* J. Murray, London, 1956.
◆ GRIFFITH (M): *India's Princes, Short Life Sketches of the Native Rulers of India,* W.H. Allen, London, 1894.
◆ HENDLEY (THOMAS HOLBEIN): *Rulers of India and Chiefs of Rajputana, 1550–1897,* W. Griggs, London, 1897.
◆ IVORY (JAMES): *Autobiography of a Princess,* Harper & Row, New York, 1975.
◆ LORD (JOHN): *The Maharajahs,* BI Publications, New Delhi, 1982.
◆ MASTERS (BRIAN): *Maharana,* Mapin Publishing, Ahmedabad, 1990.
◆ PATNAIK (NAVEEN): *Desert Kingdom,* Wiedenfield & Nicholson, London, 1990.
◆ ROUSSELET (LOUIS): *India and its Native Princes,* Bickers, London, 1882.
◆ SINGH (DHANANJAYA): *The House of Marwar,* Roli Books, Delhi, 1994.
◆ VAN WART (R.B.): *The Life of Lt. General H.H. Sir Pratap Singh,* Oxford University Press, London, 1926.

PHOTOGRAPHY

◆ BENY (ROLOFF): *Rajasthan, Land of Kings,* Frederick Muller, London, 1984.
◆ GUTMAN (JUDITH MARA): *Through Indian Eyes, 19th & Early 20th Century Photography from India,* Oxford University Press & International Centre for Photography, New York, 1982.
◆ MITCHELL (GEORGE) AND MARTINELLI (ANTONIO): *The Royal Palaces of India,* Thames & Hudson, London, 1994.
◆ MORAES (DOM) AND GAJWANI (GOPI): *Rajasthan, Splendour in the Wilderness,* Himalayan Books, New Delhi, 1988.
◆ PATANKAR (ADITYA) AND NINAN (SEVANTI): *Rajasthan,* Lustre Press, New Delhi, 1988.
◆ NATH (AMAN) AND JODHA (SAMAR): *Jaipur, the Last Destination,* India Book House, 1992.
◆ SINGH (RAGHUBIR): *Rajasthan, India's Enchanted Land,* Perennial Press, Hong Kong, 1981.
◆ TOUTAINE (PIERRE) AND BUSQUET (GERARD): *Rajasthan,* Harrap Columbus Ltd., London, 1988.
◆ UCHIYAMA (SUMIO) AND ROBINSON (ANDREW): *Maharaja, The Spectacular Heritage of Princely India,* The Vendome Press, New York, 1988.

WILDLIFE

◆ ISRAEL (SAMUEL) AND SINCLAIR (TONY) (ED.): *Indian Wildlife,* APA Productions, Hong Kong, 1987.
◆ GEE (E.P.): *The Wildlife of India,* Dutton, New York, 1964.
◆ SINGH, LT. COL. (KESRI): *The Tiger of Rajasthan,* Jaico Publishing House, 1967.
◆ THAPAR (VALMIK) AND RATHORE (FATEH SINGH): *Tigers, The Secret Life,* Elm Tree Books, London, 1989.

◆ LIST OF ILLUSTRATIONS

Front cover: Artist unknown, Private Collection
Back cover: Palace Complex with Moata Lake in Foreground by Nitin Rai
1 Elephants' stable at the City Palace, Udaipur, photo courtesy of A.L. Syed.
2–3 General view of lake and city from north, Udaipur, photo courtesy of H.N. Ghiya © Raja Deen Dayal.
4–5 Bagpipers at Bikaner Fort, photo © A.L. Syed.
6–7 Tiger hunt, photo © Sudhir Kasliwal.
9 Street scene, Kota, photo © A.L. Syed.
12–3 Map by Anuar bin Abdul Rahim. Locator map by Tan Seok Lui.
15 Drawings by Anuar bin Abdul Rahim.
16–7 Landscape drawings by Anuar bin Abdul Rahim. Locator map by Ang Teck Beng. Mount Abu, stabilized sand dunes, longitudinal sand dunes, photos © Benoit Juge. Aravelli mountains, sandy plain, photos © Roy Lewis. Shell fossil, photo © Kailash Sankhala.
18–9 All photos by Kailash Sankhala. Maps by Tan Seok Lui.
20–1 Drawing water from well, crossed furrows, weeding hoe, sickle, pick, rake, drawings by David Rankin. Irrigation by mote, drawings by Ang Teck Beng. Wooden pitch forks, photos © Roy Lewis. Monsoon ploughing, ploughing with camels, photos © Raghu Rai. A shard bearing remains of millet grains, remains of rice in shard, photos from *Excavations at Ahar*, pp. 229-35.
22–3 Drawing showing how the Persian wheel method works, bullock ploughing, wooden plough, drawings by David Rankin. Map showing distribution of crops by Tan Seok Lui. *Bajra*, *juar*, cotton, wheat, groundnut, maize, gram, barley, sesame, drawings by Tricia Moore. Irrigation by electric pump, irrigation by mote, drawings by Ang Teck Beng. Irrigation by Persian wheel, photo © Roy Lewis. Selling sugar cane, photo © Raghu Rai.
24–5 Drawings by Amy Tan. *Chinkara, chital, blackbuck, nilgai, Indian otter.* Other drawings by Anuar bin Abdul Rahim. Map showing distribution of nature reserves by Ang Teck Beng.
26–7 Drawings by Anuar bin Abdul Rahim.
28–9 Drawings by Lim Yew Cheong.
30 All drawings by Anuar bin Abdul Rahim.
31 Portrait of a Rajput, photo © A.L. Syed.
32–3 Sculpture from Kalibangan, Harivansh Puran manuscript, Chandravati stone sculptures, photos © R.C. Sharma. Chandravati sculpture of woman figure, photo © M.D. Sharma. Rajput noblemen, photo © A.L. Syed. Colonel Tod at Mewar court, painting from City Palace Museum, Udaipur, photo © Resource Foto. Harappan seal, photo © Kailash Sankhala.
34–5 Sun symbol of the Sisodias, photo © Chelna Desai. Maharaja Sawai Jai Singh II's portrait, Rao Bikaji of Bikaner transporting heirlooms of Jodhpur, Ram Singh of Jaipur's seal, photos © Sudhir Kasliwal. Prithviraj Chauhan's portrait, photo © M.D. Sharma. Battle scene at Jaisalmer fort, painting, photo Nitin Rai. Jodhpur fiscal stamp, photo © Phillips Antiques, Bombay. Jat nobles, photo © Radhika Dwivedi.
36–7 Haldighati battle scene, painting from City Palace, Udaipur, photo © Resource Foto. Shah Jahan's Palace, photo from Louis Rousselet, *India and its Native Princes*, courtesy of Radhika Kwivedi. Farmaan of crown prince Salim, dated 1605, photo courtesy Sudhir Kasliwal. Akbar's portrait, photo private collection. Portrait of Rana Sanga of Mewar, photo private collection. Shah Jahan's portrait, photo private collection.
38–9 Rajputs and the British hunting together, photo © Phillips Antiques. Maharaja Ganga Singh's portrait, photo © Sudhir Kasliwal. Maharaja Bhupal Singh with the British in court, painting from City Palace Museum, Udaipur, photo © Resource Foto. Imperial Assemblage, New Delhi, 1877, photo City Palace Museum. Maharaja of Jaipur's first interview with the British Political Agent, photo Manu Kaul. Lord Mountbatten, photo © A.L. Syed.
40–1 Maharana Bhupal Singh of Udaipur and Maharja Ganga Singh of Bikaner, 1920's, photo © A.L. Syed. Gayatri Devi's portrait, photo taken from *Lives of Indian Princes*, p. 206. Samode Palace, photo © Roy Lewis. Blue pottery sign, photo Nitin Rai.
42 Students in Islamic school near Alwar, photo © Raghu Rai. Calligraphy, Jaipur School, photo © Sudhir Kasliwal. Mewari script, photo private collection.
43 Ramayan feast, photo coll. © Sally Holkar.
44–5 Incarnations of Vishnu, gouache on wood, cover from a Vishnu Purana manuscript, photo © Victoria & Albert Museum. Trinity of Brahma, Vishnu, and Shiva and their consorts, painting from M.S.M.S. II Museum, Jaipur. Krishna and the *gopis*, painting, detail of Krishna addressing devotees, miniature, Jaipur school, from City Palace Museum, Jaipur, photos © Sudhir Kasliwal. Saraswati, painting, *Bhagavad Gita*, photos © R.C. Sharma. Figure of goddess Kali, figure of Brahma at temple in Pushkar, photos © Roy Lewis. Krishna as infant, photo © Sudhir Kasliwal. Figure of Shiva at temple in Chittorgarh, photo © Benoit Juge.
46–7 Worship of rats at Karni Mata Temple, Deshnoke, dressed up idol at Surya Temple, Jhalrapatan, photos © Nitin Rai. *Gita-Govinda*, from M.S.M.S. II Museum, photo © Sudhir Kasliwal. Priest worshiping *linga*, photo © Tripti Pandey. Lakeside at Pushkar, statues of Shiva, puja with offering, Ganesh, Nandi, figure of Shiva, photos © Roy Lewis.
48–9 Two masked women, Jain statue, temple of Rishabhadev, Jain worshiper, photos © Roy Lewis. Jains carrying five essential items, painting, photo private collection. A group of Jain nuns, Jain monk, photos © M.D. Sharma. Jain statue in procession, photo © John Falconer. Statues of *tirthankaras*, photo © Benoit Juge.
50–1 Muslim pilgrims paying obeisance at *dargah*, Ajmer, rose offerings, photos © Roy Lewis. Muharram in Jaipur, photo © Tripti Pandey. Other photos by Nitin Rai.
52–3 Baba Ram Deo, terracotta plaque of snake god, photos © M.D. Sharma. Tattooed woman, photo © Sudhir Kasliwal. Ancestor shrine, painted cow, *lingam* and *yoni* shrine, *sadhu*, photos © Roy Lewis. *Pabuji ki phad*, Jats worshiping at street shrine, photos © Tripti Pandey. Snake god being taken to temple, photo © Raghu Rai.
54–5 Bhopa and Bhopi storytellers, photo © Tripti Pandey. Narrating the story of Pabuji, Prithviraj Chauhan, taken from Hendey's Book, photo © M.D. Sharma. Manuscript on Dhola Maru folk legend, photo Sudhir Kasliwal. Figure of Karni Mata on door, photo © Raghu Rai.
56–7 Block printer in Barmer, photo Raghu Rai. Carving of printing block, washing screen printed textiles, block printing by hand, Jaipur, drying block printed textiles, photos © Jon Burbank. Sanganer and Bagru block prints, *Ajrakh* print, photos © Chelna Desai. Screen printing in Sanganer, photo Nitin Rai. Drying dyed cloth on racks, photo © Roy Lewis. Flower motif, photo © John Falconer.
58–9 Woman doing embroidery, animal embroidered design, appliqué work, tie-and-dye turban, embroidered elephant detail, photos © M.D. Sharma. Tie-and-dye design, *gota* work, embroidered mirrorwork detail, embroidered quilt design, Jaipur, photos © Chelna Desai. Costume

with *zari* embroidery, photo © Suresh Cordo. *Zari* embroiderer, photo © Aman Nath. Woman tying and dyeing material, photo © Roy Lewis. *Laharia, photo* © Tripti Pandey.
60–1 Rajput costume of Maharao S. Bani Singh of Alwar, photo © Sudhir Kasliwal. Women wearing *odhnis*, men's attire, *pila*, turbaned man, photos © Tripti Pandey. Female attire, photo © Raghu Rai. Men tying their turbans, photo © Nitin Rai. Royal women's costumes, photo © Suresh Cordo. Block print, photo © Chelna Desai.
62–3 Turban jewel, photo © Victoria & Albert Museum. Goldsmith, Jaipur, photo © Phillips Antiques, Bombay. A team of *minakars*, enameling tools, photo © Farooq Issa. Silver lion chair from Fateh Prakash Palace, feet jewelry, photos © Roy Lewis. Tribal jewelry, liqueur sipper in bird design, enameled goblet, enameled chess pieces, photos taken at Gem Palace © Sudhir Kasliwal. Body jewelry worn by woman, photo © Tripti Pandey. Inlay work, setting stones, photo © Jitendra S. Olaniya. Kitchen utensils, photo © Roy Lewis. Pehari woman, *minakari* woman's necklace, photo © Amar Nath.
64–5 Painting of Ras-lila dance, photo taken at Maharaja Sawai Pratap Singh Museum, Jaipur © Sudhir Kasliwal. Painting of Maharana Fateh Singh's durbar, painting of Maharana Fateh Singh crossing a river, photos © Resource Foto. Painting of Radha, photo © Asok Das. Painting of court scene, Jodhpur 1800, photo © M.D. Sharma. Painting of ranis and raja at palace courtyard from Chitrashala, Bundi, photo Nitin Rai. Painting of tiger hunt from City Palace, Kota, photo Nitin Rai.
66–7 Wall painting of assembly of deities, wall painting of female dancers with musicians and painting of a dancer, Kota mural, wall painting of goddess Lakshmi, wall painting of Krishna with cowherd girls from Chitrashala, *pichhavai* showing Lord Krishna with cowherd girl swinging on a tree, *phad* portraying Pabuji, photos © M.D. Sharma. *Pichhvai* painter at Nadhwara, photo © Amir Nath.
68–9 A-shaped Mughal carpet, *surahi*, leather shield from Maharaja Sawai Man Singh II Museum, Jaipur, photo © Sudhir Kasliwal. Modern Rajasthani carpet, handmade durrie, carpet-weaving, camel and horse saddles, photos Nitin Rai. Durrie-making, *jootis*, photo © M.D. Sharma. Knuckle pad from City Palace, Jaipur, photo © Asok Das. Man playing musical instrument, photo © Tripti Pandey.
70–1 Sculpture from Karni Mata Temple, Deshnoke, detail of *jali* work, photo © M.D. Sharma. *Jali*-carved balcony of *haveli*, Jaisalmer, gateway with elephant sculpture at City Palace, Jaipur, panel showing elephants in high relief from Sat Bis Deorhi Temple, Chittorgarh, photos © Benoit Juge. Sculpture of a row of figures from Surya Temple, Jhalarapatan, stone carver, photo Nitin Rai. Slabs of carved stone, photo © Tripti Pandey. Sculpture of row of dancing figures from Jagdish Mandir, Udaipur, photo © Jon Burbank.
72–3 Pair of handpainted water pots with raja and rani designs, puppet show, man playing *dholak*, photo © Nitin Rai. Molela terracotta, drawing design on a piece of blue pottery, earthen figures of folk divinities, photos © M.D. Sharma. Potter molding clay into pot, pill containers made of blue pottery, puppeteer, photos © Tripti Pandey. Row of puppets, photo © Roy Lewis. Manuscript on folklore of Dhola-Maru, photo © Sudhir Kasliwal.
74–5 Woman of desert area preparing home-cooked meal, photo © Roy Lewis. Frying *puris* in house, woman preparing a pot of *lassi*, the Indian kitchen, making *chappatis*, photos courtesy pte coll. of Sally Holkar. Rajasthani feast, photo taken from Prince of Wales Museum, Bombay. *Khar khargosh*, line drawing, photo courtesy pte coll. of Sally Holkar.
76–7 Painting of a picnic with *sula* and *khud khargosh* being prepared, photo taken from Prince of Wales Museum. Roasting *sulas*, photo courtesy pte coll. of Sally Holkar. All other photos by Nitin Rai.
78–9 Group of musicians, photo © John Falconer. *Kamaycha*, snake dance, fire dance, *kanjar* dance, *Kamaycha* dholl musican, *satara*, *chari* dance, *terah tali* dance, photos © Tripti Pandey. *Gair* dance, *morchang*, photo Nitin Rai.
82–3 Decorated elephant for Holi, women in festive dress during Gangaur, folk dance at Desert Festival, Sheetla fair, photos © Tripti Pandey. Camel polo, *dargah* at Urs Gharib Navaz, Teej festival, Jaipur, dancer at Desert Festival, Nagaur fair, photos Nitin Rai. Painting of celebration of Holi by the throwing of colored powder, photo © Resource Foto. Painting of procession during Gangaur at Udaipur, photo © Asok Das. Tightrope walker at Pushkar fair, photo © Roy Lewis. Visitors traveling to Pushkar fair on camels, photo © Raghu Rai. Ravana effigy being prepared to be burnt at Dashera festival, Kota, photo © Aman Nath.
83 *Haveli*, drawing by Kathryn Blomfield. Details from Sir Swinton Jacob's Jeypore portfolio of architectural details.
84–5 Drawings by Kathryn Blomfield.
86–7 Drawings by Kathryn Blomfield.
88–9 Drawings by Kathryn Blomfield. Detail of window at Hawa Mahal, Jaipur, photo © Jon Burbank
90–1 Drawings by Kathryn Blomfield.
92–3 Drawings by Kathryn Blomfield. Plan of Jaipur city, from City Palace Museum, Jaipur, photo © Asok Das.
94–5 Drawings by Kathryn Blomfield. Intricate panel carving from Ranakpur temple, photo Nitin Rai.
96 Drawings by Kathryn Blomfield. Architectural details from Sir Swinton Jacob's Jeypore portfolio.
97 Miniature, Mewar, photo © M.D. Sharma.
98–9 Paintings from Victoria & Albert Museum.
100–1 Paintings photographed by Resource Foto.
102–3 *The Palace of Amber*, photo © British Library. *The Village Well, Dust storm coming on near Jeypore, Rajputana,* Paul Mellon Collection, Yale Center for British Art. William Simpson's portrait, photo © John Falconer.
104 *Jaipur*, Paul Walter Collection.
105 Elephant polo, photo © A.L. Syed.
106–7 Rajputs, lithography by Louis Rousselet. Street scene, Udaipur, from *Illustrated London News*, photo courtesy of Radhika Dwivedi Col. James Tod's portrait, photo courtesy of City Palace Museum, Udaipur. Turban styles of Rajasthan, postcards printed by Mehrangarh Museum, Jodhpur Fort. Aldous Huxley's portrait, photo courtesy of Chatto & Windus.
108–9 Nautch girl of Alwar, lithography by Louis Rousselet. Sheesh Mahal, Amber Fort, painting from City Palace, Kota. Aldous Huxley's portrait, photo courtesy of Chatto & Windus. Satyajit Ray's portrait, photo © Nemai Ghosh.
110–1 Lake Palace, Udaipur, photo © A.L. Syed. Bundi Palace, lithography by Captain Waugh, Jimmy Ollia Collection. Rudyard Kipling's portrait, photo courtesy of Library of Congress.
112–3 Heralds at court, photo © A.L. Syed. Travelers in a bullock cart, Jaipur, photo © Phillips Antiques.
114–5 Portrait of Maharana Fateh Singh of Mewar, photo © Maharana of Mewar Collection. Portrait of Sir

◆ LIST OF ILLUSTRATIONS

Pratap Singh of Jodhpur, photo © S. Dutt. Maharaja Ganga Singh of Bikaner, photo © Phillips Antiques. Sharada Dwivedi's portrait, author's own. Portrait of Charles Allen, courtesy Sharada's Dwivedi's collection.
116–7 Lord Hardinge in the sport of pig-sticking, private collection. *Peacocks in Rajasthan*, paintings by David Rankin.
118–9 Temple of Vrij in the fort of Chittor, the sacred lake of Pushkar, from Louis Rousselet, *India and its Native Princes*, Ameneh Ahmed Collection. Louis Rousselet's portrait, photo © John Falconer. Sister Nivedita's portrait, reproduced from *Studies from an Eastern Home*.
120 Man leading camel, photo, Nitin Rai. Dominic Moraes' portrait, photo © Fawzan Husain.
121 Boats near Lake Palace, Udaipur, photo © Phillips Antiques.
122–3 All photos by Photobank.
124–5 Dancers at Pushkar fair, woman doing embroidery, photos © Raghu Rai. Woman at Udaipur, fetching water in the Thar Desert, Ramdeora Fair, photos © Benoit Juge.
126–7 Tilwara horse fair at Luni river, buying and selling of camels at Pushkar fair, photos © Roy Lewis. Peafowl at Sariska wildlife sanctuary, photo © Raghu Rai.
128 Camels, photo © K.B. Kothady. Gathering by the fire on a winter morning at Nagaur fair, photo © Nitin Rai. Sand dune patterns, photo © Raghu Rai.
129 Interior and gate of Amber Fort, photo © Sudhir Kasliwal.
130–1 Raja Man Singh I's portrait, photo © Sudhir Kasliwal. Street scene, Jaipur, photo © Sudhir Kasliwal. Itinerary map by Anuar bin Abdul Rahim. Locator map by Ang Teck Beng.
132–3 Portrait of Vidyadhar Bhattacharya, photo © S. Dutt. Portrait of Maharaja Sawai Man Singh II, photo courtesy of Brig. Maharaja Sawai Bhawani Singh of Jaipur, Chairman Maharaja Sawai Man Singh II Museum Trust, City Palace, Jaipur. The maharaja in his royal carriage, photo © Sudhir Kasliwal. Raja Jai Singh's *firman*, photos © R.C. Sharma Vyakul S.R.C. P.V.P.S. Trust, Jaipur. Elephant procession, photo © A.L. Syed. Jaipur's coat of arms, coin used during Maharaja Man Singh II's time, photos © Sudhir Kasliwal. Two flags of Jaipur rulers, photo Nitin Rai.
134–5 Sir Swinton Jacob's portrait, photo © John Falconer. Old map of Jaipur city, photo © Sudhir Kasliwal, courtesy of Brig. Maharaja Sawai Bhawani Singh of Jaipur, chairman, Maharaja Sawai Man Singh II Museum Trust, City Palace, Jaipur. Pink gates of Jaipur city, stone sculpture in wall niche, photos Nitin Rai. City map by Anuar bin Abdul Rahim. Miniature painting of Jaipur before the city was painted pink, photo © Aman Nath.
136–7 City Palace, Jaipur, photo © M.D. Sharma. Raja Sawai Madho Singh I's portrait, photo © John Falconer. Other photos by Nitin Rai.
138–9 Hawa Mahal, Jaipur, photo © Phillips Antiques, Bombay. Painting showing birth of Christ, from City Palace Museum, Maharaja Ram Singh's camera, photos © Sudhir Kasliwal. Other photos by Nitin Rai.
140–1 Raja Sawai Jai Singh II with Portuguese astronomers, photo © Sudhir Kasliwal. Jai Singh II's manuscript on astronomy, photo © Sudhir Kasliwal. Other photos by Nitin Rai.
142–3 Natani ki Haveli, photo © John Falconer. Manek Chowk, Jaipur, photo © Phillips Antiques. Necklace and forehead ornament, photo © Farooq Issa. Jaipur bazaar, photo © K.B. Jothady. Chand Pol bazaar street sign, photo © Jon Burbank. Other photos by Nitin Rai.
144–5 Rambagh Palace, Albert Hall Museum, Moti Dungri Palace, photos © Nitin Rai. *Polo Players on Elephant's' Back*, from the Rambagh Palace collection, photo © Sudhir Kasliwal. Rambagh Palace, drawing, private collection. Raj Mandi, façade © Ghislaine Bellemin.
146–51 Amber Fort, 3D-illustration by Anuar Abdul bin Rahim. Sheesh Mahal, elephants transporting tourists to Amber Fort, Jaleb Chowk, garden of Dilaram Bagh, Ganesh Pol, *jali* screens of Ganesh Pol, roof with Bengali eaves, Sukh Mandir with Jaigarh Fort in background, ghats leading to Maota Lake, photos © Benoit Juge. Detail of door in Sukh Nivas, photo © Sudhir Kasliwal. Other photos by Nitin Rai. Painting of elephant parking lot at Amber, photo © David Rankin.
152–3 Black and white print of Amber Fort, courtesy Radhika Dwidevi. All other photos by Nitin Rai.
154–5 Fort at Jaigarh, Jalban cannon, murals at the palace at Nahargarh, frescoes at Nahargarh © Nitin Rai.
156–7 *Chhatris* at Gaitor, photo © Phillips Antiques, Bombay. General view of Galta, circa 1902, photo © John Falconer. Other photos by Nitin Rai.
158–9 Jain temple in Sanganer, photo © John Falconer. Other photos by Nitin Rai.
160–1 All photos by Dr. A.K. Das.
162–3 Fortress and town of Ajmer, lithograph by Capt. Waugh, photo © Jimmy Ollia. Degs ceremony, photo © Tripti Pandey. Other photos by Nitin Rai.
164–5 Town of Pushkar, photo © Sharada Dwivedi. Temple of Rama, Pushkar, photo courtesy of Radhika Dwivedi Camel race, temples of Pushkar, photos © Raghu Rai. Other photos by Nitin Rai.
166–7 *Darwaan* outside Kishangarh Fort, photo © A.L.Syed. Marble mine, photo © M.D. Sharma. Postage stamp showing painting of Bani Thani, photo © Sudhir Kasliwal. Miniature of the Maharaja of Kishangarh, photo © Aman Nath. Doorways, photos © Benoit Juge, © Jon Burbank, © Nitin Rai.
168–9 Alwar's coat of arms, view of principal street leading to Alwar fort, photos © Sudhir Kasliwal. Old map of Alwar city, photo courtesy Sudhir Kasliwal. Maharaja Jai Singh's portrait, photo © M.D. Sharma. Temple tank at the Vinai Villas Palace, photo courtesy of Radhika Dwivedi.
170–1 Jewelry of Alwar's royal family, jade vase of Alwar's treasury, seal of Alwar state, photos © Sudhir Kasliwal. Miniature paintings, photo © Tripti Pandey. Other photos by Nitin Rai.
172–3 Rajgarh Fort, photo courtesy Sudhir Kasliwal. Akbar and Abu'l Fazal in court, private collection. Other photos by Nitin Rai.
174–5 All photos by Nitin Rai.
176–7 Beaters for the hunt, elephant *howdah*, maharaja's *shikar* party, photos courtesy of H.N. Ghiya. Sculpture of tiger mauling a European, photo © Victoria & Albert Museum. Other photos © Kailash Sankhala.
178 Neemrana Fort, photo © Samar Singh Jodha. Other photos by Nitin Rai.
179 Wall painting from Sone-Chand ki Haveli, photo Nitin Rai.
180–1 Itinerary map by Anuar bin Abdul Rahim. Locator map by Ang Teck Beng. Marwari businessman, painted frescos of Biyani Haveli, Sikar Fort, photos Nitin Rai. Book cover of *Rajasthan – The Painted Walls of Shekhavati*, courtesy of Aman Nath.
182–3 Poddar Haveli, cenotaph of Shardul Singh, Mandawa Castle, striking the gong, frescos at Mandawa Haveli, portrait of Maharaja Ram Singh II, portrait of Maharaja Madho Singh II, photos by Nitin Rai © Editions Didier Millet. Piramal Haveli, photo © Namas Bhojani.

184–5 Frescos from Poddar Haveli, Biyani Haveli, Mandawa Haveli, Shardul Singh's cenotaph. All photos by Nitin Rai.
186–7 All photos by Nitin Rai.
188–9 All photos by Nitin Rai.
190 Lachhmangarh Fort, photo © A.L. Syed. Fresco from Poddar Haveli featuring Ramayan scenes, photo © M.D. Sharma. Other photos by Nitin Rai.
191 Painting of daily life in village homes, photo © National Museum, New Delhi.
192–3 Itinerary map by Anuar bin Abdul Rahim. Bikaner's coat of arms, photo © R.C. Sharma. Desert in Bikaner, Rao Bikaji's bed at Phul Mahal, photos by Nitin Rai © Editions Didier Millet.
194–5 Maharaja Ganga Singh, photo © S. Dutt. Officers of Bikaner Camel Corps, c. 1902, photo © John Falconer. Fort walls of Bikaner town, *jootis*, Rao Bikaji's sandalwood throne, photos by Nitin Rai.
196–7 All photos by Nitin Rai. *Swords, Suraj Pol, Lal Niwas, frescos at Lal Niwas, Phul Mahal, Anup Mahal, Chandra Mahal, rain motif.*
198–9 Lal Niwas dining room, smoking room, Bikaner Palace, photos © John Falconer. All other photos by Nitin Rai. *Antique Rajput weaponry, Lallgarh Palace, wooden swing, drums of Jambhoji, Ganga Niwas' sandstone hall, Bikaner miniature painting.*
200–1 Raja Anup Singh's armor, photo © Nitin Rai. Armory with Mughal influence, photo © Phillips Antiques. Shields and swords, swords and scabbards, photo © Sudhir Kasliwal. Warrior in armor, Raja Man Singh I's sword, *katar*, mace, from M.S.M.S. Museum, photographed by Sudhir Kasliwal. Powder horn, from *Decorative Art of India*, London: Studio Editions, p. 174.
202–3 *Rampuria haveli, Camel breeding farm, khejri tree, Gogaji idol, water melons,* photos by Nitin Rai. Painting of *khejri* tree, photo © Aman Nath.
204–5 Officer on camel, 1950's, photo © A.L. Syed. Members of Bikaner's border security force, photo © Roy Lewis. Ganga Risala ceremonial parade, photo © Tripti Pandey. Military review of Bikaner camel corps, row of camels from the Camel Corps, c. 1902, 'Ships of the desert', photos © John Falconer. Cigarette packs featuring the Bikaner camel corps, photo © Phillips Antiques. Officers of Ganga Risala, photo © Sudhir Kasliwal.
206–7 Maharaja Ganga Singh of Bikaner with the viceroy on a hunt at Gajner, photo © A.L. Syed. All other photos by Nitin Rai. *Gateway to Karni Mata Temple, façade of Karni Mata Temple, rats at Karni Mata Temple, silver door with figure of Karni Mata, cenotaphs at Devikund, lake and lodge at Gajner, Shiva Temple at Kolaya.*
208–9 Jaisalmer's coat of arms, photo © Sudhir Kasliwal. Rao Jaisal's portrait, photo © Raghu Rai. All other photos by Nitin Rai. *Wall painting of a battle scene at Jaisalmer Fort, Bhawani idol, flag of Jaisalmer, desert minstrels.*
210–11 City map by Anuar bin Abdul Rahim. Locator map by Ang Teck Beng. Opium boxes, photo © Raghu Rai. Other photos by Nitin Rai. *Gadsisar lake, Jaisalmer Fort, puppets for sale at Jaisalmer Fort.*
210–11 Walls of Jaisalmer Fort, photo © M.D. Sharma. Hawa Pol, stone balls at Jaisalmer Fort, weather forecast device, old cannon at Jaisalmer Fort, old manuscripts at fort museum, photos © Raghu Rai. Life inside Jaisalmer Fort, photo Nitin Rai. Jaisalmeri style turban, reproduced from postcard printed by Mehrangarh Museum, Jodhpur Fort.
214–15 Patwon ki Haveli, sale of handicrafts in alley of Patwon ki Haveli, stone carver, photos © Raghu Rai. Nathmalji ki Haveli, façade of Patwon ki Haveli, photos by Nitin Rai. Camel saddle, lithography R.C. Sharma Vyakul, S.R.C. P.V.P.S Trust, Jaipur. Salim Singh's *haveli*, photo © Aman Nath. *Torana* doorway, photo © Tripti Pandey.
216–7 Bara Bagh, shrine at Bhattiani Sabi Rani, Jain temples at Lodurva, *torana* archway of Jain temple at Lodurva, wayside shrine to Bhaironji, photos © Raghu Rai. Chhatri Vyas, photo © Nitin Rai.
218–9 Sand dunes at Samm, Pokharan Fort, courtyard of Pokharan Fort, clay pitchers of Barmer, painted walls and floor of village house, woman doing embroidery, photos © Raghu Rai.
220–1 Jodhpur's coat of arms, seal of Jodhpur, photos © Sudhir Kasliwal. Rao Jodha's portrait, photo © Raghu Rai. Sir Pratap Singh's portrait, photo © Phillips Antiques, Bombay. Fish-shaped imperial standard from Jodhpur Museum, photo © Roy Lewis. Riding with jodhpurs, drawing by Raven Hill. Jodhpur city, c. 1900, photo © John Falconer.
222–3 Itinerary map by Anuar Abdul bin Rahim. Locator map by Ang Teck Beng. Maharaja Umaid Singh of Jodhpur with his sons by his aircraft, photo private collection. Clock tower in bazaar, Jodhpur, aerial view of houses in Jodhpur, photos © Jon Burbank.
224–5 Mehrangarh Fort, 3-D illustration by Anuar bin Abdul Rahim. Cannons on Mehrangarh Fort, photo © Raghu Rai. Close-up view of fort ramparts, photo © Benoit Juge.
226–7 Façade of palace at Mehrangarh Fort, close-up of *jali* window at Mehrangarh Fort, photos © Benoit Juge. Mehrangarh Fort, lithograph by Capt. Waugh, photo courtesy of Jimmy Olia. Palaces at Mehrangarh Fort, old print, photo © John Falconer. Stained-glass windows of royal bedroom in Mehrangarh Fort, photo © Jon Burbank. Palanquin in fort museum, old weaponry at museum in Mehrangarh Fort, photos © Raghu Rai. Gold wooden trone, mirrored interior, photos © Aman Nath.
228–9 Shringar Chowk, Jaswant Thada, courtyard of palace complex at Mehrangarh Fort, photos © Benoit Juge. *Jali* designs, 8 photos © Jon Burbank. 1 photo © Tripti Pandey. 1 photo © Benoit Juge. 1 photo Nitin Rai. 1 photo © Raghu Rai.
230–1 Umaid Bhawan Palace, Jodhpur, photo © Roy Lewis. Royal railway saloon of Maharaja of Jodhpur, private collection. Puppets, photo © M.D. Sharma. Crest of Umaid Bhawan Palace, Jodhpur, reproduced from a greeting card. Maharaja Gaj Singh II, private collection.
232–3 Cenotaphs at Mandore, stairway at Sachiya Mata Temple, Hindu deities, photos © Benoit Juge. Hall of Heroes, photo © John Falconer. Bishnoi farm, durrie being woven at desert village near Jodhpur, photos © Roy Lewis. Ceiling of Mahavira Temple, photo © Raghu Rai.
234–5 Figure in niche, *devakulikas,* pillars, photos © Benoit Juge. Mahavira temple, strut figures, shrine chamber and portico, photos © Saryu Doshi.
236–7 Woman preparing *rangoli* design with rice paste, applying henna to hands, woman decorating the wall of a house, clay figures, photos © Tripti Pandey. Decorating elephant, rural house with painted design, painted wall designs, photos © Raghu Rai. Square motif, photo © Roy Lewis. Wall painting of elephant god, wall painting of horse, hand pattern, folk art wall designs, photos © Jon Burbank. Folk art motif, photo © Sudhir Kasliwal.
238 Nagaur Fort, fresco of Krishna and *gopis*, medieval cooling system at Nagaur Fort, photos © Tripti Pandey.
239 Maharana Bhupal Singh in a state barge on Pichola Lake holding a durbar on a Gangaur evening, photo © A.L. Syed.
240–1 Itinerary map by Anuar Abdul bin Rahim. Locator map by Ang

◆ LIST OF ILLUSTRATIONS

Teck Beng. Udaipur's coat of arms, photo © Sudhir Kasliwal. Street scene, Udaipur, photo © Raja Deen Dayal. Old coins of Udaipur, courtesy Shriji Arvind Singh Mewar's private collection.
242–3 Haldighatti battle scene, detail from painting, from City Palace Museum, Udaipur, miniature painting of courtly procession, miniature painting of durbar scene, photos © Resource Foto. Maharana Pratap of Mewar, photo Nitin Rai. Durbar of maharana of Udaipur, painting courtesy of Manu Kaul.
244–5 City map by Anuar Abdul bin Rahim. Locator map by Ang Teck Beng. Vendor in bazaar, photo © Benoit Juge. Buildings at Lake Pichola , photo © Jon Burbank. Old city gate, photo Nitin Rai.
246–7 City Palace, Udaipur, photo © M.D. Sharma. Elephant fight, photo courtesy of H.N. Ghiya, photo © Raja Deen Dayal. Bari Mahal, miniature painting, from City Palace Museum, Udaipur, photo © Pankaj Shah. Chini Chitrashala, chair of Maharaja Fateh Singh, European-influenced tile work, Sheesh Mahal, City Palace, Udaipur, photos Nitin Rai.
248–9 Maharana Bhupal Singh of Mewar, photo courtesy City Museum Udaipur. Belgian glass crystal furniture at Fateh Prakash Palace, Udaipur, photo © Roy Lewis. Other photos by Nitin Rai. *Moti Mahal, relief of peacock at Mor Chowk, courtyard of City Palace, Maharana Pratap's horse, swimming pool at Shiv Niwas.*
250–1 Lake Palace, Udaipur, 3-D illustration by Anuar bin Abdul Rahim. Jag Mandir, lithography courtesy Jimmy Ollia. Jag Mandir, miniature painting, photo © Resource Foto. Other photos by Nitin Rai. *View of ghats and Lake Pichola , Natani ka Chabutra, ceiling of banquet hall in Jag Niwas, Sajjan Niwas, a guest room in Jag Niwas, Lake Palace.*
252–3 Maharaja of Jaipur sending off British guest at railway station, c. 1902, photo © John Falconer. Lord Mountbatten with Indian princes, British Political Agents and guests on elephants, photos © A.L. Syed. Maharaja Ganga Singh of Bikaner with King George V, photo © S. Dutt. Painting © John Falconer.
254–5 Cenotaphs at Ahar, photo © Phillips Antiques. Girl with clay doll, photo © Tripti Pandey. Other photos by Nitin Rai. *Jagdish Temple, Saheliyon ki Bari, palace at Sajjangarh, Garuda statue, kavadh, gateway, Shilpagram village.*
256–7 Eklingji Temples, photo © John Falconer. Other photos by Nitin Rai. *Sas Temple, image of Nathdwara, pichhwai, framed photos of Nathdwara sold in bazaar, details of sculptures at Sas Temple, torana archway of Bahu Temple, terracotta from Molela.*
258–9 Hunting in forest, Jaisamand, miniature painting from City Palace Museum, Udaipur, photo © Resource Foto. Irrigation by Persian wheel method, near Ranakpur, photo © Roy Lewis. *Nilgai*, photo © Kailash Sankhala. Other photos by Nitin Rai. *Carved façade of Dayal Shah Mandir, terraced embankments of lake at Jaisamand, entrance of Rishabdeo Temple, carvings at Jagat Ambika Mata Temple.*
260–1 Kumbhalgarh Fort, lithograph by Capt. Waugh, photo courtesy of Jimmy Ollia. Other photos by Nitin Rai. *Kumbhalgarh Fort, Paghra Pol, Vedi building, Neelkant Temple, wall painting of Badal Mahal.*
262–3 Interior view of Adinath Temple, Jain pilgrims visiting Adinath Temple, photos © Benoit Juge. Other photos by Nitin Rai. *Façade of Adinath Temple, carved columns of Adinath Temple, panel carvings depicting legend of Nemi, Parshva statue.*
264–5 Pillared hall, pillars, spine and ceiling at Adinatha Temple, photos © Benoit Juge. Statues and carvings, photos © Roy Lewis.
266–7 Erotic painting, photo © Nitin Javeri. Durbar hall in Juna Mahal, Juna Mahal, photos © Roy Lewis. Thema work, photo © Aman Nath. Other photos by Nitin Rai. *Udai Vilas, six examples of frescos from Juna Mahal, trophy room.*
268–9 Lake at Mount Abu, painting , sketched by Capt. Grindlay, taken from Phillips Antiques. Jain pilgrims, photo © M.D. Sharma. Gothic style palace, view of city of Mount Abu, photos, Nitin Rai.
270–1 Spectacularly carved marble pillars at Dilwara Temple, interior of Vimala Vashi Temple, intricately carved ceiling, exterior view of temples at Dilwara, photos © John Falconer. Jain monk, photo © M.D. Sharma
272–3 Divinities, photo © Roy Lewis. All other photos © John Falconer.
274–5 Gomukh Temple, line drawing by Raven Hill. Mount Abu mountain peaks, photo © Benoit Juge. Other photos by Nitin Rai. *Nakki Lake, damascened swords of Sirohi, deity in Gomukh Temple, plains near Achalgarh Fort, Achalgarh Fort, Kasar Vilas Palace.* Throne, photo © Aman Nath.
276–7 Siege of Chittorgarh, miniature painting © Victoria & Albert Museum. View of Chittorgarh, with Tower of Victory rising above city, from James Tod, *Annals and Antiquities of Rajasthan*, photo © John Falconer. *Mirabai* playing instrument, painting © Kailash Sankhala. Other photos by Nitin Rai. *Chittorgarh Fort, Tower of Victory, spring water from "cow's mouth".*
278 Palace of Padmini, Tower of Fame, photos © John Falconer. Other photos by Nitin Rai. *Kalika Mata Temple, Patta's palace, painting of Gadholia Lohars.*
279 Princely procession, photo © A.L. Syed.
280–1 Itinerary map by Anuar bin Abdul Rahim. Locator by Ang Teck Beng. Country seat of the Kota princes, photo courtesy of Jimmy Ollia. An artist's impression of Kota city, Kota's coat of arms, photos courtesy of R.C. Sharma, photo © Sudhir Kasliwal. Miniature paintings of Kota school, photo Nitin Rai.
282–3 All photos by Nitin Rai. *Solar clock, City Palace, bhujtras, interior of Umed Bhawan Palace, ivory palanquin, Jagmandir.*
284–5 Temple ruins at Barolli, lithography by Capt. Waugh, photo courtesy of Jimmy Ollia. Other photos by Nitin Rai. *Kansuan Temple, Baroli Temples, Kota Doria cloth, Ghateshwara Temple, Bhensrorgarh Fort, erotic sculpture at Ramgarh, temple at Ramgarh.*
286–7 Ravi Shankar, photo © Avinash Pasricha. Other photos by Nitin Rai. *Garh Palace, interior of Surya Temple, opera theater, façade of Surya Temple, details of sculptures from* Surya Temple. Prithvi Vilas, courtesy Prithvi Vilas.
288–9 Mangos, photo © Dinodia. Parrots, photo © Tripti Pandey. All other photos by Nitin Rai. *Doorway of Chandravati Temple, a view of temple grounds, Gagron Fort, Ganesha statue in temple at Kakuni, temple ruins at Kakuni, doorway to temple at Kakuni.*
290–1 Bundi town, dominated by Taragarh Fort, painting by Capt. Grindlay, taken from Phillips Antiques. Bundi's coat of arms, photo courtesy of R.C. Sharma © Sudhir Kasliwal. Step well, photo © John Falconer. Other photos by Nitin Rai. *Town of Bundi, tank inside Taragarh Fort, cityscape as seen from fort.* Portrait of Maharao Raja Sir Raghubir Singh Baradur of Bundi, photo © Lensville.
292–3 Garh Palace, Bhim Burj, wall paintings at Garh Palace, photos Nitin Rai.
294–5 Palace of Bundi, drawing, photo courtesy of R.C. Sharma © Sudhir Kasliwal. Taragarh Fort, along the fort walls, photo Nitin Rai. Different

styles of turbans, 14 photos © Jon Burbank, 1 photo © Tripti Pandey. Group shot of turbans, photo © Raghu Rai.
296–7 All photos by Nitin Rai. *Ranjii ki Baori, Chaurasi Khambon ki Chhatri, Bundi miniature painting, Keshar Bagh, Sukh Niwas, Chaumukha bazaar, tank inside palace of Bundi, Bijoliyan Temples.*
298 Menal Temples, photo courtesy of Jimmy Ollia. Hindoli Fort, photo Nitin Rai.
299 Rajput *raja*, lithgraphy by Louis Rousselet.
300–1 Itinerary map by Anuar bin Abdul Rahim. Locator map by Ang Teck Beng. General view of Bharatpur, lithograph from Louis Rousselet's *India and its Native Princes*. Residence of the British Political Agent in Bharatpur c. 1900, photo © John Falconer.
302–3 Palace of Durjau Sal, from Louis Rousselet, *India & Its Native Princes*. Raja Badan Singh's palace, Lord Lake, photo © John Falconer. Other photos by Nitin Rai. *Ashtadhati Gate, garden within Raja Badan Singh's palace, close-up of Astadhati Gate, Vijay Stambha.*
304–5 Lawns of Sawai Madhopur Lodge, Ranthambhor Fort, private collection. Tiger in Ranthambhor, gray partridges, animals grazing at Ranthamhor, photos, Raghu Rai. Sambar, photo © Mahipal Singh.
306–7 Duck shoot, photo © John Falconer. Lord Linlithgow's portrait, large cormorants, spoonbills, red-crested pochard, white ibis, white-breasted kingfisher, openbill stork, sarus cranes, Siberian cranes, black-necked storks, photos © Daulat Singh. Graylag geese, nesting painted storks, photos © Kailash Sankhala.
308–9 Bharatpur's bird sanctuary, painting by David Rankin. Duck shoot, photo © John Falconer. Snake bird, migratory birds, photos, Raghu Rai. Record of highest number of ducks shot, entrance sign of Keoladeo National Park, wetland landscape of Keoladeo sanctuary, photos © Kailash Sankhala. Painted storks, bar-headed goose, photos © Daulat Singh. Sign showing different bird species, photo © Raymond Chua. Wetlands, photo © K.B. Jothady.
310–1 Gopal Bhawan, from Louis Rousselet, *India & Its Native Princes*. A royal carriage at Deeg, c. 1902, photo © John Falconer. Other photos by Nitin Rai. *Palace complex at Deeg, Keshav Mahal, Badal Mahal, frescos at cenotaph at Govardhan.* Site plan of Deeg Palace complex, from M.C. Joshi, *Dig.*, published by Archaeological Survey of India.
312 Babur's garden, miniature painting, photo © Victoria & Albert Museum.

Practical information
315 Jaisalmer, J.L. Nou's coll., © Government of India Tourist Office.
316 City traffic, photo ©Government of India Tourist Office.
317 Antoine Perigot's coll., © Government of India Tourist Office.
318 Rajasthani musicians, © Government of India Tourist Office.
319 Jodhpur, Patricio Estay's coll., © Government of India Tourist Office.
320 Hot-pepper doughnuts (*michi bala*), J.-L. Moreau 's coll.© Government of India Tourist Office.
321 Jaipur's blue pottery, Antoine Perigot's coll., © Government of India Tourist Office.
326 Lakshmi Vilas Palace Hotel © Lakshmi Vilas Palace Hotel
329 Jai Mahal Palace Hotel © Government of India Tourist Office.
333 Lalgarth Palace, Bikaner © Government of India Tourist Office.
334 Jaisalmer, J.-L. Moreau's coll. © Government of India Tourist Office.
335 Jodhpur, J.-L. Moreau's coll. © Government of India Tourist Office.
336 Khimsar Fort; Sardar Samand Palace Lake Resort © Government of India Tourist Office.
338 Connaught House, Mount Abu; Umed Bhawan Palace, Kota © Government of India Tourist Office.
340 Lake Palace, Udaipur © Government of India Tourist Office.

We have not been able to trace the heirs or publishers of certain documents. An account is being held open for them at our offices.

A

Aath Haveli, 182
Achalgarh Fort, 274, 275
accomodation 318, 326–340
Adinatha, 255, 264, 270-2, 278
Adinatha Temple, Ranakpur, 262-3, 265, 272
Adresses, 314, 318
Agni (Hindu deity), 44
Agnikula (Rajput clans), 32, 268-9, 274, 280, 290
agriculture, 20, 22-3, 41
Ahar, 255, 257
Aheria, 290, 296
air travel, 315, 316
Ajit Bhawan Palace, 233
Ajit Vilas, 227
Ajmer, 35, 38, 51, 122, 130, 162-3
ajrakh fabrics, 56, 219
Akal Fossil Park, 217
Akbar, Emperor, 26, 34, 36, 50, 99, 130, 152, 162, 178, 193, 220, 238, 242-3, 260, 277-8, 289, 290, 298, 304
Akbar's Palace, Ajmer, 163
Albert Hall Museum, Jaipur, 96, 135, 144
All India States Peoples' Conference, 39
Allen, Charles, 114-5
Alwar, 130
Amarsagar, Jaisalmer, 96, 216
Amber, 35, 114, 130, 132, *see also* Jaipur
Amber Fort, Jaipur, 122-3, 135, 146-7, 152-3
Ambika Mata Temple, 258-9
ancestor worship, 52
Annals and Antiquities of Rajasthan, 33, 200, 209, 284, 293
Anup Mahal, Junagarh Palace, 197
Aravalli Range, 16, 28, 130, 146, 162
arayish (plasterwork technique), 155
Archeological Museum, Ahar, 255
Archeological Museum, Bharatpur, 303
archeological sites, 20, 32, 192, 207
architecture, forts, 90-1
architecture, *havelis*, 86-7
architecture, palaces, 88-9, 136, 199, 246
architecture, rural houses, 84-5
architecture, temples, 94-5, 234-5, 265
architecture, urban houses, 86-7
Ardhanarisvara (Hindu deity), 45
Arjuna, 208
Arhai Din ka Jhonpra, 51, 162-3
armory exhibits, 137, 171, 226, 282
arts and crafts industry, 41
Aryans 32
astronomical observations, 93, 135, 140-1
Aurangzeb, Emperor, 37, 152, 162, 175, 220, 257-8, 280, 291
Ayurveda Center, 245

B

Baba Ram Deo, 53
Babur, Emperor, 36, 203, 220
Badal Mahal, Kumbhalgarh Fort, 261
Badal Mahal, Nagaur Fort, 238
Badan Singh (Raja) Palace, 303
Baggar, 183
Bagru, 158-9
Bahu Temple, 257
Bairat, 178
Bala Qila Fort, Alwar, 169, 172
Bala Qila Fort, Shekhavati, 182
Balsamand Lake Palace, Jodhpur, 96, 232
Banai Vilas Palace, 168-9
bandhani, 58-9
bandhej, 58-9
Bapu Bazaar, Jaipur, 143
Bapu Bazaar, Udaipur, 244
Bara Bagh, Jaisalmer, 96, 216
Bara Bazaar, 244
Bardai, Chand, 33
bargaining, 318
Bari Chaupar, 143
Bari Mahal, Udaipur, 111, 247
Barlai Bhatts, 230
Barmer, 192, 219
Baroli Temple Complex, 284
Battle of Deorai, 175
Battle of Haldighati, 36, 242
Battle of Khanwa, 36
Battle of Panipat, 35-6
Battle of Tarain, 35

BAZAARS

Bapu Bazaar, Jaipur, 143
Bapu Bazaar, Udaipur, 244
Bara Bazaar, 244
Bundi bazaars, 297
Chandpol Bazaar, 143
Chaumukh Bazaar, 297
Indira Bazaar, 143
Johri Bazaar, 142
Jaipur bazaars, 142-3
Jaisalmer bazaars, 211, 215
Jhalrapatan bazaars, 287
Jodhpur bazaars, 223
Kishanpol Bazaar, 143
Mount Abu bazaars, 269
Nathdwara bazaars, 257
Nehru Bazaar, 143
Pushkar bazaars, 165
Sadar Bazaar, Jodhpur, 223
Sadar Bazaar, Bundi, 297
Sireh Deorhi Bazaar, 142
Tripoli Bazaar, 143
Udaipur bazaars, 244

Behror
Bhadon Bhawan, 310
Bhagavad Gita, 45, 138
Bhagavata Purana, 44, 64
Bhairon, 217
Bhandeshwar Temple, 202-3
Bhangarh, 178
Bharatiya Lok Kala Mandal, 254-5
Bharatpur, 27, 35, 37, 38, 300-11
Bharatpur Fort, 300-1
Bharatpur Museum, 300
Bharmal, Raja, 35-6
Bhattacharya, Vidyadhar, 92, 132, 143
Bhattis, the, 33
Bhawani (Hindu deity), 209
Bhawani Natya Shala, 287
Bhensrorgarh Fort, 285
Bhils, the, 52
Bhim Burj, 292, 294
Bhim Vilas, Udaipur, 248
Bhima, 276
Bhimgarh Fort, 289
Bhopas, the, 54
bicycles, 316
Bijoliyan Temple, 297
Bika, Rao, 34-5, 192, 204
Bikaji, Rao, 46, 204
Bikaner, 34-5, 65, 115, 130, 192-207
Bikaner Camel Corps, 194, 203-5
Bikaner Museum, 199
Bikaner Palace, 269
bird migration, 28, 108
birdlife, 28-9, 117, 285, 301, 305-9
Bishnoi farms, 232-3
Bissau Lodge, 145
Biyani Haveli, 181
blue pottery, *see* pottery, blue
Boat Procession, Udaipur, 81
Brahma (Hindu deity), 45, 66, 164, 257, 284
Brahma Temple, Pushkar, 164
Brijraj Bhawan Palace, 283
British Political Agents, 38, 209, 253
British rule, 38, 133, 193-4, 209, 243, 268, 275, 281, 291, 301
Budget, 314
Bundi, 290-8
Bundi School of Miniatures, 293, 296
Bundi-Kota, 35, 280
Burton, Major Charles, 283
buses, 316

C

Camel Corps, *see* Bikaner Camel Corps
Camel Fair, *see* Pushkar Fair
Cameron, Roderick, 111
Cannon foundry, Jaigarh Fort, 155
carpet weaving, 68
car rental, 316
Cattle Fair, Nagaur, 82, 128
Chakri dance, 79
Chambal Valley, 16, 41
Chamwar Walon-ki Haveli, 152
Chand, Nihal, 64
Chandpol Bazaar, Jaipur, 143
Chandra Mahal, Jaipur, 92, 138-9
Chandra Mahal, Junagarh Palace, 197
Chandramauleshwar Temple, 288
Chandravati Temple, Kota, 96, 288
chappati, 74
Char Chowki Haveli, 190
Charans, the, 33
Chari dance, 79
Chauhans, the, 33, 35
Chauhan, Prithviraj, 33, 34-5, 55, 162, 282, 298, 305
Chauhata Square, 212-3
Chaumukh Bazaar, 297
Chaurasi Khambon ki Chhatri, 296
Chhatris, 89
Chhawchhariya Haveli, 182
Chhe Haveli, 183
Chhipa community, 56
Chini Chitrashala, 247
Chisti, Khwaja Mu'in-ud-din, 51, 81, 162
Chittor, 34, 36
Chittorgarh, 220, 240-3, 255, 276-8
Chittorgarh Fort, 276
Chitrashala, Bundi 293
Chokhani Haveli, Mandawa, 182
Chokhani Haveli, Lachhmangarh, 190
City Palace, Alwar, 170
City Palace, Jaipur, 71, 80, 92, 96, 103, 135-9
City Palace, Kota, 282
City Palace, Udaipur, 89, 114, 123, 246-9
City Palace Museum, Jaipur, 136-9, 141
City Palace Museum, Udaipur, 246, 249
climate, 314

COAT-OF-ARMS

Alwar, 168
Bharatpur, 300
Bikaner, 193
Bundi, 290
Jaipur, 132
Jaisalmer, 208
Jhalawar, 286
Jodhpur, 220
Kota, 280
Udaipur, 241

colonial rule, *see* British rule
Congress Party, 40
costumes, local, 60-1
cranes, *see* Siberian cranes
crops, cereal, 22
Crossthwaite Institute, 282
cuisine, 74
Currey, R.N., 113
Curzon Wylie Memorial, 282

D

Dargah Sharif, 162
Darrah Wildlife Sanctuary, 285
Das, Bhagwan, 35-6
Dashhera Festival, 101
Dayal Shah Mandir, 258
Deeg, 300, 310-1
Deeg Fort, 300, 311
Deolia, 267
Desert Festival, 80-1, 211
Desert National Park, 24, 30, 192, 218
Deshnoke, 192
Devi (Hindu deity), 44, 71
Devi, Gayatri, 40, 133, 145
Devikund, 206
Devnagari, 42
Devra Haveli, 183
Dewa, Rao, 35
Dhrupad music, 36
Dhundhari dialect, 42
Dhuni Mata Temple, 246
dialects, 42
Digambaras, 48-9, 271
Dilaram Bagh, 149, 152
Dilkhush Mahal, 247
Dilwara, 94-5, 163, 258, 269-70
Dingal, 42
Doctrine of Paramountcy, 301
Dola-lila, *see* Holi
Dung beetle, 216
Dungarpur, 240, 266-7
Dunlod, 182
Durga (Hindu deity), 45, 258
Durga Niwas, Junagarh Palace, 196
durrie making, 68, 232
Dwarakadhish Temple, 258
dyeing, textile, 57

E

East India Company, British, 36, 38, 300
ecosystems, natural, 16-7
Eesul, 208, 213
Eklingji Temple, 240, 256
elections, general, 40
electricity, 318
elephants, in stone relief, 71, 137
Elephant Festival, 80
elephant fights, 246-7
embassies, 314
embroidery, 58-9, 143, 165, 215
etiquette, 318

F

fabrics, *see* textiles

FAIRS

Boat Procession, Udaipur, 81
Dassehra Festival, 101
Desert Festival, 80-1, 211
Elephant Festival, 80
Gangaur Festival, 80, 250
Holi, 45, 81
Kumbh Mela, 52
Nagaur Fair, 82, 128, 238
Pushkar Fair, 82, 124-5, 126-7, 164-5
Ramdeo-ka-Karni, 53, 124
Sheetla Fair, 82
Teej, 81
Tilwara Horse Fair, 126-7

Fateh Prakash Palace, 249
Fatehpur, 183
fauna, 24-5, 258-9
festivals and celebrations, 319, *see also* Fairs
fire dance, 79
flora, 30
folk art, 236-7 *see also* cultural performances
folklore, 54-5 *see also* cultural performances
food, local, 74, 319, *see also* cuisine
formalities, 314
Fort Museum, Mehrangarh, *see* Mehrangarh Fort Museum
Fort Museum, Junagarh, 198
Fossil Park of Akal, 217

G

Gadholia Lohars, the, 278
Gadsisar Lake, 210
Gagron Fort, 288-9
Gair dance, 79
Gaitor, 157
Gajner, 24, 192, 206
Galta, 156
Gandhi, Indira, 40-1
Gandhi, Mahatma, 39-40
Ganesh Pol, Amber Fort, 146, 153
Ganesha (Hindu deity), 44, 47, 66, 258, 289, 298, 303
Ganga Canal, 115, 194
Ganga Niwas, Junagarh Palace, 198
Ganga Risala, 194, 203-4 *see also* Bikaner Camel Corps
Ganga-Jaisalmer Risala, 205
Gangabhar Kund, 255
Gangaur Festival, 80, 250
Garasia, 52
Garbh Gunjam, 292, 294
Garh Palace, 110, 286-7, 291, 292-3
Garuda, 280
Gatodji (snake god), 52
Gee, E.P., 117
Geet Govinda, 138
Gem Palace, Jaipur, 142
geography, 328
geology, 18-9
Ghateshwara Temple, 284
Ghevar, 143
Ghori, Mohammed, 220
Goenka Haveli, Fatehpur, 183
Goenka Haveli, Mandawa, 182
Gogaji (folk deity), 52, 203
Gogamedi, 203
Golbagh Palace, 303-4
Gomukh, 274, 277
Gomukh Temple, 274
Gopal Bhawan Palace, Deeg, 96, 310
Gopinath Temple, 178
Gota work, 59
Govardhan, 311
Government Museum, Ajmer, 163
Government Museum, Jhalawar, 287
Govind Devji Temple, Jaipur City Palace, 139
Great Indian Bustard, 27, 285
Gurushikhar Peak, 17, 274

H

Hadi Rani Mahal, Nagaur Fort, 238
Hadoti dialect, 42
Haj pilgrimage, 50
handblock printing, 56-7, 143, 158
Hanuman (Hindu deity), 66, 184, 300
Haras, the, 33
Hara Chauhans, 269, 290
Harappan civilization, 20, 32, 207
Harappan seal, 32
Haravati, 35, 290
Hari Hara (Hindu deity), 45
Harideva Temple, 311
Harihara Temples, 233

HAVELI

Aath Haveli, 182
Bissau Lodge, 145
Biyani Haveli, 181
Chamwar Walon-ki Haveli, 152
Char Chowki Haveli, 190
Chhawchhariya Haveli, 182
Chhc Haveli, 183
Chokhani Haveli, Mandawa, 182
Chokhani Haveli, Lachhmangarh, 190
Devra Haveli, 183
Goenka Haveli, Fatehpur, 183
Goenka Haveli, Mandawa, 182
Khatri Haveli, 183
Kothari Haveli, 202
Madanlal Haveli, 182
Narian Niwas, Jaipur, 145
Natani-ki Haveli, Jaipur, 143
Nathmalji-ki Haveli, 71, 214
Nawab (Faiz Ali Khan) Haveli, 143
Newatia Haveli, 182
Patwon-ki Haveli, 71, 214
Piramal Haveli, 183
Poddar Haveli, 182, 190
Rampuria Haveli, 202
Rathi Haveli, 190
Ruia Haveli, 190
Salim Singh-ki Haveli, Jaisalmer, 71, 96, 215
Samode Haveli, 145
Saraf Haveli, 182
Singhania Haveli, 183
Soné Chandi-ki Haveli, 190
Tibdiwala Haveli, 183
Vidyadhar Bhattacharya Haveli, 143

Hawa Mahal, Jaipur, 88, 93, 139
Hawa Pol, Jaisalmer Fort, 212
health, 314, 319
health insurance, 314
Herbert College, 282
Hindi, 42
Hindoli Fort, 298
Hindu pantheon, 44, 232
Hindu Trinity, 45, 164, 257, 274
hinduism, 44-7
history, 32-39, 130-3, 192-5, 240-5, 280-1, 300-1
Holi, 45, 81
Horse Fair, Tilwara, 126-7

HOTELS

Achrol House 328
Aditya Hotel 328
Ajit Bhawan Palace Hotel 335
Ambassador 326
Anand Bhawan Hotel 340
Apani Dhani 332
Aravalli Hotel 326
Arya Niwas 328
Ashirwad Palace 332
Balsamand Lake Palace 335
Bhadrawati Palace Hotel 326
Bhanwar Niwas 333
Bhanwar Vilas Palace 330
Bissau Palace Hotel 328
Brijraj Bhawan Palace 337
Caravanserai Hotel 340
Castle Awan 337
Castle Bijaipur 336
Castle Jhoomar Baori 331
Castle Mandawa 332
Chambal Hotel 337
Chandravati Hotel 337
Chetak Rest House 337
Choki Dhani 328

Clark's Amer Hotel 328
Colonel's Desert Camp 331
Connaught House 338
Darbargadh Posina 339
Delight Rest House 333
Deogarh Mahal 337
Dhola Maru Hotel 333
Diamond 337
Diggi Palace 328
Dundlod Castle 331
Durg Nahargarh 328
Eagle's Nest Hotel 326
Fateh Prakash Palace Hotel 340
Forest Lodge 326
Fort Chanwa Hotel 336
Fort Khejarla 335
Fort Pokaran 336
Fort Uniara 328
Fort View Hotel 334
Gajner Palace 333
Gangaur Hotel 328
Gavri Hotel 339
Ghoomar Hotel 335
Gokul Hotel (Nathdwara) 339
Gokul Vilas (Deogarh) 337
Gorbandh Palace 334
Govind Niwas 326
Haveli Braj Bhushanji 337
Heritage Inn Hotel 334
Heritage Resorts 339
Hillock Hotel 338
Hilltop Hotel 340
Hiltone Hotel 338
Himmatgarh Hotel 334
Holiday Inn Jaipur 329
Hotel Haveli 332
Inder Lodge 333
Ishwari Niwas Palace 337
Jagat Niwas Palace Hotel 340
Jagram Durg Fort 330
Jaipur Ashok Hotel 328
Jaipur Palace Hotel 328
Jaisar Castle Hotel 334
Jal Mahal Palace Hotel 328
Jamuna Resort 332
Jangid Haveli Hotel
Jawahar Niwas Palace 334
Jhalamand Garh 334
Jheel Tourist Hotel 331
Kajri Hotel 340
Karan's guest House 329
Karni Bhawan Hotel (Jodhpur) 335
Karni Bhawan Palace Hotel (Bikaner) 333
Kesar Bhawan Palace 338
Khadim Hotel 326
Khasa Kothi Hotel 329
Khimsar Fort 336
Kotri Raola 338
Lake Palace (Udaipur) 340
Lake Palace Hotel (Siliserh) 331
Lake Pichola Hotel 340
Lakend Hotel 340
Lakshmi Vilas (Jaipur) 329
Lakshmi Vilas Palace Hotel (Bharatpur) 326
Lakshmi Vilas Palace Hotel (Udaipur) 340
Lalgarh Palace 333
Lalghat Guest House 340
Laughing Camel Inn 334
LMB Hotel 329
Madhuban (Jaipur) 329
Madhuban Hotel (Mont Abu) 338
Maharani 329
Mandawa 329
Mansingh Hotel (Ajmer) 326
Mansingh Hotel (Jaipur) 329
Meenal Hotel 326
Megh Niwas 329
Meghsar Castle 333
Moomal Hotel 334
Motel Bar 326
Motel Behror 326
Motel Chinkara 332
Motel Deogarh 337
Motel Godavan 336
Motel Mahuwah 330
Motel Shahpura 331
Mukundgah Fort 332
Narain Niwas Hotel 329
Narayan Niwas Palace 334
Neemrana Fort Palace 331
Oriental Palace Resort 340
Padmini Hotel 340
Panna Chitor Hotel 337
Park Palace Hotel 327
Paying guest scheme (Jaipur) 328 :
Madame Bhagwati Indra Naraih 328
Madame Chhaya Kumari 328
Gharonda 328
Col. O. P. Drall 328
Madame Kamla Singh Gaur 328
Hemant Royal 328
M. S. D. 328
M. Bhuvaneshwari Kumari 328
Piramal Haveli 331
Pleasure Hotel 334
Pratap Country Inn (Titardi) 339
Pratap Palace (Chittorgarh) 337
Prithivi Raj Hotel 326
Pushkar Palace Hotel 331
Raj Darshan Hotel 340
Raj Vilas 329
Rajmahal Palace Hotel 329
Rajputana Palace (Jodhpur) 335
Rajputana Palace Sheraton (Jaipur) 329
Rambagh Palace 329
Rang Niwas Palace Hotel 340
Ratanada Polo Palace 335
Rawala Narlai 339
Regency Hotel 326
Rohet Garh 336
Roop Niwas Palace 332
Rose Hotel 329
Royal Castle 330
Rupangarh Fort 330
Safari Club (Pushkar) 331
Safari Club (Ranthambor) 331
Sagar Hotel 333
Sai Niwas Hotel 340
Saket 330
Sam Dhani Hotel 336
Samode Bagh (Samode) 332
Samode Haveli (Jaipur) 330
Samode Palace (Samode) 332
Sangam Hotel 332
Saras Hotel 327
Sardar Samand Palace Lake Resort 336
Sariska Palace Hotel 331
Sarovar Hotel 331
Savera Palace 338
Sawai Madhopur Lodge 331
Shikarbadi Hotel 337
Shikhar Hotel 338
Shilpi Hotel 339
Shiv Nivas Palace Hotel 340
Shiv Shekhavati Hotel 332
Shri Shanti Niwas Hotel 333
Sona Hotel 334
Spoon Bill Hotel 327
Sunrise Palace 338
Sunset Inn 338
Suraj Hotel 334
Swagatam Hotel 330
Teej Hotel 330
Thar Hotel 333
The Desert Resort 332
The Hill Fort 330
The Palace 338
The Ramgarh Lodge 330
The Royal Castle 330
The Safari Club 335
The Trident 330
Tiger Den Hotel 331
Tiger Moon Resort 331
Tourist Guest House (Bharatpur) 327
Tourist Hotel (Jaipur) 330
Tourist Village (Pushkar) 331
Udai Vilas Palace 337
Umaid Bhawan Palace Hotel (Jodhpur) 335
Umed Bhawan Palace (Kota) 338
Vinayak Hotel 331
Vrindawati Hotel 337
Y Atriki Niwas 333
Youth hostel (Jaipur) 328

Humayan, Emperor, 34-6, 278
hunting parties, 26, 65, 101, 175-6, 206-7, 248, 258, 305
Huxley, Aldous, 106, 109

I

Imperial Assemblage, 38
independence, 39-40
Indian bustard, 27, 285
Indian National Congress, 38-9
Indian Union, 40
Indira Bazaar, Jaipur, 143
Indira Gandhi Canal, 41, 211
Indra (Hindu deity), 44
Indus Valley Civilization, 32
Instrument of Accession, 40
internet 320
irrigation, 20, 22-3, 258
Islam, 50-1

J

Jacob, Sir Swinton, 96, 134, 136, 144, 162, 198, 283
Jag Mandir, Amber Fort, 101, 153
Jag Mandir, Udaipur, 37, 100-1, 157, 250-1
Jag Niwas, 41, 111, 250-1
Jagat, 258
Jagat Shironmani Temple, 152
Jagdish Mandir, 254
Jagmandir, Kota, 283
Jahangir, Emperor, 36-7, 138, 173, 220, 243, 251
Jaigarh Fort, 148, 154
Jaigarh Palace, 154-5
Jaimal, 196, 277-8
Jaimal's Palace, 278
Jainism, 48-9, 268
Jaiprakash Yantra, 140
Jaipur, 36, 38, 41, 92-3, 104, 113, 130-45
Jaipur School of Arts, 145
Jaisal, Rao, 34, 208, 209, 213
Jaisalmer, 34, 122, 130, 192, 208-17
Jaisalmer Fort, 90, 212-3
Jaisalmer Palace, 213
Jaisamand Lake, 240, 259
Jait Bund, 216
Jal Mahal, 157
Jalandarnath, 231
Jaleb Chowk, 152-3
Jali works, 71, 87-8, 91
Jambhoji (saint), 198
Janamashtami, 45
Jantar Mantar Observatory, 93, 135, 140-1
Jas Mandir, 153
Jaswant Thada, 228
Jats, the, 35, 53, 300
Jauhar, 208, 213, 277, 289
jewelry, 62, 135, 142, 165, 215, 244
Jhalawar, 281, 286-7
Jhalrapatan, 287
Jhanki Mahal, 228
Jhunjhunu, 183
Jodha, Rao, 34, 220
Jodhpur, 34, 38, 65, 113, 122-3, 130, 192, 220-33

Jodhpur Lancers, 220
Jogi Nath, 231
Johri Bazaar, Jaipur, 142
Juna Mahal, Dungarpur, 266
Juna Mahal, Jaisalmer Palace, 213
Junagarh Fort, 196
Junagarh Palace, 196-7
Juni Dhanmandi, 222-3

K

Kachhawahas, the, 33, 35, 152
Kakuni, 289
Kalbeliyas, 52, 79, 216
Kali (Hindu deity), 45
Kalibangan, 20, 32, 192, 207
Kalika Mata Temple, Chittorgarh, 278
Kamaycha, 79
Kamra Palace, 303
Kanch ki Burj, 247
Kandiala, 217
Kankroli, 258
Kankwari Fort, 175
Kannauj, 220
Kansuan Temple, 284
Kapil Muni, 206
Karan Mahal, 196
Karkhanas (craft workshops), 36
Karni Mata (Hindu deity), 46, 55, 192-3, 206-7
Karni Mata Temple, Bikaner, 46, 55, 70, 206-7
Kathputlis, 73
Kavadh, 255
Keoladeo Ghana Sanctuary, 25, 306-9
Kesar Bagh, 296-7
Kesar Vilas Palace, 275
Keshav Mahal, 310-1
Khab ka Mahal, 228
Khan, Amir, 159
Khan, Behram, 36
Khatri Haveli, 183
Kheji, 202
Khilji, Sultan Alauddin, 34, 208, 256, 276, 278, 289, 303, 304
Khimsar, 192, 238
Khud khargosh, 75
Khurri, 192, 219
Kipling, Rudyard, 110, 133, 208, 293
Kirtishtambha, 34, 278
Kishan Bhawan, 310
Kishangarh, 64, 130, 166
Kishangarh School of Miniature Paintings, 166
Kishanpol Bazaar, Jaipur, 143
Kishnai Mata Temple, 285
Kishor Sagar Lake, 283
Kolayat Temple, 206
Kota, 38, 65, 280-9
Kota Palace Museum, 282
Kota School of Art, 281
Koteya, 35
Kothari Haveli, 202
Krishna (Hindu deity), 44, 132, 137, 139, 175, 183-4, 189, 208, 210, 238, 248, 257-8, 267, 274, 276, 282, 287, 311
Kshatriyas, the, 32
Kumbh Mela, 52
Kumbha, Rana, 34, 242, 260-1, 263, 268, 274, 277, 298
Kumbhalgarh, 24, 34, 224, 240, 260-1
Kumbhaswami Temple, 261
Kundankari technique, 63
Kunja pots, 195
Kunwar Pade ka Mahal, 277
Kushanas, the, 33

L

Lachhmangarh Fort, 190
Larani Sati Bhattinni, 216

LAKES

Amarsagar, 216
Balsamand, 232
Gadsisar Lake, 210
Jaisamand Lake, 240, 259
Kishor Sagar Lake, 283
Man Sagar, 157
Maota Lake, 147, 152
Nakki Lake, 269, 274
Pichola Lake, 81, 250
Pushkar Lake, 119, 165
Rajsamand Lake, 258
Sambhar Lake, 166
Sukh Sagar Lake, 296
Vijay Sagar Lake, 173

Lake Palace, Udaipur, 41, 111, 250-1
Lakshmi, 271
Lakshmi Mishtan Bhandar, 142
Lal Niwas, Junagarh Palace, 196
Lallgarh Palace, Bikaner, 96, 198-9, 206
languages, official, 42
lassi, 74
literacy rate, 42
Lodurva, 217
Lohagarh Fort, 302-3
Lua Vasahi Temple, 271

M

Maan Vilas, 226
Madanlal Haveli, 182
Madhavendra Bhawan, 155
Mahabharata epic, 32, 45, 171, 182, 200, 208, 276
Mahadev Temple, 261
Mahadeva Temple, 165
Mahal Khas, 303
Mahamandir Temple, 231
Mahasati, 277
Mahavira, 48, 49
Mahavira Temple, Osiyan, 233-5
Makrana, 166
Maldev, Raja, 34
Malwi dialect, 42
Man Sagar, 157
Manak Chowk, 215
Manak Mahal, Udaipur, 249
Mandalgarh Fort, 298
Mandana decorations, 218-9, 236
Mandawa Castle, 182
Mandore, 220, 232
Manganiyars, the, 79, 208, 216
mangos, 289
Maniharon-ki Gali, Jaipur, 143
Maota Lake, 147, 152
Maru Bhasha, 42
Marwar, 34, 130, 192-238
Marwari dialect, 42
matrimonial alliances (for political ends), 36-7, 130, 156
Marwaris, 180-1
Matsyadesh, 300
Mawe ki kachori, 223
Mayo College, 162, 194
Mehendi decoration, 236
Mahensar, 190
Mehrangarh Fort, Jodhpur, 91, 96, 114, 122-3, 222, 224-7
Mehrangarh Fort Museum, 226
Melas, *see* Fairs
Menpes, Mortimer, 104
metal mining, 18-9
Mewar, 33, 34, 36, 240-67
Mewar School of Miniatures, 243-4, 267
Mewari dialect, 42
Mewati dialect, 42
minakari (enamel works), 62, 135, 142, 257, 341
mineral mining, 18-9, 41
miniature paintings, *see* paintings, miniature
mining, mineral, 18-9, 41
Mirabai, 255, 276
Mirabai Temple, 277
Misra Yantra, 141
Mohan Bari, 152-3
Mohangarh, 211
mojri slippers, 143, 195, 215, 221, 341
Molela, 256
money, 314, 320
Mor Chowk, Udaipur, 248
Moraes, Dominic Frank, 120
Morchang, 79
Moti Doongri Palace, Alwar, 172
Moti Doongri Palace, Jaipur, 145
Moti Mahal, Jodhpur, 228
Moti Mahal, Udaipur, 248
Mount Abu, 17, 28, 32, 240, 258, 269-75, 290
movies 320
Mubarak Mahal, Jaipur City Palace, 71, 136
Mughal Empire, 34-7, 50
Mughal invasions, 34-5, 193, 209, 275
Muharram, 51
Murlimanohar Temple, 190

MUSEUMS

Albert Hall Museum, Jaipur, 96, 135, 144
Archeological Museum, Ahar, 255
Archeological Museum, Bharatpur, 303
Bharatpur Museum, 300
Bikaner Museum, 199
City Palace Museum, Jaipur, 136-9, 141
City Palace Museum, Udaipur, 246, 249
Fort Museum, Junagarh, 198
Government Museum, Jhalawar, 287
Kota Palace Museum, 282
Mehrangarh Fort Museum, 226
Pokharan Fort Museum, 218-9
Rajputana Museum, Ajmer 163
Vidyadhar Bhattacharya Haveli, 143

music and dance, 78-9
Muslims, the, 50-1
Muslim invasions, 33, 36, 275

N

Nabobs, the, 252
Nagaur, 192, 238
Nagaur Fair, 82, 128, 238
Nagaur Fort, 238
Nagda, 256-7
Nahargarh Fort, 155
Nainsi, 33
Nakki Lake, 269, 274
Nandi, 47, 256, 275
Narian Niwas Haveli, Jaipur, 145
Narivalaya Yantra, 140
Nasiyan Temple, 163
Natani ka Chabutra, 250
Natani-ki Haveli, Jaipur, 143
Nathdwara Temple, 240, 257
Nathmalji-ki Haveli, 71, 214
Nauchowki, Rajsamand, 258
Nawab (Faiz Ali Khan) Haveli, 143
Nawalgarh, 182
Neelkanth, 175
Neelkant Temple, 261
Neelkantheshwar Temple 175
Neemrana Palace, 178
Nehru Bazaar, Jaipur, 143
Nehru, Jawahar Lal, 40, 41
Neminatha (Jain saint) 202, 272
Newatia Haveli, 182
newspapers 320
Nikumbh Mahal Palace, 172
nilgai, 175
Noble, Margaret, 118
nuclear testing, 211, 218

O

odhnis, 60-1, 135
opening times, 320
opium, 210, 286
Oppenhejm, Ralph, 112
Osiyan Temple, 192, 233-5

P

Pabuji, 53, 55, 144
Padmini, Rani, 276, 277-8
paintings, miniature, 64-5, 134, 138, 166, 171, 193, 198, 227, 244, 247, 249, 251, 276, 281-2
paintings, wall, 66-7, 108, 154, 184-9, 208-9, 211, 237, 267

PALACES

Ajit Bhawan Palace, 233
Akbar's Palace, Ajmer, 163
Anup Mahal, Junagarh Palace, 197
Badal Mahal, Kumbhalgarh Fort, 261
Badal Mahal, Nagaur Fort, 238
Badan Singh (Raja) Palace, 303
Balsamand Lake Palace, Jodhpur, 96, 232
Banai Vilas Palace, 168-9
Bari Mahal, Udaipur, 111, 247
Bikaner Palace, 269
Brijraj Bhawan Palace, 283
Chandra Mahal, Jaipur, 92, 138-9
Chandra Mahal, Junagarh Palace, 197
City Palace, Alwar, 170
City Palace, Jaipur, 71, 80, 92, 96, 103, 135-9
City Palace, Kota, 282
City Palace, Udaipur, 89, 114, 123, 246-9
Dilkhush Mahal, 247
Fateh Prakash Palace, 249
Garh Palace, 110, 286-7, 291-3
Golbagh Palace, 303-4
Gopal Bhawan Palace, Deeg, 96, 310
Hadi Rani Mahal, Nagaur Fort, 238
Hawa Mahal, Jaipur, 88, 93, 139
Jaigarh Palace, 154-5
Jaimal's Palace, 278
Jaisalmer Palace, 213
Jal Mahal, 157
Jhanki Mahal, 228
Juna Mahal, Dungarpur, 266
Juna Mahal, Jaisalmer Palace, 213
Junagarh Palace, 196-7
Kamra Palace, 303
Karan Mahal, 196
Kesar Vilas Palace, 275
Keshav Mahal, 310-1
Khab ka Mahal, 228
Kunwar Pade ka Mahal, 277
Lake Palace, Udaipur, 41, 111, 250-1
Lallgarh Palace, Bikaner, 96, 198-9, 206
Madhavendra Bhawan, 155
Mahal Khas, 303
Manak Mahal, Udaipur, 249
Moti Doongri Palace, Alwar, 172
Moti Doongri Palace, Jaipur, 145
Moti Mahal, Jodhpur, 228
Moti Mahal, Udaipur, 248
Neemrana Palace, 178
Mubarak Mahal, Jaipur City Palace, 71, 136
Nikumbh Mahal Palace, 172
Patta's Palace, 278
Phool Mahal, 227
Phul Mahal, Junagarh Palace, 197
Raj Mahal Palace, 153
Rajmahal Palace, Jaipur, 145
Rambagh Palace, Jaipur, 41, 144
Rana Kumbha Palace, 277
Randiyon ka Mahal, 178
Rang Mahal, Jaisalmer Palace, 213
Rani Padmini Palace, 278
Rupangarh Palace, 166
Samode Palace, 41, 159, 180-1
Sariska Palace, 175
Shiv Niwas Palace, 249
Sisodia Rani ka Bagh, 156
Sukh Mahal, 296
Takhat Mahal, 227
Umaid Bhawan Palace, Jodhpur, 41, 88, 96, 230
Umaid Bhawan Palace, Kota 283
Zenana, 153

Palace on Wheels, 41, 231
Panna Mian ka Kund, 152
Parashvanath, 203
Parasrampura, 182
Parshva, 265
Parshvanatha, 271, 303
Parshvanatha Temple, Lodurva, 217
Parshvanatha Temple, Ranakpur, 263
Parvati (Hindu deity), 45, 298, 303
Parwan River, 289
Patta, 196, 277-8
Patta's Palace, 278
Patwa, Guman Chand, 214
Patwon-ki Haveli, 71, 214
peacock, national bird, 28
Pellenc, Baron Jean, 107
Persian wheels, 21, 23, 258
phad, 67
Phool Mahal, 227
Phoolgarh Fort, 166
Phul Mahal, Junagarh Palace, 197
Pichhvais, 66-7, 244, 257
Pichola Lake, 81, 250
Pingal dialect, 42
Piramal Haveli, 183
Poddar Haveli, 182, 190
Pokharan, 211, 218
Pokharan Fort Museum, 218-9
polo, 135, 144
population, 41
post offices, 320
pottery, 72
pottery, blue, 145, 158
Prasad, Dr Rajendra, 40
Pratap, Maharana, 36, 242, 298
Pratapgarh inscription, 21
Precious stones, mining of, 18-9, 41
Prince Khurram, *see* Shah Jahan
Prince Salim, *see* Jahangir, Emperor

PRINCELY STATES

Ajmer, 35, 38, 51, 122, 130, 162-3
Amber, 35, 114, 130, 132, *see also* Jaipur
Bharatpur, 27, 35, 37-8, 300-11
Bikaner, 34-5, 65, 115, 130, 192-207
Bundi-Kota, 35, 280
Jaisalmer, 34, 122, 130, 192, 208-17
Marwar, 34, 130, 192-238
Mewar, 33-4, 36, 240-67

printing, handblock, 56-7
Pritam Niwas Chowk, Jaipur City Palace, 138-9
Priyatam Niwas, Udaipur, 248
Project Tiger, 174, 176-7, 304-5
puppetry, 73, 230, 238
puris, 75
Pushkar, 130
Pushkar Fair, 82, 124-5, 126-7, 164, 165
Pushkar Lake, 119, 165

R

Radha, 248
Rai, Duleh, 35
Raj Mahal Palace, 153
Raj Mandir cinema, Jaipur, 135
Raj Prashasti, 258
Rajasthali, 341
Rajasthan Canal, *see* Indira Gandhi Canal
Rajgarh Fort, 172-3
Rajmahal Palace, Jaipur, 145
Rajpramukh, 40
Rajputana, 38, 130
Rajputs, the, 32-3
Rajsamand Lake, 258
Ram, Raja, 35
Ram Niwas Gardens, 144
Ram Yantra, 141
Rama (Hindu deity), 66, 274
Ramavaikunth Temple, 165
Ramayana epic, 32, 45, 64, 136, 171, 182, 190, 219-20, 255, 286, 302
Ramazan, 50-1
Rambagh Palace, Jaipur, 41, 144
Ramdeo-ka-Karni Fair, 53, 124
Ramgarh, 190, 285
Rampuria Haveli, 202
Rana Kumbha Palace, 277
Ranakpur, 262-5
Ranakpur Temple, Mount Abu, 94, 163, 240, 262
Randiyon ka Mahal, 178
Rang Mahal, Jaisalmer Palace, 213
Rani Moosi Chhatri, 170
Rani Padmini, 276-8
Rani Padmini Palace, 278
Rani Sati Temple, Jhunjhunu, 183
Raniji ki Baori, 296
Ranthambhor Fort, 304
Ranthambhor National Park, 24, 130, 176, 305
Ras-lila, 45, 64
Rathi Haveli, 190
Rathors, the, 33-4, 275
rats, sacred, 46, 206, 345
Rattan Bihari Temple, 203
Rawal, Bappa, 34, 255, 256, 276
Ray, Satyajit, 108, 212, 215
Rebaris, the, 53
Reed, Sir Stanley, 112
religion, 44-53, 329

RESTAURANTS

8th July 333
Aangan (Jaipur) 327
Aangan (Mont Abu) 338
Amber 332
Angithi Maharani Palace 327
Annapurna (Bikaner) 332
Annapurna (Jaipur) 327
Aravalli 327
Baithak 337
Balsamand Lake Palace 334
Berry's 339
Bhola 326
Bhuwaneshwari 327
Brijraj Bhawan Palace 337
Bundi Cafe and Crafts 336
Chanakya 327
Chandralok 327
Chandravansh Pavilion 327
Cheetal 337
Chotu Motu 332
Cloud 9 338

Copper Chimney 327
Courtyard Restaurant 334
Deepali 326
Dhola Maru 332
Diamond 337
Dining room 333
Fort Pokaran 336
Fort View 333
Gallery Restaurant 339
Garden cafe (Jaipur) 327
Garden Restaurant (Udaipur) 339
Gauri 327
Gay time 333
Golden Sands 327
Gulab Mahal 327
Haveli 338
Honey Dew 326
Jai Hind 326
Jal Mahal 327
Jhalamand Garh 334
Jharokha 339
Jungle Corner 338
Kalinga 334
Kalpana 333
Khamaghani 334
Khasa Rasoda 327
Khimsar Fort 336
Kohinoor 326
Kumbha Palace 339
Lakshmi Misthan Bhandar 327
Lakshmi Niwas 333
Madhuban 338
Madras cafe 338
Maharani Bagh Orchard 339
Marwar Hall 334
Midtown 334
MK 338
Morcha 337
Moti Mahal 333
Natraj 333
Niros Restaurant 327
On the Rock 334
Oriental Palace Resort 339
Padmani 339
Palms 327
Park View 339
Prince's Restaurant 330
Reggie's Restaurant 335
Risala 335
Roof Garden cafe 339
Roop Niwas Palace 332
Sai Niwas 340
Sardar Samand Palace Lake Resort 336
Shakti 336
Sher-e-Punjab 338
Shilpi Village Restaurant 340
Shish Mahal (Ajmer) 326
Shish Mahal (Samode) 332
Shivir 327
Spoon Bill 326
Surya Mahal 328
The Hill Fort 330
The Pillars 335
The Trio 333
Top Deck 333
Toran 335
Veena 338
Zaika 328
rickshaws, 316
Rig Veda, 32, 44
Rishabdeo Temple, 258-9
Rishabhdevji Temple, Jaisalmer, 213
Rishabhdevji Temple, Udaipur, 48
river Kak, 217
Rousselet, Louis, 119, 132
Ruia Haveli, 190
Rupangarh Palace, 166

S

Sachiya Mata Temple, 233
Sadar Bazaar, Jodhpur, 223
Sadar Bazaar, Bundi, 297
sadhu, 53
safaris, 316
Sah, Dharna, 262-4
Saheliyon ki Bari, 254
Sajjan Niwas, 251
Sajjangarh, 255
Sal, Rao Chhatar, 290-2
Salim Singh-ki Haveli, Jaisalmer, 71, 96, 215
Sambhar Lake, 166
Sambhavnath Temple, Jaisalmer Fort, 213, 217
Samm, 192, 218
Samode Haveli, 145
Samode Palace, 41, 159, 180-1
Samrat Yantra, 141
Sandeshwar Temple, 202
Sanga, Rana, 34, 36, 220, 242
Sanganer, 57, 158
Saraf Haveli, 182
Saraswati River, 219
Sardar Vilas, 228
Sariska Palace, 175
Sariska Wildlife Sanctuary, 24, 126-7, 130, 174-5
Sarneshwar Mahadev Temple, 275
Sarus cranes, 307
Sarvottam Vilas, 213
Sas Temple, 257
Sat Bis Deorhi, Chittorgarh, 71
Satara, 79
sati, 38, 91, 213, 216, 225, 228
Sawan Bhawan, 310
Sepoy Mutiny, 38, 251
Shah, Dayal, 258
Shah, Sher, 34, 289
Shah, Sultan Bahadur, 34
Shah, Vimala, 270-1
Shah Jahan, 34, 36-7, 220, 251, 280, 290
Shakti (Hindu deity), 45
Shankar brothers, 286
Sharada Dwivedi, 114-5
Sheesh Mahal, Amber Fort, 109, 152-3
Sheesh Mahal, Nagaur Fort, 238
Sheesh Mahal, Samode Palace, 181
Sheetla Fair, 82
Shekhavati, 130, 180-90
Shergarh Fort, 289
Shikar Burj, 296
shikar parties, *see* hunting trips
Shila Devi Temple, 153
Shilpa Shastra, 132-3
Shilpagram, 254
Shiva (Hindu deity), 44, 45, 47, 66, 71, 132, 164, 256-7, 259, 284, 289, 298, 303
Shiv Niwas Palace, 249
Shiva Purana, 138
Shiva Ratri, 47
Shivalinga, 47
Shrinathji Temple, Nathdwara, 257
Siberian cranes, 27, 306-7
Sikar, 181
Sikar Fort, 181
Sileh Khana, Jaipur City Palace, 137
Siliserh, 174
Simpson, William, 103
Singh, Ajit, 37, 232
Singh, Amar, 36, 216, 228, 230, 243, 255
Singh, Amar II, 37
Singh, Anup, 35, 198, 199, 201
Singh, Ari, 101
Singh, Badan, 35, 310
Singh, Bakhta, 238
Singh, Bakhtawar, 169, 170
Singh, Balwant, 303
Singh, Banai, 169
Singh, Bhagwat, 249
Singh, Bhawani, 137, 287
Singh, Bhopal, 40, 101, 248
Singh, Fateh, 65, 114-5, 246
Singh, Gaj, 202, 220, 228
Singh, Ganga, 39-40, 115, 194-5, 198, 203-4, 206, 207, 220, 252, 269
Singh, Hanuwant, 223
Singh, Jagat, 250-1
Singh, Jai, 93, 131, 153, 168-70, 172, 173-5, 259, 269
Singh, Jai II, 35, 37, 131-4, 136, 139-41, 152, 155-7, 165
Singh, Jaswant, 34, 37, 220, 228
Singh, Jaswant II, 228
Singh, Jawan, 101
Singh, Karan, 36, 251
Singh, Karni, 40
Singh, Kirpal, 145
Singh, Madho I, 137, 157, 280
Singh, Madho II, 136-7, 157, 183
Singh, Man I, 35-6, 40, 62, 131-2, 146, 152-3, 242
Singh, Man II, 133, 144-5
Singh, Nahar, 155
Singh, Pratap, 93, 114, 172-3, 220-1
Singh, Rai, 34-5, 154, 196
Singh, Raj, 37, 258
Singh, Ram, 139, 145, 183
Singh, Rana Karan, 247
Singh, Rawal Sabal, 209
Singh, Sadul, 40, 206
Singh, Salim, 210, 215
Singh, Sangram, 255
Singh, Sardul, 40, 182
Singh, Sawant, 166
Singh, Swarup, 210, 233
Singh, Udai, 34, 243, 246
Singh, Umaid, 221, 223, 294, 296
Singh, Zalim, 281, 286
Singh, Zorawar, 202
Singhania Haveli, 183
Sireh Deorhi Bazaar, Jaipur, 142
Sirohi, 274-5
Sirohi Fort, 275
sirohis (swords), 274
Sisodia dynasty, 33-4, 240, 255, 266
Sisodia Rani ka Bagh, 156
Sita (Hindu deity), 66
Sitamata, 24
Sitar, 286
Siyaji, Rao, 34, 220
snake cult, 52
Someshwar Temple, 178
Soné Chandi-ki Haveli, 190
Sorsan, 285
souvenirs, 320
stone carving, 70-1
storks, 306-7
Sukh Mahal, 296
Sukh Mandir, 148, 153
Sukh Sagar Lake, 296
Sulas, 76-7
Sun Temple, Jhalrapatan, 71, 286-7
Sun Temple, Osiyan, 233
Sun Temple, Ranakpur, 263-5
Sunehri Kothi, 159
Sunni Muslims, 51
Surahis, 69
Suraj Mahal Pavilion, 311
Surajmal, 35, 302
Surya (Hindu deity), 44, 156, 255, 278
Surya Gokhra, Udaipur, 248-9
Surya Temple, *see* Sun Temple
Suryamal, 33
Svetambara, 48-9, 271
Swatantra Party, 40

T

Takhat Mahal, 227
Tal Chappar, 24
Taragarh, 162
Taragarh Fort, 291, 294, 297
Taxes, 321
taxis, 317
Teej, 81
Tejaji (folk deity), 238
Tejpala, 272
telecommunications, 327
telephone, 315, 321
Telia, 210

◆ INDEX

TEMPLES

Adinatha Temple, 262-3, 265, 272
Ambika Mata Temple, 258-9
Bahu Temple, 257
Baroli Temple Complex, 284
Bhandeshwar Temple, 202-3
Bijoliyan Temple, 297
Brahma Temple, Pushkar, 164
Chandramauleshwar Temple, 288
Chandravati Temple, Kota, 96, 288
Dayal Shah Mandir, 258
Dhuni Mata Temple, 246
Dwarakadhish Temple, 258
Eklingji Temple, 240, 256
Ghateshwara Temple, 284
Gomukh Temple, 274
Gopinath Temple, 178
Govind Devji Temple, Jaipur City Palace, 139
Harideva Temple, 311
Harihara Temples, 233
Jagat Shironmani Temple, 152
Jagdish Mandir, 254
Kalika Mata Temple, Chittorgarh, 278
Kansuan Temple, 284
Karni Mata Temple, Bikaner, 46, 55, 70, 206-7
Kishnai Mata Temple, 285
Kolayat Temple, 206
Kumbhaswami Temple, 261
Lua Vasahi Temple, 271
Mahadev Temple, 261
Mahadeva Temple, 165
Mahamandir Temple, 231
Mahavira Temple, Osiyan, 233-5
Mirabai Temple, 277
Murlimanohar Temple, 190
Nasiyan Temple, 163
Nathdwara Temple, 240, 257
Neelkantheshwar Temple 175
Nilkanth Temple, 261
Osiyan Temple, 192, 233-5
Parshvanatha Temple, Lodurva, 217
Parshvanatha Temple, Ranakpur, 263
Ramavaikunth Temple, 165
Ranakpur Temple, Mount Abu, 94, 163, 240, 262
Rani Sati Temple, Jhunjhunu, 183
Rattan Bihari Temple, 203
Rishabdev Temple, 258-9
Rishabhdevji Temple, Jaisalmer, 213
Rishabhdevji Temple, Udaipur, 48
Sachiya Mata Temple, 233
Sambhavnath Temple, Jaisalmer Fort, 213, 217
Sandeshwar Temple, 202
Sarneshwar Mahadev Temple, 275
Sas Temple, 257
Shila Devi Temple, 153
Shrinathji Temple, Nathdwara, 257
Someshwar Temple, 178
Sukh Mandir, 153
Sun Temple, Jhalrapatan, 71, 286, 287
Sun Temple, Osiyan, 233
Sun Temple, Ranakpur, 263-5
Teli ka Temple, 139
Varah Temple, 165
Vimala Vasahi Temple, 270, 272-3
Vraj-ji Temple, 277

temple culture, 47
textile industry, 56-9, 158, 160, 244
Thar Desert, 28, 30, 32, 120, 124, 162
Tibdiwala Haveli, 183
tie-and-dye textiles, 58, 143, 215, 223, 244
tigers, endangered species, 26-7, 176, 304
tiger hunt, 38
Tilwara Horse Fair, 126-7
time difference, 315
tipping, 321
Tirthankara (Jain saint), 49
Tirtharaj, Pushkar, 47
tobacco, 321
Tod, Lt.-Colonel James, 32-3, 106, 157, 166, 192, 200, 203, 209, 212, 232, 251, 283-6, 293, 298
Tonk, 159
tourism, 41
trains, 317
travel agent, 315
tribal practices, 52-3
Trikuta Hill, 212
Trinity, the Hindu, 45 *see also* Brahma, Vishnu, Shiva
Tripolia Bazaar, Jaipur, 143
turbans, 58, 61, 106, 112, 135, 226, 231, 295

U

Udai Vilas, Dungarpur, 266-7
Udaipur, 34, 38, 107, 125, 240-67
Umaid Bhawan Palace, Jodhpur, 41, 88, 96, 230
Umaid Vilas, 226-7
Umed Bhawan Palace, 283
Uprising of 1857, 38, 251-2, 281, 283
Uttarian Haveli, 182

V

Vagadi dialect, 42
Varah Temple, 165
Vastu Shastra, 260
Vastupala, 272
Vedas, the, 32, 44
Vedi building, 261
Vedic religion, 32
Vijay Mandir, 173
Vijay Sagar Lake, 173
Vijaystambha, Chittorgarh, 277
Vimala, 272
Vimala Vasahi Temple, 270, 272-3
Viratnagar, 168, 178
visa regulations, 314
Vishnu (Hindu deity), 44, 66, 71, 164, 256-7, 259, 274, 280, 284, 287
Vidyadhar Bhattacharya Haveli, 143
Vraj-ji Temple, 277
Vyas Chhatri, 216

W

Wagh Nakh, 200
water, 321
weaponry, 200-1, *see also* Armory exhibits
what to pack, 315
when to go, 315
wildlife, *see* Fauna

WILDLIFE SANCTUARIES

Darrah Wildlife Sanctuary, 285
Desert National Park, 24, 30, 192, 218
Gajner, 24, 192, 206
Jaisalmer Forests, 258
Keoladeo Ghana Sanctuary, 25, 306-9
Kumbhalgarh, 24, 34, 224, 240, 260-1
Ranthambhor National Park, 24, 130, 176, 305
Sariska Wildlife Sanctuary, 24, 126-7, 130, 174-5
Sitamata, 24
Tal Chappar, 24

World War One, 39

Y

Yama (Hindu deity), 44
Yeshwant Niwas, 173

Z

zari embroidery, 59
Zenana, 153